The
Psychoanalytic
Study
of the Child

VOLUME FIFTY

Kindly submit seven copies of new manuscripts to

Albert J. Solnit, M.D.
Yale Child Study Center
P.O. Box 207900
New Haven, CT 06520-7900

The Psychoanalytic Study of the Child

VOLUME FIFTY

New Haven and London
Yale University Press
1995

Correction notice for volume 49 (1994):
In the article " 'The Widening Scope' Reconsidered," by Pietro Castelnuovo-Tedesco, M.D., the
footnote labeled and placed as note 1 (p. 164) actually should be note 2 , and, conversely, note 2
(p. 169) should be note 1.

Designed by Sally Harris
Set in Baskerville type by The Composing Room of Michigan, Inc.
Printed in the United States of America by Vail-Ballou Press, Inc., Binghamton, N.Y.

Library of Congress catalog card number: 451-11304
International standard book number: 0-300-06471-3
A catalogue record for this book is available from the British Library.

The paper in this book meets the guidelines for
permanence and durability of the Committee on
Production Guidelines for Book Longevity of the
Council on Library Resources.

10   9   8   7   6   5   4   3   2   1

Contents

APPLIED PSYCHOANALYSIS

PSYCHOANALYTIC THEORY

Freud's Psychology

Can It Survive?

CLIFFORD YORKE, FRC PSYCH., DPM

The increasing diversity of, and disparities between, psychoanalytic theories raises the question of whether, and to what extent, these various formulations remain firmly rooted in Freud's basic psychoanalytic concepts. Many analysts believe that these theories exemplify "unity in diversity." This view is contested in this paper. It is argued that Freud's basic concepts are his metapsychological *concepts which, although capable of modification in the light of fresh clinical and theoretical findings are, in their fundamentals, indispensable. It is contended that it is precisely these fundamentals that are dislodged or put at risk by a great deal of current psychoanalytic thinking, and that it is in this (negative) respect that many diverse approaches are in concert. The argument is pursued with special reference to infant observational research, contemporary affect theory, and the neuroscience of Luria.*

I

THE PAST QUARTER CENTURY HAS SEEN A PROLIFERATION OF PSYCHO-analytic theories, many of them, like the Kleinian system before them, resting on fresh formations of psychological development in infancy. The self psychology of Kohut (1971) quickly made inroads into recognized theory and practice and divided psychoanalytic societies in the United States, but splits and factions rapidly arose even within well-established psychological frameworks that already differed radically

---

Hon. consultant psychiatrist, Anna Freud Centre, London; formally, psychiatrist-in-charge.

The Psychoanalytic Study of the Child 50, ed. Albert J. Solnit, Peter B. Neubauer, Samuel Abrams, and A. Scott Dowling (Yale University Press, copyright © 1995 by Albert J. Solnit, Peter B. Neubauer, Samuel Abrams, and A. Scott Dowling).

from the Freudian tradition. The Kleinian group, for example, is no longer unified, though it is more cohesive in London than in Buenos Aires. And although there have been sharp differences of theory and practice in psychoanalysis since the days of the early schismatics, the growing diversity of opinion has in some quarters occasioned alarm and led to a search for what Wallerstein (1988, 1990) has called the "common ground." For my own part, I find it hard to see how this can be found without blurring or even obliterating some cardinal distinctions.

For all that, there *is* a common if negative factor that unites the majority of dissident groups: the insistence on the irrelevance of Freud's metapsychology for the understanding of mental functioning. Departures from Freud's psychological system are in themselves nothing new, but earlier criticisms of metapsychology are thought by some to be given added weight by more recent developments in neighboring fields. Observational research in child development (especially infancy), the neurosciences, and so-called cognitive science are among the disciplines whose findings are nowadays invoked to pronounce the demise of metapsychology. But since the infant's mind cannot be reached by psychoanalysis of any description, infant research in particular has attracted attention for the light it is hoped it may cast on this most obscure phase of development.[1]

Over a century ago Freud (1891), following Hughlings Jackson (e.g., 1884), warned against the dangers of confusing brain with mind. Yet a great deal of argument that reaches the literature today rests on an unwary inclination to cross disciplines without respect for their boundaries. In the applied science that ought to inform the practice of the clinical psychiatrist, a working knowledge of the relevant anatomy, physiology, biology, genetics, neurology, sociology, epidemiology, and, for that matter, statistics, to name some examples, is indispensable. But none of these can do duty for psychology itself.

The difficulties posed by healthy collaboration have in some instances led to a false dichotomy between "organic" and "dynamic" psychiatry in which the one is embraced and the other spurned. It was this spurious and fruitless opposition that led Eisenberg (1986) to entitle one of his papers "Mindlessness and Brainlessness in Psychiatry." So it seems unfortunate to have to reassert that, while the cooperation of

---

1. It is in this early phase that the contributions of neuroscience seem less extensive and more indirect than they are for the understanding of later phases, though Luria (e.g., 1982) insisted on the developmental point of view and sought to understand it more fully.

interrelated disciplines is necessary and legitimate, their findings are not interchangeable and generally defy simple translation from the language of one to that of another. To treat them as if they were amounts to a misuse of valuable information.[2]

II

The risk of such misapplication has a particular bearing on the way we understand the relationship between psychoanalysis and infant observational research. Child observation has always been of great interest for students of human development; and Phyllis Tyson (1989) has recently presented a succinct historical summary acknowledging the contributions of Anna Freud and Dorothy Burlingham in their wartime nurseries, of James and Joyce Robertson, Bowlby, Ainsworth, Stroufe, Fraiburg, Winnicott, Spitz, Greenacre, Mahler, Roiphe and Galenson, and many others. The findings of infant research in recent years have been particularly impressive, even spectacular. Such well-known facts as the infant's selective response to the sound of the mother's voice or the smell of her milk, his capacity to fix his gaze in response to the mother's singing or smiling, and the reciprocity involved with the mother's response are repeatedly used to support the viewpoints of object relations and self psychologists alike. And they have led many others to question some of the basic assumptions of Freudian psychology and the clinical practice identified with it. But if, as seems to me evident, no one can really know what goes on in the mind of a baby, inferences drawn from observational data must be assessed for their compatibility with what *is* known about psychological development. Hypothetical reconstructions are of a different order from clinical (analytic) observations; at best, they can increase the credibility of a clinical interpretation, as Glover (1947, 1961) has pointed out. And here, it can be argued, as Glover did argue, that Freud's metapsychology can provide a useful check on the validity of hypotheses not directly amenable to clinical accountability.

For all that, the degree to which observed *behavior* can be used to infer concomitant *psychological processes* remains a matter of some disagreement. For, although Blum (1989) has emphasized that "interdisciplinary studies entail a mysterious leap between different domains of discourse" (p. 159), there are many who make the leap with no real sign of discomfort.

---

2. I have discussed the implications of all this for general psychiatry elsewhere (Yorke, 1988).

In my own clinical practice I have not found the new observations of any great value, but that is by no means every psychoanalyst's experience. In his introduction to a collection of papers devoted to the subject (Dowling and Rothstein, 1989), Rothstein points out that, although almost all psychoanalytic practitioners value the genetic perspective, "there is a significant difference of opinion as to the value of the data derived from outside the clinical situation for theory building, for interpretation, and for reconstruction" (p. xv). The contributors to the volume in question represent a broad spectrum of opinion. At one end Cooper and Lichtenberg find their respective approaches to clinical work profoundly affected by the new findings; at the other, Glenn and Scharfman, while acknowledging the importance of these observations, find little use for them in their clinical strategies. (Scharfman concedes—I think correctly—that the new findings could be of didactic value for the training of those who take care of the very young.) A less unequivocal view is taken by Silverman (1989), and McLaughlin (1989) has a very personal approach to his clinical work, locating in his patients' idiosyncratic movements or mannerisms allusions to or enactments of an early infantile past.

The views of Cooper and Lichtenberg merit attention since they raise important issues pertinent to the purposes of this paper. Cooper (1989), working with adults, asks how it comes about that the "Freudian baby" is different from the "Kleinian baby," and the "Kohutian baby" is different from either. His answer is clear: Freud "patterned the patient's associations according to his own vision of the infant's early life, as have all analysts since" (p. 80). This statement is questionable, to say the least; and the generalization derived from it must be strongly challenged. All analysts, it seems, impose their view of childhood on their adult patients. Theory governs technique in what presumably is a one-sided process. I found no reference to the *mutual* understanding that comes about through effective interpretation. The patient associates, but the analyst, it seems, reshapes the material in accordance with his own theoretical preconceptions.[3] But "baby watching" is free from the handicap of therapeutic aims: it tries to find out what a baby actually *does* (Cooper's word, my italics). It has challenged and changed some "core theories" in important ways that influence therapeutic endeavor. It helps us he adds, toward a far richer and more varied view of baby life, thus changing the way we listen to our patients' associations.

---

3. Does not this imply that the adult patient regressively replicates the (caricatured) "Freudian baby" as passive and totally at the mercy of analyst-induced events, i.e., as the victim of *suggestion*?

It provides more interpretative possibilities than were previously available, and it has helped us to know that certain adult constellations are unlikely to appear without accompanying childhood circumstances. Later, Cooper continues: In our inevitable attempts to impose some intellectual and affective order on the unfolding life story, we call upon the familiar picture in our mind of the circumstances of pain and suffering that we imagine might endanger our patients' neurotic patterns, and that make our empathic responses possible" (pp. 81–82). And so on: infant research provides "the biological underpinning" for modern analytic work, and in doing so it replaces instinct [drive] theory. But there is more to psychoanalytic clinical work than empathy and a knowledge of "biological underpinning." Cooper seems more concerned to detect the material realities of the patient's early life than the psychic reality with which many analysts would be concerned.

Lichtenberg (1989a) expresses, through a different theoretical framework, what is in some ways a similar view. He uses a concept of transference based on his own theory of motivational systems—a theory in turn based on infantile observational research. While Cooper speaks of ordering the patient's "story" in line with a global view, Lichtenberg writes of "model scenes."[4] There are "classical" model scenes and "new" model scenes. The latter are based on direct observational research and are closer to the child's lived experience in his first two years. In each motivational system Lichtenberg finds in infancy, experiences are amplified by affects, and these serve as signals to caregivers and self. In analysis they serve as goals for the recreation of past experiences and the affective states that go with them.

Views such as these reflect an approach to clinical practice that, inter alia, fails to allow for the fact that mental organization in the very young child is subject to transformations as development proceeds. Other writers do acknowledge this. Glenn (1989) points out that the oedipal child has both transformed and incorporated preoedipal configurations. Silverman (1989) has a similar point in mind when he cautions against excessive clinical enthusiasm for the new findings, and Shane (1989), commenting on Silverman's paper, emphasizes the latter's acknowledgment of "the complexities and complications of developmental progression." With echoes of Hartmann, he stresses "the danger of reductionist genetic fallacies" (p. 154). Blum (1989) points to the problem of continuity versus discontinuity in clinical work; Meissner (1989) and others have comparable concerns. Rangell (1989), with customary clarity, elaborates a position in line with these views.

---

4. See also Lichtenberg, 1989b, 1989c.

The importance of early affective attunement has long been acknowledged and repeatedly discussed. For the infant to function effectively, the programmed capacities with which he enters the world need
stimulation. With stimulation, he can respond and make forward progress; without it his capacities fall into desuetude and may atrophy.
Spitz's work on anaclitic depression pointed long ago to a dramatic
consequence of the loss of a caregiver, and the Robertsons have illustrated it in harrowing film reportage. But infant observational research has emphasized and particularized the point in ways not hitherto possible. Emde (1988), for example, has shown that infants can
both recognize and express the facial patterns of basic emotions in the
first year of life, but, if the mother is emotionally unavailable and
cannot respond in turn, the child's development may be set at risk.

The enthusiastic welcome given by so-called object relations group
of analysts and by self psychologists to findings of this kind has kept
company with a belief that defects in early mothering and affective
attunement can somehow be put right by an analyst who offers the
human interchange his patient has lacked.[5] Scharfman (1989) questions this view, since "developmental processes are time-related," and a
failure of attunement at an early stage cannot necessarily be compen-
sated by an empathic relationship at a later one. What Balint (1968)
called the "basic fault" cannot necessarily be put right.

Psychoanalysts who work with children find the face-to-face relationship of great value. The young patient may conceal the content of his
thoughts but not the affect that can give it away. Nonetheless, the
interchange between child and analyst is no simple matter of reciprocity of the kind to be sought in infancy. The child's expression may
convey the delight or the misery he feels, but the analyst's affective
display has to be controlled in the interest of the treatment. It would,
for example, be no great service to the child if the analyst lost all
professional detachment. The analytic situation is not, and never was, a
mere replica of an infant-to-parent relationship. The belief that it is
dies hard. Deeply rooted in early Kleinian theory, it has plenty of
followers. If it were such a replica, however, what kind of "mother"
would see her child, at fixed times, for just fifty minutes on five out of
seven days in the week?

Among the many clinical problems posed by infant research, and
one to which Blum (1989) has pointed, is that great care is called for in
trying to refer to preverbal experience in verbal terms in therapies that

---

5. This view was long ago held, articulated, and organized into a personal system by
Fairbairn (e.g., 1944, 1958). For a recent succinct review, see Freeman (1994).

rely primarily on words for communication. When, as sometimes happens, we dramatically reduce an adult patient's anxieties by interpreting his fear of merging with the couch and hence with the analyst's body, we refer to a preverbal experience (although we cannot be sure of what is replicated in the transference) in a form of words that the patient can understand and to which he responds. We do not use words that prejudice the issue, and we are careful to refer only to a fear the nature of which is on the verge of accessibility. We have certainly not answered the related theoretical question, also put by Blum, of how the prerepresentational later achieves representation. In my view, we cannot approach that matter without the help of Freud's metapsychology. It is surely the setting-aside of metapsychology that allows Meissner (1989), for example, on the one hand to say that psychoanalysis is essentially a developmental psychology and that its most powerful tools are its understanding of psychopathology and personality functioning at all levels of development, and on the other to aver that the shift from the "Freudian baby" to the "modern baby" involves an equally decisive change on the part of both theory and technique toward an object relations model.

Daniel Stern's contributions to infant research are massive. He has also constructed, on the basis of his findings and those of other investigators in the field, a map of child development that amounts to a metapsychology of his own. The sense of self is a developmental organizing principle. Stern's account, "centering on the sense of self-and-other, has as its starting place the infant's *inferred* subjective experience. It is unique in that respect. Subjective experiences themselves are its main working parts, in contrast to the main working parts of psychoanalytic theories, which are the ego and id from which subjective experiences are derived" (Stern, 1985, p. 26; italics are mine).

It is beyond the scope of this paper to review the systematized inferences drawn by Stern from child observation, but Zuriff (1992) has brought a critical acumen to bear on the general questions raised by them, and I will summarize his conclusions: The empirical data from the research under scrutiny do not establish that infants possess a self or are capable of self/other differentiation in a psychological sense. Statements about the intrapsychic experiences of infants based on such data are theoretical postulates, not empirical generalizations or metaphors. The new theories differ from traditional theories of infancy in their criteria for attributing selfhood and self/other differentiation to the infant. Earlier theories require the possession of concepts and schemata not required by the former, and the former neither refute the latter nor put them to the test.

Finally, Novick (1989) has done a useful service in drawing attention to Freud's own experience with children—after all, he had six of his own (three of each sex), was a remarkably alert observer of what went on in the nursery, and painfully scrutinized his own childhood through the rigors of self-analysis, to say nothing of the significant and sustained neuroscientific work with children that preceded this period. In showing just how extensively and consistently Freud made use of child observation as well as of the findings of child analysis, Novick calls on key papers by James Anthony (1986) and Ruth Mack Brunswick (1940). He also includes the contributions made in Vienna by those close to Freud, in particular by Bernfeld and by Freud's daughter Anna. All this is a useful corrective to those who unaccountably believe that Freud's knowledge of child development was restricted to the vicissitudes of the oedipus complex. That view was and still is common among those who, for whatever reason, read or recall Freud only selectively. The error is widely asserted as almost self-evident fact. In the context of baby research, Cooper (1989) and Silverman (1989) come uncomfortably close to repeating it. Treurniet (1993), in a paper aptly entitled "What Is Psychoanalysis Today?," baldly states that "the first object was for Freud determined by the Oedipus and castration complexes." Many papers in many psychoanalytic journals contain statements of this kind.

III

The comprehensive study by Darwin (1872) of the expressions of emotions in man and animals attracted widespread attention beyond the field of biology itself and continues to do so. (It was once the subject of a series of seminars at the Anna Freud Centre). This interest underlines the fact that the wider study of affects has profited from biobehavioral research. Psychology has not been slow to turn to such studies for fresh enlightenment, and the result can be seen in a rapidly expanding literature.[6] But the necessary safeguards in respecting interdisciplinary boundaries are not always applied. Person (1990) has neatly summarized an accelerating trend. "Affects," she says, "so long neglected by virtue of the psychoanalytic pre-occupation with the discharge and transformation of libidinal energy, have been, so to speak, rediscovered in the context of object relations theory and the increasing attention paid to the self and to issues of narcissism" (p. ix). There is no doubt

---

6. Recent collections of papers include those edited by Glick and Bone (1990), to which Person contributed a foreword, and by Shapiro and Emde (1992).

that much of the persuasive force of this line of thinking derives from the impetus lent it by the study of affective attunement and related matters of biobehavioural research.

The dangers of emphasizing biological factors at the expense of the psychological are illustrated in various degrees by a large number of investigators, and I select one or two examples. Although Stern (1990) tries to stay on psychological ground, and in discussing pleasure draws a distinction between *joy* and *satisfaction,* he gives, as the prototype of *psychological* satisfaction at the mother's breast or its substitute, the meeting of a *biological* need—hunger—even though he deals with the regulation of states of excitation in pleasurable satisfaction. Joy is conceptualized as "a discrete organization of patterned activation accompanied by specific qualities of subjective experience" manifest particularly in patterns of facial expression. There are other discrete patterns in "classical affect states in the Darwinian tradition."

A more florid confusion between biology and psychology is demonstrated by Hofer (1990), who draws on experimental biology, including work with typhoid bacilli and infant rats, in attempting to explore the development of affect from an evolutionary and biological point of view. As might be expected, he has some impossible leaps to make when it comes to matters of human psychology, and although he acknowledges a distinction between mind and brain, he avoids the former and talks only in terms of the latter when he formulates his conclusions.

Some writers set great store by the affect theory of Tomkins (1962, 1963)—a theory open to serious criticism and one incompatible with psychoanalysis (see Yorke et al., 1990). In a recent paper that champions Tomkins's theory (Nathanson, 1990) Freud is not so much criticized as ill-used. The author does not seem to have understood Freud very well: the account of his scientific development in the last decade of the nineteenth century lacks rigor and sounds at times as if it were founded on hearsay. Nathanson has an unfortunate habit of relying on others whose own assessments, at least in this context, are open to objections (e.g., Basch, 1983; Brenner, 1955; Radó, 1962). This kind of criticism, unhappily, exemplifies a growing trend.

In his analysis of the Count Thun dream, Freud (1900, pp. 216–17), described associations that included his own recollection of urinating in his parents' bedroom and his father's scornful response: "The boy will come to nothing!" This remark acted as a spur to Freud's ambition. The painful affect of wounded self-esteem led to a wish for revenge: in Freud's dream he exchanged positions with his father. Shengold (1993) has based a book on Freud's account of his experience, considering in fascinating detail "Freud's ego ideal and Freud as ego ideal." He brings to life the motivating power of affect while ceding nothing to critics of drive theory or metapsychology, though the book is written in terms of human conflict and interplay and not theoretical exposition. In contrast, Schwartz (1990) sees in Freud's dream story "a view of 'aggression' as a *defensive reaction* to 'self'-involved injury or threat" and an idea that "endures in later publications (Freud, 1916, 1925) despite the concurrent development of the death instinct speculations (Freud, 1920) and derivative notions of an almost appetitive 'aggressive instinctual drive'" (p. 114). Schwartz builds on a "psychobiological" theory of motivation he has elaborated elsewhere (Schwartz, 1987, 1988) in which he seeks a synthesis of Freud and "new neurobiological understanding." His work, for all its interest, amply demonstrates the confusion to which I have referred.

Lastly, not all contemporary thinkers on these matters fall into the trap of disciplinary interchangeability even when their views differ from the Freudian tradition in substantial particulars. Doige (1990), for example, who seeks a "psychobiological model" of pleasure states and their regulation, makes extensive use of the work of Donald Klein (e.g., 1974, 1987) and his theory of appetitive and consummatory pleasure systems, but he does not regard different disciplines as interchangeable. He adopts the "dual track" method of Reiser (1984) by which "the separate languages of neuroscience and psychoanalysis are applied to a single clinical phenomenon": the two "can be looked at simultaneously to raise important questions." And Doige is aware, as some other writers are not, of the importance of Freud's remarks on pleasure and unpleasure in his paper on the economic problem of masochism (Freud, 1924).

In some of the papers I have mentioned (e.g., Schwartz, 1990) drive theory is under heavy attack and is replaced by a new "dynamism" based, for example, on affects as motivators—a view as often as not founded on a failure to distinguish between motivation and drive.[7] Let me exemplify the point. Shame, or its avoidance, is a great motivator, though not a drive, but there is a complex relation between the two. A few years ago at the Anna Freud Centre a study group reached the conclusion that, from a psychological point of view, shame involved a regressive breakdown of anal defensiveness[8] not always apparent from

---

7. Rapaport (1960), in a comprehensive and searching paper, says in a closing resumé, "the instinctual drives and their derivatives are causes which are also motives, and some motives may not be such derivatives" (p. 906).

8. We found the contributions of Shengold (1985, 1988) invaluable in reaching our formulations.

later transformations. As we tried to show, its development is highly complex (Yorke et al., 1990). Once fully developed, however, the affect of shame is such an overwhelmingly unpleasant experience that people go to great lengths to avoid it, and this very avoidance points to the fact that *anxiety* plays a major part in the motivation. It is generally acknowledged that shame has a special relationship to guilt, though the difficulty in defining the difference in meaningful psychological terms has likewise been recognized. Guilt, however, is often thought of as a poor motivator, since it may be experienced quite intensely at the very moment when the act that occasions it is being committed. But that everyday observation refers to conscious, not unconscious, guilt, and it is the latter that plays such an important part in mobilizing defenses against its full conscious experience and for the most part prevents incest and murder—that is, unmodified drive discharge.[9] But guilt is essentially "moral anxiety," as Anne Freud (1936) observed; and it is anxiety that brings about the steps taken by the ego to keep at bay a basic danger situation. So the motivating affects of guilt and shame both operate through the anxiety to which the forces that call them up give rise. Freud (1926) identified (in guilt) the danger of loss of the superego's love. But, in terms of the superego complex with a punitive superego on the one hand and an ego ideal on the other, it is perhaps rather more accurate to say that guilt is closely identified with the fear of punishment and shame with the fear of the loss of love of the ego ideal.[10] In this instance the ego ideal retains the *external* origins that give the affect its characteristic sense of exposure.[11]

It seems necessary to reassert, then, that while any affect can influence behavior, can be motivated and motivational, and can call into being defenses against psychic pain of all kinds, it is signal anxiety that mobilizes defenses against the more direct derivatives of the drives that threaten a basic danger situation. This distinction is one of the most

---

9. In view of the mass mayhem that is a matter of everyday report, these remarks refer to individual, not group, psychology.

10. There is, in effect, a superego complex that involves, for example, the ideal self and related ideals (see Sandler, Holder, and Meers, 1963). The idea of links between shame and the ego ideal and between guilt and the superego is rightly associated with the work of Piers and Singer (1953), though the present outline is set in the developmental context provided by the AFC study.

11. To put the matter in terms of metapsychology, the *economics* of shame involve a distribution of cathexis that borders intensely on the demarcation between self and object; the *dynamics* involve its striking links with drive derivatives; and the *structural* involvement has to be placed in accordance with the relevant point on its line of development. Each of these points of view has to be understood within the context of *regression*.

important points made in Anna Freud's book (1936). Anxiety is an affect biologically and psychologically different from any other (see Yorke et al., 1990; Yorke and Wiseberg, 1976).

It is important to note that the Anna Freud Centre study was based on observational data on mothers in relation to their toddlers and on detailed observations from the nursery school as well as on extensive reports from both child and adult analyses. It would not have been possible to construct a line of development, however imperfectly, without the help of observational records kept over many years.

Some of the controversies so far addressed are not entirely new. Over thirty years ago the reactions of Anna Freud, René Spitz, and Max Schur to the work of John Bowlby[12] provided a counterpart to the current disputes over the psychological significance of the work of such investigators as Stern and Emde. At that time, too, there was no disagreement about observational data: the point at issue was the significance for psychoanalysis of findings drawn from biology and ethology. For present purposes, one or two points made by Anna Freud may suffice. She was concerned with the repercussions in the mind of the child of biological interplay—satisfactions and frustrations. The pleasure/pain principle as such was not a drive representation at all but embraced all mental processes including those reflecting the tie to the mother. The analyst did not deal with the drives directly [that would not be possible] but with their [mental] representations. And a potent source of misunderstanding was the concept of infantile narcissism: Bowlby was using the term descriptively, referring "to a state in which the infant is supposed to be withdrawn, self-sufficient and independent of the object world," and he maintained that no normal infant displayed behavior of this kind. Anna Freud agreed with this last assertion, but pointed out that, "metapsychologically speaking, the concept of infantile narcissism refers not to behaviour but to an early phase of libido distribution and organization" (p. 56). It seems to me that misunderstandings of this kind—of which these are but examples—permeate a good deal of current controversy.

IV

Of the major schismatics, Adler and Steckel left the psychoanalytic movement on clinical grounds. Jung was the only one of the early

---

12. Bowlby (1960) read a paper on grief and mourning in infancy to one of two Sandor Radó Lectures at Columbia University in New York in April 1960. Anna Freud (1960), René Spitz (1960), and Max Schur (1960) were the discussants.

defectors to construct a new metapsychological system, and one that has some interesting affinities with the very much later one devised by Melanie Klein[13] (Glover, 1950). But whereas Jung *left* the psychoanalytic movement, Klein created a precedent by remaining within the formal psychoanalytic organization. Since then, further splits have occurred on clinical or theoretical grounds, as well as for other reasons discussed in this paper. But it is not very often that Freud's metapsychology, including its relevance for the theory of affects, is reassessed and rejected on psychological grounds alone, in its own terms, and with nothing more than the selective use of Freud's own theoretical writings. Yet that is precisely what Patricia Herzog (1991) has recently chosen to do. Philip Holzman, in a preface, considers her views to be of some interest to both the psychologist and neuroscientist, as well as the "cognitive scientist"; and as it seems possible that they may provide some affect theorists with a psychological basis for their speculations, they need at least brief mention.

If it is true that the concept of a dynamic Unconscious (*Ucs.*) is a cornerstone of Freudian psychoanalysis, no model of the mind that dispenses with it can claim to be psychoanalytic. But the gravamen of Herzog's argument is that Freud, on his way to the concept of the dynamic force of repression, shed insights indispensable to a proper understanding of consciousness and perception. He abandoned the pretopographical formulations set out in "The Neuro-Psychoses of Defence" (Freud, 1894), in which the psychoneuroses were understood in terms of "pathological defence" without any explicit or implicit reference to a psychological "unconscious." Freud argued that when the ego encountered an "incompatible idea"[14] that idea was robbed of its *affect*—the "sum of excitation" to which it was attached and which gave the idea its force or "associative strength." For Herzog, "this important albeit elusive conception of affect . . . has been completely overshadowed by Freud's far less subtle energic conception—which latter, incidentally, almost no one today finds useful" (p. 6).

Herzog could not accept the concept that affect could be detached from the idea to which it was related. She turned to the *Studies on Hysteria* (Breuer and Freud, 1895) to support her view that, in conversion hys-

---

13. For a discussion of Klein's psychological system see Yorke, 1971, and for some clinical implications of post-Kleinian developments see Yorke, 1994.

14. Here the ego is the "I" (self). In his paper Freud gives examples of "incompatible [unacceptable] ideas." One of these is "the case of a girl who blamed herself because, while she was nursing her sick father, she had thought about a young man who had made a slight erotic impression on her" (p. 48). The case was discussed as that of Fraulein von R. in the *Studies on Hysteria* (Breuer and Freud, 1895).

teria, it was not detached affect that gave rise to the somatic symptom, but the *associative*[15] or *symbolic* links between affect and idea. There was no separation between the two: rather, they were "*together transformed.*" A somatic symptom like Frau Cäcilie's difficulty in swallowing was a somatic representation of a hurtful thought. Herzog turns to the "Project" (Freud [1895] 1950) and with the aid of an extensive quotation finds further support for her view that, "as a result of the experience of satisfaction, ideas get attached to *one another.* Hunger, satiety, the breast: all are on a par as constituents of the drive" *understood as facilitation* [my emphasis]. There is no 'quota of affect' to which the drive constituents are attached. Nor is affect itself one of the constituents. Hunger . . . is not an affect but a mental representation,[16] a sensation or inner perception which has entered into the configuration of ideas constituting the drive. Affect "*cannot be conceived apart or in abstraction from idea.*"[17] It is the "*glue that holds ideas together*" (p. 14).

From all this Herzog argues that pathological defense "effects a dissociation of ideas, it breaks apart the existing structure of thought." And in the pretopographical works the concept of consciousness is theoretically central and the splitting of consciousness is the basis of psychopathology. Yet, in "Further Remarks on the Neuro-Psychoses of Defence" (Freud, 1896a) as well as in "The Aetiology of Hysteria" (1896b) there is "a clear terminological departure from that [1894] paper and from the *Studies.*" But in between "Further Remarks" and "Aetiology" came the "Project" (Freud [1895] 1950), and it was the difficulties Freud encountered there—difficulties not properly dealt with by Herzog—that led him to abandon the line of reasoning of which Herzog so strongly approves. She rejects Freud's explanation made in 1906 and in 1912 that we had no right to extend the meaning of the word conscious "so far as to make it include the consciousness of which its owner himself is not aware" (Freud, 1912a, p. 263).

I have outlined only the basis for Herzog's thesis and have tried with brief quotations to give the flavour of her argument. Because it gives

---

15. Unless otherwise stated, italics are those of the author to which a passage refers.

16. In an endnote Herzog says it is a biological need as well, but she wants to elucidate its *psychological* significance.

17. Herzog (1991, p. 14) quotes with approval a statement by George Klein (1967) that the concept of drive "as a distinct entity which 'interacts' with thought creates all sorts of mischief. It is only as affective-cognitive-motor events that drives are knowable as motivation and definable at all. To the extent that thought records the directed relationship of knower to object, to event, to self, and to other, it *is* a unit of motivation" (p. 84). Put in Herzog's terms, "affect" (Klein's "drive") does not interact with "idea" (Klein's "thought"), but rather *constitutes* the drive as such (Klein's "unit of motivation").

the appearance of scholarship, it needs to be read with a vigilant eye. Her thesis is beguiling, but only within the narrow focus through which she views it. For Herzog ignores the fact that, for all the imperfections of its formulations, Freud's *analytic* model of the mind casts light on normal behaviour and development, on the dream, and on mental disturbance of all kinds that cannot be matched by a theory of dissociation. Herzog loses sight of the wider context in which Freud's ideas developed; in her historical account there are some serious lacunae. There is, for example, no consideration of Freud's *On Aphasia* (1891) and, consequently, no acknowledgement of Freud's debt to Hughlings Jackson. Indeed, Jackson is not even mentioned. For a more accurate picture of these historical developments, the reader is advised to consult Solms and Saling (1986).

V

Apart from her very brief references to one or two cases in the *Studies*, Herzog makes no use of clinical material in her argument. To that extent hers is an armchair exercise. And it is a mater of some moment that the concept of the case history as a route to knowledge is currently under fire. Case histories are dismissed as anecdotal, with no part to play in empirical investigation—which, in some quarters, is considered the only legitimate form of research. Furthermore, Freud's particular case histories are themselves under attack; it has even been proposed that studying them should no longer be a requirement of psychoanalytic training. Mahony (1993) has examined these charges and provided a very convincing defense, which should perhaps be required reading in analytic institutes. I want now to consider the matter from a different, though related, point of view, and to look at the old distinction between nomothetic and idiographic approaches to psychology.

Early in this century the German scholar Max Verworn suggested that in their approach to their subject scientists fell into two groups: classical and romantic. Luria (1979) recalls this in his autobiography, in which he too adopts the same terms. His discussion of the issue is of considerable interest. Classical science is akin to the nomothetic: events are broken down into their constituent parts, and the study of significant elements permits the formulation of abstract general laws. These are then regarded as the agents of the phenomena observed in the field of investigation. The living whole is reduced to the abstractions of schemata. The romantic scientist, on the other hand, takes an opposite path, one akin to the idiographic approach. He does not want "to split living reality into its elementary components nor to represent the

wealth of life's concrete events in abstract models that lose the proper-
ties of the phenomena themselves" (p. 174).

As Luria so clearly describes it, the distinction between classical and
romantic science is similar to that drawn between Newtonian science
and science in the tradition of Goethe, so very well described by Kaufmann (1980) in his indispensable study of the minds of Freud, Adler,
and Jung. It was hearing a recitation of "Goethe's beautiful essay on
Nature" that decided Freud to study medicine (Kaufmann, 1980, p. 11).
And indeed, in defining romantic science, Luria quotes from Goethe:
"Gray is every theory, but ever green is the tree of life." Luria, nonetheless, sees difficulties and limitations of method arising from both
camps and describes the problem of "a reformulation of the conflict
between nomothetic and idiographic approaches to psychology" as a
concern for him during the early years of his intellectual life. He tells us
that one of the major factors that drew him to Vygotsky was "his emphasis on the necessity to resolve this crisis. He saw its resolution as the
most important goal of psychology in our time" (Luria, 1979, p. 175).

It is not easy to summarize Luria's extensive discussion without diminishing it, but paraphrase with selected quotations may help to convey its force. He describes how nomothetic reductionism in the study of
learning had led to "an emphasis on contiguity and reinforcement as
the basic elements, the combination of which could explain even the
most complex forms of behaviour, including human conscious[18] activity. In this atmosphere, the rich and complex picture of human behaviour which had existed in the late nineteenth century disappeared
from psychological textbooks" (pp. 175–76). Spectacular advances in
biophysics followed, and "the study of human conscious activity became submerged in a sea of molecular speculation." Then came "what
was perhaps the most striking breakthrough of all. Electronic devices
whose detection capabilities and speed greatly exceeded those of individuals were invented, and self-regulating computers became one
of the basic tools of science. Many scholars began to suppose that observation could be replaced by computer simulation and mathematical
models." Psychological textbooks and monographs overflowed with
models and schemas. "This deluge brought a still graver danger: the
reality of human conscious activity was being replaced by mechanical
models" (p. 176).

Some of Luria's most forceful arguments are reserved for the practice of medicine. He considers that the reduction of living facts to

---

18. To put the argument in psychoanalytic language, for "conscious" in Luria's terminology, read "mental."

mathematical schema and the tendency in investigation to rely heavily on instruments were accompanied by the relative neglect of the clinical observation that used to be thought essential for diagnosis and treatment. He has no objection to clinical tests as such, nor to their analysis by mathematical techniques, but insists they should not be central. They should be "servants to clinical thought." In opposition to the trends he condemns, he cites the vanishing art of the case history, which reached its acme in the case descriptions of such great physicians as Charcot, Wernicke, Korsakoff, and Henry Head, among many others, and "the beauty of the art of science" that they reveal (p. 177). (Here I would like to add a personal comment. For several years, I acted as a scrutineer for papers submitted to the British Psychoanalytical Society for their annual clinical essay prize. In the last year I served, only three papers were submitted, none of them outstanding. There were no submissions in the following year, and the prize was discontinued.)

Luria adds a word of caution to the passage I have just quoted. Simple observation and description also have their shortcomings. Observers can be seduced by a description of immediately perceived events into "pseudo-explanations based on their own phenomenological understanding." Errors of this kind jeopardize the essential role of scientific analysis. But this is only a danger when phenomenological description is superficial and incomplete. Truly scientific observation avoids such dangers because it is not simply pure description of separate facts: "Its main goal is to view an event from as many perspectives as possible. The eye of science does not probe 'a thing', an event isolated from other things or events. Its real objective is to see and understand the way a thing or event relates to other things or events" (Luria, 1979, p. 177).

Looking back on his own earlier research Luria examines the part played in it by clinical and psychological observations. He has sought out the primary basic factors that have immediate consequences and then considered the secondary or "systemic" ones. The entire picture cannot become clear until these basic factors and their consequences have been identified. In this way observations are used to establish a network of significant relations. "When done properly," Luria adds, "observations accomplish the classical aim of explaining facts, while not losing sight of the romantic aim of preserving the manifold richness of the subject" (p. 177). On the other hand, he is entirely prepared to use instrumental laboratory techniques for "meaningful scientific advancement" and insists that in a good deal of work his approach has been "as much that of the classical scholar as the romantic one." Two of his books have resulted from his efforts to revive the tradition of romantic science: *The Mind of a Mnemonist* (1969) and *The Man with a Shattered World* (1972). These are in the line of the great case histories of the past that he so much admired and of which Freud (with whom he had once corresponded) was such a striking exponent. Case *illustrations* may be dismissed as anecdotal, since they are meant only to clarify a point and not to prove it. Psychology can only be the poorer if it turns its back on case *studies*.

While putting together this account I recalled an endnote by Sacks (1985) to a popular book of his, full of richly informative neurological case studies. There he referred to Hughlings Jackson, Kurt Goldstein, Henry Head, and A. R. Luria as the fathers of neurology, seeing in the writings of each the attraction and influence of both classical and romantic science. If Jackson, for example, was a great logician he was also "a poet"—that is, a *poetic scientist*. In Luria, however, the dual nature of his scientific impetus was conscious: he felt he had to write two different kinds of books—the formal and structural, for example, his *Higher Cortical Functions in Man* (1980), and the "biographical 'novels'" to which I have referred.

Influential academic psychiatrists (for example, the late Dennis Pond, 1986) have repeatedly stated that psychoanalysis is out of step with contemporary neuroscience. A historical survey of the facts does not support this conclusion. During his many years as a neurologist and neuropathologist, Freud was deeply influenced by Hughlings Jackson and acknowledged his indebtedness—notably in *On Aphasia* (1891). That book, however, was in advance of its time (see Jelliffe, 1937; Stengel, 1953; Jones, 1953), and the significance of Jackson's work was not otherwise recognized for half a century (see Head, 1926; Luria, 1980). Freud was in complete accord with the English neurologist's rejection of the predominating cerebral localization hypothesis of the day that was so well in tune with its contemporary associationist psychology. On the basis of his *clinical* observations Jackson (e.g., 1884) came to understand nervous functioning in terms of a complex "vertical" organization. According to this hierarchical model the process of dissolution in nervous disorder led to two kinds of symptoms. *Negative,* or pathological, ones came into being through the loss of higher levels of organization. *Positive* symptoms, in contrast, were not intrinsically pathological at all: they came about simply from the operation of developmentally older but persisting structures whose operation came to light only when the ontogenetic process was in reverse.

Freud's *psychoanalytic* thinking was profoundly influenced by these new ideas, and their impact is conspicuous in his formulations of fixation and regression. Freeman (1969) has emphasized the importance of "the factors of insanities" (Jackson, 1894) for Freud's thinking about psychosis. Although their impact on neurology was long delayed, the influence of Jackson's ideas through Head and others on modern neuroscience was immense and ultimately led to our contemporary understanding of the working brain (Luria, 1973, 1980) with its concepts of functional systems and primary, secondary, and tertiary areas of cortical functioning. In their important historical paper Solms and Saling (1986) concluded that there was no good reason for the continuing mutual mistrust between neuroscience[19] and Freudian psychoanalysis.

The romantic tradition bequeathed by Freud to psychoanalysis should be a matter for pride. For clinical psychoanalysis depends above all on intensive and sustained study that, with the help of a treatment alliance, gives the analyst the most highly privileged view of his patient's internal functioning. It must be remembered, however, that the slowly unfolding picture is no simple "story," as some analysts seem to suggest. It does not and cannot have an orderly narrative sequence. Like development itself, it reveals continuities and discontinuities, with changes, transformations and, for that matter, transmogrifications.

VI

It seems strange, in the light of these considerations, that the value of clinical work can be used as an argument against Freud's metapsychology, but that is indeed a common strategy. So it was that although in studies at the Anna Freud Centre on the psychology of the common psychiatric disorders, Yorke, Wiseberg, and Freeman (1989) found Freud's metapsychology an indispensable conceptual tool, they felt forced to defend it in the light of an accumulating body of criticism, some of which was based on its alleged impoverishment of clinical data. Those arguments need to be repeated and extended in the present context.

The notion that metapsychology, in its seeming aridity and undoubted abstraction, depreciates the value of clinical observation, continues to grow. Critics say that Freud's concepts maintain a nineteenth-century view of mental life based on the physics and chemistry of the day and expressed in the language of forces, energies, and structures.

---

19. Neuroscience is not here identified with what has come to be called cognitive science. Some analysts feel that models constructed on the basis of computational research can and should replace Freud's metapsychology. Much will no doubt be learned from these new developments, but in the absence of machines that can develop and grow up in a social context it is difficult to see how they can acquire "internal speech" (Luria, 1982) and thus be able to think.

Yet these critics seem not to take into account the fact that metapsychology was brought into being by an outstanding clinician whose case histories recreate with unsurpassed vividness and clarity the human complexities of their subjects. Jones (1955, p. 47) tells us that Freud talked for several hours on the Rat Man in 1908 to an audience held in rapt attention, but *Studies on Hysteria* of 1893–95 had long before displayed his mastery of the case presentation. And that work, too, involves a conceptual achievement in formulating the psychological processes that seemed to shape the movement of clinical events, for Freud made a pioneering link between aetiology (seduction in childhood), psychopathology (strangulated affect), and symptom (hysteria), although this first preanalytic model could not survive the stringency of further investigation. It was Freud's painful realization of this fact that led to the inspired struggle resulting in *The Interpretation of Dreams* (1900) and with it the birth of metapsychology proper. None of this, incidentally, is reflected in Herzog's account of events.

Other charges against metapsychology have been laid by writers like Holt (1981) and Peterfreund (1975). Yorke, Wiseberg, and Freeman acknowledged that "some of the accusations have weight because undisciplined use of metapsychological concepts has encouraged [some] analysts to regard explanatory concepts as facts" (1989, p. 213). But, they continued, "the basic objection to metapsychology, common to every critical publication (Gill, 1976[20]; Lidz, 1972), is that this approach to clinical phenomena is rendered redundant by advances in contemporary psychobiology (Hill, 1971)" (ibid). Some of these charges may already have been met, but it seems to me more than ever necessary to go back to the dream book itself, for it is surely worth recalling the careful and guarded words with which Freud introduced his model of the mind:

> I shall entirely disregard the fact that the mental apparatus with which we are here concerned is also known to us in the form of an anatomical preparation, and I shall carefully avoid the temptation to determine psychical locality in any anatomical fashion. I shall remain upon *psychological* ground. (p. 536, my emphasis)

Drawing a comparison between operations of the mental apparatus and those of certain optical instruments, he went on:

> I see no necessity to apologize for the imperfections of this or of any similar imagery. Analogies of this kind are only intended to assist us in

---

20. Gill's criticism of metapsychology is of special interest since he was once one of its distinguished supporters (e.g., Gill, 1963). He has recently described his present views in *Psychoanalysis in Transition* (Gill, 1994).

our attempt to make the complications of mental functioning intelligible by dissecting the function and assigning its different constituents to different component parts of the apparatus. So far as I know, the experiment has not hitherto been made of using this method of dissection in order to investigate the way in which the mental instrument is put together, and I can see no harm in it. We are justified, in my view, in giving free rein to our speculations so long as we retain the coolness of our judgement *and do not mistake the scaffolding for the building*. And since at our first approach to something unknown all that we need is the assistance of *provisional ideas*, I shall give preference in the first instance to hypotheses of the crudest and most concrete description. (ibid., my emphases)

These words seem to me a wonderful combination of daring and caution, free from the dogmatism of some of Freud's critics, or the cocksure tone that characterizes Herzog's book.

But this early model of the mind—expanded and further developed in later papers, and to which the economic point of view, though adumbrated in earlier writings, was added in 1915—sprang from the clinical study of dreams and, in particular, Freud's courageously clinical scrutiny of his own dreams in the course of his self-analysis. But clinical concepts are not metapsychological concepts. Metapsychology is conceptualized at a high level of abstraction. It is more akin to the nomothetic than the ideographic method of psychoanalytic practice. It is not, and never was supposed to be, equated with the realities of clinical interchange; and the idea that it was led many, misguidedly, to oppose what they call Freud's "one-person psychology" with a "two-person psychology." Clinical observations in the process of analysis are the bedrock on which the abstractions of metapsychology (which is, after all, only another word for Freud's theory of mind) are firmly rooted. It is for this reason that new clinical findings may call for modifications of the abstract model, and Freud did not hesitate to change it in the light of clinical necessity.[21]

Critics of metapsychology seem to lose sight of the purpose of metapsychological concepts. They are explanatory concepts, means to an end and not ends in themselves. When they are abandoned clinical practice may follow erroneous lines: if, for example, the distinction

---

21. The reformulation of the theory of anxiety (Freud, 1926) is a striking example. Of course, a theoretical difficulty or inconsistency may also call for change. The structural model (Freud, 1923) came into being on both counts: the theoretical anomaly that defenses could not be located in the system *Pcs.*, but must themselves be dynamically unconscious, and the clinical observation of the negative therapeutic reaction. But basic mental concepts—concepts incapable of further reduction—persist through these changes of model (Glover, 1947).

between primary and secondary process were no longer drawn, a patient's dream material might be treated like any other communication from the couch. And this, sadly, is all too often the case. We need explanatory concepts. Noy (1977) has suggested that metapsychology offers a framework for a series of models illustrating aspects of mental phenomena, models that can be likened to topographical, geologic, and climatic maps.[22]

Of the metapsychological *points of view,* the least controversial seems to be the structural one. Inasmuch as the dynamic point of view is closely linked with the theory of instinctual drives, it is strongly under attack; I have already discussed the offensive in an earlier section and the equation of motivation and drive that so often lies behind it. The economic point of view is also a target of criticism, criticism originating, I believe, in a misunderstanding of part of Freud's argument on narcissism (Freud, 1914), a matter I have considered elsewhere (Yorke, 1991). Freeman (1992) has discussed in some detail the theoretical value of the economic concept. Many analysts, some inspired by Hartmann, have thought it necessary to add an adaptive and a developmental point of view, though these rest on the other three. So, too, does the "object relations point of view," though it is often used to imply an endopsychic representation free of metapsychological distinctions.

There is one question that, during my analytic training, puzzled me deeply. How can analysts differ so drastically from each other in their understanding of a patient's material? The differences between the seminar leaders I met then and some of the authors I have mentioned now are by no means trivial. Here, I believe, the principal culprit is the tool of observation. It has often been said that what most distinguishes psychology from other sciences is that the mind is both the subject and object of its own investigations. That is true: Luria knew it well and it is a point to be kept firmly in mind in considering his statements on scientific observation. But the observing mind in psychoanalysis is both an *analyzed* mind and a mind that listens in a very special way. This fact confers advantages, and these go some way to meet the difficulties, providing certain conditions are met by both patient and analyst. Once a treatment alliance has been won and the patient tries to follow his associations to the best of his ability, his recumbent posture, the an-

---

22. Many who consider the topographical model outmoded and totally replaced by the structural model still have recourse to a topographical point of view in explaining the dream process. The topographical *point of view* must however be distinguished from the topographical *model.* Noy (1977) offers a related, if somewhat different, approach to the conceptual difficulties arising from the change of models.

alyst's comparative silence and invisibility, and the lack of other dis-
tractions fosters regression. *Formal* regression permits a measure of
primary-process intrusion to color the patient's material, and *temporal*
regression means that partial replication of past experience in the
present helps to bring about the transference situation. The many
forms of resistance to be detected in the thought and feelings of even
the most cooperative of patients reveal the conflictual nature of the
analysand's efforts to follow the basic rule. It is the collective presence
of these subtle but powerful factors that give every analytic hour an
underlying theme. To detect that theme the analyst, whose repression
barrier should have been loosened by his own analysis, listens with *free-
floating attention*.[23] This permits and furthers the analyst's intuitive
responses to his patient, by means of which he is better able to detect
the underlying theme of the associations with which he is presented.[24]

I have long thought it likely, however, that not all analysts adopt this
technical procedure. They do not relax and give themselves up to free-
floating attention. They do not, for example, find that appropriate
associations attuned to those of the patient come readily to mind, that
one of the patient's remarks recalls another that gives it fresh meaning,
or that a fleeting thought touches something in their own unconscious
that points to a deeper or more primitive context than the one which
the patient consciously presents, or that a patient's immediate fantasy
spontaneously recalls in the analyst's mind something said in a session
days or weeks ago. Rather, as a colleague once remarked, they give the
impression of sitting on the edge of their seats as they try to make sense
of what the patient tells them. They try to fit it into a theoretical framework and feel vindicated when the "fit" is a good one. If the fit isn't
there, they may explain this in a way that depends on their theoretical
predilections. That, presumably, is what Lichtenberg (1989a,b,c) is getting at. So they may assume, for example, that the patient is trying to
make them feel what it is like not to be understood, or to convey to
the analyst (some would say through the "countertransference") the
mother's lack of attunement when the patient was an infant, or to put
his own confusion into the analyst, to trick him in order to triumph over

---

23. Freud (1912b, p. 111) uses the term *evenly hovering attention*, which conveys very well
what he has in mind. But I prefer the term *free-floating:* I believe it conforms more closely
to what, in practice, the analyst is able to achieve.

24. This is a highly condensed and simplified account of the analytic interchange that
may suffice for present purposes but is otherwise inadequate. A much fuller account
(Yorke, 1965) illustrates the value of metapsychology for understanding clinical processes. That account needs updating, but its basic tenets are not to my mind overruled by
subsequent developments.

him, or whatever else is plausible within their frame of reference. The fact that these processes, or something akin to them, may indeed take place does not, I submit, invalidate the point.

These differences in technical approach may be fostered by a further factor. Metapsychology is a theoretical model of the mind, and to that extent is basic to further psychological constructions. It is closely related to, but by no means identical with, a model of illness on which a model of treatment has to be based. Ignoring the logical distinction creates problems. If, for example, a borderline or psychotic patient is treated in accordance with a model of neurosis, the analyst is bound to be disappointed with the result. But, failing to recognize where the error lies, the analyst may seek a different basic model of mind rather than a more accurate model of illness and treatment. He may be all to ready to embrace a "new" and ostensibly more attractive mental system, which is apt to lack the explanatory power and wide applicability— to both normal and abnormal development—of the metapsychology that Freud's thinking set in train.[25]

The continuation of this tendency would mark a real and perhaps irretrievable loss for psychology. For if, as I believe, Freud's metapsychology ranks in achievement with the self-analysis on which it was founded, then the most important clinical case study yet undertaken and the basic mental concepts derived from it could be consigned to a history impervious to effective rediscovery.

BIBLIOGRAPHY

ANTHONY, E. J. (1986). The contributions of child psychoanalysis to psychoanalysis. *Psychoanal. Study Child*, 41:61–87.

BALINT, M. (1968). *The Basic Fault*. London: Tavistock.

BASCH, M. F. (1983). The concept of self: An operational definition. In *Developmental Approaches to the Self*, ed. B. Lee & G. G. Noam. New York: Plenum.

BLUM, H. (1989). The value, use, and abuse of infant developmental research. In Dowling and Rothstein (1989).

BOWLBY, J. (1960). Grief and mourning in infancy and early childhood. *Psychoanal. Study Child*, 15:9–52.

BRENNER, C. (1955). *An Elementary Textbook of Psychoanalysis*. New York: Int. Univ. Press.

BREUER, J., & FREUD, S. (1893–95). *Studies on Hysteria. S.E.*, 2.

---

25. There is a related kind of error that also has had great influence. Developments in Kleinian theory have increasingly relied on models of adult psychosis to further their conceptualization of child development (Spillius, 1988)—a curious inversion of Klein's own procedure.

BRUNSWICK, R. M. (1940). The preoedipal phase of the libido development. *Psychoanal. Q.*, 9:293.

COOPER, A. M. (1989). Infant research and adult psychoanalysis. In Dowling and Rothstein (1989).

DARWIN, C. ([1872] 1979). *The Expression of the Emotions in Man and Animals.* London: Julian Friedmann.

DOIGE, N. (1990). Appetitive pleasure states: A biopsychoanalytical model of the pleasure threshold, mental representations, and defence. In Glick and Bone (1990).

DOWLING, S., & ROTHSTEIN, A. (1989). *The Significance of Infant Observational Research for Clinical Work with Children, Adolescents, and Adults.* Madison, Conn: Int. Univ. Press.

EISENBERG, L. (1986). Mindlessness and brainlessness in psychiatry. *Brit. J. Psychiat.*, 48:497–508.

EMDE, R. N. (1988). Development terminable and interminable. *Internat. J. Psycho-Anal.*, 69:23–42.

FAIRBAIRN, W. R. D. (1944). Endopsychic structures considered in terms of object relations. In *Psychoanalytic Studies of the Personality.* London: Routledge and Kegan Paul.

——— (1958). On the nature and aims of psychoanalytic treatment. *Int. J. Psycho-Anal.*, 39:374–85.

FREEMAN, T. (1969). *Psychopathology of the Psychoses.* New York: Int. Univ. Press.

——— (1992). Psychiatric perspectives on Freud's metapsychology. *Int. Rev. Psycho-anal.* 19:497–502.

——— (1994). Melanie Klein & W. R. D. Fairbairn: The clinical foundations and explanatory concepts of their theories. In *Centres and Peripheries of Psychoanalysis*, ed. R. Ekins & R. Freeman. London: Karnac.

FREUD, A. ([1936] 1937). *The ego and the mechanisms of defence.* London: Hogarth.

——— (1960). Discussion of Dr. John Bowlby's paper. *Psychoanal. Study Child.*, 15:53–62.

FREUD, S. (1891). *Zur Auffassung der Aphasien.* Translated by E. Stengel as *On Aphasia.* London: Imago, 1953.

——— (1894). The neuro-psychoses of defence. *S.E.*, 2:45–61.

——— ([1895] 1950). Project for a scientific psychology. In *The Origins of Psycho-Analysis*, ed. M. Bonaparte, A. Freud & E. Kris. London: Imago.

——— (1896a). Further remarks on the neuro-psychoses of defence. *S.E.*, 3:162–85.

——— (1896b). The aetiology of hysteria. *S.E.*, 3:191–221.

——— (1900). *The Interpretation of Dreams. S.E.*, 4 and 5.

——— (1906). My views on the part played by sexuality in the aetiology of the neuroses. *S.E.* 7:271–79.

——— (1912a). A note on the Unconscious in psycho-analysis. *S.E.*, 12:260–66.

——— (1912b). Recommendations to physicians practising psycho-analysis. *S.E.*, 12:111–20.

——— (1914). On narcissism: An introduction. *S.E.*, 14:73–102.

——— (1915). The Unconscious. *S.E.*, 14:166–204.

———— (1916). Some character types met with in psychoanalytic work. *S.E.*, 14:311–33.

———— (1920). *Beyond the Pleasure Principle. S.E.*, 18:7–64.

———— (1923). *The Ego and the Id. S.E.*, 19:12–66.

———— (1924). The economic problem of masochism. *S.E.*, 19:159–70.

———— (1925). Some psychical consequences of the anatomical distinction between the sexes. *S.E.*, 19:248–58.

———— (1926) *Inhibitions, Symptoms and Anxiety. S.E.*, 20:87–172.

GILL, M. M. (1963). *Topography and Systems in Psychoanalysis.* New York: Int. Univ. Press.

———— (1976). Metapsychology is not psychology. In *Psychology v. Metapsychology*, ed. M. M. Gill & P. S. Holzman. New York: Int. Univ. Press.

———— (1994). *Psychoanalysis in Transition: A Personal View.* Hillside, N.J: Analytic.

GLENN, J. (1989). The significance of infant observational research with prelatency children. In Dowling and Rothstein (1989).

GLICK, R. A., & BONE, S., eds. (1990). *Pleasure Beyond the Pleasure Principle: The Role of Affect in Motivation, Development, and Adaptation.* New Haven: Yale Univ. Press.

GLOVER, E. (1947). *Basic Mental Concepts.* London: Imago.

———— (1950). *Freud or Jung.* London: George Allen and Unwin.

———— (1961). Some recent trends in psycho-analytic theory. *Psychoanal. Q.,* 30:86–107.

HEAD, H. (1926). *Aphasia and Kindred Disorders of Speech.* Cambridge: Cambridge Univ. Press.

HERZOG, P. (1991). *Conscious and Unconscious: Freud's Dynamic Distinction Reconsidered.* Madison, Conn: Int. Univ. Press.

HILL, D. (1971). On the contribution of psychoanalysis to psychiatry: Mechanism and meaning. *Int. J. Psycho-Anal.,* 52:1–10.

HOFER, M. A. (1990). Early symbiotic processes: Hard evidence from a soft place. In Glick and Bone (1990).

HOLT, R. R. (1981). The death and transfiguration of metapsychology. *Int. Rev. Psycho-Anal.,* 8:129–43.

JACKSON, J. H. (1884). Evolution and dissolution of the nervous system. In *Selected Writings of John Hughlings Jackson.* New York: Basic.

———— (1894). The factors of insanities. In *Selected Writings of John Hughlings Jackson.* New York: Basic.

JELLIFFE, E. S. (1937). Sigmund Freud as neurologist. *J. Nerv. and Ment. Diseases,* 85:696–711.

JONES, E. (1953). *Sigmund Freud: Life and Work.* Vol. 1. London: Hogarth.

———— (1955). *Sigmund Freud: Life and Work.* Vol. 2. London: Hogarth.

KAUFMANN, W. (1980). *Discovering the Mind. Vol. 3: Freud versus Adler and Jung.* New York: McGraw-Hill.

KLEIN, D. F. (1974). Endogenomorphic depression: A conceptual and terminological revision. *Archives Gen. Psychiat.,* 31:447–54.

—— (1987). Depression and anhedonia. In *Anhedonia and Affect Deficit States*, ed. D. Clark & J. Fawcett. New York: PMA Publishing.

KLEIN, G. S. (1967). Preemptory ideation: The structure and force in motivated ideas. In *Motives and Thought: Psychoanalytic Essays in Honor of David Rapaport*, ed. R. R. Holt. *Psychological Issues*, Monogr. 18/19. New York: Int. Univ. Press.

KOHUT, H. (1971). *The Analysis of the Self*. New York: Int. Univ. Press.

LICHTENBERG, J. (1989a). Model scenes, motivation, and personality. In Dowling and Rothstein (1989).

—— (1989b). *Psychoanalysis and Motivation*. Hillsdale, N.J.: Analytic.

—— (1989c). A theory of motivational-functional systems as psychic structures. *J. Amer. Psychoanal. Assn.*, 37:55–70.

LIDZ, T. (1972). Schizophrenic disorders: The influence of conceptualization on therapy. In *Schizophrenia*, ed. D. Rubinstein & Y. O. Alanen. Amsterdam: Exerpt Medica.

LURIA, A. R. (1969). *The Mind of a Mnemonist*. London: Jonathan Cape.

—— (1972). *The Man with a Shattered World*. London: Jonathan Cape.

—— (1973). *The Working Brain: An Introduction to Neuropsychology*. London: Penguin.

—— (1979). *The Making of Mind: A Personal Account of Soviet Psychology*, ed. M. & S. Cole. Cambridge, Mass.: Harvard Univ. Press.

—— (1980). *Higher Cortical Functions In Man*, 2d ed. New York: Basic.

—— (1982). *Language and Cognition*. New York: Wiley.

MCLAUGHLIN, J. T. (1989). The relevance of infant observational research for the analytic understanding of adult nonverbal behaviour. In Dowling and Rothstein (1989).

MAHONY, P. J. (1993). Freud's cases: Are they valuable today? *Int. J. Psycho-Anal.*, 74:1027–35.

MEISSNER, W. W. (1989). The viewpoint of a devil's advocate. In Dowling and Rothstein (1989).

NATHANSON, D. L. (1990). Project for the study of emotion. In Glick and Bone (1990).

NOVICK, J. (1989). How does infant research affect our clinical work with adolescents? A case report. In Dowling and Rothstein (1989).

NOY, P. (1977). Metapsychology as a multimodel system. *Int. J. Psycho-Anal.*, 4:1–12.

PERSON, E. S. (1990). Foreword to Glick and Bone (1990).

PETERFREUND, P. (1975). The need for a new general theoretical frame of reference in psychoanalysis. *Psychoanal. Q.*, 44:534–49.

PIERS, G., & SINGER, M. (1953). *Shame and Guilt*. Springfield, Ill.: Charles C. Thomas.

POND, D. (1986). Prospects and opportunities for research in psychiatry and clinical psychology. *Brit. J. Clin. and Soc. Psychiatry*, 4:45–49.

RADÓ, S. (1962). *Psychoanalysis of Behaviour*. Vol. 2 of *Collected Papers*. New York: Grune and Stratton, 1956–61.

RANGELL, L. (1989). The significance of infant observation for psychoanalysis in later life. In Dowling and Rothstein (1989).

RAPAPORT, D. (1960). On the psychoanalytic theory of motivation. In *The Collected Papers of David Rapaport*, ed. M. M. Gill. New York: Basic.

REISER, M. (1984). *Mind, Brain, Body: Towards a Convergence of Psychoanalysis and Neurobiology*. New York: Basic.

SACKS, O. (1985). *The Man Who Mistook His Wife for a Hat*. London: Duckworth.

SANDLER, J., HOLDER, A., & MEERS, D. (1963). The ego ideal and the ideal self. *Psychoanal. Study Child*, 18:139–58.

SCHARFMAN, M. A. (1989). The therapeutic dyad in the light of infant observational research. In Dowling and Rothstein (1989).

SCHUR, M. (1960). Discussion of Dr John Bowlby's paper. *Psychoanal. Study Child*, 15:63–84.

SCHWARTZ, A. (1987). Drives, affects, behaviour—and learning: Approaches to a psychobiology of emotion and to an integration of psychoanalytic and neurobiological thought. *J. Amer. Psychoanal. Assn.*, 35:467–506.

—— (1988). Reification revisited: Some neurobiologically filtered views of "psychic structure" and "conflict." *J. Amer. Psychoanal. Assn.*, 36 (supp.):359–85.

—— (1990). On narcissism: An(other) introduction. In Glick and Bone (1990).

SHANE, M. (1989). The challenge posed by infant observational research to traditional psychoanalytic formulations: A discussion of the papers. In Dowling and Rothstein (1989).

SHAPIRO, T., & EMDE, R. (1992). *Affect: Psychoanalytic Perspectives*. Madison, Conn.: Int. Univ. Press.

SHENGOLD, L. (1985). Defensive anality and anal narcissism. *Int. J. Psycho-Anal.*, 66:47–63.

—— (1988). *Halo in the Sky*. New York: Guilford.

—— (1993). *"The Boy Will Come To Nothing!" Freud's Ego Ideal and Freud as Ego Ideal*. New Haven: Yale Univ. Press.

SILVERMAN, M. A. (1989). Infant observation and the reconstruction of early experience. In Dowling and Rothstein (1989).

SOLMS, M., & SALING, M. (1986). On psychoanalysis and neuroscience: Freud's attitude to the localization tradition. *Int. J. Psycho-Anal.*, 67:397–416.

SPILLIUS, E. B. (1988) *Melanie Klein Today*. (2 vols). London: Routledge.

SPITZ, R. (1960). Discussion of Dr. John Bowlby's paper. *Psychoanal. Study Child*, 12:159–63.

STENGEL, E. (1953). Introduction to *On Aphasia*, by S. Freud. London: Imago.

STERN, D. N. (1985). *The Interpersonal World of the Infant: A View from Psychoanalysis and Developmental Psychology*. New York: Basic.

—— (1990). Joy and satisfaction in infancy. In Glick and Bone (1990).

TOMKINS, S. S. (1962). *Affect/imagery/consciousness 1: The Positive Affects*. New York: Springer.

—— (1963). *Affect/imagery/consciousness 2: The Negative Affects*. New York: Springer.

TREURNIET, N. (1993). What is psychoanalysis now? *Int. J. Psycho-Anal.*, 74:873–91.

TYSON, P. (1989). Two approaches to infant research: A review and integration. In Dowling and Rothstein (1989).

WALLERSTEIN, R. S. (1988). One psychoanalysis or many? *Int. J. Psycho-Anal.*, 69:5–21.

——— (1990). Psychoanalysis: The Common Ground. *Int. J. Psychoanal.*, 71:3–20.

YORKE, C. (1965). Some metapsychological aspects of interpretation. *Brit. J. Med. Psychol.*, 38:27–42.

——— (1971). A critique of Kleinian psychology. *Psychoanal. Study Child*, 26:129–55.

——— (1988). A defect in training. *Brit. J. Psychiat.* 152:159–63.

——— (1990). (In collab. with T. Balogh, P. Cohen, J. Davids, A. Gavshon, M. McCutcheon, D. McLean, J. Miller, & J. Szydlo). The development and functioning of the sense of shame. *Psychoanal. Study Child*, 45:377–409.

——— (1991). Freud's "On Narcissism": A teaching text. In *On Freud's "On Narcissism: An Introduction."* ed. J. Sandler, E. S. Person, & P. Fonagy. New Haven: Yale Univ. Press.

——— (1994). Freud or Klein: Conflict or compromise. *Int. J. Psycho-Anal.* In press.

YORKE, C., & WISEBERG, S. (1976). A developmental view of anxiety. *Psychoanal. Study Child*, 31:107–35.

YORKE, C., WISEBERG, S., & FREEMAN, T. (1989). *Development and Psychopathology: Studies in Psychoanalytic Psychiatry.* New Haven: Yale Univ. Press.

ZURIFF, G. E. (1992). Theoretical inferences and the psycho-analytic theory of infancy. *Psychoanal. Q.*, 61:18–36.

Resistance Analysis and Psychic Reality

Per R. Anthi, Cand. Psychol.

The purpose of this paper is to elucidate some aspects of our mode of working; how we as analysts listen, observe, and collect information to formulate appropriate resistance interventions. Analytic exploration and technique should to a greater extent than what is usual include a careful analysis of verbal and nonverbal resistance expressions, as these may contain important material related to the analysand's psychic and historical reality. Our theoretical and technical conceptualization of how a systematic and consistent resistance analysis is performed should be improved. Our listening and observing attitude involves the simultaneous use of various forms of auditory, visual, and enactive data. This is exemplified by an excerpt from an analytic hour in which a specific resistance problem—an analysand's suppressed response to crying—is examined and linked to specific preverbal experiences.

THE CONCEPT OF RESISTANCE HAS ALWAYS BEEN A BASIC ELEMENT IN OUR technical theory. Freud's early technical rationale emphasized the importance of lifting the repression of experiences and memories in such a way that "strangulated affects" were released. Later the abreaction model was replaced by a model in which the resistance itself was regarded as containing significant information about the analysand's pathology. Although Freud used the concept in different contexts, one may say that in both the topographic and the structural models resistances were treated as obstacles to the analytic process. "Whatever interrupts the process of analytic work is a resistance" (1900, p. 517).

Training and supervising analyst, Norwegian Psychoanalytic Institute, Oslo.

I am grateful for the support I have received from the Research Fund of the Norwegian Psychoanalytic Institute during the preparation of this paper.

The Psychoanalytic Study of the Child 50, ed. Albert J. Solnit, Peter B. Neubauer, Samuel Abrams, and A. Scott Dowling (Yale University Press, copyright © 1995 by Albert J. Solnit, Peter B. Neubauer, Samuel Abrams, and A. Scott Dowling).

Although his second theory of anxiety (1926) implied a reconceptualization of how resistances were mobilized and activated, Freud did not seem to have made major changes in his technical approach to analyzing resistance phenomena. One might have expected this, since the theoretical implications of the structural model represented a development in which the significance of investigating ego processes and of analyzing resistance as the *ego's* unconscious response to a danger situation became essential for attaining true insight and psychic change. Freud's *technical* considerations about resistance, however, remained drive-oriented, focused on analysing the unconscious phantasies behind the resistance (Busch, 1992).

Wilhelm Reich (1933), Anna Freud (1936), and Otto Fenichel (1941) made the first systematic studies of how resistance as a technical problem was related to the workings of the analysand's ego functions and defense activities. They insisted that the threat to the ego and the dangerous affects that mobilized the resistance should be analyzed first if the resistance was to be thoroughly understood. Resistance was a sign that the analysand felt threatened by his ideas and impulses, and the aim of the resistance was to keep these from awareness. M. N. Searl (1936) also emphasized that it was an adaption derived from a danger from the past.

Reich (1933) described how the resistance often was expressed through the analysand's character and mode of behaving, "not in the content of the material, but in the formal aspects of the general behavior, the manner of talking, of the gait, facial expression and typical attitudes" (p. 47). The repressed affects and phantasies behind the resistance were maintained by the analysand's specific mode of associating and behaving.

Fenichel (1941) agreed in principle with Reich's technical approach, emphasizing the importance of analyzing resistance before content, ego before id, working with "the layers accessible to the ego at the moment" (p. 44) and seeking out "the places where the affect was situated." According to Fenichel, the principle of beginning at the *surface* should be taken seriously and implemented consistently.

In spite of Freud's second anxiety theory and the technical recommendations of Reich, Anna Freud, and Fenichel, psychoanalysts of all schools tend to ignore concrete manifestations of resistance phenomena. The content of the analytic data takes precedence when clinical material is discussed in journals, scientific proceedings, supervision, and technical seminars (Stone, 1973; Gray, 1987; Anthi, 1989). Analysts have always been fascinated by the id, in contrast to the resistances, and many treat the resistances primarily as a hindrance to the analysis of unconscious content (Sandler, 1992). Some hermeneutically oriented analysts take an exceedingly content-oriented stance, maintaining that the essence of the analyst's work is the interpretation of meaning. Ricoeur (1970), for example, asserts that there are no "facts" in psychoanalysis, "for the analyst does not observe, he interprets" (p. 365). The focus of analytic work is to uncover "the semantics of desire" concealed in the analysand's verbalizations. The data are not *observed* behavior, but what can be said about it. This standpoint implies that the analysand's behavioral expressions of resistance based on the analyst's observations are ignored.

Marshall Edelson (1988), an advocate for a more scientifically based psychoanalysis, argues against analysts of a hermeneutic bent. Nevertheless, he seems to have much in common with those he criticizes when he writes that the aim of psychoanalysis is to explain mental *contents*, "in particular those that are mystifying to the persons in whose mental representation they appear. Not *how* someone is able to believe, but *why* does he believe just *that?* Not *how* someone is able to remember, but *why* does he remember just *that?* Not *how* is he able to form or carry out *intentions*, but *why* does he intend doing, or why does he carry out the intentions to do, just *that?*" (p. 332). The formal aspects of analytic data are thus downgraded. Resistance phenomena, which often materialize through the analysand's *mode* of expression, are accordingly neglected in Edelson's definition of the aim of psychoanalysis.

Although most non-Kleinian analysts theoretically are aware that one usually should start from the surface and analyze resistance first, they often have an unclear conceptualization of what this means in practice. We often mix the concepts of defense and resistance, inferring that resistance is expressed by means of either defense or transference (Gill, 1982). In this manner we may confuse the intrapsychic perspective with the interpersonal. We may believe we are making resistance interpretations when in reality we are simply interpreting defense manifestations which at the moment are not activated in the transference.

In what follows I will present a fragment of a resistance analysis. Since systematic observations of bodily based resistance data in many cases are ignored, I shall emphasize the relevance of taking such data into consideration when the analysand's pathology is linked to traumatizations and constellations of conflicts dating back to the preverbal[1]

---

1. The preverbal period is that time of life when speech has not yet taken over the major expressive function (Mahler, Pine, Bergmann, 1975). Various forms of nonverbal behavior represent the main channel of communication during this period, which usually covers the first two years of life.

and preoedipal period. I will use the following extract from an analytic hour as a focus for discussing the significance of exploring the analysand's body experience. The verbatim excerpt centers on a specific phonetic-somatic aspect of her voice, which proved to play a prominent part in her resistance behavior. Brief comments on her behavior and on my various interventions will appear in italics within parentheses. In addition, I will summarize how the material from this hour was worked through and subsequently elaborated. Finally, I will discuss some fundamental technical problems related to resistance analysis raised by this dialogue.

CLINICAL MATERIAL, INTERVENTIONS, AND COMMENTS

Mrs. C., a thirty-one-year-old married woman, sought analysis because of depression. In her daily life she was reserved and had difficulty establishing an intimate relationship with her husband. Her relationship both to him and to her parents was ambivalent and marked by detachment. She also was troubled by eczema and bronchial asthma. She grew up in a remote forested district as the eldest of five children. For the past four years she has been working as a bookkeeper in a timber firm. Mrs. C. has two sons.

For the first 235 hours I listened to her verbalizations and made hardly any comments on her nonverbal behavior and body experience, since she apparently had no difficulty keeping to the basic rule by associating freely. But she had a tendency to rationalize and intellectualize. On the whole her affective expression was restricted and somewhat flat. I wouldn't say there was an absence of affective arousal, but the spontaneous expression of her emotionality was held back and toned down in such a way that it was difficult to explore the psychic meaning of what she was feeling. Instead, she was inclined to complain about unpleasant bodily feelings. For example, she had for some time been complaining about feeling worn out and stifling an impulse to cry. Trying to work more directly where the resistance was expressed and "where the affect really was anchored," I changed my technique and began focusing my interventions more directly on her body experience and the protective function of her resistance against crying.

Patient (P): *(in a voice stifled by suppressed crying):* I can't cry. Then I'm overflooded. It is too overwhelming. My throat is like a big lump of pent-up feelings.

Analyst (A): It sounds as if you are feeling that lump in your throat quite concretely. *(I invite her to explore an emotional and* bodily *based experience related to a specific resistance manifestation.)*

P: Yes, becoming strangulated, losing my breath. Something bottomless about that feeling, something endless if I give myself up to crying and screaming. Instead, I become harder and harder in my body and just sob. Except that time when I cried my eyes out and howled. *(She is referring to an episode that occurred at her home).* Then I didn't get a headache. That howling really came from the depths of my heart. Afterwards I didn't have that lump feeling; the tears just flowed and flowed. They poured down. I was soaking wet. *(After a short pause she starts talking about her eczema, which is bothering her just now.)* It is as if I had bubbles of pus on my hands. Full of shit. I'm trying to get away from something. *(Her stomach begins to rumble. She beats herself on her stomach with a clenched fist as if she might stop the rumbling by her pummeling. I get the impression that she is attempting to tame something wild and uncontrollable inside herself. Her beating, commanding hand movements remind me of a dog owner who orders his dog to be quiet. Her stomach continues to rumble, and she goes on striking herself rather harshly and determinedly on her belly.)*

A: You are beating yourself on your stomach. *(Again I am focusing on an unpleasant aspect of her body experience.)*

P: *(in a condemnatory, rebuking tone indicating that the rumbling ought to be extinguished):* It's making so much noise. It's roaring.

A: You behave as if you were able to get rid of that rumbling and control it.

P: You use the word *control*. That makes me think of Mama. Her rigidity. I was brought up well. Stopped using diapers before I was one year old. When I come to X *(a small sawmill town)* people remember me as the little girl who became clean so early. . . . I'm not able to feel and accept my needs, rationalize them away. . . . I'm the matter-of-fact-oriented girl and, at the same time, the very sensitive girl. I have done what my mother said I should do. My needs and problems have never been accepted. My parents couldn't cope with me. If I was sad and cried, they said, you mustn't be sad. I see how they are treating Knut and Arne *(her sons).* They don't allow any opposition or sadness, just like they treated me. My feelings have been manipulated. Mama refuses to listen to the difficult things. She says, I don't want to talk about this, and then she changes the subject. It is an avoidance of truth and reality.

A: You must be afraid of crying here, too, then. *(I am bringing in a central aspect of her transference resistance.)*

P: Oh, yes, I would be overwhelmed, flooded with tears. I would be afraid of not being able to stop.

A: It sounds as if the whole room here would then be flooded, so that I, too, would go down the drain. *(I must have sensed a humorous undertone in her voice, as my response is tinged with humor.)*

P: *(Chuckling, with her breath drawn into her respiratory passage):* Yes, it almost feels that way. I would drown in tears. *(Pause.)* There is a need to cry locked up in my throat. It's so strong that it frightens me. I can weep until I become quite stiff in my body. Then I suddenly decide to stop, and then the tears stop. I'm tired of my scratching, my asthma-spraying, all this psychosomatics, this bad body of mine. I can't call in sick again. *(She scratches her eyelid intensely.)*

A: You are scratching yourself on your eyelid. *(I call her attention to a tactile sensation.)*

P: I woke up this morning scratching myself on my eyelids. I have eczema there. I have something inside myself. I use the asthma spray so much. Must break myself loose in the morning. My body is so stiff. My cheeks are quite stiff. Takes some time before I come to my senses and can start functioning. I'm angry when I wake up and have a headache.

A: That you feel so angry and have a headache must be connected to something. *(I invite her to explore an underlying anger and unpleasant body experience and their possible resistance implications.)*

P: Loneliness—that has a stranglehold on me. *(Pause.)* I have so many nightmares about Greyboy.

A: Greyboy?

P: My cat that died when I was ten years old. I was so alone at that time. Father didn't like my cat and wouldn't have anything to do with it. Greyboy was my closest friend. I took his life.

A: You took his life?

P: I took it to the vet. It was blind and had turned aggressive. If frightened, it would scratch. That wasn't Greyboy's fault. It was I who wasn't able to take care of it. Reproached myself. Felt I killed myself in a way. I cried for a week. Wasn't able to stand on my own feet. Mourned and wept so that the quilt was soaking wet. I still have nightmares in which Greyboy is about to die while I'm trying to take care of it. Have much the same feelings toward Knut and Arne. I'm afraid of losing them like Greyboy. They have also been much petted.

This excerpt gives us a certain picture of how the patient's transference readiness is activated and the repressed hatred of her mother mobilized. We can also form an idea of how her restrained response to crying is related to the traumatic loss of her cat. Some hours later it was possible to discover another source of her resistance against crying in the analysis. She told me that when she was between one-and-a-half and two years old she was hospitalized for nearly four weeks because of eczema. Her parents were not allowed to visit her. While informing me of this, she said she felt "tied up" on the couch, with a faint memory of her hands being fastened to prevent her from scratching her skin. She also recalled that long after her discharge from the hospital she went around with "boxing gloves" and that in the morning her bandages were loosened by water vapor through holding them over a steaming saucepan. After telling me this, she kept silent for several minutes. I could faintly hear the spasmodic sound of her obstructed respiration; simultaneously I saw that she was holding her breath. I had long observed her inhibited respiratory pattern without commenting on it. It had become increasingly clear that her mode of breathing represented a *bodily* based resistance against crying. I had expected that the ongoing analytic process centered on her verbal material and my various transference interpretations sooner or later would lead to a release of her suppressed urge to cry. But this had not happened. Therefore, I now decided to describe the specific resistance aspect of her respiratory attitude and said, "You are holding your breath." This simple intervention proved to be very potent. After a short pause she responded by beginning to cry. Soon her whole body was trembling, and her teeth were chattering. She was freezing, in a cold sweat, and began biting the pillow she had under her head. A picture of Mama flashed through her mind. She had a "shirtcuff sensation" around her wrist and started to scratch herself on one of her knuckles until it bled, saying, "I understand now that there is a connection between my feeling of emptiness and my itching, the clawing raw flesh, all the sores." She felt quite alone, and "a pillar of hate" arose in her, making her feel "enclosed in black emptiness." Then came a roar of rage, and she shouted furiously, "Nobody here, nobody here," accusing me of being unable to help her. She cried, screamed, and howled for several minutes. Afterwards she cried silently, and the hour ebbed out in weeping and sobbing.

In subsequent hours we were able to work in peace and quiet on what she had experienced during the hour described. Her problems were expressed partly through various screen representations. Her blocked respiration, shivering, biting of the pillow, scratching of her knuckles, "shirtcuff feeling," and quelled impulse to cry were concrete and tangible phenomena. These varied behavioral responses could be interpreted as a condensed motor and tactile screen memory in which primitive affects and reaction patterns were enacted. Reconstructive work indicated that this particular screen memory was derived to a large extent from the rough treatment of her eczema and her traumatic experiences of being alone and lost in connection with the hospitalization when she was a small child. In the course of this hospitalization she appeared to have suppressed her urge to cry and scream in order to defend herself against unbearable psychic pain related to separation, sorrow, and anger. Instead she resigned herself to not being taken care of and protected by her mother. Her transference behavior toward me supported such a genetic interpretation. Her skin sensations and enacted reaction pattern functioned as cues, helping me to explore how she experienced the current transference situation. On the couch she felt alone and "tied up," longing almost desperately for closeness and fearful of being left in the lurch by me as she felt she had been by her mother.

DISCUSSION

The excerpt and my clinical account of the dynamic and genetic sides of Mrs. C.'s difficulty in crying do not include my "inner analytic monologue" and countertranference (in the broader sense), as the leading idea of this paper is to illuminate the significance of a systematic resistance analysis that does not bypass the formal expressive aspects of the resistance. For that reason, I have also excluded from discussion material related to her oedipal conflicts and her father.

My interventions directed at her bodily based resistance phenomena were primarily the result of a deliberate technical method. Some may assert that the analysand's suppressed urge to cry would have been released and her resistance against reliving preverbal traumatizations would have been overcome without the interventions aimed at making the analysand attentive to what she was doing with and to her own body. I doubt whether this would have been achieved without such interventions. Before discussing this issue, it is necessary to describe the biopsychological significance of crying.

There are two basic elements in crying: vocalization and weeping. Screaming, groaning, wailing, and moaning represent different acoustic aspects of crying (Sadoff, 1966). Weeping can be defined as the shedding of tears caused by an underlying emotional experience. Crying was linked to many somatic sensations in the patient under discussion. Besides changes in voice quality, there were changes in body tonus, posture, and respiration, often with jerky inspiratory movements and deep expirations and more or less spastic contractions of the glottis.

Sorrow and anger seem to be the primal affects expressed during the act of crying—sorrow at the loss of the love object and anger at being left alone. One function of weeping is the attempt to eliminate emotional pain. Tears are a biopsychological response aimed at washing away painful feelings and getting rid of unpleasant body tensions (Sadoff, 1966). I would assume that a more complete crying reaction in which the angry vocalized aspects of crying are included may also be an attempt to eject intensely hated self and object representations.

Bowlby (1958, 1960, 1969, 1973, 1980) and Robertson (1952, 1958) have investigated the central role of crying when the child over the age of six months is separated from its mother. At the beginning there is a period of protest accompanied by loud cries. This behavior is superseded by a phase of despair and distress in which the child wails and laments in a monotonous tone. If this situation is prolonged and the child is separated from its primary objects over a long period, the child often will reject the parents when they later appear.

The restraint of the vocal aspects of her crying posed a difficult problem for Mrs. C. Why was she so afraid of screaming and crying? Her stifled impulse to cry was frozen into a defensive respiratory attitude that represented a formidable affective resistance against reliving preverbal traumatic experiences and articulating unconscious transference phantasies. But this attitude also had an important *communicative* function, as it was a mode of mobilizing within the transference resistance the body's memories of these preverbal experiences. In analysis Mrs. C. *behaved* as if she were lying in a hospital bed feeling "tied up" and alone. At this phase in the analysis she didn't have any verbalized fantasies or memories of lying in a hospital bed, separated from mother and compelled to suppress her urge to cry and scream. There are essential dynamic and structural differences in the level of concept formation, memory, and attention functioning (Anthi, 1989) between a train of thought that results in a specific fantasy or memory content that is verbalized and *unverbalized* resistance phenomena, which only bring about a specific mode of behaving, speaking, breathing, and so forth.

Mrs. C. was not aware of the meaning of her specific behavior in the transference. First, I had to describe the resistance manifestations to her and focus her attention on them. Then the analytic process took another course, as she came closer to the resistance implications of her body experience and was thus able to *feel* more tangibly how she withheld important material by talking with tears in her eyes and holding her breath. My interventions, determined by my observations of the manifest "phenotypical" features of her resistance pattern as a particular concrete reality, helped her to explore how her body behavior and mode of speaking reflected important traumatic experiences that she was unable to convert and describe in words.

The suppressed vocalized aspects of her impulse to cry represented an attempt to quell her primitive rage and hate against her mother, who she felt had abandoned her not only when she was hospitalized but also later. The hospitalization, however, represented a prototypical experience of being abandoned.

Mrs. C.'s defensive respiratory attitude and the particular timbre of her voice represented a resistance against expressing her archaic transference hate since representations of her abandoning mother were displaced to me. She felt she would destroy the analytic relationship if she expressed her preoedipally determined hateful affects and phantasies in relation to me—that is, by *vocalizing* and articulating her rage and hate through crying in the analysis. She was almost literally afraid of being dissolved in tears, screaming, and anger. She imagined I wouldn't be able to stand her fury and would react by stopping the treatment and leaving her alone; that is, the danger to the ego was the threat of going to pieces and being left in a distressful void (Leira, 1980).

The totality of her affective communication was restricted, as the underlying anger of her suppressed urge to cry was split off from her sorrowful weeping. The physical concomitants of crying were also split off. She could weep and experience sorrow, but she was not able to cry and vent her anger. There was a division of the affects involved in crying on the bodily level.

In my opinion, she would have been unable to voice and articulate her archaic rage and hate if I had not intervened and made her aware of the specific nonverbal aspects of her resistance pattern. Years might have passed without the release of the central repressed experiences, phantasies, and affects. The analysis consequently would have come to a permanent standstill, while the psychic meaning and reality of her resistance manifestations would have remained unexplored.

TECHNICAL CONSIDERATIONS

To Kris (1982) the hallmark of resistance is the analysand's lack of freedom of association due to unconscious obstacles and conflicts. One way of identifying resistance phenomena is to observe their specific mode of expression. I concur in believing that this is a fruitful general guideline and will therefore try to elaborate further the relevance of this general principle.

We lack a systematic rationale and terminology for analyzing resistance phenomena. But the basic point of departure is *how* the analyst is observing and being attentive toward what goes on in the analytic situation. The resistance is chiefly expressed formally. Detecting and listening for resistance phenomena require that the analyst's free-floating attention be able to localize and catch up specific *formal* aspects of the analysand's mode of associating and behaving. The formal organization of cognition and phantasy life sometimes may function as a chronic resistance pattern. We do not know how to proceed if we attempt to analyse the resistance through the *manner* in which the analysand organizes his/her perceptual impressions, affects, phantasies, chains of thoughts, attention, and memory functioning. The ingrained and often subtle organized cognitive and affective patterns are very difficult to grasp when they appear as a resistance pattern in the transference. Nevertheless, they influence the quality of the transference and play a significant role in determining the analyst's responsive feeling and countertransference. Further, it is rather uncommon for us to take notice of the *syntactic* pattern of the analysand's formulations. The analyst may, for example, notice that aspects of the analysand's resistance are expressed through a specific verbal style characterized by "if" sentences—utterances beginning, for instance, with a doubtful "perhaps," a reserved "but," or a negation.

Intonation, rhythm, pitch, loudness, and other personal voice characteristics that give the analysand's verbalizations a certain affective value and communicative function represent another expressive side of the analysand's "resistance language" (Anthi, 1986, 1989; Killingmo, 1990). The analysand also may communicate with his whole body. Gestures that accompany and qualify the semantic content are visible, but the specific sound pictures he/she creates by modulating and regulating his/her voice and breathing often may pass unnoticed.

Though we pay insufficient attention to the formal expressive sides of the analysand's language and speech and their possible resistance implications, the analytic setting may nevertheless help us to improve our ability to collect and make use of such behavioral data. This setting, with its physical restriction of perceptual stimulation together with our free-floating attention, induces us to be more aware of the formal expressive resistance sides of the analysand's verbalizations. Our receptivity to nuances in syntax and phonology is increased as the main channel of communication is the vocal-auditory. But in many cases we appear to be unaware of how we are influenced by such affective and expressive resistance qualities, and we perceive them more or less unreflectingly. Moreover, both the syntactic and phonetic resistance characteristics of the analysand's verbalizations are, for the most part, unconsciously determined. For that reason, it is often difficult to comprehend how a specific verbal formulation and way of speaking may have an unrecognized resistance significance.

Gray (1987, 1990) has further refined Fenichel's technical principles and has attempted to develop a more modern rationale for analyzing resistance phenomena. The essence of his approach is to listen alertly to those concrete moments when a specific resistance expression materializes and is audible in the analysand's associations. At such moments there is a "change of voice" that reflects a regressive "breaking point" in the analysand's psychic functioning. The change may vary from the hardly discernible to the obvious. But, in principle, it is an audible and objective phenomenon relatively independent of the analyst's unconscious and speculative inferences. Being a behavioral and perceptual fact, it is commonly more accessible and perceptible to the analysand's conscious experience when the analyst, from the position of an outside observer, calls attention to what is noticed. Interventions based on listening to such "breaking points" aim at drawing the analysand's ego into conscious participation in the analytic process and thus integration of the warded-off impulses through *experiencing* the ego's own active controlling ability.

In order to supplement and clarify the resistance significance of various forms of verbal-vocal data, it may also be fruitful to extend our basic analytic attitude and technique from listening to include visual observations of resistance manifestations related to the analysand's body behavior. If one's mode of observation is limited to introspective data and the expressive qualities of the analysand's verbalizations, one inevitably will restrict the psychoanalytic universe of data and exclude some resistance phenomena from consideration. We are not only listeners, we are observers as well, utilizing our visual observations, the basic instrument in clinical science (Anthi, 1983).

Early experiences and representations of self and object have a particular proximity and affinity to affects and the body. Early affective development is to a large extent derived from emotionally invested object relation experiences. Research on infants indicates that a form of affective memory is established very early and that such a mode of remembering simultaneously involves the activation of specific body responses and internalized object relation experiences (Stern, 1985; Emde, 1988). Affects are early object-related modes of communication.

Besides, not infrequently we can substantiate the correctness of an intervention directed at the analysand's resistance on the basis of visual and auditory observations of nonverbal expressions. Changes in respiration and voice quality, the appearance of tears and crying, and so on, are affective responses that can be used in estimating to what extent our interventions are appropriate (Gullestad, 1993). They often can function as convincing standards of measurement, as they have a genuine and authentic quality linked to specific observable body phenomena. Therefore, they are especially relevant data when testing the validity of our resistance interventions and reconstructive assumptions.

The analyst's listening and observing attitude is manifold and complex. It reflects a creative and two-sided relational process involving several interacting factors. Variables of our personality, the extent of our knowledge and experience, and the quality of our relationship(s) and countertransference to the analysand will influence how we perceive the resistance implications of the analysand's cognitive and emotional communications.

Resistance reveals itself simultaneously through various forms of verbal and nonverbal expressions. From a linguistic viewpoint the division of vocal and nonvocal, verbal and nonverbal into separate vehicles of communication may be expedient. However, from a psychoanalytic standpoint, such a delimitation is too narrow, as the unique interaction in analysis is derived from different forms of communication acting in parallel. If we separate them, the general effect is lost. Body language and other nonverbal expressions are an intrinsic part of both the analysand's and the analyst's speech and behavior; they are parts of a larger and more comprehensive communicative process. Sometimes the verbal and nonverbal expressions act as synergic and consistent resistance configurations, but frequently the underlying resistance is exclusively conveyed through specific nonverbal expressions that contradict the analysand's seemingly unambiguous verbal message.

If the analyst describes or comments on specific resistance aspects of the analysand's nonverbal behavior, the analysand is distracted and diverted from following his or her own associations. This fact raises a more general question: to what extent, when, and in what way should the analyst take note of such forms of resistance and direct his or her interventions in order to explore them? The traditional analytic attitude implies that the analyst should wait and ask himself, "Will I hear something that will make the possible resistance aspect of this specific nonverbal behavior more comprehensible?" The analyst waits to see whether the actual resistance manifestation is spontaneously followed by relevant reminiscences and verbalizations that may illuminate what is expressed nonverbally. Or is it necessary to intervene and comment on such resistance phenomena and ask for associations to them in order to analyze them more directly?

Child analysts have always known that nonverbal behaviors are an invaluable source of material. In the analysis of adults we have no clear conceptualization of when it is indicated or contraindicated to make interventions aimed at the resistance aspects of the analysand's nonverbal behavior. There is no doubt that such interventions can be very potent agents and can provoke intense affective and vegetative reactions. Furthermore, the analysand may feel under surveillance and reproved. Although interventions are phrased and expressed in a neutral, noncriticizing manner, the analysand may still feel that his or her self-image, appearance, and narcissistic representations are being attacked and may experience the analyst as a persecuting, rebuking object. Therefore, many analysts abstain from making such interventions. On the other hand, if the analyst is too afraid of provoking the analysand or disturbing his or her chain of associations and avoids making comments on the resistance aspects of the analysand's nonverbal behavior, the analyst may miss important material that is inaccessible via verbal communication, as such resistance configurations may reflect conflicts and traumatizations stemming from the preverbal period.

Observations of body-based resistance patterns pose problems similar to those related to infant observation, as they too have a behavioral basis that cannot be directly translated into psychoanalytic language. Both research and practice indicate that there is no direct link between adult pathology and preverbal traumatizations (Thomä and Kächele, 1985; Blum, 1989; Dowling, 1989). Besides, reconstruction of early pathogenic object relation experiences and conflicts may be contaminated by attributing adultomorphic concept formation to the preverbal child. A given disturbance may not be the result of specific early influences and traumatizations but rather the outcome of much later, or even recent, pathogenic circumstances or retrospective revisions of early traumatic impressions (*Nachträglichkeit*).

Though there is no simple cause-and-effect link between preverbal impressions and pathological formations in adulthood, psychoanalytic developmental theory has always stated that there is a causal relevance between early infantile experience and later development. Therefore, beneath a present resistance configuration there is usually a concealed layer of infantile desires and pathogenic object relation experiences displaced and distorted into the transference situation. A given resistance determined by specific preverbal circumstances certainly may have undergone several transformations, but in principle there is a continuity between the preverbal past and the present.

In addition, infant and child research has provided a better theoretical framework for our technical interventions and understanding of various resistance phenomena. For instance, Robertson's films (1952, 1958) of how small children contend with the double experience of being hospitalized and being separated from their primary objects and Bowlby's work (1958, 1960, 1969, 1973, 1980) on the child's tie to its mother represented a useful conceptual frame of reference in my transference interpretations and clinical reconstruction of the basically preoedipal determinants of Mrs. C.'s resistance against crying in the analysis.

The verbal/semantic content of the analysand's associations is just the tip of the iceberg, as the analysand expresses himself or herself simultaneously through body language and other nonverbal expressions. We need to develop a systematic technical rationale that can improve our ability to catch, decode, and make use of such forms of communication.

Preverbal experiences can only fragmentarily or partially be put into words and articulated. But the analysand's enactive and affective responses may express what is not possible through verbalizations; such responses can function as nonverbal vehicles for specific, bodily based memories, experiences, and resistance configurations derived from the preverbal period.

BIBLIOGRAPHY

ANTHI, P. R. (1983). Reconstruction of preverbal experiences. *J. Amer. Psychoanal. Assn.*, 31:33–58.

—— (1986). Non-verbal behaviour and body organ fantasies: Their relation to body image formation and symptomatology. *Int. J. Psychoanal.*, 67:417–29.

—— (1989). Formal defensive aspects of cognition and modes of thinking exemplified by Freud's case history of the rat man. *Scand. Psychoanal. Rev.*, 12:22–37.

BLUM, H. (1989). The value, use and abuse of developmental research. In *The Significance of Observational Infant Research for Clinical Work with Children, Adolescents, and Adults*, ed. S. Dowling & A. Rothstein. Madison, Conn.: Int. Univ. Press.

BOWLBY, J. (1958). The nature of the child's tie to its mother. *Int. J. Psychoanal.*, 39:350–73.

—— (1960). Grief and mourning in infancy and early childhood. *Psychoanal. Study Child.*, 15:9–52.

—— (1969). *Attachment and Loss*, vol. 1, New York: Basic.

—— (1973). *Attachment and Loss*, vol. 2, New York: Basic.

—— (1980). *Attachment and Loss*, vol. 3, New York: Basic.

BUSCH, F. (1992). Recurring thoughts on unconscious ego resistances. *J. Amer. Psychoanal. Assn.*, 40:1089–1117.

DOWLING, S. (1989). Epilogue. In *The Significance of Observational Research for Clinical Work with Children, Adolescents and Adults*, ed. S. Dowling & A. Rothstein. Madison, Conn.: Int. Univ. Press.

EDELSON, M. (1988). *Psychoanalysis: A Theory in Crisis*. Chicago: Univ. of Chicago Press.

EMDE, R. N. (1988). Development terminable and interminable: Innate and motivational factors from infancy. *Int. J. Psychoanal.*, 9:125–45.

FENICHEL, O. (1941). *Problems of Psychoanalytic Technique*. Albany, N.Y.: Psychoanalytic Quarterly.

FREUD, A. (1936). *The Ego and the Mechanisms of Defense*. New York: Int. Univ. Press, 1966.

FREUD, S. (1900). The interpretation of dreams. *S.E.*, 5.

—— (1926). Inhibitions, symptoms and anxiety. *S.E.*, 23.

GILL, M. (1982). *Analysis of Transference*. Madison, Conn.: Int. Univ. Press.

GRAY, P. (1987). On the technique of analysis of the superego. *Psychoanal. Q.*, 56:130–54.

——— (1990). The nature of therapeutic action in psychoanalysis. *J. Amer. Psychoanal. Assn.*, 38:1083–98.

GULLESTAD, S. (1993). Psychoanalysis—a hermeneutic discipline? In *Psychoanalysis in Norway*, ed. P. R. Anthi & S. Varvin. Oslo: University Press.

KILLINGMO, B. (1990). Beyond semantics: A clinical and theoretical study of isolation. *Int. J. Psychoanal.*, 71:113–27.

KRIS, A. (1982). *Free Association: Method and Process*. New Haven, Conn.: Yale Univ. Press.

LEIRA, T. (1980). The release of tears. *Int. Rev. Psychoanal.*, 3:299–309.

MAHLER, M., PINE, F., & BERGMANN, A. (1975). *The Psychological Birth of the Human Infant*. New York: Basic.

REICH, W. (1933). *Character Analysis*. 3d edition. New York: Farrar, Straus & Giroux, 1949.

RICOEUR, P. (1970). *Freud and Philosophy: An Essay on Interpretation*. New Haven, Conn.: Yale Univ. Press.

ROBERTSON, J. (1952). *A Two-Year-Old Goes to Hospital*. (Film). London: Tavistock Institute of Human Relations. New York University Film Library.

——— (1958). *Going to Hospital with Mother*. (Film). London: Tavistock Institute of Human Relations. New York University Film Library.

SADOFF, R. L. (1966). On the nature of crying and weeping. *Psychiat. Q.*, 40:490–503.

SANDLER, J. (1992). Reflections on developments in the theory of psychoanalytic technique. *Int. J. Psychoanal.*, 73:189–99.

SEARL, M. N. (1936). Some queries on principles of technique. *Int. J. Psychoanal.*, 1:471–93.

STERN, D. (1985). *The Interpersonal World of the Infant*. New York: Basic.

STONE, L. (1973). On resistances to the psychoanalytic process. *Psychoanal. Contemp. Sci.*, 2:42–73.

THOMÄ, H., & KÄCHELE, H. (1985). *Psychoanalytic Practice*, vol. 1. Berlin, London, New York: Springer, 1986.

Loewald's "Positive Neutrality" and the Affirmative Potential of Psychoanalytic Interventions

JUDITH GUSS TEICHOLZ, ED. D.

Patients who suffer from severe vulnerability in the narcissistic realm but who otherwise enjoy impressively intact ego functioning can sometimes be helped to endure the rigors of psychoanalysis in the early months of treatment by the analyst's emphasis on, or even exaggeration of, the affirmative elements in ordinary psychoanalytic interventions. Loewald's (1960) concept of "positive neutrality" is explored in an effort to determine an acceptable element of affirmation in the initial analytic stance taken toward these patients, and case material is offered to illustrate the application of these principles in the first fifteen months of psychoanalytic work with a high-functioning but narcissistically vulnerable man. It is thought that this stance, used judiciously, does not compromise the full emergence and analysis of the transference but rather enhances the process. To illustrate this progression, a session is presented from the thirtieth month in the treatment of the same analysand, when the affirmative emphasis had receded and more ordinary interpretive activity had begun to dominate the analytic interchange.

Faculty member and supervising analyst at the Massachusetts Institute for Psychoanalysis; clinical instructor in psychiatry/psychology, Harvard Medical School/Massachusetts General Hospital.

The author would like to thank Gerald Adler, M.D., Howard Corwin, M.D., Ralph Engle, M.D., and Sam Kaplan, M.D. for their helpful responses to an earlier version of this article.

The Psychoanalytic Study of the Child 50, ed. Albert J. Solnit, Peter B. Neubauer, Samuel Abrams, and A. Scott Dowling (Yale University Press, copyright © 1995 by Albert J. Solnit, Peter B. Neubauer, Samuel Abrams, and A. Scott Dowling).

Between the lips and the voice
Something goes dying.
Something with the wings of a bird,
Something of anguish and oblivion.
The way nets cannot hold water.
                              —Pablo Neruda (1969)

OUR CLINICAL MATERIAL IS RICH, VERY RICH, AND EVEN WHEN EVERY word is transcribed, much is lost in the transcription. The unique affective qualities of every session, every analysis, have a life of their own that cannot be fully conveyed by the words alone. Just as the clinical material has a richness that is a challenge to communication among analysts, so our analytic interventions have a complexity of intent and of action that may elude our awareness and defy theoretical categorization. In spite of these limitations, I am going to try to shed light on a quality of our interventions which I believe contributes to the establishment of therapeutic alliance and is instrumental in diminishing resistance in some cases. Indirectly, then, it facilitates the psychoanalytic process through the further unfolding of transference and the deepening and broadening of affect.

What I am about to focus on is not something new and is not even an intervention in its own right. It is simply an element that can be implicit or explicit in any psychoanalytic intervention, including cognitive/affective clarifications, dynamic interpretations of transference or extratransference material, and genetic reconstructions. I shall call this quality the affirmative potential of ordinary psychoanalytic interventions. Although it is inherent in the analyst's accepting neutrality toward all of a patient's material, this potential has its primary relevance within the "widening scope" and is of particular importance in the early phases of treatment with patients who suffer from severe narcissistic vulnerabilities.

Such vulnerability often presents in the context of intact ego functioning and a high level of performance in relation to the external world. This level of functioning is, however, accompanied by a chronic sense of precariousness, with intense shame and anxiety about exposure of the vulnerability. It seems in many cases to be related to a history of early deprivation or of parental hostility toward early dependency needs, and in the adult patient it often resides in an intrapsychic climate of extreme hostility toward the patient's own affective life and attachment needs. In the treatment of analysands who share these attributes of vulnerability, an early emphasis on, or even a slight exaggeration of, the affirmative elements of psychoanalytic interventions can sometimes enable an otherwise unanalyzable patient to establish a therapeutic alliance, and it can ameliorate for the analysand what might have been either an initial atmosphere of frozen terror (presenting as intractable resistance) or an intolerably shame-filled development of the analytic process.

This emphasis on the affirmative tends not to be useful in the treatment of more massive structural deficit, which can require a very different emphasis in the analytic stance (not discussed in this paper), and this approach is not usually essential to the analysis of patients who enjoy the benefits of a more intact sense of self, who from the outset can make use of the implicit acceptance conveyed by any tactful, accurate, and well-timed interpretation given from a position of more ordinary neutrality. Thus, what is to be discussed, though perhaps of general theoretical and technical interest, may have a quite limited application in actual psychoanalytic practice: it is useful in the early phases of the treatment of quite severe narcissistic vulnerability when this vulnerability occurs in the context of adequate or even superior ego functioning and some degree of structural cohesion. High levels of achievement and one or two stable object relationships may at first mask the reality that for these individuals, everyday life involves an intensity of psychic effort which is unrelenting, herculean, and shame-filled. Such patients often are assessed initially as being eminently analyzable, but once the psychoanalysis has begun, the patient's narcissistic vulnerability may present a technical challenge to the development of a viable analytic process. It is in this context that the need for an emphasis on the affirmative elements of our ordinary psychoanalytic interventions might arise. However, the concept of affirmation alone does not do justice to what I am trying to identify in the analytic process and may even be misleading in this context.

Perhaps we can best introduce affirmative potential of psychoanalytic communication by looking at Loewald's (1960) emphasis on the "positive nature of the neutrality" (p. 230) required of the analyst in relation to his patients. Loewald's introduction of the adjective *positive* to his discussion of neutrality highlighted aspects of the analyst's stance that had always been recognized as inherent in the analytic situation but had not previously been identified as important contributions to the therapeutic action of psychoanalysis. For some analysts, the introduction of the concept of something actively "positive" in the analyst's stance of "neutrality" toward his patients might even represent a contradiction in terms. But Loewald was able to emphasize the positive aspects of the therapeutic action without arousing undue alarm about loss of neutrality, precisely because he refused to separate the two concepts. While introducing the positive components as contributors to the therapeutic action, he was careful to underscore the importance of neutrality as a way of both protecting the patient from "the analyst's own emotional intrusions" (p. 233) and creating a space in which the transference could develop and be explored.

Loewald placed a clear emphasis on traditional concerns for the analyst's neutrality and objectivity, yet he also expressed concern that the analyst not equate such neutrality and objectivity with the "avoidance of being available to the patient as an object" (p. 225). He went on to spell out some of the concrete ways in which the analyst can, and should, become a new object for the analysand. These ways included the analysis of the patient's distortions in the transference, but in his view, this analysis could lead not only to insight, but to the possibility for a "new object relationship." He drew our attention to certain parallels between early childhood development and the psychic development that takes place in successful analytic treatment. Like Winnicott (1954, 1956), Emde (1990), and many others, Loewald emphasized the regression involved in successful analytic treatments, which tends to set in motion developmental processes similar in some ways to the developmental processes of childhood. An example of the many links Loewald made between the infant-mother and the patient-analyst relationships is his emphasis on the importance for development of the mother's role in the "recognition and fulfillment" (p. 237) of the infant's needs. Integrative experiences in analysis, he continued, "are experiences of interaction, comparable in their structure and significance to the early understanding between mother and child" (p. 239). By linking the mother's recognition and fulfillment of the infant's needs to the analyst's recognition and fulfillment of the adult patient's needs in treatment, Loewald might have seemed to be stretching traditional analytic discourse beyond acceptable boundaries (see Cooper, 1988). However, he made it clear that he was not advocating the analyst's direct satisfaction of the patient's libidinal needs but rather was referring strictly to the indirect or symbolic fulfillment of the patient's developmental, psychic needs as an integral aspect of the interpretive-reconstructive process in psychoanalytic treatment.

This distinction—between instinctual needs, on the one hand, and developmental psychic needs, on the other—has also been made by Winnicott (1958), Kohut (1977, 1984), and others. To the extent that the distinction is accepted, analysts can feel more confident that both appropriate neutrality and an interpretive focus can be maintained, even while certain developmental psychic needs of the patient are being met through treatment. Examples of such needs that might be met in the context of a properly conducted analysis are the patient's transient needs for omnipotence (Winnicott, 1960b), his dependency needs in regression (Winnicott, 1954), his needs for the analyst's emotional availability and empathic responsiveness (Kohut, 1982, 1984; Emde, 1990), his needs for mirroring and idealization (Kohut, 1977, 1984), and, in the more primitive patient, the need for containment of affect through the analyst's processing of projective identifications (Ogden, 1982; Adler, 1989). Some of these needs normally arise in the process of all analytic treatments, and they do sometimes have to be met by discrete, noninterpretive verbalizations on the part of the analyst. However, the point being made here is that they can often be met in the ordinary course of clarifying, interpreting, and reconstructing, provided that the analyst is oriented toward recognizing such needs when they emerge and is able to maximize the affirmative potential of the usual psychoanalytic interventions in order to respond to them.

In addition to his emphasis on the analyst's "recognition and fulfillment" of the patient's developmental psychic needs, Loewald (1960) emphasized identification and other internalization processes as the central processes through which structural development and change go forward in psychoanalytic treatment. McLaughlin (1981), Kohut (1984), Blatt and Behrends (1987), Cooper (1988), Emde (1990), and others have also identified internalization as a central process in the therapeutic action of psychoanalysis, which can both enhance and be enhanced by interpretation and insight. McLaughlin (1981) tells us that analysis produces change by means of "the internalization, as new psychic structures, of attitudes and values experienced in the relationship to the analyst" (p. 655). Loewald (1960) had reminded us that all processes of internalization are dependent on interaction. He said: "This identification [in the psychoanalytic process] does have to do with the development of a new object-relationship . . . [and] is the foundation for it" (p. 227). In this view, internalization processes do not replace interpretation of resistance and transference as the central tasks of psychoanalytic work but rather are silent, internal accompaniments to the interpretive-reconstructive process.

As an example of the "positive nature" of what might get internalized in the process of treatment, Loewald (1960) told us that a child begins to experience himself as a "centered unit" by internalizing repeated experiences of "being centered upon" by the parents (p. 230). He added: "In analysis, if it is to be a process leading to structural changes, interactions of a comparable nature have to take place" (p. 230). Although the analyst's attentiveness has been recognized as an inherent aspect of the analytic experience from Freud's time to the present, Loewald gave it a role in therapeutic action by linking it to early, structure-building experiences in childhood. For patients whose early structure-building experiences were faulty, the experience of being centered on in the analytic situation becomes a major content of the analytic work rather than a silent backdrop. The actual differences between the early and the current experience tend to facilitate the patient's insight into his psychic history, thus enhancing the interpretive reconstructive process. An example: A patient who had just been speaking of his pleasure in having received positive attention at work lapsed into a long silence. When the analyst inquired about this, after several minutes, the patient replied that he had begun to experience anxiety in the session because he'd been "the center of attention for too long," thus bringing the extratransference theme affectively into the transference. The patient was able to link the transference feeling with his father's humiliating responses to his childhood bids for attention— he labeled them as "showing off." The patient's recognition that these responses were not being repeated in the analytic relationship helped him to develop insight into the reactive, characterological inhibition of his own talents and capabilities with authority figures. This insight became a first step in the working through toward a fuller expression of the patient's creative powers in his work and other settings. As Loewald suggested, in such cases it is essential not only that the analysand gain insight into the faulty childhood experiences of being centered on by the parents but also that he "internalize" the experience of being the center of the analyst's positive and neutral attention.

Loewald also spoke of "certain qualifications" required of the analyst in order to promote the analytic process: among these were an ability and a willingness to imply "aspects of undistorted reality" to the patient (p. 225). Often included in these aspects of undistorted reality would be communications to the analysand that convey what he might become through treatment (Loewald, 1960). This image of what the patient might become is based not on the values and desires of the analyst but on the analyst's recognition in the patient of that which has not yet been developed, because of his psychopathology. This means that the analyst might at times make implicit or explicit reference to qualities and potential that he sees in the patient and that the patient does not yet consciously recognize as his. It means also that, in reconstructions, the analyst might imply (hurtful or helpful) aspects of personality or functioning in the patient's parents or siblings that the patient has not quite yet seen clearly. The analyst bases these communications on his ability to identify latent perceptions and experiences of the analysand in relation to self and others and to see in them something "positive" or affirmative for the patient's development.

Loewald's positive neutrality seems to refer to the analyst's deepest acceptance of the complex totality of the patient and his unique potential for growth. However, for the patient whose internal life tends to be dominated by nonacceptance and self-loathing, the inability to feel the analyst's acceptance becomes one of the central treatment issues. In such cases, the analyst's acceptance must sometimes become a more explicit aspect of the interpretive process in the early stages of treatment. This can be thought of as having a two-pronged effect: (1) helping to detoxify the negative or destructive introjects while interpreting them, and (2) helping to shore up fragile psychic structure externally, until over time the interpretive process has worked to solidify it internally. With these patients, the analyst will need to convey her deep acceptance of the halting, infinitesimal steps involved in the lurches toward growth and development in the course of an analysis and of the inevitable steps backwards; of the defensiveness and resistance with which the analysand protects his "true self" at the outset of treatment (Winnicott, 1960b); and of the regression that is necessary in treatment in order for integration and healthy development to take place (Loewald, 1960).

Loewald hardly needed to remind us that the "new object relationship" the analyst makes possible for the patient has nothing to do with meeting the libidinal desires of the patient and nothing to do with the analyst's expressing or revealing the facts of his own life or the nature of his experience to the analysand. The new object relationship in analysis is also unlike ordinary friendship or romantic and sexual love in that the analyst is guided exclusively by the understanding of and response to the patient's developmental needs and does nothing within the analysis that would have as its purpose the meeting of the analyst's own libidinal, affective, or other psychic needs. This analytic ideal—of putting aside the analyst's own interests and needs for the purposes of helping the patient find the pathway to his own development—resonates with important aspects of the parent's attitude toward the child. In both the parent-child dyad and the early stages of analyst-patient relationship there is an element of "sacred trust." (This is made complicated, and all the more essential, in the psychoanalytic situation by the fact that many patients enter treatment with a major deficit in the capacity for trust or in the ability to make judgments about others' trustworthiness.)

Loewald (1979) has used the word *sacred* in his attempt to identify the essence of "the bond between parent and child" (p. 387). To the extent that the regressed patient transfers to the analyst the trust that once was directed toward the parents, the analyst as well must be held to a code of sacred trust, until such time as the interpretive process and the totality of the therapeutic action have enabled the analysand to make more mature judgments and to take more responsibility for his own life and experience. All this is not to suggest that the adult patient is an "innocent." Through analysis, he may well find out that he is in some ways far more "guilty" (though in other ways far more innocent) than he once thought. But by coming to us for help, the patient is to some extent putting himself in our hands; and in fostering the development of an "infantile neurosis," the analyst needs to adopt an attitude that will protect the analysand from harm that may come from his preexisting vulnerability or from the vulnerability created by the psychoanalytic situation itself. This can be thought of as part of the analyst's "diatrophic attitude" (Spitz, 1956; Gitelson, 1962) toward the analysand, usually seen as appropriate to the early stages of treatment, but exaggerated or extended for the patient population under discussion.

There are, of course, limitations to the parallels that can be drawn between the infant-mother dyad and the analytic relationship (see Abrams, 1990; and Fonagy et al., 1993, for further important discussion of these limitations, beyond the scope of this paper). For instance, the analyst, unlike the parent of a very young child, has to deal somehow with the analysand's complex structural overlay, his defensive functioning, and his previously internalized object relations; and, unlike parenting, analytic treatment is carried out primarily on a symbolic plane, so that the parallels between psychoanalysis and childhood experience refer largely to the patient's (often unconscious) experience of the meaning and significance of the relationship rather than to the virtual care given. Transcending all these differences, however, is the recognition that certain basic intrapsychic processes of development are set in motion similarly during childhood and during psychoanalysis (Emde, 1990). Thus—although the analyst offers primarily symbolic care, in a sharply delimited setting, through verbally expressed understanding, acceptance, clarification, and interpretation—this relationship may be experienced and used by the analysand as an opportunity for renegotiating earlier developmental challenges. It is above all this facilitation of new development in an intrapsychic context of early trauma and defense that requires the analyst's positive neutrality.

How does this concept of positive neutrality, with its command that the analyst "love and respect . . . the individual and individual development" (Loewald, 1960, p. 229), on the one hand, and its demand for scrupulous self-restraint and delimitation, on the other, translate into the analyst's technical stance toward her patients? How, as analysts, can we express this "positive" aspect of our attitude toward our patients, this deep acceptance, while maintaining the neutrality necessary to safeguard our patients against unwanted intimacy in the transference, against overstimulation of hopes and fears related to the treatment, and against undue pressure from the analyst for self-responsibility, for goodness, for health, or for development, before the patient himself is ready? These concerns have always been part of the classical emphasis on neutrality, but perhaps the widening scope of psychoanalysis makes us more aware of a need to find the right balance, with each patient, between the "positive" elements required to sustain the patient through the rigors of the psychoanalytic process and the "neutral" elements required to safeguard the patient's security and autonomy in the analytic relationship. As analysts, we strive toward a certain ideal of neutrality with all patients: to be emotionally available and responsive, but not to intrude our own feelings into the relationship; to be alive to our own feelings, yet not to act on them; to accept the patient's negative or destructive feelings and impulses, but not to retaliate; to receive the patient's transference love, yet not to return it in kind (Freud, 1915). But with patients for whom an early history of deprivation or trauma has resulted in significant narcissistic vulnerability, the effects of that history need somehow further to be *neutralized* in the analytic situation before the patient can experience these more ordinary expressions of the analyst's neutrality as a safe-enough milieu in which to tolerate the analytic work.

Early environmental failures in the fulfillment of developmental psychic needs are often the essence of the psychopathogenic cumulative trauma or strain which have brought the patient to treatment. Withholding such fulfillment of these needs, as would be possible within the frame of a properly conducted analysis, might, therefore, constitute an unnecessary retraumatization of the patient within the treatment situation. Klauber (1980) has spoken of the need for the analyst's active "de-traumatization" of the transference (p. 197) in some cases. And both he and Rangell (1991) have suggested that the analyst must become the "antidote" for anxieties that the patient brings to treatment, anxieties that are understood to have their origins in the relationships of early childhood. The concepts of positive neutrality (Loewald, 1960), of the detraumatization of the analysis (Klauber, 1980), and of the analyst as antidote to childhood anxieties (Rangell, 1990) all tend to suggest that with some patients the analyst must take an active stance toward reversing the negative effects of earlier structure-thwarting or structure-distorting experience. These suggestions are based on the conviction of many analysts that "later relationships can induce profound salutary influences on early internalized relationships that are problematic" (Emde, 1990, p. 884). With severe narcissistic vulnerability, these salutary influences often must first be used to overcome prolonged "resistances" related to early deprivation or abuse: toward this end, the "positive" aspects of the analyst's neutrality can sometimes be emphasized without compromising a disciplined exploration of the patient's intrapsychic and interpersonal functioning.

Killingmo (1989) has elucidated the concept of affirmative interventions, but he characterizes them in sharp contrast to interpretive interventions. He suggests that interpretive interventions relate to conflict and involve the analyst's assisting the patient's ego "in the risky venture of confronting archaic impulses and affects towards internalized object representations which are projected onto the analyst" (p. 67). In contrast, he sees affirmative interventions as being aimed more at "correction and separation of distorted or diffused self-object representations" and "bringing about structuralization of aspects of object relations which has not yet been accomplished in the previous development" (p. 67). Although these are important discernments to be made in thinking about the goals and intents of specific interventions, the view taken here does not technically separate out interpretive from affirmative interventions. Rather, affirmation is seen as a quality that can be inherent in any psychoanalytic intervention, including clarifications, genetic reconstructions, and dynamic interpretations.

Killingmo identified four aspects of human experience that can be addressed by what is affirmative in our interventions. These are (1) the patient's existence, (2) his relatedness, (3) his sense of worth, and (4) the validity of his experience. Killingmo upheld affirmative interventions addressing these areas of experience as the technique of choice when prevailing transference manifestations represent structural deficit more than they do conflict. However, to the extent that, as Killingmo described, the intrapsychic ramifications of conflict and deficit interpenetrate and are indissolubly interwoven in the layers and fabric of the personality throughout development, aspects of this approach sometimes may be found to have broader application. Myerson's (1990) discussion of how the analyst responds to analytic "strain," which can emerge in the work with any patient, points to a need for the judicious use of interventions that serve to reestablish the analytic relationship in addition to the interpretation of unconscious wishes. In the re-establishment of the relationship between patient and analyst, the patient's relationship to self is also restored, so that he can then resume the more "purely analytic" work. The affirmative stance will not need to be sustained throughout the course of any analysis, because the patient's need for it will diminish as the analysis progresses.

The emphasis on what is affirmative in analytic interventions sometimes has raised legitimate concerns that such a stance might inhibit the emergence of the patient's more negative transferences. This could no doubt be so, if what were being "affirmed" included only the analysand's most positive or pleasant feelings. The point being made here, however, is that what is consistently and repeatedly affirmed is whatever latent, nascent, emergent, or full-blown affect or ideation the patient reveals (or that can appropriately be interpreted on the basis of the associative material or transference behavior), from the pleasantest to the nastiest, from the most loving to the most hateful. Particularly with patients whose childhood forays into the expression of negative affects were repeatedly experienced as being met with punitive hostility, the analyst sometimes must provide something that borders on explicit permission for the expression of negative transference feelings in the analytic situation. Even some of our more intact patients on occasion require that the interpretation of latent "negative" affects (such as disappointment in the analyst, competitive aggression, resentment, hostility, anger, hatred, sadism, and rage) be made in the most affirmative climate. Although such affects may appear evident to the analyst on the basis of dreams and other associative material, the negative regard in which such feelings often are held, the extent to which they have been systematically repressed or disavowed, the lack of confidence in the capacity to self-regulate once they begin to emerge, and the fear of punishment or retaliation which they tend to evoke can make them feel unacceptable and dangerous even to our healthier patients. Furthermore, for the patient population under discussion, not just negative transferences but also authentic positive transferences (in the forms of attachment needs, desires for mutual idealization, or romantic and erotic passions) are frequently disavowed, feared, or avoided. The technique of emphasizing the affirmative elements of psychoanalytic interventions seems to facilitate emergence of the full range of potential transferences, positive or negative, when these have been blocked by an intrapsychic atmosphere of severe narcissistic vulnerability, intense shame, and vicious self-criticism (see also Kris, 1982, 1990). With this stance affectively frozen, flat, or constricted patients move toward more authentic, more differentiated, and broader affective expressiveness both inside and outside of the treatment and eventually toward confrontation and grappling with the full range of oedipal strivings.

This affirmative quality of the analytic stance seems to have much in common with Kohut's (1977, 1984) self-object function of mirroring. In Kohut's view of therapeutic action, the analyst's mirroring (or self-affirming function) contributes to intrapsychic structuralization through the analysand's internalization of a two-step interpretive process, repeated throughout the analysis (1984). This involves a phase of understanding and a phase of explaining. The understanding stage of the process precedes the interpretation proper and might correlate with Killingmo's concept of discrete affirmative interventions. The explaining stage of the process constitutes the interpretation itself and leads to insight as it also entails "optimal frustration" of the analysand's transference wishes. Kohut believed that the inevitable but manageable frustration involved in repeatedly having transference needs and wishes understood and interpreted, rather than fulfilled, would facilitate a process of internalization whereby the analyst's self-affirming function (or empathy) and his analytic function (or capacity for observation and insight) could gradually be taken over by the analysand (1984). He pointed out that some narcissistically fragile patients require longer periods of noninterpretive understanding before they can tolerate and use the interpretive process. What I am suggesting is the possibility of enabling patients with quite severe narcissistic vulnerability to use interpretive interventions right from the start, by capitalizing on or exaggerating the affirmative elements of our usual repertoire of interventions.

If, then, an affirmative stance toward our patients need not be communicated through a discrete, "affirmative" intervention, nor through a period or phase of noninterpretive understanding, but rather can be expressed from the start in the course of our ordinary psychoanalytic activities, how can we exploit this affirmative potential? Every intervention by the analyst that isn't an accurate reflection of exactly what the patient has communicated about himself represents some new information or involves some degree of questioning of the patient's former assumptions about himself. No matter how highly motivated a patient is in his analysis, there is often an unwelcome element in this newness, or in this opening up of the psychic status quo to questioning. Thus, with some patients it becomes important to be able to affirm where the patient is now, or where he has been, even as we present that piece of newness or that questioning of the old that asks him to reach for change. Besides the usual considerations of tact, timing, tone, and wording of our interventions, one further way to help the patient feel affirmed in what he is experiencing and in what he has communicated is by staying very close to the patient's material and to his language

(Winnicott, 1960b). The greater theoretical leaps away from the patient's material the analyst makes, the greater the risk of undermining the patient's sense of being affirmed. In addition to staying close to the associative material of the patient, the way we mix and combine the techniques in our usual analytic repertoire can make an important difference in whether a vulnerable patient feels validated, justified, and accepted (Killingmo, 1989) by an intervention or somehow hurt, stung, or alienated by it. In particular, the routine psychoanalytic mix of the intrapsychic with the interpersonal in our interpretations, and the mix of the psychodynamic with the psychogenetic, seems to hold a potential for an affirmative effect on many patients when it is most needed.

In Loewald's (1960) statement, "Nothing is introjected by the infant that is not brought to it by the mother" (p. 238), we have a reminder of the indissolubility, in development and in treatment, of the intrapsychic and the interpersonal. Historically, there has tended to be some dichotomization in analytic discourse between concepts which relate to the intrapsychic, on the one hand, and to the interactive or interpersonal, on the other.

The analyst's appreciation of the indissolubility of intrapsychic and interpersonal phenomena and of psychodynamic and psychogenetic phenomena can become an important contributor to her capacity to take an affirmative stance toward his analysands. Many patients hear analytic interventions that place a seemingly exclusive emphasis on the intrapsychic and psychodynamic components of the patient's material as containing some degree of criticism, or as an occasion for self-criticism. A communication that focuses on the patient's intrapsychic functioning and psychodynamic motives tends to demand that the patient in the here and now take full responsibility, alone and by himself, for whatever way he is functioning, or for whatever motivations, instincts, or affects are being revealed. Although such responsibility may be an ideal of mature adulthood, given the state of narcissistic vulnerability with which some patients begin treatment, or the regressed state which many analysands achieve within the treatment, when they are asked to take this degree of responsibility they may feel blamed or humiliated.

One particular effect of integrating an intrapsychic interpretation with an interpersonal component is to give the patient the message that the analyst includes himself in the consideration of how the analysand came to feel how he is feeling in the here and now, whether the feeling is primarily instinctual, affective, or defensive. Freud (1905) articulated his recognition of the importance of the analyst's contribution to transference in the Postscript he wrote after Dora had fled treatment. He wrote: "I ought to have said to her, '. . . have you been struck by anything about me or got to know anything about me which has caught your fancy, as happened previously with Herr K.?'" Schwaber, 1986, and Jordan, 1992, both cite this passage, making several points that, in part, overlap with my thesis here. Schwaber suggests that we "consider our participation, as the patient has perceived it and as a central element in the transference" (p. 929). She shows that this tends to deepen the realm of psychic experience and to increase the access to genetic material. Jordan holds that this approach to transference, which includes recognition of its potential as "plausible conjecture" (p. 729), serves to communicate the analyst's respect for "the patient's sense of reality," and for his "sanity" (p. 734). He goes on to say that when the perceptual basis for the transference, or its "perceptual edge" (Smith, 1990), is acknowledged, the patient is better able to distinguish the distortions that remain to be analyzed. I am suggesting that an additional, unintended effect of an intervention in which the analyst draws attention to how he might inadvertently have triggered a transference reaction in his patient is that, at a symbolic level, it can give the analysand a transient sense of shared responsibility for what he is feeling, and for how he has responded intrapsychically and interpersonally, and that this can facilitate the analytic process.

Of course many transference triggers are predominantly intrapsychic and not significantly evoked by the interpersonal in the here and now. But if we assume that all triggers are intrapsychic only, we may fail to give our analysands implicit permission to include their perception or experience of our behavior in their accounting for shifts in affect during an analytic hour. Without this permission, some patients may never let us know what it was in our interventions that was the Proustian madeleine for their affective experience, memory, or fantasy. This can be a loss, because the identification of the here-and-now trigger is often the "royal road" back to the genetic material, which was long ago transformed to become a part of the patient's dynamic unconscious. The patient may vehemently deny the relevance of the analyst's behavior, words, or person, or he may elaborate in a most surprising way on how something about the analyst has indeed triggered the current affect or defensive constellation. But in either case, the suggestion by the analyst that she may have contributed to what the patient is experiencing usually has a liberating effect on the analysand and his subsequent associations. The implicit message is that the analyst might have said or done something in the current situation that would make understandable the patient's new version of old familiar feelings. This frequently leads to new material related to the origin of the current transference feelings and to eventual insight into the patient's characterological way of dealing with these feelings. This approach is useful with patients who have a history of feeling alone in the face of overwhelming affect and who tend to take shame-infused responsibility for both their own and their objects' experience. The relief from the sense of sole responsibility for everything that has happened paradoxically can increase their capacity to make fine discernments concerning the ultimate responsibility for events and situations in their lives and enable them finally to take that responsibility which they themselves judge to be theirs.

Although ultimately the patient's feelings, needs, instincts, and fantasies can belong only to him, there is a theoretical rationale for allowing him transiently and symbolically to feel that the analyst in some way shares in the responsibility for aspects of his experience. In his 1979 article "The Waning of the Oedipus Complex," Loewald proposed that the capacity for self-responsibility is an achievement of the optimally resolved oedipal crisis, through the establishment of an internalized, autonomous superego. By definition of what constitutes neurosis, most patients entering analysis have not "optimally" resolved the oedipal crisis of their childhood; that task, in all its complex and multivarious ramifications, eventually becomes the focus of the work to be done in psychoanalytic treatment. Until such time in the course of an analysis that this structural achievement of an internalized, autonomous superego with its concomitant capacity for self-responsibility is achieved, asking our patients alone to bear the sense of responsibility for all that they feel and do is giving them a task beyond their capacity. Before the establishment of a mature superego, says Loewald (1979), we are all "more or less fortunate victims . . . victims of our instincts and of those of others, not to mention other forces of nature and social life" (p. 392). Not only Loewald, but Winnicott (1960a) as well, has pointed out the paradox involved in the sense of responsibility for what happens in one's life, both in childhood and in analytic treatment. He points out that in infancy, "good and bad things happen to the infant that are quite outside the infant's range" (p. 37). He goes on to say the the "ego-support of the maternal care enables the infant to live and develop in spite of not yet being able to control, or to feel responsible for what is good and bad in the environment" (p. 37). The patient feels less that he alone is being held responsible for the unacceptable or intolerable aspects of his experience when the analyst stays close to the patient's material, language, and view of reality (Kohut, 1984; Schwaber, 1986 and 1990) and when the analyst integrates the interpersonal, intrapsychic, dynamic, and genetic components of the patient's experience within a series of communications to the patient. This seems to strengthen the patient to do the analytic work and to facilitate the ongoing development of more differentiated, autonomous, and flexible ego and superego functioning.

So far, I have addressed the facilitating effect on analytic process of interventions that combine intrapsychic and interpersonal elements in the here and now. The patient's ability to accept interpretation of his current psychic functioning and motivation is also often furthered by an extension of the analyst's interventions to include a genetic reconstruction. The genetic reconstruction makes further sense of the patient's current psychic functioning and experience by identifying the childhood origins of the current experience (Blum, 1980), which often include hurtful aspects of the patient's human environment in childhood. Thus, the sum total of an intervention which includes the intrapsychic and dynamic plus the interpersonal and genetic will be a communication which says in effect to the patient: "I can certainly understand why you would feel this way right now, because it seems that you experienced what I just did or said as being similar to some specific hurtful thing that your mother or father repeatedly said or did in the past." Of course with each individual patient in each instance, the analyst would have the specific details to make a very particular, detailed, and personally nuanced intervention of this kind. Examples of this kind of integration of the intrapsychic, the interpersonal, the psychodynamic, and the genetic, within one series of interpretive communications are to be found in Schwaber's (1986) discussion of reconstructive work, and in her (1990) discussion of interpretation. Schwaber describes the analyst's consistent attention to shifts in the analysand's tone or mood of communication—which often signal the emergence of a resistance within an hour—followed by the analyst's interpretive attention to the here-and-now interpersonal triggers of these shifts, as well as to the psychogenetic roots of the patient's current vulnerability to these particular triggers. What follows is a further example of the analyst's blending of the intrapsychic and the interpersonal in the here and now with acknowledgment of psychogenetic forerunners of the patient's current dynamics, fostering intrapsychic integration.

A patient starts an hour by saying that he almost canceled the session even though he doesn't have a very bad cold, and he doesn't think the cold is really the problem. The patient goes on to elaborate on some very frustrating developments in an important project he has been trying to complete at work, leading to feelings of disappointment in himself and to a generalized sense of futility. Because the patient, most unusually, had thought of canceling the session and because the analyst hears the patient's discouragement and frustration at work as part of what he might be feeling about the analysis, the analyst thinks back to the end of the previous hour to search for possible triggers of the patient's current mood and remembers having noticed that the analysand had seemed surprised when the analyst announced the time was up. At the time, the analyst had wondered, but only to herself, if perhaps she had failed to make a needed intervention toward the end of the hour to help the patient better understand the confusing and conflicting feelings and self-representations that he had been elucidating. The content of the patient's associations at the end of the previous hour had had to do with contradictory experiences, in relation to both his wife and his mother, of feeling at some times very special and favored and at other times totally disregarded and left out while others replaced him in the most favored position.

A recent vacation of the analyst had been preceded by the patient's questions in the associative material concerning whether his mother ever thought of him when he was not in her presence. The analyst had linked this to the patient's possible concerns about whether the analyst would think of him while she was away. This kind of wondering aloud was new for the patient, who had made an early adaptation of selfsufficiency and denial of dependency needs by looking after others and walling himself off from any intimacy in which his own needs would be acknowledged. Very early in this hour, then, the analyst responded to the patient's information that he had thought of canceling the session by sharing her observation that the end of the previous session had seemed difficult for the patient and asking the patient if that observation fit with his experience. The patient acknowledged that he had experienced the ending the day before as very abrupt, and that he had left feeling very frustrated and discouraged, with a sense of futility about his own capacity to do analysis. He thought that there had been a point in the session when the analyst had made an intervention which should have been able to move him beyond his pathological position and that instead of using the analyst's help he had gone right on in the same track and had failed to do his part.

The analyst responded by telling the patient that she had noticed his distress at the end of the previous session and had wondered afterwards if maybe the patient might have felt in need of a clarification that had never come concerning the many confusing and contradictory feelings he had been talking about in relationship to his wife and mother. The analyst went on to say that if that were the case, the failure on the analyst's part to make such a clarification might understandably have left the patient feeling frustrated and discouraged, but the interesting thing was that, instead of considering the possibility that the analyst had failed to respond to a felt need of his, the patient had focused on his own inadequacies and on what *he* had failed to do, thus becoming depressed about himself, about the analysis, and about many other things in his life. The analyst further suggested that her lack of response at the end of the hour might even have felt to the patient like a concrete enactment of exactly what he'd been talking about in the hour—the experience of losing a special position that he had thought was his and of expecting something that never came. While the analyst explicitly acknowledged a possible role for her own, interpersonal contribution to the patient's "transference resistance," she kept the analytic focus on helping the patient understand more about the genetic roots of his affective response and the pattern of intrapsychic mechanisms by which the patient had come to deal with the particular affects evoked by the analyst's triggering behavior.

This intervention, which included but was not limited to a transference interpretation, acknowledged the patient's current psychodynamic state of dejection in the analytic and extraanalytic experience. It linked this internal state both to the analyst's (interpersonal) behavior at the end of the previous hour and to certain (psychogenetic) recurring features of his mother's behavior toward him in childhood. It drew attention to the early (structuralized) establishment within the patient of a certain intrapsychic dynamic whereby the patient would become self-critical and depressed in the face of an interpersonal disappointment, which he then tended to disavow, explaining the interpersonal disappointment to himself in terms of his own inadequacies. The patient was visibly moved by this intervention because he had been unaware that his wish to cancel the session might have anything to do with feelings he had in relationship to the analyst which had been triggered by the previous hour. He went on to report in new and more differentiated ways childhood experiences of his mother's attentions to his brothers and of his own tendency for self-blame when he felt his mother had turned away from him. He seemed to be seeing clearly and articulating forcefully for the first time highly differentiated aspects of her mothering that had only been expressed in the vaguest of terms in the past. Some of these elaborations were manifestly about his mother's indirectness in communicating her feeling for the patient. The analyst heard and interpreted in this material the patient's transference frustration due to the characteristic indirectness of the analyst's communications about how she views the patient. Thus the hour elucidated in great detail both psychogenetic and here-and-now interpersonal components of the transference. The patient also began to speak of aspects of his current (extratransference) relationship with his wife, seeing new ways in which he had chosen a mate who had similarities to his mother and seeing also that in some inappropriate ways he carried over the intrapsychic solutions that he had developed in reaction to his mother's (pathogenic) idiosyncrasies into his relationship with his wife.

Even if the primary mode of functioning or motivation in a given analytic hour is largely in the service of resistance—such as, in this case, the patient's desire to cancel the session—the analyst communicates her understanding and her acceptance of the patient's attitude and behavior through placing it in the context of both the interpersonal experience in the here and now of the transference and the earlier childhood experience with the parents and siblings. This goes a long way toward enabling the patient to accept and understand it as well and thus facilitates the patient's ability to take the next step. Freud (1937), Blum (1980), Ornstein and Ornstein (1980), Kohut (1984), Schwaber (1986), and others have drawn our attention to the importance of genetic (re)constructions as a part of the interpretive process—a process which enables the patient to increase his understanding, acceptance, and integration of ever-broadening and deepening areas of his experience, past and present. Behind every link that the analyst makes between a current dynamic constellation and a psychogenetic experience lies a metacommunication that says to the patient: "No wonder you feel what you feel now, or do what you do! Look at what happened to you when you were two or three or four or five. Now we can begin to understand the ways (intrapsychic and interpersonal) which you have found to deal with this." This latent message within the interpretation that makes the dynamic/psychogenetic link seems to contribute to the patient's feeling of justification, validation, and acceptance (Killingmo, 1989) by capitalizing on the affirmative potential inherent in ordinary interpretive and reconstructive interventions without having to rely on discrete affirmative statements. The feeling of validation inherent in this process seems to enable the patient to look more objectively than before at his objects and at himself and to express more freely what comes to mind, thus facilitating the psychoanalytic process.

The integration described above of the intrapsychic, interpersonal, dynamic, and genetic components of the patient's experience need not be made in one overwhelming communication to the patient but is often conveyed in dialogue form in a series of brief communications in which only a part of the analyst's understanding is conveyed in any one intervention, to be refined, corrected, or rejected by the patient before the next "installment" from the analyst. In fact, at certain well-chosen points in a session or in an analysis, the dialogue form of communication also goes a long way toward conveying a sense of affirmation to the patient. Ordinarily, we are quiet in order to allow the patient's associations freely to develop. But we are also responsive to those moments when the patient needs to hear something from us. In order for our patients to be able to hear the clarifying and affirming nature of our understandings of them, we must feel free to communicate the complexity of that understanding over a series of communications. At these moments, the dialogue style allows the analyst to communicate the richness and complexity, the detail and the nuance of what she understands and also allows the patient to confirm, elaborate, correct, or disagree with the analyst as the communication progresses. When the analyst amends what she is saying about the patient on the basis of the patient's further communication, this also has an affirmative effect and enables the patient to access and express more of the previously hidden wells of his experience. Further affirmation of the patient is provided by the analyst's success in using creatively the subtle details of the patient's life and the increasingly fleshed-out view of the patient's original objects, as these have emerged and are revised over the course of a treatment.

To illustrate these technical considerations, I present material from the analysis of a high-functioning businessman in his mid-fifties who was married with two grown children. He began treatment suffering from intense feelings of vulnerability related to a chronic sense of anxiety and inadequacy in his work setting, where he had been unable to attain recognition in keeping with his potential. He also suffered from intense shame at the degree of emotional dependency that he felt on his wife and from unbearable feelings of inferiority in relation to colleagues and friends. His wife had recently become less available due to a promotion that would involve extensive international travel for her. In spite of a difficult beginning, related to an intensified sense of vulnerability and fears of dependency, the patient responded very positively to initiation of analytic treatment. Following the first year of analysis, he was better able to tolerate his wife's absences for professional travel, and his career took a dramatic upturn. In my comments on the material that follows, I will use the term *transference* to refer to the intrapsychic and dynamic meanings and motivations which the patient brings to the analytic situation from his past. I will use the term *interpersonal* to refer to the interactions (verbal and nonverbal exchanges) that take place between patient and analyst. The term *here and now* will refer to the analytic relationship in both its interpersonal and transference aspects.

The first session to be presented occurred during the fifteenth month of a four-year analysis. It is the second hour after a one-week interruption, and two weeks before a scheduled two-week interruption. The degree and quality of analyst activity and interaction in this hour were deemed essential to facilitating the analysand's capacity to identify and work through his painful transference-based affective experience of the analyst's absences, one just past and the other looming ahead. This degree and quality of analyst activity and interaction would be inappropriate with many other analysands and after the second year of treatment was no longer necessary with this particular patient. Issues of separation emerge, along with the theme of "being centered upon" (Loewald, 1960, p. 230). In this segment, the analyst is uncharacteristically engaged in active dialogue with the patient because of apparent resistance at the start of the hour. The patient lies down on the couch, is silent for five minutes, and then says, "Well, I don't have anything to say," followed by a further five-minute silence. The analyst then intervenes:

A: Did somebody here say something disturbing yesterday? *(Allows for an intrapsychic or interpersonal explanation of the patient's silence.)*

P: I don't think so. The silence seems more related to your absence—still feeling disjointed, disconnected—it has a sense of "I can't get back in gear."

A: But the word *disconnected* could also mean that it has something to do with your sense of what's *between* us, as well as with your sense of getting back in gear internally. *(Again allows for an interpersonal component as one aspect of the patient's difficulties in getting started in the current hour.)*

P: Yes, it does. I am aware—there are two levels—feeling disconnected does have to do with the relationship. And getting in gear has to do with the content.

A: So that yesterday you were in gear with the content, but you still felt disconnected from me?

P: That's right. And I guess what comes to mind is, I am aware of the upcoming absence—separation's a better word. I say to myself, "Well, Peter, are you angry? Are you angry at her?" But it feels more like, dead. It has more a sense that I was alive, the connection was alive, and the separation deadened it, and I can't get it alive again . . . *(three-minute silence.)* . . . It takes *time* to look ahead at the next separation. Yesterday was helpful—the content was helpful, but again, it's the two weeks looming ahead. I need the content and activity, over time, in order to get back the connectedness.

A: It must be very hard to need the connectedness, to feel that it's helpful over time, but to know that we just came back together after a break, and that we'll be separating again after next week.

P: There was a sense of feeling more connected as you were saying that.

A: Would it have something to do with feeling understood in your difficulty with my going away again?

P: Time is the opportunity to feel understood again and again with you— it's as if, coming back, that has to happen all over again.

A: You mean, after an absence, whether you're in my physical presence or not, you feel isolated and alone, or disjointed and disconnected, until proven otherwise by my understanding, again and again, over time?

P: I hadn't thought of it that way, but that fits. Because just before you said that, I was thinking "GOD! How regressed and shameful!" I feel surprised that I can't have a feeling of being connected because of a separation of one week! But what you said made me realize that I'm not talking about connection per se, but about a level of *vitality* in connection that's lost. My experience, I think, *has* been that I *am* alone, and that's what I've come to believe, until proven otherwise. This is the reason for giving it time—time is something that in the larger picture of my life I wasn't given a lot of. *(This self-observation by the patient comes after months of slowly building psychogenetic reconstructions.)* I was really working hard, in yesterday's hour, to understand that stuff about envy.

A: And I think we could say that in yesterday's hour we didn't give you enough time, after the one-week break, to reestablish your sense of connection with me before we plunged into talking about a content area—envy—that you had to work too hard to understand. *(The analyst makes an interpersonal formulation in which she takes some responsibility for allowing the previous hour to get into difficult content before dealing with the patient's feelings about the absences behind and ahead in the treatment. This is then linked with the intrapsychic sense of disjointedness and the interpersonal sense of disconnection that the patient has been describing in the current hour. The patient himself has brought in the genetic component with his reference to the phenomenon of his childhood, having to do with not being given enough time for his development.)*

P: When you say that, I feel, "Whew! I don't always have to work on problems here!"

The analyst and patient have interpreted the resistance (the patient's silence and words, "I have nothing to say") in terms of the genetic contribution of the patient's chronic childhood feeling of being pushed beyond his developmental capacity by a reluctant mother who had seven children, very close in age, and who justified the resultant deprivation of her children with a child-rearing philosophy expressed in the words, "It's good for you! It'll make you tough." The analyst has further suggested that this transference-based resistance was triggered by the analyst's failure in the interpersonal field of the previous hour to recognize the patient's postvacation sense of disjointedness and disconnectedness, leading to his feeling pushed to deal with difficult content while feeling a lack of affective response. The combination of the genetic and interpersonal understanding of the patient's transference feelings and resistance seems to have helped the patient to feel affirmed, and the resolution of that particular resistance was expressed in the patient's "Whew!" The patient was then able to go on with transference and extratransference associations about longing for attention and continued until shame emerged at his impulse to tell the analyst about every single thing that happened while the analyst had been away. The patient then spoke of his own pleasure in sharing in the mundane details of his children's lives and of the impossibility of imagining that anyone could take pleasure in hearing the everyday details of his own life. The analyst responded by inquiring about possible genetic roots of these feelings, implying that the shame legitimately derived from early experience, but might not be justified in the here and now. The patient responded that in a recent conversation with his mother he had felt deadened at her leaden recital of her own activities. He then went on:

> P: When I was thinking yesterday of my impulse to say to you, "This happened and this happened and this happened," what stopped me was the thought that you would feel the same way toward me that I would feel toward my mother. But today, I get the *two* images: the one that's like with my mother—it's deadening; the other is like with Jeremy and Ashley (his two grown children), because it *is* enlivening.
>
> A: So today, you can have the *two* images. But yesterday, you were afraid that I would react only *one* way to you, the way you react to your mother; *and* I might add, possibly the way your mother might've reacted to *you* when you were a child? *(The analyst takes on what she imagines is the mother's voice, from the patient's childhood):* "I can barely survive just seeing that you seven kids are clean and clothed and fed! So *don't* ask me to just *sit* here and watch you *grow*. I'm already *doing* all I *can*." *(Bringing the previous genetic reconstructions together with the intrapsychic and interpersonal here and now of the transference.)*
>
> P: (The patient tears up.) (Pause.) That's right. That's how she talked.
>
> A: Yes. And it seems that that is how you keep expecting me to talk. (This brings together the intrapsychic with the interpersonal here and now and the genetic reconstruction.)
>
> P: I know you're right.

The analyst, in a quite ordinary analytic way, has attempted meaningfully to relate the patient's extratransference and transference experience (of desire, shame, and disavowal, related to longings for loving attention) to current interpersonal phenomena within the analytic relationship (the analyst's absences, and the analyst's neglect of the patient's heightened need for a sense of connectedness in the first postvacation hour by a too-exclusive focus on content) and to the relevant psychogenetic experiences of childhood. Such parallels can be drawn because the internalizations of childhood produce enduring psychic structures. These structures dictate that the adult individual will exhibit reactions in adulthood that are structural elaborations of the original childhood reactions. The phenomena of internalization will also lead each individual to be particularly sensitive to disruptions which seem similar to the specific impingements that affected his development in childhood (Winnicott, 1958). The adult patient will be alert to such similarities, even when they are not obvious to outside observers. It is for this reason that it is important that the analyst think in terms of the similarities between the patient's current and past objects, and help the patient direct his own attention to these similarities, rather than focusing immediately or exclusively on helping the patient to differentiate between old and new (Schwaber, 1990). Thus, in the material presented above, the analyst was alert to the similarity that the patient felt between his emotionally unresponsive mother of childhood and the analyst's unresponsiveness to the patient's feelings of disconnectedness and need after the disruption in the treatment. Through this analytic understanding and how it was conveyed, the analyst affirmed the patient's past and present experience of longing and shame while also bringing together elements of the patient's experience in a way that might foster insight and integration.

During the third and fourth years of analysis, the analysand did more and more of the work independently, and the analyst's affirmative stance receded into the background to be replaced by a more purely "analytic" stance. A summary of a session two and a half years into the analysis illustrates the patient's increasing self-confidence, greater recognition of aggressive strivings, and increased capacity for self-reflection. The session to be described, like the one above, also took place on the first day back after a one-week disruption, but this time the interruption of treatment had come at the patient's initiative. While his wife had been on a business trip, the patient had spent the week doing renovations on their vacation home. He began by reporting that it had been a good week and by describing the pleasure he had felt in his solitude and in his physical labors. He then reported two dream fragments. From the first dream, he could remember only "the image of a two-by-four." In the second dream, someone he knew "was badly hurt in something like a car accident." There were emergency vehicles, and the analysand asked the emergency personnel why they were not taking the victim to the hospital. He got a reply that the injury was not that serious, but he did not feel reassured. In his associations, the

analysand spoke of a boxing match he had watched on TV the evening
before the dream.

> **P:** Something very clear about the aggression, and also the skill involved.
> You don't just go out and bludgeon someone. (Pause.) There's some-
> thing missing here. How did I get on to this? (Pause.)
>
> **A:** Well, if we put the dream about the two-by-four together with the
> dream in which someone gets badly hurt, it might fit with what you were
> talking about before you went on vacation: how can you find a way to
> assert your own interests, or to use two-by-fours to create structures in
> your own life, without ending up feeling that you have badly hurt some
> other person?
>
> **P:** I think that's probably right. Actually the boxing match—the guy who
> ended up winning—he was more skilled. And also pretty intelligent for
> a boxer. Involved with youth groups, quite personable, savvy, and con-
> cerned. When he looked his opponent in the eye, he would back off. I
> thought: how is he negotiating this very aggressive stance with these
> other parts of himself? After he won, he kept going over to the other guy
> to see if he was all right.
>
> **A:** The way you did with the person who was hurt in the second dream last
> night?
>
> **P:** Yeah. I could relate to *that!* I keep thinking that the two-by-four thing in
> the earlier dreams was there for a reason, but I can't figure it out.
>
> **A:** Well, what are two-by-fours used for?
>
> **P:** (Laughs.) They're really used to build structures *(The patient just added a
> structure to his vacation home)*—or, to hit somebody with. (Pause.) It's
> puzzling—that visual image—I can't blink it away—I've got to find
> some way to make sense of it. (Long pause.)
>
> **A:** Well, it seems to me that in the two uses you came up with for the two-by-
> four, you've just crystalized your own dilemma. Because for you, when-
> ever you use a two-by-four to build structure in your life, you end up
> feeling as if you've just used it to hit somebody else over the head. And
> then you have to send for the emergency vehicles, like in the dream.
> From your wording about the dream, it sounds like you were not com-
> pletely convinced that it was an "accident."
>
> **P:** (Pause.) I think that's true. (Pause.) I think this is true. It's pertinent.
>
> **A:** It's still hard for you to believe you're not hurting people by your new-
> found success and independence. You may feel that I'm like the emer-
> gency personnel in the dream, who reassure you, but don't convince
> you, that the "victim" is not so badly hurt.
>
> **P:** That's right!

The patient continued to free-associate for the rest of the session,
moving on to speak of annoyance with his boss for an incident that
suggested poor judgment and weak leadership. The patient was silent
and then said, "I guess it's better for me to do what I can do, well, than

to sit around being disappointed and angry at how other people are doing things." The previous analytic work on the patient's associative link between his own achievements and other people's hurt or destruction seems to have allowed him to think more freely about empowering himself in relation to his boss and about taking more pleasure in a fuller use of his own capacities at work. This theme had been worked and reworked previously in relationship to his father and to current authority figures, but at the end of this session the analysand seems to be reaching for a new level of integration.

During he fourth year of analysis, the patient continued the move toward greater autonomy, self-acceptance, resilience, and insight, with the analyst playing a decreasing role, even in the need for interpretation. We thus arrive at a reiteration of tried-and-true psychoanalytic principles to be used with selected patients in the early phases of treatment. In particular, the analyst stays close to the patient's material, and any leaps that are taken are leaps to the details of what the analyst and patient have already shared together about the patient's past, including the accruing details concerning the patient's experience of the analytic relationship. The analyst participates at times in a dialogue with the patient, presenting her understanding of the patient in manageable increments and showing the patient that she is refining her understanding interactively in her ongoing verbal exchanges with the patient. The analyst also shows the patient that she has grasped the essence of his experience by making creative use in interpretations and reconstructions of the shared, accruing knowledge of the patient and his original objects. Finally, the analyst transiently takes a certain pressure of responsibility off the patient by placing intrapsychic and dynamic interpretations within an interpersonal and/or a psychogenetic context. All these ordinary technical guidelines can tend to maximize the affirmative effect of the analyst's communications, minimizing resistance derived from transference of affect and defense related to early deprivation or trauma. The reduction of this source of resistance facilitates the analytic process and enhances the therapeutic action of psychoanalysis.

BIBLIOGRAPHY

ABRAMS, S. (1990). The psychoanalytic process: The developmental and the integrative. *Psychoanal. Q.*, 59:650–77.

ADLER, G. (1989). Transitional phenomena, projective identification and the essential ambiguity of the psychoanalytic situation. *Psychoanal. Q.*, 58:81–104.

BLATT, S., & BEHRENDS, D. (1987). Internalization, separation, individuation and the nature of therapeutic action. *Int. J. Psycho-Anal.*, 48:279–97.

BLUM, H. (1980). The value of reconstruction in adult psychoanalysis. *Int. J. Psycho-Anal.*, 61:39–52.

COOPER, A. (1988). Our changing views of the therapeutic action of psychoanalysis: Comparing Strachey and Loewald. *Psychoanal. Q.*, 51:15–27.

EMDE, R. (1990). Mobilizing fundamental modes of development: Empathic availability and therapeutic action. *J. Amer. Psychoanal. Assn.*, 38:881–914.

FONAGY, P., MORAN, G., EDGECUMBE, R., KENNEDY, H., & TARGET, M. (1993). The roles of mental representations and mental processes in therapeutic action. *Psychoanal. Study of the Child*, 48:9–48.

FREUD, S. (1905). Fragment of an analysis of a case of hysteria. *S.E.*, 7:3–122.

―――― (1915). Observations on transference love. *S.E.*, 12:159–71.

―――― (1937). Constructions in analysis. *S.E.*, 23:255–69.

GILL, M. (1982). *Analysis of the Transference*. New York: Int. Univ. Press.

GITELSON, M. (1962). The curative factors in psycho-analysis: The first phase of psycho-analysis. *Int. J. Psycho-Anal.*, 43:194–205.

JORDAN, J. (1992). The transference: Distortion or plausible conjecture? *Int. J. Psycho-Anal.*, 73:729–38.

KILLINGMO, B. (1989). Conflict and deficit: Implications for technique. *Int. J. Psycho-Anal.*, 70:65–79.

KLAUBER, J. (1980). Formulating interpretations in clinical psychoanalysis. *Int. J. Psycho-Anal.*, 61:195–201.

KOHUT, H. (1977). *The Restoration of the Self*. New York: Int. Univ. Press.

―――― (1982). Introspection, empathy and the semi-circle of mental health. *Int. J. Psycho-Anal.*, 63:395–408.

―――― (1984). *How Does Analysis Cure?* Chicago: Univ. of Chicago Press.

KRIS, A. (1982). *Free Association: Method and Process*. New Haven: Yale University Press.

―――― (1990). Helping patients by analyzing self-criticism. *J. Amer. Psychoanal. Assn.*, 38:605–36.

LOEWALD, H. (1960). On the therapeutic action of psychoanalysis. *Int. J. Psycho-Anal.*, 41:16–33.

―――― (1979). The waning of the Oedipus complex. *J. Amer. Psychoanal. Assn.*, 27:751–77.

MCLAUGHLIN, J. (1981). Transference, psychic reality, and countertransference. *Psychoanal. Q.*, 50:639–64.

MYERSON, P. (1990). Managing strain in a classical analysis: Re-establishing the therapeutic relationship or interpreting unconscious wishes. *J. Amer. Psychoanal. Assn.*, 59:741-65.

NERUDA, P. (1969). I have gone marking. In Neruda, *Twenty Love Poems and a Song of Despair*, trans. W. S. Merwin. London: Jonathan Cape Ltd.

OGDEN, T. (1982). *Projective Identification and Psychotherapeutic Technique*. New York: Jason Aronson.

ORNSTEIN, P. & ORNSTEIN, A. (1980). Formulating interpretations in clinical psychoanalysis. *Int. J. Psycho-Anal.*, 61:203–11.

RANGELL, L. (1991). Castration. *J. Amer. Psychoanal. Assn.*, 39:3–24.

SCHWABER, E. (1986). Reconstruction and perceptual experience: Further thoughts on analytic listening. *J. Amer. Psychoanal. Assn.*, 34:911–32.

―――― (1990). Interpretation and the therapeutic action of psychoanalysis. *Int. J. Psycho-Anal.*, 71:229–40.

SMITH, H. (1990). Cues: The perceptual edge of the transference. *Int. J. Psycho-Anal.*, 71:219–28.

SPITZ, R. (1956). Countertransference. *J. Amer. Psychoanal. Assn.*, 4:256–65.

WINNICOTT, D. (1954). Withdrawal and regression. In Winnicott, *Through Paediatrics to Psychoanalysis*. New York: Basic.

―――― (1956). Clinical varieties of transference. In Winnicott, *Through Paediatrics to Psychoanalysis*. New York: Basic Books.

―――― (1958). The capacity to be alone. In Winnicott, *The Maturational Processes and the Facilitating Environment*. New York: Int. Univ. Press.

―――― (1960a). The theory of the parent-infant relationship. In Winnicott, *The Maturational Processes and the Facilitating Environment*. New York: Int. Univ Press.

―――― (1960b). Ego distortion in terms of true and false self. In Winnicott, *The Maturational Processes and the Facilitating Environment*. New York: Int. Univ. Press.

DEVELOPMENT

A Childhood Gender Identity Disorder

Analysis, Preoedipal Determinants, and Therapy in Adolescence

JOHN B. McDEVITT, M.D.

This paper is about a four-year-old boy's wish to be a girl. This wish was a compromise formation, the consequence of intrapsychic conflict. Using reconstructive inferences and research findings, I suggest a line of development in the boy's femininity, beginning with constitutional and maturational factors, with being shaped in a feminine direction by his environment, and with shaping himself internally in the form of a compromise formation in that direction by the time he was two to three years of age. The disorder began to acquire a persistence and stability during the preoedipal phase and, with minor changes in its components, remained operative during the oedipal phase, latency, and adolescence.

IN THIS PAPER I PRESENT AND DISCUSS DATA FROM AN ANALYSIS OF A FOUR-
year-old boy who wanted to be a girl, the preoedipal determinants of
this wish, and his therapy in adolescence.

Billy's mother consulted me when he was aged four because she was
concerned that his wish to be a girl and his preference for playing with
girls indicated that he was not happy with himself as a boy. He wanted to
use her makeup, wear her clothes, and put his own hair as well as hers in

Director of research, Margaret S. Mahler Psychiatric Research Foundation; training
and supervising analyst in adult and child analysis, New York Psychoanalytic Institute.

A shorter version of this paper was first presented at the International Symposium of
the Margaret S. Mahler Psychiatric Research Foundation, Paris, November 3, 1985.

The Psychoanalytic Study of the Child 50, ed. Albert J. Solnit, Peter B. Neubauer, Samuel
Abrams, and A. Scott Dowling (Yale University Press, copyright © 1995 by Albert J.
Solnit, Peter B. Neubauer, Samuel Abrams, and A. Scott Dowling).

a ponytail. He insisted that girls were stronger than boys, could do more, and had more—jewelry, clothes, hair. She added that he had always been quiet, shy, passive, and compliant. He had avoided boyish activities from the time he was two, had shown an interest in jewelry and girls' clothes from two and a half, and had liked to dress up as a girl from the age of three.

When I first met Billy, he told me that he would like a magic fairy to turn him into a girl and that playing with boys gave him a headache because they made too much noise. He then chose to play with two Barbie dolls. He was particularly interested in their dress, hair, and high-heeled shoes.

THE HISTORY

Billy's mother, an attractive, reserved, articulate young woman, hid her femininity. She preferred slacks and jeans to skirts and dresses. Looking at herself in a mirror or going to a beauty shop to make herself attractive made her uncomfortable. She had always felt shy, insecure, and insignificant, and she had always felt the need to please others and depreciate herself. Asserting herself made her feel uneasy, and she was frightened by her own anger.

In her weekly meetings with me she cried when she talked about Billy's wish to be a girl. She abhorred homosexuality and felt extremely guilty thinking that she had damaged him, as if he had cancer. For this reason, in the second year of Billy's analysis, I recommended that she begin analysis herself. She was dedicated to Billy's analysis, driving miles from the suburbs to appointments.

Her own mother had been similarly restrained and reserved but also cold and distant, which she was not. By contrast, her father, who became ill with cancer when she was eleven and died when she was fourteen, was warm, loving, and ebullient but had a temper that frightened her. Both parents, as they already had a daughter, had wanted her to be a boy.

As a child, the mother, like Billy, was shy, self-sufficient, and happy to play alone for hours in her room. During latency, she was a tomboy, which pleased her father, but no matter how much she tried to gain his love, she was always disappointed and enraged by his strong attachment to her pretty and popular sister, six years older. Her father and sister were in constant battle, but the father always gave in to his daughter's demands. The sister was preoccupied with her dress and appearance, especially her breasts, and frequently preened in front of the mirror. Dominating and temperamental, she belittled Billy's mother, humiliated and demeaned her. Yet Billy's mother thought her sister was beautiful, particularly admired her breasts, and envied and idealized her. She was also jealous and afraid of her.

For many years Billy's mother was subordinate and submissive to his father. At first, she thought that her husband was as strong, capable, and reliable as her father had been, but subsequently she was disappointed and angry because he was not. For all her shyness, she eventually became the dominant partner in the marriage, the disciplinarian in the family, and a successful businesswoman.

Although the father hoped to have a better relationship with Billy than he had had with his own father, he did not. Like his father he traveled frequently and was emotionally distant and unavailable during Billy's first three to four years. He left on a long business trip the day after Billy was born, was away 80 percent of Billy's first year, and by his fourth year was still away 40 percent of the time. He had not wanted a child and paid little attention to Billy. Not being of a very domestic temperament, he often found interests outside the family. Unlike his own father, when he did begin to pay attention to Billy, when the boy was four, he was overly permissive rather than critical and dictatorial. He related to Billy more like a pal or brother than a father, often providing gifts and treats. He was more tolerant and permissive with Billy than his wife, who was more serious and the disciplinarian. He also did more with Billy—ice skating, sledding, football, and baseball— and he took Billy to the barbershop, bathed him, and read to him at bedtime. Up to the age of four Billy preferred his mother; after that he preferred his father.

The father had been in therapy for several years prior to Billy's treatment, for reasons unrelated to any concern about Billy. In fact, he told me that he was not concerned about nor did he feel any responsibility for Billy's femininity, recalling that he himself had often dressed in his mother's clothes as a child—once in his mother's fur coat, when his parents were away on a trip when he was three. He added that if Billy became a homosexual he would still love him. Soon after Billy began his analysis, the father stopped his own therapy. Before Billy was six the father began to take him to sexually stimulating movies. I saw Billy's father every month or two.

Three years after the parents were married the mother had her first abortion. She was afraid that she could not care for a baby adequately. Billy, an only child, was born as planned, two years later. The mother would have preferred a girl. Although she felt happy and excited during her pregnancy, she was also apprehensive, afraid that she wasn't prepared to raise a child, particularly a boy, who would become too wild and sexually aggressive (as his father had been in adolescence) and who would stimulate her own sexual impulses. But she was delighted with Billy, a sweet, sensitive, happy infant, much like herself when she was a child. Until he was six months old she dressed him in a niece's pink clothes.

The mother recalled being happy most of the time during Billy's first year and a half. At times, however, as a young, insecure new mother whose husband was away most of the time and who was without family or friends nearby, she was both angry with her husband and overly anxious about Billy's welfare, particularly on the few occasions when he was sick. In her husband's absence she was lonely, and she liked to hold, cuddle, and cling to Billy, fostering, she thought in hindsight, undue dependence. She also recalled that she was too rigid in her control of Billy and in his schedules of eating and sleeping. Since Billy was developing normally and was an easy and compliant baby to care for, the mother, despite her concerns, hired a babysitter twice a week when he was two months old so that she could have time to herself, and she returned to work part-time when he was two years old.

The mother never thought of her child as baby boy or baby girl, just as baby. She did not recall difficulties, conflicts, or confusion in her mind between herself and Billy during the first year and a half. From her description I could infer that Billy had been appropriately attached and responsive to her; it seemed that his separation and stranger reactions had been mild to moderate; and the practicing subphase, although subdued, seemed to have been otherwise normal. Billy was described as a graceful, sensitive, cooperative, good-natured infant—a joy to be with.

Shortlived difficulties began when Billy was one and a half. He went through a period of coercing and clinging, insistently demanding his mother's attention and, on occasion, attacking other children—for example, pulling their hair. The mother could not understand or tolerate this behavior any more than she could tolerate her own anger, nor could she understand the "unreasonable demands" he made on her. Billy's behavior sounded fairly typical of the rapprochement subphase. In hindsight the mother wondered if she had conveyed to Billy the idea that it was bad to lose control of one's temper: "Maybe Billy went through a period of defiance after which he might not have dared to be defiant." In fact, Billy was not defiant during the remainder of the rapprochement and phallic-narcissistic phases from one and a half to four years; it sounded as if he was too subdued and reasonable. Although he went through a brief stage of saying no and had a few mild temper outbursts, he rarely resisted his mother's requests.

The mother had always assumed that Billy was very vulnerable, and she had been overly concerned about his welfare with each childhood illness and with each step in his development. Billy's resentment of what he experienced as controlling and intrusive behavior was masked, only to come out later in his analysis. The mother became even more concerned when Billy found it difficult to separate from her when he attended a play group at the age of two. As a result of her concern, the mother thought the most difficult aspect of caring for Billy was saying no to him. The first time she recalls being really angry was when Billy at two and a half was demanding and cranky. She lost her patience, said no, and sent him to his room. Another result of the mother's concern was a second abortion, when Billy was two years old. She feared that their having a new baby would damage Billy.

Rigidity in controlling Billy's schedules in the first eighteen months shifted to an inability to be firm when the mother was confronted with Billy's own wishes. Asked about toilet training, she said, "God forbid, push Billy into toilet training when he wasn't ready? I suppose it was I who wasn't ready." Bill trained himself by age three. He sat on the toilet to urinate until he was three and a half. When he did stand he did not hold his penis to direct the stream of urine. He gave up his strong attachment to his bottle when he was three and a half, his thumb and blanket three years later.

The mother did not recall sexual curiosity, erections, or masturbation. She ignored and devalued Billy's masculinity and phallic urges, and, as a consequence, Billy seems to have similarly ignored and devalued the masculinity and sexuality that he was just becoming aware of. Billy did not express curiosity or ask questions about being exposed to the primal scene on at least six occasions between the ages of one and a half and four or about daily exposure to his mother's nude body and showers with his father.

When Billy was two years old, the mother noticed that he did not like to play with cars and trucks as boys usually do. She attributed this to his "artistic" nature. Billy did not like the Superman outfit that he received as a gift for his second birthday, nor did he like football T-shirts. It soon became apparent that Billy preferred to play with girls and liked jewelry, the colors pink and purple, and the feel of such fabrics as velvet. She recalled buying him a pink bracelet and a "pull-string egg-beater" toy, and she thought it cute that he liked to play with an old straw handbag of hers.

The months prior to taking a two-week vacation without Billy when he was almost three were very difficult for her. She was extremely angry that her husband had forced her to choose between him and

Billy by threatening to leave her if she did not go on the trip. The disagreements and the fights—and especially the anxiety that something terrible might happen to Billy while she was away—were so great that she entered psychotherapy. She was also concerned that Billy, like herself when she was three, would be too anxious to attend nursery school the next fall. Although his maternal grandmother said that Billy had gotten along very well during his parents' absence, on their return he was no longer spontaneously affectionate, nor would he respond to their affection. He would turn his head away and become "limp." His apparent lack of interest in sex and his fear of expressing aggression may have increased at this time. There was no change, however, in his friendliness with playmates. Occasional brief vacations before and after this one did not upset the mother or Billy, who was always cared for by his grandmother. Only gradually during the second and third year of his analysis did Billy begin to show affection again toward his mother.

When Billy as three and a half he was hospitalized for an adenoidectomy. The procedures were carefully explained to him beforehand, and his mother stayed with him in the hospital. Soon after the operation, he was given a haircut in a barbershop for the first time. Before this he had been frequently mistaken for a girl because of his looks and his long hair. The father had not wanted Billy's hair cut, partly as an expression of rebellion toward his own father. From three and a half to four Billy became overly anxious about minor cuts and bruises and liked to look up women's dresses. Following a myringotomy at age four, Billy appeared excited when blood was drawn from a vein, played that his gown was a dress while in the hospital, and became "swishy" in his movements. A few months later he started treatment.

In addition to crying when speaking of her guilt at Billy's wish to be a girl, the mother also cried when she spoke of her father's illness and death, her guilt over her two-week vacation and Billy's two operations, even though he appeared to manage these experiences better than children ordinarily do. She wondered why her anxiety was so intense prior to leaving Billy to go on a vacation, before he went to nursery school, and when he was hospitalized. She recalled her distress when her parents went on vacation when she was almost three. "I must have identified with this child, from two to three, without knowing it—because he did have a lot of me in him, and possibly I encouraged him to be artistic and gentle as a mother might do with a daughter—creating a mirror image of herself."

Billy did have an "artistic" nature. According to the mother he had always been sensitive to noise, color, texture, and visual nuances. On psychological testing at age six, he showed an extraordinary perception of visual nuances of shading, texture, and shape. The mother not only identified with Billy, she had a very special relationship with him, and he with her. She had an "uncanny" ability, she thought, to know what Billy was feeling or thinking, an unusual sensitivity to nonverbal cues. When she brought him Matchbox cars after her vacation, she sensed that he would not like them. Billy developed the same "spooky" ability to know what she was thinking. The closeness between them was "creepy." She had to discourage him from sewing and cooking with her. When Billy got older, she said that the two of them could enjoy going to the theatre together every night.

According to Billy's teacher, the mother worried too much about his minor difficulties with separation when he started nursery school at age three. The teacher had told her that Billy coped with separation well enough. Soon after treatment began, his nursery school teacher reported that he was gentle, unaggressive, and creative, had difficulty asserting himself, and preferred to play with girls in the doll corner. She noticed a strong and unique interaction between Billy and his mother. It was not that Billy was dependent on his mother, but rather that they were very tuned in to each other. (I was also impressed with how each seemed to know what the other was thinking or feeling, particularly about Billy's feminine wishes. The mother and son often chatted in a manner more typical of a girl with her mother than a boy with his mother.) According to this and all subsequent school reports, Billy did well academically, was friendly and cooperative with adults and peers, was well liked, and was often the creator of play activity—especially art projects, games, and theatrical productions.

By four Billy was more outgoing and friendly in his manner. As he became more feminine he became less shy, enjoying acting out TV roles for parents and guests. At home he played happily for long periods of time in his room. He also became more assertive, battling with his mother over TV and schedules. She found his "greediness" for things difficult to take; his father his "whinyness." Each of them on occasion referred to Billy as "she." He sometimes called his mother "Daddy."

Although Billy got along well on play dates, he was excessively agreeable and submissive, needing, like his parents, to please, and he took physical abuse from a close girl friend, less from a boy friend. Billy had a unique ability to imitate and to play different roles with different children. He hid his femininity sufficiently so that no one other than his parents and I knew about his gender disorder.

THE ANALYSIS

At four years Billy was a good-looking, likable, considerate, well-behaved boy with feminine speech and gestures, his hands drooping in an exaggerated manner, a caricature of femininity, quite the opposite of his mother.[1] From the beginning of treatment, separating from her was too easy for a child of his age. In fact, he always looked forward to becoming grown up and independent, to extricating himself from his close tie to her.

Billy's four-year-long analysis consisted largely of fantasies expressed in doll play. In the first year there were two main characters: Barbie and Ken. Billy's main interest was in playing the role of the Barbie doll, who, after several months, became a sexy adolescent girl. He put her hair in a ponytail, her feet in high-heeled shoes, and soon introduced Ken, a handsome adolescent boy to whom Barbie displayed her beauty and her remarkable abilities to perform. Barbie was portrayed as an all-powerful female who humiliated Ken. Nonetheless, Ken and other male dolls admired and experienced Barbie as captivating, and they envied her clothes, the attention she got, and the fact that she was so superior to them. Billy had me play the role of the Ken doll, who was portrayed as weak and helpless.

Billy's doll play seemed to give him great pleasure; it also had a driven quality, was repetitive, and occupied most of his sessions. He completely avoided boyish play or activities because they frightened him; they made him noticeably anxious. In the first two years, although fond of me, he maintained a physical and emotional distance, not engaging me directly in play or other activities. He did, however, speak to me as he played—as an accompaniment, a communication, or an explanation—and he shared his feelings with me. Billy spoke for all the dolls, although I sometimes asked questions or made comments in the role of the Ken doll, which he did not object to. Billy did not share with me the scary dreams, fears of ghosts and monsters, and fears of injury his parents reported. In fact, he was always in a good mood and rarely complained.

In play, Billy attributed to Barbie everything that he envied, admired, or found pleasurable, and to Ken everything unsatisfactory and unpleasurable. Barbie expressed Billy's exhibitionistic, narcissistic, possessive, aggressive, and sexual impulses as well as his wish to be grown up and independent. Ken expressed Billy's envy of Barbie's beauty, her breasts, and her power to attract men; of her strength and

---

1. The material here is derived from notes dictated after each session.

ability to dominate them; and of such of her possessions as dresses and cosmetics. And Ken expressed everything Billy disliked about himself—his doubts, anxieties, and inhibitions. At home and at school Billy, like Ken, showed no curiosity or interest in his own body or genitals and was unable to assert himself.

One theme in Billy's play in the first year was the fear of object loss. Barbie not only repeatedly ignored Ken, she also frequently left him. For example, when Barbie was taking off in an airplane on a trip similar to a trip recently taken by Billy's mother, Ken strenuously objected and tried to grab Barbie, particularly her breasts, in order to keep her from leaving. When Ken failed, Billy had a magic fairy change him into another Barbie doll, undoing the separation. On another occasion when Barbie was away, Ken became so enamored of the clothes in her room that Billy turned him into another Barbie, making up for his envy and loneliness.

In the second year Billy began to touch his penis and to have erections at home and in the office for the first time. Experiencing pleasurable sensations in the penis and beginning to value it caused Billy to view the male role more favorably, or perhaps was the result of this view. After Ken injured his penis in play and Billy reassuringly replaced it with a plastic tube, he reported a scary dream. A purple-people-eater monster grabbed Billy's penis, pulled it and bit it off, and put a plastic tube where the penis had been so that Billy could urinate. Billy then stole the penis from the monster and put it back on himself. The tube was similar to the one used in his Eustachian canal at the time of the myringotomy a year earlier.

In the first year Billy had wanted to be the phallic Barbie, not a boy with a penis. Now, in the second year, he was uncertain about who he wanted to be. He said he had both a penis and a vagina, that he was half-boy, half-girl. This was the same expression his mother had used a year earlier when she told me how sad she felt looking at a photograph of Billy when he still had long hair.

Soon after Billy began to value his penis, he introduced competition between the Ken doll and the Bionic Man doll for Barbie's hand in marriage. This oedipal theme, along with the question of whether to be Barbie or to marry Barbie, whether to be a woman or a man, were Billy's major concerns for the remainder of the analysis. And it as not only a question of whether to be a woman or a man; it was also a question of how to be a man. Billy said he knew how to be a woman, but he did not know how to be a man or how to compete with a man.

The Ken doll, now played by Billy, was repeatedly beaten up by the Bionic man, a role Billy had assigned to me; or, almost as frequently, the Ken doll won out over the Bionic Man and stole his heart, power, and penis so that he could marry Barbie, just as a year earlier Barbie had stolen Ken's penis and power. Another Ken doll, also speaking for Billy, said that he would prefer to be a girl rather than marry Barbie.

Soon after the onset of the oedipal competition between Ken and the Bionic Man, sadomasochistic qualities became more prominent in Billy's play. Barbie made believe that she loved the Bionic Man and seduced him, with the purpose of teasing, belittling, and rejecting Ken. This hurt Ken and made him angry. He dramatically and excitedly put Barbie to sleep by pricking her finger, threatened her with monsters, threw her off cliffs into water full of sharks, and stuck her in the heart with thousands of needles so she would die. Although Barbie had repeatedly belittled Ken in the first year of treatment, Billy had not experienced sexual excitement and erections until now. The Bionic Man was not included in these scenes, but, at the same time that Ken was forcibly wooing, subduing, and torturing Barbie in order to get control over her and marry her, he was also fighting the Bionic Man for her hand in marriage, with one or the other winning out at different times. On one occasion, after being tortured, Barbie claimed that Ken was responsible for the operative procedures performed on her, the same procedures earlier performed on Billy, procedures he said had turned him into a girl. When Billy rubbed his hands over Barbie's breasts, he also rubbed his hands over his own breasts. He was both Barbie and Ken but never the Bionic Man.

In the first year of treatment Barbie had been active, sadistic, and phallic but not maternal. Ken had been passive and masochistic, but neither castrated nor feminine. In the second year Barbie became masochistic, Ken sadistic. The roles were reversed. Ken had become more masculine and was able to stand up to and challenge Barbie, and the Bionic Man as well. This picture could change quickly, however, with Barbie once again gaining the upper hand and belittling Ken. On one occasion Ken's only recourse was to turn himself into another, stronger Barbie who shot a bullet from her breast and hit the breast of the Barbie who had belittled him. On occasion Billy played a more subdued family game in which a girl doll who represented Billy sat quietly and happily beside her father, who was driving a car.

Toward the end of the second year Billy invited me to play with the construction toy Lego. He was quite skilled at this and did not seem at all feminine while playing. This play was an acceptable boyish activity, compared with play with cars and trucks or superhero figures, which made him visibly anxious. This boyish behavior must have been what he showed to others in his everyday life—at school, for example. A few sessions later, however, he acted both the female and male roles in a show he performed for me. He danced like a seductive girl and also played that he was her lover, using a masculine voice and manner.

At the end of the second year Billy told me that, even though he still wanted to be a girl, he did not want to lose his penis; that he was not able to understand why, despite his best efforts at learning how to be a boy, he unintentionally continued to make movements like a girl; that he did want to know how to be a boy, to know what love is, and to learn how to love and marry a woman.

At the beginning of the third year, Billy talked more about his fears—of death, robbers, monsters—and he worried that his parents would die in a plane crash or that a stranger would shoot and kill his father. He explained that he could protect himself from being shot by robbers by dressing as an old woman with a long skirt. Even so, he was not safe because the robbers might see his pants underneath his skirt. After saying this he immediately began to play that he was a coy, seductive, charming, and beautiful girl who would captivate the robbers. When asked if the purpose of the disguise and the play was to avoid being shot, he said that it definitely was.

Billy then proceeded to put on many dramatic, romantic plays in which a seductive lady was treated badly by men. The plays were exciting, exhibitionistic, sadomasochistic, repetitive, and often accompanied by erections. Billy said that he enacted such frightening plays in order to get over the fears he had at night. Throughout the analysis, whenever Billy experienced castration anxiety he played that he was a girl. In the plays Barbie masochistically loved men who rejected, hurt, raped, and killer her, or, alternatively, she seduced and tricked men, throwing them in the water to be eaten by sharks, just as Ken had done to her the previous year.

On several occasions during the analysis Bill had walked into his parents' bedroom and observed them having intercourse. The room was dark and they were under a blanket, with one or the other on top. Once he said that he saw their genitals and thought the sight was funny. Billy acknowledged that he masturbated, but when asked about details or fantasies he told me that it was none of my business.

Although previously Billy had hated and ignored babies, he now introduced them briefly into his play. In one scene Billy, in the role of a girl, said that he missed his lover, pulled a string from his vagina, fainted, and said that a baby was kicking in his stomach. In another he played that he had given birth to two small dolls, a male and a female, but the father wanted them killed. The boy died after his penis was cut off; the girl died after she was poisoned. There was no direct evidence that Billy knew of his mother's abortion two years before he was born or of the other abortion when he was two.

In his plays Billy became more openly attracted to me. He wrapped himself in a blanket, which he used as a skirt, and danced like a girl in a nightclub. He then quickly removed the blanket, exhibiting an erect penis underneath his underwear. He told me that he preferred to exhibit his penis to men rather than to women. For a few months Billy was a transvestite in his play. On another occasion, while staging a sexy dance, he suddenly and impulsively planted a kiss on my cheek. He insisted that I was a prop in the play and that his behavior did not mean that he had feelings about me. He staged many seductive plays for me, always insisting that I was not his love. Billy also denied that he had feelings about me when he called my answering machine several times from his home and asked in a seductive feminine voice to see me on Saturday nights to talk about his problems. Billy did acknowledge, however, his love for his friend Tom. For example, Billy pretended he was a girl called Judy. She and Tom lay on a pillow expressing their love for each other. Judy first said, "Hands up. Your money or your life," but then changed it to, "Or kiss me." There were other scenes in which Judy was married to Tom. She (Billy) was a loving wife who wanted to have babies by Tom.

In addition to being a transvestite, Billy liked to trick me: he was a girl, yet he had a penis; he played that he had a broken foot, or that he was pregnant. In a play, Billy as a girl killed the male director and sang, "I kiss only men." He then found a gun and stood on his head, revealing an erection underneath his underwear. The robbers said, "Get that chick. Take her gun. Take her skirt off." Billy answered, "Don't you dare. Not on your life." So Billy, in the role of a girl, exposed his penis and at the same time was afraid that a robber would put his penis in her (his) vagina. He said, "Don't worry, it's just make-believe."

Billy rarely expressed anger directly. He could do so only in the role of Barbie or in a play. Early in the analysis, after his mother took his temperature rectally one evening, Barbie ignored the male doll, stole his penis, and took his temperature rectally. Not until the end of the hour was Billy able to say that he would like to tear his mother into pieces and make a jigsaw puzzle out of her. As he said this he ripped the male doll's arms off. Later in the analysis, when he was angry with a male friend, he expressed it by having Barbie take revenge on Ken. When he was angry at his mother he played that a husband stabbed his wife after he found out she was unfaithful. He then wrote a play called "How I Killed My Wife." One of the few ways Billy could express his anger toward his mother directly was by flaunting his femininity—for example, walking into the waitingroom with a ball under his shirt, saying he was pregnant. On two occasions, immediately following a disagreement with her that angered him, he impulsively hurled a girl doll and a toy plastic gun across my office room.

One day toward the end of the third year of Billy's analysis, his mother told me that she had dreamt that Billy was holding her sports brassiere and was wearing her blue running suit. When she returned home after a session early in the second year of her analysis, she was horrified to find Billy in the bathroom sink wearing her underwear and her brassiere, looking in the mirror and applying her makeup. Billy had carefully assembled the clothes he wanted to try on. They were soft, satiny, and flashy.

In the fourth year Ken and the Bionic Man continued to fight for Barbie's love, with Ken often winning. This could readily change, however. For example, when the Bionic Man returned from a trip he forced his love on Barbie, after she had put up a half-hearted resistance. She was not totally unresponsive even though she said she preferred Ken. Billy explained that the Bionic Man was Barbie's father, who, in disguise, had come to make love to her and to tell her that her mother had died in an accident. Barbie's father, in this session, died soon after of a heart attack. When his own father traveled, Billy missed him, feared that he might die, and began to express affection for his mother more openly.

Toward the end of treatment, as Billy entered latency, his play became more subdued, and he began to assume the male role almost exclusively. For a while he spoke appropriately for each role, but he then spoke only as a male. He spent less time in imaginative play and talked with me about such interests as traveling, reading, and movies. He hoped to be an airline pilot, an actor, or a lawyer when he grew up. He enjoyed swimming and bicycling and was chosen captain of this class soccer team.

Billy was able to hide his continuing feminine identification by weaving it into acceptable masculine play and behavior. He combined ballet or modern dancing with gymnastics, so that he looked masculine. In playing with Star War figures, he appeared to behave like a boy, but to him it was more important to dress the figures in fancy ways—for example, in purple pants—than to have the good guys beat the bad guys. His mother always saw through this disguise, his father never did.

When Billy was almost eight, he told me that he wanted to be a boy but often thought of himself as a girl. As an example, he explained that while on vacation he felt like a girl for two days, but the rest of the time he felt like a boy. He illustrated the difference with slightly different movements in a gym routine, one female and the other male. A few months later, he said that he no longer wished to be or thought of being a girl. The only thing that bothered him were occasional dreams of being badly treated, such as being attacked or shot by bad guys. After he heard on the new that a man had slashed a number of people with a knife, he woke with the fear that a robber would attack him with a knife. He associated the knife to a machete that his father used in the country.

During his analysis Billy became more aware of his anger toward his father and his mother. He was not, however, able to acknowledge feelings of longing or love for his father or his analyst. The changes that had occurred in Billy were the result of entering latency, his mother's firm opposition to his femininity, his acceptance as a boy in school, his social and academic success, and his analysis. His parents were pleased that he appeared to be more boyish.

Billy continued to be remarkably adaptable in his ability to enjoy a variety of play activities and roles with close friends. On the one hand, this adaptability was the result of his wit, charm, and intelligence; on the other, it was due to his unique ability to imitate and to assume and play a variety of roles. The parents reported that he imitated actors and performers on TV and that these imitations were often the "essence" of Billy. His acting was not limited to putting on plays, however; in a sense he was always acting. He needed "instant gratification"—for example, by imagining that he was a star on Broadway. On a few occasions his mother questioned the depth of his attachments and emotional commitments. She thought that his expression of his feelings was shallow and that they did not last long enough. The father believed that not until he was eight was Billy finally able to "integrate" what he had taken in from others so that his own personality could begin to emerge.

DISCUSSION

When Billy began analysis at age four, he was in the phallic-narcissistic phase; his object relations were dyadic. It is likely that he regressed to this phase from the early oedipal phase. His wish to be a girl, portrayed by Barbie, was a compromise formation that provided the best available solution to his conflicts. It protected his mother against his phallic, destructive wishes while, at the same time, permitting him to use his femininity to express his hostility toward her. It gained her approval and maintained his close tie to her but was not incestuous. It warded off separation and castration anxiety, made up for his dissatisfaction at being a boy, and allowed him to gratify narcissistic and sadomasochistic wishes, including the wish to seduce the father he loved. Its repetitive and driven expression in play was an effort to master trauma. What he had endured passively he initiated actively, saying at the same time, "Don't worry, it's not real," thereby reassuring himself that the female genitals were not real and that he had not been castrated. Additional mechanisms operative were inhibition, reaction formation, submission, and masochism.

Early in the second year of treatment, when Billy reentered the oedipal phase, the compromise formation changed from the wish to be a girl to the wish to be both a girl and a boy—a bisexual solution. This new bisexual compromise formation—expressed in the endless battles for Barbie between Ken and the Bionic Man, and in the sadomasochistic sexual relations each of them had with her—consisted of a striking reshuffling of the developmental opposites of active-passive, sadistic-masochistic, phallic-castrated, and masculine-feminine, which had earlier been so out of kilter. Barbie, who had previously been active, sadistic, and phallic in her relation to Ken, became passive, masochistic, and castrated in relation to Ken and to the Bionic Man. Ken became active and sadistic with Barbie and competitive with the Bionic Man. In other words, Billy, who in the phallic phase had envied and identified with the phallic Barbie, now, in the oedipal phase, identified either with the masochistic Barbie, experiencing pleasure and excitement when she was mistreated by Ken or by the Bionic Man, or with Ken, who competed with the Bionic Man for Barbie and who treated her sadistically, which also excited him sexually. The oscillating shifts in these roles accounted for the bisexuality, with each of the three roles—phallic-narcissistic, negative and positive oedipal—serving as a defense against the others.

Although in the first year of the analysis Billy had turned Ken into another Barbie when Barbie left him, separation anxiety—the result of intense hostility toward the mother—was not a major issue in his analysis. His major concern was castration anxiety. Whenever it increased, it inevitably triggered his compromise formation: Billy became Barbie. And, conversely, Billy's compromise formation and its endless repetition in play minimized his castration anxiety. Early in the analysis the mother as the castrator; later, it was the father. Billy was afraid that his father would be killed when he traveled, and the robber in his nightmares was his father.

Although Billy's compromise formation at the time of his analysis was determined by the anxieties and conflicts of the phallic-narcissistic and oedipal phases, it had its roots in the entire preoedipal phase (see McDevitt, 1967, 1971). Since his wish to be a girl and his equally important fear of being a boy started when he was two years old, there must have been important preoedipal determinants for both the wish and the fear. The first such preoedipal factor was Billy's constitutional endowment—his passivity and compliance; his heightened visual, tactile, and auditory sensitivity, particularly to noise; and his appearance as an infant as a "mellow" baby with a "sweet" disposition. These qualities not only had a direct effect on Billy's development but also influenced the mother's attitude toward him. Had Billy been more assertive, his mother would have found it more difficult to mold him in a feminine direction.

The second determinant was the mother's unconscious need to shape Billy in a feminine manner. Her neurotic personality disorder and uncertain gender identity seriously interfered with Billy's masculine sexual development. The mother cared very much for Billy. She was loving, available, and reliable, and she was a consistent and efficient caretaker. Although she was empathic, her empathy was skewed in the direction of seeing her own wishes and needs in Billy. He was an extension of herself, of her own phallic-narcissistic wishes. In the first year and a half she was too controlling of Billy. In the next year and a half, during the anal and phallic phases, she found it difficult to be firm, fearing she would damage him. Later she became a strict disciplinarian, the "heavy."

The mother's preference for a girl, her fear of being sexually attracted to a boy child's developing phallic sexuality, and her hostile, competitive impulses toward men and toward Billy—all of which were very subtly expressed in her behavior—caused her to selectively respond to, mirror, and attune herself to those aspects of Billy's behavior that would later contribute to femininity. Her ambivalence and feminine shaping intensified in Billy's second and third year because her anxiety was intensified by Billy's emerging expression of his masculinity. She once said that if Billy were more masculine she would be tempted to seduce him. As a consequence of the conflict between his mother's preference and the onset of his awareness of his masculinity, Billy had to choose a feminine identity in order to assure himself of her love.

It was not only the external shaping that laid down a pathway for Billy's identification with his mother; internal forces also contributed: his temperament, his extraordinary visual and tactile sensitivity, his attunement with and closeness to his mother, and his remarkable imitative ability all fostered identification with her. An essential aspect of this closeness was the unconscious communication between the two, in which the mother saw herself Billy, confusing herself with him, and Billy saw himself in her, confusing himself with her. The closeness, however, made him uncomfortable and caused him to struggle to free himself.

Another related internal force may have been a disturbance in self-object differentiation in the first two years of life. The first motive for identification with the mother seen in Billy's analysis was the fear of object loss. Ken became another Barbie in order to undo the separation brought on by Barbie's airplane trip. A disturbance in self-object differentiation would have created an uncertain, unstable mental representation of the mother and of the self. Identification with the mother may have taken place to relieve this uncertainty and may have prepared the ground for the subsequent use of identification with the mother as his main defense mechanism. Billy was said to have been shy between ages one and three and to have clung to his mother. As he became more feminine in behavior, he also became more certain of himself and less shy, and more certain of his mother, clinging to her less. In fact, he became a "ham," acting TV roles for his parents and guests and putting on plays in nursery school.

By age two to three years another powerful internal force—intrapsychic conflict—caused Billy to shape himself in a feminine direction in order to protect himself from the dangers of object loss and castration brought on by his hostility toward his mother. This was the first version of the compromise formation that was present when Billy entered analysis.

A third determining factor was trauma and overstimulation. On the one hand, the mother was prudish, anxious, and intolerant of sex in herself and Billy, and she devalued and depreciated his developing phallic sexuality. On the other, she overstimulated him by exposing herself to him, by exposing him to the primal scene, and by arranging for his operations. Billy reacted with excitement and fright, frustration and rage, especially since he was so sensitive to sights and sounds. He turned away from and devalued the masculine body, genitals, and the phallic urges he was just becoming aware of; he repressed and inhibited sexual curiosity, interest, and excitement, as well as aggression.

A fourth determining force was constituted by the father's absence, unavailability, and indifference; his sibling relationship and rivalry with Billy; his permissiveness, especially his sexual permissiveness; and, significantly, his own unconscious gender confusion. When Billy was four his father began to spend more time with him and encouraged Billy to prefer him to his mother. He not only competed with Billy for his wife's attention, he also competed with his wife for Billy's attention. As mentioned earlier, when Billy was five to six years old his father began to take him to sexually stimulating movies. In addition to being seductive in his behavior, the father was not a reliable masculine figure with whom Billy could identify. And Billy's marked fear of anything masculine, which he equated with aggression, made it impossible for him to identify with his father.

In fact, instead of identifying with his father, as boys ordinarily do, Billy identified with the mother. But in contrast to the little girl, who usually identifies with the maternal qualities of the mother, Billy identified with his mother's phallic qualities. This diminished his concern over losing his penis. These qualities stood for the penis, just as an inanimate object or clothes stand for the penis in the fetishist and the transvestite, respectively. In his analysis Billy temporarily became a transvestite, displaying his erect penis underneath a make-believe skirt.

A fifth determinant was Billy's fear and intolerance of his hostility. This fear caused him to forgo phallic and masculine activity and to be willing to give up his penis because he evidently experienced it as a destructive weapon. In his analysis he was visibly frightened by boyish activities or toys—superheroes, cars, weapons—which he avoided. He took extreme measures to contain hostility by modifying it sado-masochistically and by attributing it to Barbie, and then alternately to Barbie, Ken, and the Bionic Man. In his everyday life he was unassertive and submissive.

Billy's intense, sadistic hostility was directed toward his mother, not his father, just as Ken's hostility was directed toward Barbie, not the Bionic Man, although he fought and competed with him. Billy was enraged with his mother for hampering his autonomous strivings, for squelching his masculinity, for preferring his father, and for the operative procedures, which left him feeling castrated. His view of her as an extremely strict, uncaring, and ungiving woman, as unfaithful as Barbie, was not correct. It was the result of his projection.

On the Rorschach at age six Billy viewed the mother as having the power to destroy the father and as the parent most implicated in his fear of his aggression and his fear of castration. The father barely appeared on the tests; he seemed hidden, mysterious, almost unknown. On the Rorschach at age eight Billy viewed the mother figure as demanding, destructive, powerful, cold, and rejecting. He was both fearful and antagonistic toward her. Fathers were considered capable, good, and strong.

Billy identified with Barbie, rather than with the actual mother, who was shy and inhibited. I think it reasonable to infer that one of the mother's unconscious sexual fantasies was portrayed by the powerful, exhibitionistic, seductive, and captivating Barbie doll. These were the qualities that Billy envied. I assume that another sexual fantasy of the mother that Billy identified with was portrayed by the passive and masochistic Barbie.

Barbie's seductive exhibitionism, which Billy envied, resembled his mother's description of her sister. She particularly liked to exhibit her breasts, which the mother envied. Just as Billy was caught dressing in his mother's clothes and using her cosmetics while in her bathroom, the mother had been fearful as a child that she would be caught in her sister's bathroom using her cosmetics.

In exposing herself to Billy the mother may have done to him what her sister did to her and unknowingly may have imposed her fantasies on him. Barbie's breasts were important to Billy. When he staged plays he taped paper over his own breasts in order to draw attention to them. Furthermore, there was a similarity between Barbie's demeaning attitude toward Ken in Billy's play and his aunt's humiliating behavior vis-à-vis Billy's mother and also with Billy's mother's occasionally demeaning attitude toward Billy when she was angry with him.

OTHER STUDIES

In order to examine the origin and meaning of Billy's disturbance more closely, it might be helpful to compare Billy with children who have similar disorders and with children in research studies.[2]

Billy's disorder was remarkably similar in age of onset, manifestations, and treatment to the data on twelve other gender-disordered boys familiar to me: ten were in analysis, two in intensive therapy; nine of the total group of thirteen, including Billy, were presented and discussed in a study group.[3] Most of the mothers of these boys strongly repressed—in fact, squashed—their son's masculinity. They either preferred girls, were hostile to the idea of a son, or, as in Billy's case, were afraid of their son's phallic sexuality and aggression. The expression of these attitudes ranged from open to subtle, and the degree of disturbance in the mother-child interactions varied from moderate to marked, as did the degree of the sons' pathology. The sons expressed their femininity either openly and publicly, or privately, as did Billy. A number of the boys, like Billy, showed a heightened sensitivity to visual and tactile stimuli. Most of the fathers were either absent or emotionally uninvolved with their sons.

---

2. For a review and overview of the literature on gender identity disorder (GID), see Coates, 1992.

3. See Galenson and Fields, 1989; Coates, Friedman, and Wolfe, 1991; Haber, 1991; and Karush, 1993.

As a result of their mothers' behavior, and of trauma, the sons gave up their biologically determined push toward autonomy and masculinity, particularly since they could not depend on their fathers' availability or support. Although separation anxiety was seen early in the treatment of these boys, castration anxiety became more significant later.

Sam (see Karush, 1993), like Billy, dressed as a woman to avoid the threat of castration.[4] And, like Billy, he "tricked" his analyst, using the word *pagina,* and played that he was the "bride" of a boyfriend. Unlike Billy, but like other boys with openly hostile mothers, Sam publicly expressed his femininity and was directly hostile toward his female analyst. Whenever his castration anxiety was stirred up he simultaneously played that he was a fancily dressed woman and excitedly and sadomasochistically attacked his analyst, identifying both with the female and with the aggressor.

By comparing Billy with boys in some research studies, we might learn more about the origins of his disorder. In a study of thirty boy and girl babies ranging in age from nine to twelve months, Olesker (1990) found that three of the boys resembled the girls in their gender behavior. That is, they showed earlier self-object differentiation, more awareness of separateness, and a greater focus on the mother than the other boys. There was evidence that these differences were in part constitutional and maturational.

At the age of two these boys showed an unusual degree of identification with the mother—playing at mothering dolls, cooking, sweeping—as a solution to their intense hostility toward their mothers and their intense castration anxiety (Wendy Olesker, personal communication). When they were six they showed a predominance of phallic-narcissistic concerns; their oedipal issues were much weaker. These boys were similar to Billy, as were their experiences with their mothers and fathers.

In a research study of the separation-individuation process (Mahler et al., 1975), it was observed that girls, and to a lesser extent boys, identified with the maternal attributes of their mothers in part as a compromise solution to the fear of loss of love by one and a half to two and to castration anxiety soon after. From one and a half to three years of age, boys began to move away from their mothers both physically and psychologically; they turned toward their fathers, toward father substitutes, and toward more masculine, phallic, aggressive activities

---

4. Disguising a male child as a girl to avoid danger—execution, death, the evil eye, abduction by fairies—is a common folktale motif.

and play. Identification with the mother was gradually replaced by identification with the father. The mother's encouragement and the father's availability were necessary for these developments to take place.

Billy identified with the maternal attributes of his mother more strongly than the study boys—for example, playing with the egg-beater toy and the mother's pocketbook—but there was no evidence that he had identified with his father at any time. He did, however, in time shift his identification from the maternal qualities of his mother to an identification with her phallic qualities.

The separation-individuation study suggested that intrapsychic conflict may begin as early as the second year of life, following the acquisition of distinct self and object representations and of representational thought. The compromise formations that become established at this time tend to persist, often becoming more fixed and more stable with each succeeding crisis in development (Mc Devitt, 1991, 1995).

The likelihood that Billy's wish to be a girl was a compromise formation which began as early as the age of two is supported in a study of young children by Roiphe (1991) and Roiphe and Spira (1991). They observed *in statu nascendi* the compromise formation of the wish to be a girl by identifying with the mother in a two-year-old boy in a nursery setting. This was Henry's method of coping with intrapsychic conflict brought on by destructive impulses toward his mother and by castration anxiety, after other methods such as erotization of aggression no longer contained his anxiety.

In Galenson and Roiphe's (1980) study of the early genital phase, during the second year of life, three of the thirty boys observed showed greater castration anxiety than the other boys, heightened aggression toward the mother, and a stronger attachment to and identification with her than with the father. Unlike the other boys, they engaged in elaborate doll play. The play, however, was rigid, repetitive, and compulsive, not resembling the more creative play of the girls, but very much resembling Billy's play. Also like Billy, these boys wore their mother's jewelry and clothes, forecasting the development of a negative oedipal constellation.

Many features of Billy's play brought to mind the fetishist (his attachment to Barbie's hair, to high-heeled shoes, to breasts, and to bras) or the transvestite (his use of the bottle, the thumb, the blanket, mother's clothes). In his wish to be mother he had given up the symbolic use of the inanimate object or a piece of clothing as a substitute for the penis or the mother and claimed instead that he preferred to be a woman. In the second year of his analysis he began to change his mind.

In contrast to that of the neurotic child, Billy's play was rigid, driven, compulsive, and repetitive. One reason was the trauma, seduction, and overstimulation he had experienced; another was the severity of his castration anxiety. As Billy explained, he took action by playing that he was a girl to overcome his nightmares and neurotic fears.

SUBSEQUENT TREATMENT

Two years after he stopped analysis, Billy, then ten, asked to see me because he had recently had five unexplainable attacks of anger. When we first met he showed feminine gestures and speech. In the second session they disappeared, as they had done soon after his analysis began when he was younger. After recalling his wish to be a girl, he said that he now preferred to be a boy, felt like a boy, had many male friends, and enjoyed playing sports. The only evidence I could see of feminine interests was his tendency to identify with the adolescent heroines of books he had read.

We learned that Billy's angry attacks occurred when he felt pushed around by his mother—for instance, when she refused to buy him faddish clothes. He recalled that when he was younger he had been afraid to express anger, worried that someone—his mother—might get angry and hurt him. When he was disappointed he used to cry or run away. Now he said he was better able to assert himself. After nine visits he stopped seeing me. He had wanted to come only a few times and resented his mother's pushing him to come more often.

Billy chose to come to see me again when he was fourteen and continued once a week for two and a half years. Once again feminine gestures and speech disappeared after we had met a few times but briefly recurred when Billy was anxious, or following a vacation. He was a handsome, likable, stylishly dressed boy, with long, wavy hair, who spoke unusually freely. He enjoyed arranging his hair and wearing showy, outlandish outfits, expressing both exhibitionistic and defiant wishes. He told me he was troubled by spells of moodiness when parents or friends criticized or rejected him. He was also distressed because he had cut the back of his wrist superficially and because he was sexually attracted to both girls and boys, which worried him. He no longer remembered his wish to be a girl.

Billy was in a hurry to grow up, as he had been when he was younger. He envied the freedom of older boys and girls. When his parents, particularly his mother, firmly but not unreasonably restricted his activities or criticized him, he quickly became angry and moody. Describing them as stupid, and demonstrating how he belittled them, especially his mother, he rolled his eyes, a movement reminiscent of his feminine gestures when he was a boy. When he cut the back of his wrist, he had been in a miserable mood because he felt hopelessly overwhelmed by a homework assignment, by his anger with his mother, and by feeling unpopular at school. Being popular and having a busy social life were more important to Billy than academic standing or success in such sports as baseball and skiing. His peers considered him one of the boys, and for five summers he had enjoyed an Outward Bound type of camp.

I understood Billy's need to be liked, to be the center of attention, as a way of boosting his low self-esteem. Although he had friends and was popular, he was easily hurt and quick to withdraw. He worried that he didn't care enough about his friends and that he was shallow emotionally, a concern his mother had told me she had about him when he was a boy.

Billy was alternately sexually attracted to women and to men and was bisexual in his masturbatory fantasies and dreams and in his choice of pornographic TV and videos. These included his father's videos. The most common sequence was sexual fantasies about women followed by fantasies about men. On occasion the two occurred in the same fantasy or dream. For example, after describing a masturbatory fantasy in which he sadistically raped an older woman in an office, he told a fantasy about a campmate who had actually approached him sexually. In the first part of a dream he fucked a female porno model, using the couch in my office; in the second part he fucked a male porno-movie cop.

After telling a fantasy of sucking a porno-movie officer's penis and screwing him in the ass, he lay face down on the couch, looked at me, felt sexually excited, felt like masturbating, and said he would like to fuck a girl. His sexual attraction to me had persisted. He asked if I had sex with my patients and wondered why he jerked off before his sessions. He then recalled seeing his parents having intercourse when he was five.

In the second year of treatment Billy fell in love with Polly, who resembled his mother. Although he enjoyed sexual play with her, he lusted for Ruth, who resembled the Barbie-like aspects of his mother. His fantasies about Polly and Ruth alternated, as did his fantasies about women and men. Fantasies about men, which were much less frequent while he was going out with Polly, returned when she ended the relationship because she was jealous of Ruth. He fantasized fucking men forcibly in the ass, or being fucked in the ass, just as he had fantasized fucking Polly and, especially, Ruth forcibly. In contrast to the previous year, when he had been enthralled with large cocks he could suck, he was now enthralled with cute butts he could fuck.

Billy's fantasies were more sadistic and belittling when a girl disappointed him, which was reminiscent of Ken sadistically attacking Barbie when she belittled him and of Billy belittling his mother when she criticized him. The young women in his fantasies were attractive, well-built, with large bosoms, like Barbie; the men had large penises, as Billy claimed he had, or they had cute asses. When he had played in his analysis that he was a boy-girl with a penis-vagina, he had been afraid that robbers would penetrate his vagina. Now, as an adolescent, he had masturbatory fantasies that a man would penetrate his anus.

One evening after having a premature ejaculation during intercourse with a girl, he impulsively called an older homosexual man he did not know but had previously spoken with on the phone; he then traveled some distance to the man's home. But after they kissed, Billy said he was frightened and fled, feeling nauseated. This was the only occasion reported in which he thought he had acted with poor judgment. As an adolescent Billy did not feel like a real man, nor did he feel that he could compete successfully with a real man, just as Ken had found it difficult to compete with the Bionic Man. He had not successfully identified with his father or his analyst.

Billy stopped treatment with me and entered therapy with a female therapist, whom he saw twice weekly for a year and a half. Later, she filled me in on his therapy with her. Although Billy continued to have exciting sadomasochistic sexual fantasies about men, he could not imagine loving or having tender feelings for a man. Such feelings would be repulsive, demeaning, disgusting. He could, wanted to, and was more capable of having loving and tender feelings for a woman, but he was not able to have an erection except on a few occasions when sadomasochistic thoughts of being abused by the woman excited him. Experiencing the female genitals as disgusting, nauseating, and horrible was the main reason for his impotence. His sexual fantasies about women continued to be sadomasochistic. Tenderness did not extend to the sexual area. Women, sensing his confusion, were not responsive to his approaches, which left him feeling puzzled and hurt.

Billy felt horrible and disgusted about himself. Although he liked his penis, and his body in general, he spoke of himself as a negative boy. One of his solutions to his dilemma was the fantasy of getting married and having children but secretly picking up men in gay bars. In many ways he was unclear about who he was or wanted to be, just as he did not have a clear sense of the nature of his relationships with other people. His real self came out most clearly when he tearfully expressed his wish to be sexually normal, to have a lasting, loving relationship with a woman, and to have a consistent, stable sense of himself.

COMMENTS

One of the most striking features in Billy's analysis and in his therapy was his inability to resolve opposing tendencies between active and passive, sadistic and masochistic, masculine and feminine. He moved between closeness and distance—struggling for independence and autonomy, fearful both of being tied down, hemmed in by his mother and Polly—and between being tender but impotent and repulsed but potent. In addition to intersystemic conflicts and compromise formation, Billy showed many intrasystemic conflicts.

Fantasy was said to play an excessive role in Billy's life from an early age, its importance persisting beyond the time it should have diminished. It was not sufficiently integrated with the real world. In his analysis Billy often told me, "It's only make-believe, it's not real." But it was becoming real. He not only wanted to be a girl, he was becoming a girl. In saying "it's only make-believe," Billy was referring not only to the distinction between idiosyncratic, egocentric make-believe and social reality, or to his denial and confusion about the female genitals; he was also expressing his problem with integrating and synthesizing these distinctions in a manner that would permit greater harmony and directedness in his feelings, thoughts, and actions. He was at the mercy of rapidly shifting contradictory feelings. Not only was he overinvolved in fantasy, but "imitations" of others were said to be the "essence" of Billy. Not until he was eight, according to his father, did he begin to integrate these "imitations" sufficiently so that his own personality began to emerge. Failure in synthesis and integration, although determined by conflict and compromise formation, may initially have been the result of a more basic underlying disturbance in the ego that preceded and shaped conflict and compromise formation.

Billy had a moderately severe character disorder based on conflict and on the same predisposing factors that shaped his conflicts and compromise formation. Manifestations of this disorder included an unstable sense of self and others, shallow object relations, sadomasochism, poor tolerance for anxiety and frustration, and a disturbance in reality testing and in synthesis and integration. Psychological tests done when Billy was eight showed confused ego boundaries, a failure in self-object differentiation, an inability to integrate his fantasy world with the real world, and a thought disorder, with loose, fluid, distorted, idiosyncratic associations. Billy's diffuse sense of identity—his insufficient differentiation from his mother—seems to have had its beginning very early in life. It may be that the only way he could separate and individuate from his mother was to identify with her femaleness and, at the same time, to be different from her in other ways and to continue to insist on his independence, fighting and opposing her.

BIBLIOGRAPHY

COATES, S. (1992). Etiology of boyhood gender identity disorders: An integrated model. In *Interface of Psychoanalysis and Psychology*, ed. J. W. Barron, M. N. Eagle, and D. L. Wolitsky, pp. 245–65. Washington, D.C.: American Psychological Association.

COATES, S., FRIEDMAN, R. C., & WOLFE, S. (1991). The etiology of a boyhood gender identity disorder: A model for integrating temperament, development, and psychodynamics. *Psychoanalytic Dialogues*, 1 (no. 4):481–523.

GALENSON, E., & FIELDS, B. (1989). Gender disturbance in a three-and-one-half-year-old boy. In *The Significance of Infant Observational Research for Clinical Work with Children, Adolescents, and Adults*, ed. S. Dowling and A. Rothstein, pp. 39–52. Workshop Series of the American Psychoanalytic Association, Monograph Five. Madison, Conn.: Int. Univ. Press.

GALENSON, E., & ROIPHE, H. (1980). The preoedipal development of the boy. *J. Amer. Psychoanal. Assn.*, 28:805–29.

HABER, C. (1991). The psychoanalytic treatment of a pre-school boy with a gender identity disorder. *J. Amer. Psychoanal. Assn.*, 39(1):107–29.

KARUSH, R. K. (1993). Sam: A child analysis. *J. Clin. Psychoanal.*, 2(1):43–63.

MAHLER, M. S., PINE, F., & BERGMAN, A. (1975). *The Psychological Birth of the Human Infant*. New York: Basic.

MC DEVITT, J. B. (1967). A separation problem in a three-year-old girl. In *The Child Analyst at Work*, ed. E. R. Geleerd, pp. 24–58. New York: Int. Univ. Press.

———(1971). Pre-oedipal determinants of an infantile neurosis. In *Separation-Individuation: Essays in Honor of Margaret S. Mahler*, ed. J. B. McDevitt and C. F. Settlage, pp. 201–22. New York: Int. Univ. Press.

——— (1991). Contributions of separation-individuation theory to the understanding of psychopathology during the prelatency years. In *Beyond the Symbiotic Orbit: Advances in Separation-Individuation. Essays in Honor of Selma Kramer, M.D.*, ed. S. Akhtar & H. Parens, pp. 153–69. Hillsdale, N.J.: Analytic Press.

——— (1995). The continuity of conflict and compromise formation from infancy to adulthood: A twenty-five-year follow-up study. *J. Amer Psychoanal. Assn.*

OLESKER, W. (1990). Sex differences during the early separation-individuation process: Implications for gender identity formation. *J. Amer. Psychoanal. Assn.*, 38:325–46.

ROIPHE, H. (1991). The tormentor and the victim in the nursery. *Psychoanal. Q.*, 50(3):450–64.

ROIPHE, H., AND SPIRA, N. (1991). Object Loss, aggression, gender identity. *Psychoanal. Study Child*, 46:37–50.

A Follow-up of Child Analysis

The Analyst as a Real Person

HELEN R. BEISER, M.D.

Thirteen cases of child analysis or intensive psychotherapy are described briefly, along with follow-up data. Seven made spontaneous contact with the analyst, some as long as thirty or forty years after the termination of treatment; three more were followed into young adulthood through reports of family, therapists, or friends; and three more made no contact. The process of internalization and preservation of the analyst as a real person is discussed, as well as why it occurs in some cases and not others. Most of the late contacts were made to obtain help in decisions regarding further treatment for self or family members.

IN THE PAST FEW YEARS THREE PERSONS WHOM I HAD ANALYZED AS CHILdren and two with whom I had conducted intensive psychotherapy have spontaneously made contact with me—some more than thirty years after the termination of treatment. This aroused my curiosity about how the person of the analyst could be retained for so long, and what the treatment had meant to the patient. Of course, it is necessary to live for quite a long time to experience such spontaneous follow-ups. Still, being of sound mind, I decided to review the literature on follow-ups, as well as my own caseload, in more detail.

LITERATURE

There is relatively little literature on the follow-up of analytic cases, adult or child. Even the literature on the follow-up of psychiatric cases

Training and supervising child and adult analyst (retired) at the Institute of Psychoanalysis, Chicago. Past president of the American Academy of Child and Adolescent Psychiatry.

The Psychoanalytic Study of the Child 50, ed. Albert J. Solnit, Peter B. Neubauer, Samuel Abrams, and A. Scott Dowling (Yale University Press, copyright © 1995 by Albert J. Solnit, Peter B. Neubauer, Samuel Abrams, and A. Scott Dowling).

is spotty. In the area of adult analysis, Schlessinger and Robbins (1983) indicate that, when contacted, analysands easily fell back into a transference mode with the analyst-interviewer, and it was obvious that all conflicts had not been fully analyzed. Contact was made with the patients by the authors, with the permission of the original analysts.

The follow-up of a single child case is reported by Hellman (1973) from the Hampstead Clinic. A two-and-a-half-year-old child was analyzed during the war years, returned home to her mother, and was seen at the age of twenty-three by her therapist from the Clinic. She showed evidence of identification with her therapist in her choice of house furnishings and also in vocation. A famous follow-up is Ritvo's (1966) analysis at age twenty-four of a man whom Berta Bornstein had analyzed as a latency child. In his sixties, Peter Heller (1983) published a book on his childhood analysis with Anna Freud. There were many complications caused by his personal relations with the Freuds and with Dorothy Burlingame. He had spontaneously consulted Anna Freud during divorce proceedings, but the book describing his analysis was prompted by *her* sending him the poems he had written during the analysis, plus her notes on the analysis. In such circumstances, there were more reasons than the childhood analysis to see her as a real person.

Probably the most extensive study of a large child population with some relevance to child analysis was conducted by Cass and Thomas (1979) at the St. Louis Child Guidance Clinic, where James Anthony did his study of the children of psychotic mothers. The effects of both evaluation and treatment were studied. The follow-up patients were young adults, none older than twenty-eight. A surprising finding was that those who had refused treatment were making a better adult adjustment than those who had been treated. There was little memory of the early experience, more of the clinic than of the therapist or evaluating professional. Possibly relevant for child analysis was the finding that results were better in the treated population if the therapist was experienced and if treatment was long-term.

A very interesting follow-up study of child analysis cases was done in Cleveland by Koch (1973). He asked Cleveland child analysts to fill out questionnaires on two completed cases. Twenty cases were studied, thirteen boys and seven girls, from two to sixteen years after termination. About half had been training cases. The main focus was on arrangements for later contact and how the patient had been prepared for this during the analysis. If somewhat older, the child usually spontaneously asked about future contacts, and there were several types of follow-up instituted. The first was formal but nonintensive weekly or monthly sessions. Second were periodic contacts at sensitive points, such as vacations or anniversaries. Third were informal contacts, really just informing the child that the therapist would be available if needed. In these arrangements the influence of the parents, as well as of the analyst, varied. Where the parents were seen as unsupportive of further development of the child, the analyst was more likely to arrange for further contact. There was a tendency for formal arrangements gradually to decrease. Most spontaneous contacts by the former child patient were made by patients who were over ten at the start of analysis and for specific help with a new problem that had arisen. The analyst at these times tended to be a sounding board, did little if any interpretation, and took the role of "interested adult," something like an aunt or uncle.

The childhood analyses were generally seen as helpful. The patients had some memory of specific incidents but also had some distorted memories. Most of the analysis had been repressed. The positive changes observed as resulting from treatment were the freeing of ego for school, hobbies, or work. If there had been an early lack of tolerance for frustration, this persisted, and old defensive features were still present, although with some modification. Ritvo observed that old phobic defenses tended to shift to obsessive-compulsive ones.

PERSONAL EXPERIENCE

My own experiences have been different from those reported in the literature. I did not plan for follow-up or even attempt it except for two boys with parent loss (Altschul and Beiser, 1988). I could find neither of them at that time, fifteen years after termination, but one spontaneously contacted me later. I also reviewed my entire caseload rather than select two cases, as Koch did in Cleveland. Unfortunately, when I closed my office several years ago, I destroyed all old records, but I did make a list of all patients, their ages and the dates at the time of start and termination, total number of hours seen, and treatment technique used. For details of referral source, presenting problem and analytic process, I must rely on my memory.

I analyzed a total of thirteen children, seven boys and six girls, ranging in age from six to fifteen at the start; most were below age ten. Although most families were middle class, I had four clinic or low-fee cases (two of them training cases) and two from quite wealthy upper-class families. Presenting problems were neurotic (old terminology): thumb sucking, enuresis, school phobia, and mild depression or unhappiness. The only children of concern to their schools were those with school phobia and those who were not working up to capacity.

Disruptive behavior problems were limited to the home, as in the case of a girl who physically attacked her mother out of anger over an impending divorce. Although all but one patient had two parents present in the home at the beginning of analysis, one had a stepmother (the biological mother had died), one father died shortly after the beginning of analysis, and at least two fathers and one mother died after treatment was terminated. There was one stepfather after two previous divorces, and one divorce occurred after termination. In addition, four of the mothers were probably psychotic. There was only one family that had no apparent marital discord. As I wish to discuss the interesting phenomenon of spontaneous contact after many years, I would also like to include two nonanalytic cases in which I did long-term intensive psychotherapy.

Twelve-year-old Alice, with whom I did residential therapy during my fellowship in child psychiatry, was a ward of a social agency, as her mother had been institutionalized for mental retardation and her father was in prison. She was raised by a senile grandmother and an alcoholic uncle, and I am sure, was sexually abused. Her problem, for which she had been expelled from several foster homes and other residences, was running away and begging money from men, then immediately running off. She was a disheveled, remarkably unattractive child, and I despaired of making her into a lady. After two years in a state children's ward run by the Institute for Juvenile Research, she was sent to a residence for adolescents. She was expelled after a week, and, by her wish, I had her committed to the same institution in which her mother resided. She did not answer my letters, and she told a visiting professional that I had abandoned her. I immediately corrected her and, on a visit to the institution with my trainees, talked with her and learned that she wished to leave because she had found that she didn't like her mother.

Several years later she called me, and I learned that she had been discharged with some vocational training. She made several contacts over a period of forty years, the last one shortly after I moved into a retirement community. We arranged to meet at a McDonald's for coffee, and I learned there that she had been married a couple of times, had had several jail experiences, had had scleroderma resulting in the loss of several digits, and had produced one daughter "out of wedlock." The daughter was graduated from college and lives and works in the town where the institution for the retarded is located. Although she is still unattractive, Alice is now neat and clean, and this, together with the success of her daughter, makes me feel that something very important took place.

Ruth, the other nonanalytic case, was the only child of two teachers who had been told, on the basis of the shape of Ruth's face, that she was probably retarded and had ignored her for the first year of her life. She was in a therapeutic nursery until age five or six and was considered psychotic. Because of financial considerations, I saw her only twice a week between the ages of six and twelve. She needed a great deal of control but was eager to learn and formed a close relationship with me. At twelve she appeared normal, and we terminated. She returned at fourteen with the usual adolescent rebellious behavior of bad companions and some drugs. When she wanted plastic surgery, which I did not feel was indicated, she told me how children had teased her about her narrow face, and called her "the witch." Because of her improvement in her senior year, we terminated formal treatment. She entered an excellent small liberal arts college and graduated with honors. In the meantime, her parents had divorced and both had remarried. After Ruth's graduation, her mother kept me in touch with Ruth's activities through an occasional interview or letter. Ruth went off to the West Coast, worked as a hotel maid, and generally disappointed her mother. A few years later I was invited to her wedding and five months after that got a birth announcement. Three years later, now aged thirty-five, she spontaneously made contact with me and requested an interview. She had tried a number of jobs, found she was not good at working with children, had been a laboratory technician, and was currently doing fairly well in the real estate business. She wished to talk to me because her daughter's biological father, who had deserted her, had reappeared and wanted to see his child. I discovered that in spite of his failure to support her treatment emotionally or financially, Ruth had always felt close to her own father. She was dissatisfied with her husband's lack of ambition in much the same way her mother had been toward her. Although Ruth obviously has poor judgment in relation to men, she seems able to work quite well, and she has no complaints about her daughter. Considering her extremely pathological start, I think she is doing well.

I describe these two cases to show both some similarities to and some differences from child-analysis cases. These children had much more severe presenting pathology, and Alice also came from a very poor, severely dysfunctional family. Nevertheless, they were able to form a strong therapeutic relationship.

I have had a wide variety of experiences with the child-analysis cases. There are those I have never heard from after termination. One was a fifteen-year-old girl of whom I have almost no memory. I think she came because she did not have friends, and I recall no pathology in her parents. I hope she benefited. Another was a twelve-year-old girl with a school phobia. I realize now that I actively disliked her and her parents. It was a low-fee case, but the mother always pushed for a still lower fee, while keeping a full-time maid. The grandfather called me once to ask whether she would "stop this nonsense" if he gave her her own television set, at a time when few children had one. She came in on her thirteenth birthday dressed like a prostitute, announcing that she was now an adult. Her characterization of adulthood was, "You smoke, drink, and go to racetracks." The third case was that of a seven-year-old girl who physically attacked her mother when she started divorce proceedings. After I advised the father to get treatment and the dissension between them eased enough so that the parents remarried, the girl's negative transference to me softened, but I don't think she ever was able to feel positively toward her mother or me.

With another group, I maintained some contact through the parents. Bob was a ten-year-old boy with a school phobia. His mother was a severe depressive who, during the course of his analysis, would call to tell me that she was in the hospital. She knew Bob wouldn't tell me. His father died of lung cancer a month into the analysis. Bob had had two hernia operations and presented as a depressed child. I helped him to work through his father's death and to be more expressive in general. He terminated on graduation from elementary school and came back once in high school and once in college, on referral from a social worker. The problem both times was an inability to succeed in courses related to his chosen vocation in science. His ambitions had always been higher than his abilities, and I had tried to help him to be more realistic. His mother frequented the Institute and would give me glowing progress reports. Some years later Bob did not respond to my letter offering a free follow-up interview for children who had suffered parent loss, but his mother told me that he was now thirty-eight years old, married, with two children under age ten, and was an accountant. I felt this vocation well matched his obsessive-compulsive personality and his level of intelligence. I thought he might contact me spontaneously, but perhaps he never forgave me for being realistic about his abilities.

I had a different experience with the mother of a six-year-old boy with enuresis. A couple of years after termination, she consulted me about the oldest of her five children. He was not as bright as my patient, Harry, and I found myself counseling the mother to help her with all of the children. Harry was doing fine. Some time later, I met her psychiatrist, and he told me that before I began to see Harry the mother had taken all the children into the garage in the middle of the night and turned on the car motor. Luckily, her husband found them before anyone was seriously hurt. This threw light on an incident in Harry's analysis during which he had drawn cars, covered them with black crayon, and had barely scratched through the black to the underlying color. I recall feeling anxious about this, but he never explained. I read about the father's death a few years later, but never heard more from the mother or Harry.

Dick was a seven-year-old boy who provoked his father to rages. He was an interesting combination of aggressive athleticism and soft sentimentality. Although quite resistant to analysis, he stopped his bedwetting and worked on his anger toward and jealousy of his younger brother. After termination, I would occasionally see both parents socially and was surprised when they divorced. Each told me that Dick had joined an evangelistic group at age twenty, a subtle way of continuing to provoke his father. I felt that he never let himself have strong feelings toward me.

Another type of follow-up was through communications with colleagues. For example, my first child analytic case had been a six-year-old girl with a thumb sucking problem. Her psychotic mother had seen a number of psychiatrists and was so intrusive in my treatment of Roberta that I arranged for her to see a social worker. Roberta was very resistant and required considerable physical control. She finally gained some respect for me because I could beat her consistently at Chinese Checkers. When I learned that she had inguinal hernias, I arranged for a repair and discovered that she had a fantasy that the surgeon would give her a penis. Needless to say, it was a stormy analysis, and when I left the state clinic for private practice, I refused the mother's request to continue without fee. It was with some surprise that I learned from a colleague that Roberta had sought treatment with him at age twenty-five because of difficulties in forming heterosexual relationships. Her IQ at six had been measured at 150. She had become a fairly successful social worker. She did not have positive memories of her childhood analysis, but I was pleased that she had been able to get help again, an indication to me that the analysis had been more successful than I expected.

Another report, from a psychiatrist neighbor of the family, was about an eight-year-old boy with a school phobia. Artie was the youngest of four children. During his mother's recuperation from an operation for cancer, he had been sent to his grandmother's because he "was a handful." The family then moved, and Artie refused to attend the new school. In spite of an early very negative grandmother transference and his continuing to be "a handful," the analysis was quite successful. I controlled his behavior, as well as analyzing his guilt over the possibility that he had caused his mother's illness and some damage to me. His way of showing love was to attack, then feel guilty. We terminated after working through the deaths of his paternal grandmother and, later, of a pet guinea pig. When his mother died three years later, he dealt with it better than some of the older siblings did. Although I have not had a long-term follow-up, I at least learned that the analysis helped him deal with the death of his mother.

The most interesting experiences were those in which the young patient spontaneously sought me out, perhaps without the help or even the knowledge of a parent. This was not easy, especially once I had moved, retired, and closed my office. Also, my name is hard to spell and find in the telephone book. Two patients made spontaneous contact with me in adolescence and/or young adulthood.

Terry was eleven when I started her analysis. The only child of a woman who had had two unsuccessful marriages but whose third marriage seemed solid. This husband had adopted Terry, but her friends commented on the discrepancy between her Jewish last name and her looks. She was very attached to her mother and could not understand her friends who talked about hating their mothers. The analysis helped her to be more expressive in a number of ways as well as to succeed in a very competitive private school.

Her mother was in treatment with a Jewish psychiatrist, and both she and the stepfather were very supportive of Terry's analysis. In midadolescence Terry had a disappointing relationship with the son of a disapproving prominent Christian clergyman. She graduated from high school and terminated analysis in a very traditional way. A few years later, probably with a push from her mother, she came in for an interview concerning a boyfriend with whom she was considering marriage. Her mother was hysterical, fearing that Terry might make the same mistakes that she had made in her two failed marriages. In listening to Terry's description of the young man and hearing of her educational progress and vocational choice, I could be neutral and let her know that I trusted her judgment. Some years later—I think she was in her late twenties at the time—I received a very formal wedding invitation from the mother and stepfather to Terry's wedding to a man with a non-Jewish last name. I am sorry now that I decided not to go, and have heard nothing since.

I had a somewhat different experience with Hector, a nine-year-old boy who did not do his school work but always passed his achievement tests at the end of the school year. I described him in greater detail in a paper on infantile omnipotence (1979). He was the oldest child in an upper-class family and bullied the servants and his younger siblings.

The parents were well-meaning but very busy with their own activities. After a stormy period in the analysis in which he tried to bully me, I obtained control, and he became more cooperative in school as well as with me. However, the principal did not think Hector was ready for the Eastern boarding school that was part of the family tradition, and the parents agreed to one more year of analysis. During that year, a very important analytic interpretation became possible. Through his play with blocks and Indian figures, I learned that an uncle had been killed during an archeological expedition and also that two of Hector's paternal grandmother's husbands had died early deaths. His paternal aunt had epilepsy, and he himself had an abnormal but asymptomatic EEG. After I was able to deal with his fears of growing up he was able to go away to school.

Two years later he spontaneously showed up at my office to thank me. He now realized that whatever he accomplished, he would have to do for himself. It became obvious that the transference to me had been that of a servant, and he was ready to give it up. Some years later, he recognized me in a public bus and told me that he had finished school, gone to England to teach American history, come back to study law, and was working as a clerk in the office of a judge. I also met his parents in church, and father was profuse in his thanks for what I had done for Hector. I have heard no more, but on the basis of a fantasy he expressed during analysis of becoming president, I suspect that he might some day run for public office.

More remarkable are the three former analytic patients who initiated contact with me twenty to thirty years after termination. One was John, whom I had seen at age ten, five years after his mother died of a mysterious illness. He had a stepmother and had given her a hard time when she was pregnant. She became pregnant again soon after the analysis started, and I helped John analyze his fears of harming pregnant women. He thought that his mother had died in childbirth and that he and his father were responsible. He became resistant to further analysis after the stepmother delivered. The family consulted me briefly when, at fifteen, he reacted to his father's having the family dog put to death without informing him. John refused to see me, so I explained the similarity of the situation to his mother's death, and the family managed to tell him the facts about the dog's death.

At age thirty-five John spontaneously contacted me about his only son, age thirteen, in whom he recognized some of the same problems for which he had originally seen me, at much the same age. I learned that he was a high school teacher in the inner city, had some credits toward an advanced degree, and had been married three times. He did not confirm my earlier prediction that he would be anxious during a wife's pregnancy. His first wife began to have trouble with drugs after the birth of the child, precipitating divorce. His stepmother had helped him raise the boy, but she died when the child was five, thereby repeating John's early trauma. I could not quite understand the problems with the next two marriages. It was obvious that his son, like John as a boy, was reluctant to learn and grow up. When I expressed surprise at John's academic achievements, he said he had begun to learn after his stepmother nursed him through a severe illness when he was thirteen. I interviewed the boy, but he was not motivated for treatment and had already failed to respond to two school psychologists. As John was in no financial position to support an analysis, I gave him a few suggestions, including considering a woman therapist for the boy. I have not heard from them since.

Laura called me after I had closed my office, twenty-eight years after termination of her analysis. I had seen her for two years starting at age seven. I do not remember a specific presenting problem, only that her mother wanted her to be happy and well adjusted—difficult goals. Laura was concerned that she could remember nothing of her analysis and wondered if she should go back into treatment in order to remember. Over the telephone I learned that she was thirty-eight years old, married with two children, and that she worked with developmentally disabled children. She had no clinical symptoms. With some hesitation, I told her why I thought she had repressed details of the analysis. About six months into her treatment her mother had asked me to sign medical permission for an abortion. The family was financially well-off, but she did not want more than her current four children. As I felt uncomfortable in this role, I suggested that she go back to the doctor who had referred her to me in the first place. For two months after this, Laura drew and played "The Murder Family." I did not feel comfortable in interpreting this play at the time. I learned at the follow-up meeting that Laura knew that her mother had had an abortion but did not remember her play. Apparently this failure did not interfere with her development, and I advised her not to have further analysis unless she became symptomatic. I have not heard from her again.

Perhaps the most interesting spontaneous long-term follow-up came just recently. I thought I heard a man's voice in my apartment. It came from my answering machine saying, "I just wanted to thank you." It was Peter, whose analysis had started when he was eight. He was planning to visit old friends in Chicago and wondered if he could see me. We arranged a three-hour lunch and interview. Now forty-two years old, he is a paralegal who has started training as a psychologist and wants to be an analyst and treat children.

He was originally referred to me by his mother's psychiatrist, who told me she was psychotic. The mother dramatically and tearfully told me that she had ruined her son, evidenced by his thumb sucking. The father asked to see me and told me about the parents' experiences as refugees and that, after the birth of their second son, his wife had had a postpartum psychosis, during which she had cut three-year-old Peter's thumb with a kitchen knife when he sucked it. Surprisingly, in spite of their disorganization in relation to time and money, both parents were very supportive of the analysis. After three years in which Peter only hinted at mother's attack on him, we terminated. He returned in an anxiety state at age fourteen, not doing as well in high school as he and the parents had expected. After reestablishing our relationship, he came in one day and paced near the door, casting sidelong glances at me. When I commented, "You look as if you expect me to hurt you," he broke out with, "Do you know that my mother almost cut off my thumb when I was little?" I said that his father had told me and that he had been unable to discuss this when I saw him before. We continued therapy throughout his high school years, mostly of a supportive and advisory sort about classes and future vocation. He came again in a panic when he was twenty, after his father told him he could die at any time from severe hypertension and it would be Peter's duty to take care of his mother and two brothers. After some support, I referred him to the low-fee clinic of the psychoanalytic institute, but he was rejected as being too disturbed. Shortly after that he came in to say goodbye, as he was leaving to go to the West Coast. There was no further contact until the follow up at age forty-two.

During our conversation I learned that the parents had been divorced, and that he had found out that his mother's accusation of his father's infidelity was true, not an effect of her paranoia. The parents had fought both verbally and physically, and his mother also had beaten Peter when he did poorly in school but then felt guilty and tried to make it up to him. She now lives near him in a retirement apartment, and all three sons support her. Peter's father remarried, but had had a massive heart attack and died about ten years before. Peter studied law and, with some delay, graduated, but he has been unable to pass the bar examination. (The next brother became a psychologist but has not been able to pass the state certifying examination. The youngest studied medicine and has not been able to pass the board examination in internal medicine. All three boys have lived with women but have not married.) Peter's girlfriend left him when he returned to school a year ago. He has been seeing a woman counselor who supported him in his desire to call me. He has some fears about being able to relate to children, and I encouraged him to combine his legal training with his interest in psychology. I also gave him the names of two child analysts in his vicinity who would be interested in his child analysis and would help him regarding his ambition to be an analyst.

We went over his memories of his child analysis. He said I had told him it was unacceptable to put his feet or chocolate-smeared hands on my desk. His parents had let him do anything he wanted, as long as he got good grades. He also remembered playing games and how, in Fox and Hounds, I gave each hound the name of an affect to help him deal with depression, envy, anger, and happiness. From his high school therapy he remembered telling me about some papers he had written, making his family battles into comedy. Although I had expressed an interest in reading them then and now, he still "forgot" to bring them. As part of his interest in psychology, he asked me questions about how I got into psychiatry and details about technique in treating children. I found myself talking to him almost as to a colleague. He gives me credit for keeping him out of a mental hospital. Although we did not arrange for any future contact, this could occur.

DISCUSSION

This review brings up some interesting theoretical considerations. What is the process that allows some patients to keep an analyst an important part of their lives without any actual contact for as long as twenty to forty years? Why do they then make contact? The two non-analytic cases give one clue. Apparently long-term intensive treatment of some sort is important. This promotes introjection or internalization of a therapist permanently. Schafer (1968) has written extensively on internalization and states that *preservation* of an external object is more mature than simple internalization, or even identification, although these may be involved in the preservation. This may be what is meant in the literature when the analyst or other therapist is described as "a real person." Schafer talks about benign parental functions, and Koch describes the analyst as an interested adult, like an uncle or aunt. This is the role in which many of my former child patients seem to have placed me.

I think it takes something more than time and interest to get into this special position. One thing that interested me was that the memories of those who made contact much later almost always included experiences in which I had limited their behavior. These were children who responded to the limits very easily, and I did not remember them, such as Peter's statement that, unlike his parents, I had let him know what was unacceptable to others. I more clearly remember the need to physically control Artie, Hector, Robert, and Ruth. Blatt and Behrends (1987) indicate that both development (Behrends and Blatt, 1985) and therapy are processes of gratification, experienced incompatibility, and internalization, followed by individuation. Treatment, or the analytic situation, has many gratifications, such as undivided attention, empathy, explanations of behavior, and, in the case of children, participation of the adult therapist in the games, art productions, and play of childhood. The "experienced incompatibility" or frustration may take many forms. I recommended an inguinal hernia repair to demonstrate to Roberta that she could not grow a penis or have one supplied by a surgeon. I took Artie's shoes off when he kicked me in the shins. Sometimes, as with Peter, a simple suggestion is enough; sometimes silence is a refusal of desired gratification. Frustration is produced sometimes by refusal to come to a party, and sometimes by an interpretation that indicates some unwanted responsibility of the patient for thoughts or acts. Whatever the specifics, this alternation of gratification and frustration does seem to result in internalization. If this process occurs within a meaningful relationship and the patient has the competencies and interests, there is also considerable identification. I was interested in how many of my former patients have or have tried vocations that help children. John is a teacher, Laura works with retarded children, and Peter wants to be a child analyst. Even those who aren't involved professionally seem to be doing a good job of raising their own children. The final phase of the developmental process, individuation, would seem to show itself in the ability of these adults to run their lives for many years without direct contact with me. All therapists are familiar with patients who, although seemingly asymptomatic, need to continue some sort of treatment or contact indefinitely. It is possible that these patients either lacked frustration in their treatment or were unable to tolerate it.

My cases indicate a number of factors in this preservation process. Most of those who never made contact after termination seemed to have difficulty finding any gratification in the treatment and had come mostly at the urging of parents. Others seemed to have difficulty dealing with frustration and could not work through it toward internalization. From Peter I learned that a psychotic parent may fully support a relationship to another adult. This means that such a parent can provide some sort of basic relationship, along with the permission to use others to complement his or her deficits in parenting. Healthier parents may also do this, such as Ruth's mother, who felt guilty for ignoring her as an infant. Some of these mothers remain the real force behind future contacts, which they see as support for themselves as well as for their offspring. Bob's mother was so needy that he may have avoided my invitation to him because he recognized his mother's greater need. The contact made by Harry's mother was obviously for herself. There may be some lack of parenting in all cases that developed a long-term "real" relationship.

The question remains as to why there was a need for further contact with the therapist. I did not have the experience of older children or adolescents making contact for new problems in young adulthood. I have had no contact from the one case I started in adolescence. On the other hand, those whom I analyzed into adolescence do seem to make relatively short-term contact to deal with new problems. Terry, for example, returned to get help when her mother feared her choice of a mate. With her wedding invitation, she let me know that I had helped. Hector made contact not to solve a problem but to let me know that his treatment had allowed him to solve problems himself. The long-term contacts seem to relate to treatment decisions, either for self or children. Laura needed to understand the repression of her reaction to her mother's abortion, which I could help her do in a brief time. John was worried about his son, and Peter was considering embarking on a career like mine, requiring a new analysis.

I think the latter cases demonstrate that an analytic experience is more than just a good and long relationship in childhood, such as many others, for instance, teachers, may provide. Even in my nonanalytic cases, I brought to the treatment an attitude of inquiry as to the meaning of behavior and feelings which the patients retained. John wanted to understand his son, Laura her amnesia. I think Peter, in his new analysis, will better understand his ambivalent relationship to his father, which seems to be present in his brothers also. He openly expresses gratitude to me, not only for my parental experiences with him but also for an attitude of curiosity and inquiry as to causes. Schlessinger and Robbins (1983) found an internalization of the observing, understanding, and integrating functions of the analyst in their follow-up study of adult analyses.

Through this study I have developed some new insights into child psychoanalysis. Although it contains gratifying and frustrating aspects that cause many analysts of adults to consider it "not analysis," it is definitely different from the nonanalytic, long-term treatments. I doubt if a child would tolerate an orthodox adult approach, with free association, abstinence, and interpretations. I recall a child-analysis seminar where the presenting analyst noted in surprise that a hysterical, silent, and hostile twelve-year-old girl had come for two years and left much improved clinically. This was in contrast to a talkative, obsessive-compulsive fourteen-year-old boy who behaved just like an adult analytic patient and showed no change at all after two years. In child analysis there might be a special need for the analyst to be a "real person," or adjunctive parent. Perhaps one or two of my cases who made no further contact had ideal parents. However, if parents with a defect in parenting skills, even to the point of psychosis, know that they have such a problem and can allow their child to make a "real" relationship to an analyst, this person can then be internalized by the child and preserved for future use. Even Alice, a waif from a poor and severely dysfunctional family, was able to internalize and preserve me for over forty years. Her need for a "real person" was truly extraordinary.

I believe my experiences also support the value of child psychoanalysis, at least for some kinds of clinical situations. Two recent studies of the efficacy of analysis and analytic psychotherapy for children from the Hampstead Clinic (Target and Fonagy, 1994, and Fonagy and Target, 1994) found that analytic therapy is most valuable for conditions usually considered neurotic or emotional rather than for pervasive pathology or disruptive behavior disorders. My cases would support that finding; Alice is the only case that might qualify as a disruptive disorder, and the clinical results of her therapy were not remarkable. The Hampstead study also notes the importance of parental support of the therapy. So far, however, they have not done any follow-up studies.

Is there some special personality or countertransference in the therapist that promotes or interferes with such "real" relationships? I can only describe myself and some therapists whom I have supervised. My principles of therapy have been a balance of gratification and frustration. I have also found that I can be empathetic to parents, even when I think they are misguided. I place high value on individuation and do not encourage long analyses or formally set up future contacts. It would be interesting to know if analysts with different values and practices have the same or different experiences with spontaneous contacts long after the treatment period.

BIBLIOGRAPHY

ALTSCHUL, S., & BEISER, H. (1988). Early and late effects of bereavement. In *Childhood Bereavement and Its Aftermath*, ed. S. Altschul, pp. 239–56. Madison, Conn.: Int. Univ. Press.

BEHRENDS, R., & BLATT, S. (1985). Internalization and psychological development throughout the life cycle. *Psychoanal. Study Child*, 40:11–40.

BEISER, H. (1979). The problem of infantile omnipotence. *Ann. Psychoanal.*, 7:113–32.

BLATT, S., & BEHRENDS, R. (1987). Internalization, separation-individuation, and therapeutic action. *Int. J. Psychoanal.*, 68:(2)279–98.

CASS, L., & THOMAS, C. (1979). *Childhood Pathology and Later Adjustment: The Question of Prediction.* New York: Wiley.

FONAGY, P., & TARGET, M. (1994). The efficacy of psychoanalysis for children with disruptive disorders. *J. Amer. Acad. Child and Adol. Psychiat.*, 33:(1)45–55.

HELLER, P. (1983). *A Child Analysis with Anna Freud.* Madison, Conn.: Int. Univ. Press.

HELLMAN, I. (1973). Hampstead nursery follow-up studies: Effects of sudden separation. *Psychoanal. Study Child*, 17: 159–74.

KOCH, E. (1973). Follow-up of child analysis patients. *J. Amer. Acad. Child Psychiat.*, 12: 223–46.

SCHAFER, R. (1968). *Aspects of Internalization.* New York: Int. Univ. Press.

SCHLESSINGER, N., & ROBBINS, F. (1983). *A Developmental View of the Psychoanalytic Process: Follow-up Studies and Their Consequences.* New York: Int. Univ. Press.

RITVO, S. (1966). Correlation of childhood and adult neurosis. *Int. J. Psychoanal.*, 47:(2)130–31.

TARGET, M., & FONAGY, P. (1994). Efficacy of psychoanalysis for children with emotional disorders. *J. Amer. Acad. Child and Adol. Psychiat.*, 33:(3)361–71.

Trauma in the Preverbal Period

Symptoms, Memories, and Developmental Impact

THEODORE J. GAENSBAUER, M.D.

In this paper, five children who experienced traumas during the preverbal period are described. The clinical presentations are oriented around three questions: (1) What are the expectable symptomatic reactions of preverbal infants to trauma? (2) To what extent and in what forms are preverbal traumatic experiences retained in memory? and (3) Does trauma in the preverbal period have enduring effects? In these five preverbal infants, symptomatology consistent with typical posttraumatic diagnostic criteria was observed. The clinical material also suggested that the capacity to encode and retain meaningful internal representations of the salient elements of a traumatic experience may be present as early as the second half of the first year of life. The developmental implications of early trauma, particularly if it is severe, appear to be significant.

THE IMPACT OF TRAUMA OCCURRING IN THE PREVERBAL PERIOD OF INfancy and the nature of its representation in memory have been subjects of interest for psychoanalysis as far back as Freud's classic case of the "Wolf Man," who was hypothesized to have been traumatized at eighteen months of age by witnessing parental intercourse (Freud,

---

Associate clinical professor at the University of Colorado Health Sciences Center; faculty member of the Denver Institute for Psychoanalysis.

The author is indebted to Dr. Jill Miller and Dr. Richard Crager for their collaboration in organizing and sharing therapeutic material utilized in this paper, and to Dr. Peter Mayerson and Dr. Sam Wagonfeld for their helpful comments.

The Psychoanalytic Study of the Child 50, ed. Albert J. Solnit, Peter B. Neubauer, Samuel Abrams, and A. Scott Dowling (Yale University Press, copyright © 1995 by Albert J. Solnit, Peter B. Neubauer, Samuel Abrams, and A. Scott Dowling).

1918). More recent clinical and research studies of infants have led to skepticism about Freud's formulation of the Wolf Man's experience, exemplified by Blum's observation that "it is extremely unlikely that a child of eighteen months, with a life-threatening illness like malaria, could see anything that discretely or in the correct sequence" (Blum, 1989). Most contemporary writers have emphasized the influence of cumulative, emotion-laden, interactive experiences between infant and caregivers rather than specific traumatic events (Dowling and Rothstein, 1989; Emde, 1981; Stern, 1985). This emphasis on relational patterns is consistent with current conceptions of the preverbal period as "prerepresentational" in nature (Emde, 1983), with the limitations in capacity for enduring memory formation and cognitive understanding that such a descriptive term implies. This shift in focus notwithstanding, questions about the carry-over effects of trauma from the infancy period are as relevant today as when Freud first raised them. My purpose in this paper is to provide clinical data bearing on this important area.

I will describe five children who experienced traumas of varying degrees of severity during the preverbal period. The case presentations will be oriented around three questions: (1) What are the expectable symptomatic reactions of preverbal infants to trauma, and to what extent are these reactions similar to post-traumatic symptomatology seen in older children and adults? (2) To what degree and in what forms are traumatic experiences in the preverbal period retained in memory? and (3) Does trauma in the preverbal period have enduring effects?

Symptomatology following trauma in the infancy period. On the basis of a recent review of the limited literature available and our own clinical experience, my colleagues and I hypothesized that a symptom complex similar to that documented in older children and adults could be observed in infants and toddlers, with some modifications owing to the young child's immature developmental level (Drell et al., 1993). This hypothesis was subsequently supported by the report of Scheeringa et al. (in press) on twelve new cases of traumatized children under the age of four. The youngest child was seventeen months, leaving open the question of whether preverbal infants would show a similar correspondence. The material presented here indicates that even prior to the onset of language fluency, symptomatology consistent with traditional posttraumatic diagnostic criteria can be observed.

Retention of memories beyond the infancy period. Perhaps the most remarkable case report of memory for preverbal trauma is that of

Bernstein and Blacher (1967), based on parental reports, of a twenty-eight-month-old child who was able to recall details from a pneumo-encephalogram carried out at three months of age. Two recent publications have provided more systematic data on memories of early trauma. The more extensive is that of Terr (1988) on twenty children who had been traumatized prior to five years of age, although only two of them had been traumatized before eighteen months of age. She found that for traumas occurring prior to twenty-eight months of age verbal memories were either absent or extremely spotty. For traumas occurring after twenty-eight to thirty-six months, children could provide more detailed verbal narratives. Observing that children who were unable to provide conscious verbal recall nevertheless were able to carry out accurate behavioral enactments, Terr concluded that even at ages younger than twenty-eight months traumas create powerful and lasting visual images. She hypothesized that the child's enactments or behavioral memories derive from these "burned-in" visual imprints rather than from verbal memory.

More recently, Sugar (1992) compared two toddlers traumatized at sixteen and twenty-four months who already had achieved verbal fluency and were subsequently able to give detailed verbal reports with a third patient traumatized at eighteen months but prior to the onset of verbal fluency, who had only a vague visual memory. Sugar concluded that the onset of speech phrases was crucial to the child's ability to relate the event in a coherent manner, particularly in regard to time sequencing.

Current conceptions of memory functioning support the distinction made by Terr and Sugar between verbal and behavioral memory. Memory researchers have conceptualized two functionally distinct systems of memory: procedural, implicit, or early memory and declarative, explicit, or late memory. These systems are believed to be mediated by different neural pathways (Cohen, 1984; Squire, 1987; Siegel, in press). Procedural or implicit knowledge refers to the largely unconscious, automatically operating memory systems related to behavioral, emotional, and sensory experience (Schacter, 1987; Clyman, 1991). Declarative or explicit memory refers to knowledge that is conscious, can be recalled as coming from the past, and can be communicated to others directly. Autobiographical memory, the ability to represent oneself as having participated in a particular activity at a particular time and place in the past, has traditionally been considered a form of declarative memory (Nelson, 1993). Consistent with Terr's and Sugar's observations, developmental researchers have generally found that children are unable to provide descriptions of personally experienced events that occurred prior to the onset of language. With the onset of language, children are able to verbally communicate fragments of memories for events that took place over previous months, with much cueing required. Only after approximately age three have children been found to be able consistently to provide coherent stories about personal events—that is, to develop stable autobiographical narratives (Nelson, 1990, 1993; Fivush, 1993).

An important limitation of the conclusions described above is the fact that to date clinical and research studies on autobiographical memory have depended almost exclusively on verbal retrieval. Efforts are currently underway to develop methods that do not depend on verbal retrieval to assess recall of past events in the preverbal period (Mandler, 1990). There is a growing literature documenting infants' capacities to recall nonverbal experiences over extended periods of time, as demonstrated by some form of behavioral recognition during re-exposure to the situation (Rovee-Collier and Hayne, 1987; Daehler and Greco, 1985). An impressive example of this literature is the report of Perris et al. (1990) demonstrating that children who experienced a single laboratory experiment at six months of age were able behaviorally to demonstrate retention of memory for aspects of the experience two years later.

The case reports presented below raise interesting questions about infants' capacities for memory of events in the preverbal period beyond simple behavioral recognition. They suggest that when provided with opportunities for nonverbal expression, children can give evidence that salient sensory and somatically based elements of a preverbal traumatic experience have been encoded and retained in memory over extended periods of time.

Developmental impact of trauma in infancy. While most clinicians would agree with Meissner (1989) that "the earliest experiences, including those of the preverbal period, antedating the advent of conscious memory, enter into the determination of evolving psychic structure and function," the manner in which such experiences might influence subsequent development remains a topic of much conjecture. Specific experiences from the infancy period have been thought to be expressed through "screen memories" (Freud, 1899; Anthony, 1962; Rycroft, 1951), nonverbal sensory and affective perceptions (Isakower, 1938; Lewin, 1946; Spitz, 1955; Dowling, 1982; Lichtenberg, 1983), dreams and visual imagery (Niederland, 1965; Mack, 1965; Pulver, 1987), and postural/behavioral enactments (Deutsch, 1947; Anthi, 1983; McLaughlin, 1989; Dowling, 1990). We know relatively little about the extent to which traumas occurring in the preverbal period may be capable of specific psychic representation or about the specific mechanisms by which they may influence subsequent development. Given the availability of data about the children's psychological functioning during the years immediately following their traumas, I believe the cases reported here will stimulate valuable hypotheses about the potential influences of early trauma.

Before presenting the cases, I would like to provide some overview information. The traumas were all relatively circumscribed and predominently physical in nature. At the time of their traumas the children ranged in age from seven to fifteen months. None of them had achieved verbal fluency beyond single words. The time elapsed from the point of the traumas to my initial contact with them ranged from thirteen months to seven years. Three of the children were seen by me directly in evaluation or therapy. One of the children was seen subsequently by another therapist. In the fourth case I was consulted by the parents in the course of the child's treatment by another therapist. The fifth child I did not see directly, but I did review her medical records.

In every case there were many factors contributing to the behavior and symptoms of the children that cannot be described here. Although every attempt was made to take these multiple factors into account in organizing the material, the presentations themselves will focus on what seemed to be trauma-specific effects. One particularly relevant factor is the degree to which the children's communications were influenced by outside sources of information, particularly since verbalizations accompanying the children's descriptions and reenactments clearly reflected subsequently gained knowledge. In each case I have described what the parents told me concerning the extent to which the traumas had been discussed with the child. There were no doubt many potential sources of information and influence that I was not able to verify. Nevertheless, the ways in which the children reenacted their traumas, the contexts in which the material emerged, the associated affects and symptomatology, and the defensive operations brought into play, all suggested to me that the primary source of their communications was internalized personal experience rather than declarative knowledge obtained from outside sources.

CASE MATERIAL

CASE 1: TOMMY

This case involves a child who at thirteen months of age took an overdose of pills requiring an emergency hospitalization. At twenty-six months he was able to play out specific details of the experience. Elements of the experience were manifested in a subsequent psychotherapy which began when he was four and one-half years old.

I saw Tommy when he was twenty-five months old because of depressive symptoms associated with his father's extended hospitalization for a serious illness, precipitated by an adverse reaction to medication. At thirteen months Tommy himself had been hospitalized for an overdose of analgesic medications taken while he was in the care of a babysitter. Emergency personnel were called, with a group of firemen providing the initial intervention. He was taken to the hospital in an ambulance, accompanied by his father. While in the ambulance, he had a respiratory arrest and was given an injection of Narcon with immediate relief of symptoms. He remained at the hospital overnight with his parents in attendance. His parents did not recall any specific posttraumatic symptoms following his return home. The only indicators of stress they noted were a mild slowing of his growth rate and an intensified dependence on pacifiers over the next several months. The parents did not remember any discussions of the experience with Tommy.

In the therapy his mother and I attempted to help Tommy understand the complicated events associated with his depression. A month or so into the therapy, we were playing out a theme related to his father's hospitalization because he had taken the wrong medicines. Tommy became fascinated with a siren that was part of the toy "town" we were using to represent the hospital. As we were playing out helping the daddy doll at the hospital, Tommy took some pieces of chalk that had served as pills in a previous session and threw them in the trash along with a pillbox, saying "Bad medicine!" apparently in reference to his father's medications. Somewhat later, his mother and I were talking about another aspect of the current family situation, but Tommy did not seem interested. He kept going back to the pillbox, saying, "All gone" as he examined it. He then began playing with an ambulance.

Impressed by the purposefulness of the play, it occurred to his mother and me that he might be trying to say something about his own experience. I made a comment about Tommy having taken medicines that made him sick and then placed the toy figure that we had been using to represent Tommy on top of the ambulance. Tommy immediately began to move the ambulance along the floor in a very animated fashion. I contributed to the sense of urgency by turning on the siren, at which point Tommy spontaneously called out, "Daddy" and placed the daddy figure on the ambulance with the little boy. We proceeded to the hospital, and I introduced some doctor figures to check on the little boy. I was approaching the examination in a generic way, but Tommy clearly had something specific in mind. He took a plastic thermometer and rubbed the side of the baby figure's face, under the chin, and down the chest. I was puzzled, but his mother immediately recognized the play's meaning. In the emergency room, Tommy had been given charcoal, had vomited frequently over the next several hours, and had required repeated cleaning up. Following this session his parents discussed the overdose and hospitalization on a number of occasions with Tommy over the next few months.

At four and one-half years, Tommy began a two-year course of therapy with another therapist for reasons related to his parents' subsequent divorce. There were several indications from this second treatment of persisting effects from the overdose. An obvious connection was a recurrent symptom of vomiting which appeared during stress, particularly at times of separation. In two sessions play references which seemed directly related to the accidental overdose appeared spontaneously.

The first occurred approximately a year into the therapy. During the previous several months Tommy had been preoccupied with a number of themes that could potentially be understood in relation to his traumatic experience. These included feelings of being unsafe and inadequately protected by caregivers and an intense behavioral regression to an infantile level at home. He would camp outside his mother's bedroom door pretending to be a "lost puppy" wanting to be taken in. During one therapy session he played out a story about a baby whose caregivers didn't pay attention to him and who was taken away by a "jail truck." The intense concern about feeling safe seemed noteworthy in that, even though there were separation issues related to the divorce, caregiving by parents and babysitters had been consistent, and except for a brief emergency room visit at age twenty months, when he fell off a wagon and cut his finger, there had been no other episodes of risk for harm. Whenever the therapist would pursue issues of safety in the present, Tommy would not appear to be anxious and would say, "My parents always take care of me."

The specific session in which Tommy spontaneously brought up the overdose occurred shortly after the therapist's vacation. His play was again focused on themes of safety and separation. He told a fantasy story about a baby who slipped out of his mother's grasp and almost drowned. He then pretended to bring a pet to the therapist to keep because he was going away. A little later he played out that he and the therapist were married and had a baby; he explained to the therapist that they needed to watch the baby closely because it could crawl out of bed and get into dangerous things. Following this, the therapist was assigned the role of a babysitter who got caught in a lie. Tommy then created a train crash with injured people having to go to the hospital. At this point he abruptly interrupted the fantasy play and told the therapist that when he was a baby he had had to go to the hospital and that he had "barfed all the time" and was very sick.

While there are many possible contributions to this material, I was struck that the play themes seen both prior to and during the session (feeling unsafe, infantile regressions in the context of separations, descriptions of inattentive babysitters and babies kidnapped by "jail trucks," babies who could get into dangerous things, and people going to the hospital) seemed to have associative links to his overdose experience. A tenable interpretation was that the unconsciously experienced themes related to the overdose were brought to the surface sufficiently by the play to evoke conscious awareness of the overdose experience, which was then shared with the therapist.

Consistent with the hypothesis that feeling unsafe at times of separation from caregivers had links to his earlier experience was a sequence of play that occurred in the next-to-last session prior to termination. In this session issues of safety were again expressed. Tommy had gathered together a variety of emergency vehicles and at one point commented, "The only thing I don't have is poison control." When the therapist observed that poison control might be important, he responded, "Yeah, in case you swallow too many vitamins." The therapist interpreted, "Or too many pills," but Tommy did not give any response indicating if the play material was linked to memory.

A brief report from his parents when Tommy was seven and one-half years of age indicated that he was doing well. There were no behaviors that could be unquestionably related to his early experience. He knew he had been hospitalized but did not seem to remember the details. The only areas noted as possible carry-overs were his continued strong fascination with sirens and rescue activities, exemplified by the fact that he had chosen to be a fireman for Halloween for three consecutive years.

CASE 2: BETH

This is the case of a child who experienced an auto accident at nine months of age and carried out an accurate play enactment of the accident thirteen months later (for greater detail see the case description in Drell, Siegel and Gaensbauer [1993]).

Beth was twenty-two months of age when I evaluated her. At nine months, she was with her mother and grandmother when their car was hit by a truck. The car rolled over, was carried over an adjacent river embankment, and fell more than twenty feet into a dry creek bed, landing on its front and then flopping right-side-up. All three passengers suffered bruises of the face and body. Beth's mother had a broken wrist, and her grandmother had significant back pain, requiring immobilization. Beth screamed for two hours.

Following the accident, Beth showed a number of symptoms related to situations reminding her of the accident. She was very frightened of being in the car and having another accident. Once she learned the word, whenever she saw a truck nearby she would scream, "Truck, mommy, truck!" She absolutely refused to sit in the back seat of the car or in her carseat. Eating also became a serious problem. She could remain in her highchair only for brief periods before becoming restless. (I thought it probable that the highchair reminded her of the carseat.) In the thirteen months following the accident she went from the seventy-fifth percentile to below the third in weight and was hospitalized on two occasions for dehydration following viral illnesses with persistent vomiting. Other symptoms included major disruptions in sleep, with frequent fearful awakenings. At the time of our meeting she still had difficulty sleeping through the night. Separation difficulties were marked for both mother and infant. Her mother had experienced a significant posttraumatic reaction as well and did not leave Beth with anyone but her father for the next ten months. Beth's personality changed from outgoing and confident to restless and whiney, although over time the overt fussiness diminished and was replaced by a very subdued demeanor.

During the first session with Beth and her mother, Beth was initially uneasy. When she had become more comfortable, I initiated a re-creation of the accident scene. I took some small doll figures to represent Beth, her mother, and her grandmother; a play automobile; a toy truck; and some flat pieces of plastic to represent the river bed and set them out as they existed prior to the accident. Beth immediately became attentive. When I asked her to show me what happened next, she carried out an accurate demonstration of what had occurred. She put the car in front of the truck, upended it on the hood of the truck, demonstrated how the car fell head first into the river bed, and completed the sequence by placing the car in its upright position on the plastic "riverbed." Having explicitly avoided any discussion of the accident with Beth, her mother was stunned by the accuracy of the portrayal. Toward the end of the session, I introduced some toy ambulances and we took the play family to the hospital.

Immediately following the session, Beth showed and upsurge in symptoms that had specific connections to the accident. During the night she woke up screaming twice, and for the next three weeks she awoke at last once a night. Her mother believed these awakenings involved nightmares of being injured, because she repeated the word "owies," the word she had used in the past to describe the injuries that she, her mother, and her grandmother had experienced in the accident. Her appetite diminished, and she was more withdrawn for the next week or so. She then became much more aggressive than usual and hit her mother on one occasion. There was a further example of memory of the accident four days after the first session. Beth and her mother were driving past the area where the accident had occurred and Beth called out, "Car in there!"

In our second session, three weeks later, Beth sought out the previous play materials and picked up where we had left off. She put the grandmother doll in the bed that had been used to represent the hospital and announced that grandmother had "owies." Soon after, she spontaneously recreated the accident and immediately activated the play siren. Later she brought the grandmother doll in the bed over to me and again said that the grandmother had "owies." When I asked her where, she pointed to the doll's face, stomach, and back, accurately indicating where her grandmother had been injured. We proceeded to put play bandages on these locations. She then spontaneously turned to her mother and put the play bandages on her mother's right wrist and both knees in the specific locations where her mother had been hurt.

There was a follow-up phone conversation with her mother four months after the evaluation was completed. Her mother decided not to follow through with recommendations for therapy, largely, I believe, because of her own anxiety related to the reenactment play. She stated that Beth was doing better, was more outgoing, was eating better, and had been talking more about the accident at home. Her mother felt that had been helpful to Beth.

CASE 3: AUDREY

This case involves a child who at twelve and one-half months observed the violent death of her mother and was able to play out and verbalize details of the event over the next three-and-one-half years (for discussions of the case by a number of contributors see Gaensbauer et al, in press). A follow-up interview at age six years documented the continued impact of her traumatic loss.

Audrey was four and one-half years old when I saw her for a forensic evaluation. At twelve and one-half months, she had watched as her mother was killed instantly in a severely mutilating fashion by a letter bomb sent by a former boyfriend (not Audrey's father). A friend of the mother's who was also injured fell to the floor screaming and died three weeks later of her injuries. Audrey was found close to her mother's body, unhurt except for some minor abrasions to her leg. Since her birth father had abandoned her mother during the pregnancy, following seven weeks of foster care she was placed with, and subsequently adopted by, one of her mother's female relatives and her husband.

On her arrival at her adoptive home, Audrey was unable to sleep, and woke up repeatedly with fearful crying. During the day she was fidgety, rocked incessantly in a self-soothing manner, and displayed intense screaming episodes lasting up to five minutes. She appeared to experience frightening, intrusive imagery, both in nightmares and in daydreams. While Audrey had not been able to describe her nightmares in detail, her adoptive mother recalled that at three years of age she awoke crying and saying, "It's messy all over!" while rubbing her head and neck. The next day she pointed to some bed sheets colored with large burgundy spots and said to her mother, "That's a bad dream." Her mother responded that the spots looked like flowers. Audrey said, "No, they're messy all over," and moved her hand in front of her. In her drawings Audrey repetitively would mix red and brown colors on the page and say, "It's icky!" In the month prior to her first visit with me, while being held she suddenly looked very terrified and said, "I'm having a bad dream about my mommy who died," but was not able to describe exactly what she was seeing.

She showed fearful reactions to a range of stimuli reminiscent of the trauma, including loud noises, Santa Claus (presumably because of the red color), rocking horses (possibly because of the vestibular sensation), fuzz- and dust-balls, flies, and on one occasion a charred piece of wood. When Audrey was two, her babysitter had a mild heart attack which required an ambulance. Audrey was so upset that she could no longer be cared for in this sitter's home, and screaming episodes, which had calmed down at that point, reoccurred for several weeks. At around age three, during the movie *Bambi*, Audrey started screaming, "Bambi's mommy shot! Bambi's mommy gone!" and couldn't bear to watch. At age three and one-half years, at a doctor's office, she heard an ambulance siren outside and spontaneously called out, "Uh oh, Mom!" She also showed repetitive patterns of play which appeared to be behavioral reenactments. She would spin until she became dizzy and fell down, or lie on the ground and thrash back and forth with her arms and legs.

Her adoptive parents had visited with Audrey and her birth mother when Audrey was nine months old. Compared to the happy, socially engaging infant they remembered from that visit, when she came to them she was serious and withdrawn. She was initially resistant to her adoptive parents' caretaking and showed a transient feeding disturbance. Over the first year, she became able to give and receive affection but continued to be restrained, particularly toward her adoptive father. Other symptoms observed both immediately and over time included marked separation anxiety, speech articulation problems, difficulties with peer relations, and disruptive, angry behavior, including the sadistic teasing of animals. One babysitter commented that Audrey was "like someone with two personalities in one body," sometimes sweet and loving, at other times hateful and mean.

Audrey was seen briefly in a behaviorally oriented therapy at age three and a half. Prior to that time, there had been no direct discussion of her mother because her adoptive parents had assumed she would not remember her. At the therapist's suggestion, she was told about "her mother who died." This information seemed helpful. Over the next year, Audrey made a number of spontaneous comments that indicated she had distinct memories of her mother. Her mother had had red hair and, looking at a picture on a T-shirt of a mermaid with red hair, Audrey said, "That's my mom!" Her adoptive parents asked her once if she remembered what she was doing when her mom died. Audrey said she was playing with a ball and that her balls had been red and yellow. Some time later, they saw a red and a yellow ball in photographs of the apartment where Audrey and her mother had lived prior to her mother's death. Shown the photographs and asked if she remembered where she was when her mother died, Audrey pointed to the spot where her mother's body had been found. While in the year prior to my evaluation there had been a great deal of discussion of her birth mother, her adoptive mother reported that there had been no discussion of the circumstances of her mother's death.

That the explosion and the death of her mother were still preoccupying Audrey was evident in her first session with me. Initially she pointed a gun at me. I asked her what happens when you shoot a gun and she said, "They die." When asked what happens then, she said, "You get a hole in your stomach," and "the police come." I asked if she knew anyone who had died. She responded, "My mommy," and told me that she felt sad. I asked some direct questions about her birth mother, but she did not seem to know how to respond. She referred to the present, clearly echoing what she had been told, that "I have a mommy now," that her other mommy was happy in Heaven, and that her "mommy now" would be sad if she (Audrey) died. At one point, I asked if she remembered how her mother had died. She didn't respond verbally but, with a dramatic shift in mood, appeared to reenact it. She jumped on an inflatable bop bag, knocked it over, and thrashed wildly back and forth on top of it in a manner similar to the repetitive play her mother had described at home. Her speech became pressured and impossible to understand.

Later in the session, after she had calmed down, I recreated a play situation reminiscent of the trauma scene, setting up dining room furniture with two female figures and a baby figure. Like Tommy and Beth had, Audrey immediately became engaged. She initially played out an affectionate scenario between the baby and one of the female figures involving cuddling and pushing the baby figure in a carriage. Suddenly, as she was holding the baby figure, she brought her hand across the scene, violently knocking over the furniture and the female doll figures. The implications of this explosive gesture left her adoptive mother in tears. When I asked what had happened and directed attention to the female figures lying on the floor, she held the baby doll within several inches of the mother figure and kept it there for several moments. She then put the baby in a bed.

Shortly after this, Audrey transferred the theme of injury into the present, showing me a scratch on her elbow and telling me she had hurt herself. A few minutes later, I returned to the play scene and, following her earlier comment that "the police come," introduced a policeman and police car. She immediately took the policeman out of the car, placed his head over the chest of the mother figure, and then stood the policeman upright alongside the "mother." Shortly thereafter, while holding the police car and policeman in her hand, she abruptly knocked down all of the remaining pieces of furniture in a repetition of the earlier explosive gesture.

After she left the session, Audrey told her adoptive mother "that doctor hurt me so bad," and described having pain in her chest, a headache, and a stomachache. Nonetheless, two days after the session, she told her mother that she wanted to come back to see "the doctor where she played with the toys to make [her] feel better." Her mother believed that the play had been relieving to her, in that for the next two days she had been noticeably calmer and better behaved.

During our second session Audrey was visibly sad. She hid behind her mother and did not want to talk or return to the play from the previous session. She did make a connection between the last session's reenactment play and her own experience, referring to the mother doll she had focused on in the previous session as "Mommy." Only as the session was about to end did she approach the furniture. She knocked over the tables and chairs with the same backhanded motion, and then placed the two female dolls in beds in a very nurturant way. As she was leaving she again sent the beds and the female figures flying.

Because the family lived some distance from Denver, I was not able to follow Audrey in therapy but was able to carry out follow-up interviews with Audrey and her mother fifteen months after my original evaluation, when Audrey had just turned six.

In the interim Audrey had had a two-week intensive therapeutic experience, during which she was for the first time officially informed about the exact nature of her mother's death. As she was told that her mother's former boyfriend had made a bomb and it "went boom," Audrey took her hand and pushed it sharply off her forehead (a gesture her adoptive mother had described in our initial interviews) and said that her mom didn't have any hair, or any hands, or any arms, or any legs. The possibility that there had been a loss of limbs was new information to her adoptive mother, who then called the police department where the bombing had taken place. The police confirmed Audrey's description.

The intensive therapy appeared to have been helpful. Audrey had been able to grieve more freely, contributing to a closer relationship with her adoptive mother and a significant reduction in separation anxiety and behavioral difficulties. Specific posttraumatic symptoms were few. There were still intermittent nightmares and occasional frightened reactions to stimuli having associations to the trauma, such as a recent panic reaction to a strong wind, felt by her adoptive mother to be related to the vestibular sensations. She also showed evidence of continued preoccupation with the explosion. At her fifth birthday party, Audrey had received a new playhouse. Her mother showed me photographs from the party, including the one showing how Audrey had knocked over the furniture in the dining room/kitchen area, with two female doll figures lying nearby.

Her adoptive mother's primary concern was the lack of integration of the "two Audreys," the Audrey who was happy and loving and the Audrey who was intermittently angry and wild. This split identity was one that her caregivers likely contributed to, in that, as noted above, it reflected their conceptions of the marked variations in her behavior. With her transition into early latency, one could see this conflict becoming internalized. Audrey herself would speak about "other Audreys" who were bad, and on one occasion told her adoptive mother that "Audrey" had died when her mother died. Her adoptive mother described overhearing Audrey talking to herself about doing bad things such as killing baby ducks and then countering this by saying that she would be good and not be like the ex-boyfriend. Her mother had not seen any recent sadism toward animals, yet destructive impulses seemed still a matter of intense internal conflict. The knowledge that her mother was killed by an ex-boyfriend was creating conflict in her feelings about her father, particularly since she had had the fantasy that the ex-boyfriend had been her real father.

In my interview with Audrey, she brought me pictures she had recently drawn of the "bomb"—splotches of color on paper of the sort previously described. She explained that one of the pictures, indistinguishable to me from the others, was a picture of herself being naughty, suggesting a connection in her mind between the violent images of the trauma and her self-image of being a bad girl. Over the next fifteen minutes, as we talked about her current life, she spontaneously described three recent events (her dog having surgery, a toy house she had built with a friend which had come crashing down, and a missile which went "pop") which appeared to have unconscious links to her trauma.

During the session, Audrey completely avoided the play scene we had used the previous year and spent most of the time standing by her adoptive mother taking toys in and out of a box. I asked her directly about her memories of her mother's death, and at that point she repeated the violent gesture of the previous year, knocking over a play swingset she had been playing with. Over the next few minutes a number of things were knocked over. She did not describe any specific memories but was able to verbalize feelings in response to questions about her birth mother. She said she thought a great deal about her mother, especially at night, and that it made her sad. She said she also thought about her mother's ex-boyfriend and that she was both scared and very mad at him. Her play became more aggressive as she began shooting a dartgun at a doll figure she used to represent the boyfriend. The anger quickly spilled over as she brought in several other doll figures, including "the moms and babies," and proceeded to shoot them all.

In summary, although Audrey had made great strides, there appeared to be a number of unresolved issues interfering with her development. Feelings relating to the gruesome circumstances of the explosion appeared to be contributing to a dissociation in her sense of self, between the self preoccupied with violent images and the self that felt loved and loving. Unless this split could be healed, she appeared to be at some future risk for the dissociated acting out of destructive impulses toward herself or others. In addition, feelings of fear and anger toward her mother's ex-boyfriend were interfering with her relationship with her father and the resolution of a number of Oedipal issues.

This is the case of an eight-year-old boy who at seven months of age experienced a week-long traumatic experience of physical and sexual abuse perpetrated by his birth father and who appeared to manifest a frightening reliving of his traumatic experience in a therapeutic session at age eight. His mother consulted me soon after this very disturbing session because of concerns about whether her child's behavior and verbalizations could legitimately be attributed to his early traumas, since "we were told that preverbal abuse can't be talked about." She said that Robert's birth father had not been discussed in the home because they had not wanted him to have a negative image of his birth parent. Nine months later I provided a medication consult. The material presented here reflects a compilation of information provided to me by the parents and his therapist.

At the time his mother consulted me, Robert had been in therapy for approximately a year because of severe mood swings and behavioral problems, including difficulties with attention, occasional defiance, episodes of agitation and uncontrollable crying which could last up to an hour, persisting intense separation anxiety, and sleep difficulties with frequent nightmares. Repetitive genital touching had also been noted. His primary play interests were dollhouses and Barbie dolls, and he frequently expressed the wish to be a girl.

Robert originally had come to live with his adoptive parents as a foster child at seven months of age. His birth mother was alcoholic and neglectful, and his birth father was both physically and sexually abusive. Little is known of his first months of life. When he was four months old, because of a conviction for sexual molestation of a minor, his father was ordered not to have contact with the family, and the mother entered a residential facility for single parents. When Robert was seven months old, his birth mother left him and his two siblings, aged two and three years, with his birth father for a week. There was strong evidence that the father physically and sexually abused all of the children during this time, with absolute physical evidence of anal penetration involving his two siblings and presumptive physical evidence that Robert too had been victimized.

When his adoptive parents received him immediately after the week with his father, he was "catatonic," didn't want to be touched, and preferred to be left in the dark. His mother and an older sister held him almost constantly over the next several weeks before he began to accept physical affection and showed his first smile. Overall, he slept excessively, but would also awaken at night crying and would panic when his adoptive mother entered his bedroom until he recognized her. He was terrified of men and would not let his adoptive father or older brothers comfort him. When the pediatrician tried to undress him at his first checkup, he cried and struggled to get away "as if he was possessed." After placement, there was no further contact with his birth father. He did have weekly visits with his birth mother for the next eighteen months, supervised by a woman named Barbara. He clung desperately to Barbara during the visits.

In his therapy, much as had happened with Tommy, themes related to the early traumas seemed to build, in this case to the point of an intense emotional breakthrough. From the beginning Robert was preoccupied with frightening imagery. He described nightmares of being chased by skeletons, of "flying beds," of being on top of a mountain that was shaking, and of ghosts and skeletons "rising." Fantasy play involved repetitive themes of parent loss and gruesome assaults with gory details. He used a variety of defensive efforts to ensure safety and survival, both in play scenarios and in direct interactions with the therapist, such as through compulsive organizing of the office furniture and the creation of forts and safe havens. The therapist was very respectful of Robert's needs to maintain his sense of safety and to go at his own pace.

In the several months prior to his frightening therapeutic session, Robert began to talk about his fears more directly. There were two episodes after being with babysitters when his mother found him cowering and crying in bed because of frightening daydreams that something bad had happened to him. During one of the episodes, as he was crying he said, "Don't let him hurt me again." In his therapy, he had been able to talk about memories of earlier fears, including fears of dying and vague but scary memories of visits to his birth mother's house. Several weeks prior to the disturbing session he told the therapist he had had a memory of his birth father hurting him, though he did not say what the memory was. In the session immediately prior, during a play scenario, Robert for the first time allowed the direct expression of anger toward a criminal.

On the day of his dramatic session, Robert came to the office in an angry mood because he felt he had been unjustly accused by a teacher. By coincidence, in the waiting room was a mother with a five-month-old infant. When the therapist came for him, Robert was sitting on the floor approximately two feet away from the infant, staring intensely. In the session, Robert refused to talk, played in an area away from the therapist, and then ran out of the office to his mother. When he and his mother returned, the therapist asked if anything had made him frightened. Robert replied that he had had a scary memory about his father hurting him, like the one he had described to the therapist several weeks earlier. Suddenly, he appeared to lose touch with the present reality. He became agitated, clung to his mother, and screamed, "You're hurting me! Why do you want to kill me!" He threw himself on the floor, sobbing hysterically. Over the next half-hour or so, he remained in what appeared to be an extreme state of dissociation. He tried desperately to crawl under the couch. At one point, as he was screaming such things as "Stop! I hurt all over! My bottom is red!" he was on his hands and knees with his rear end in the air, moving it in a very sexualized manner that communicated both an impression of anal intercourse and a chaotic sense that he did not know what to do with his body. At another point, suddenly flopping down as if his legs had been pulled out from under him and writhing on the floor, he screamed, "Don't let him hurt me! Please don't do that to me! I'm just a baby!"

The therapist and mother attempted to calm and reassure him, but he did not seem to recognize his mother and cried, "I don't know you! When the big lady comes, they don't hurt me!" His mother asked if he meant Barbara. He said, "That's right!" and immediately crawled into his mother's lap, clung to her, and sobbed, "Barbara, don't let them hurt me!" During the next few minutes he crawled around his mother like a baby and eventually lay at her feet. He was finally able to calm down, the session having lasted close to two hours. On the way home, he acted as if nothing had happened, although his mother said she felt like she "had been hit with a Mack truck." When the therapist called Robert several hours later, he seemed to have no memory of the session.

Nine months after my initial contact, in conjunction with a medication consultation, I was able to review Robert's progress. In the immediate aftermath of the frightening session, Robert had conveyed a sense that he remembered at least parts of the session but that it was too difficult to talk about. His mother believed that the session had deeply affected him. There had been an exacerbation in symptoms, including difficulties going to sleep because of fears of someone breaking into the house, difficulties concentrating at school, increased "girl play," and intensified compulsive behavior involving the need to organize his belongings in rigid ways. In the months following the traumatic session, Robert also had two more dissociative episodes at home of terrified screaming and loss of recognition of his mother. During one of these episodes, he screamed, "I'm getting shots in my bottom!" which his mother interpreted as his understanding as an infant of the sexual abuse. Nonetheless, both his parents and his therapist were persuaded that there had been something constructive about the frightening experience, in that during the next sessions he seemed more directly communicative and trustful.

At the time of my medication consultation, Robert was making progress in therapy. Symptoms had improved, although they continued to fluctuate in intensity. His play had begun to shift away from themes of danger and destruction. In doll play, he had begun to express sexual curiosity and also to carry out nurturant parental activities. He also was becoming more comfortable with age-appropriate board games involving direct competition with the therapist and showed signs of an increased positive male identification, such as playing with soldiers. Concomitantly he was showing more direct physical affection toward his father at home. Despite these very positive developments, maintaining the therapeutic alliance and a sense of safety continued to be difficult. He remained fearful of men outside the family. The recent presence of a repairman in the house had caused him to hide in terror. His mother believed that Robert's fear was related to a close physical resemblance in size, hairstyle, and facial features between the workman and his birth father. While terrifying feelings about his birth father clearly persisted, his continued intense wishes to avoid discussion made it difficult to know the exact nature of any persisting internal imagery.

CASE 5: STEPHANIE

This case involves a child who broke her leg at fifteen months. Eleven months later a minor fall appeared to stimulate the reexperiencing of memories and feelings about the previous injury and associated treatments. Occurring at the time of developing genital awareness, this reexperiencing appeared to complicate her understanding of gender differences. I did not see this child personally but reviewed her extensive medical records as part of a legal process.

At age fifteen months, under unknown circumstances, Stephanie suffered a spiral fracture of the femur at a babysitter's house. The babysitter denied knowing how the injury had occurred. The fracture required a very painful, ten-day hospitalization in traction followed by a six-week immobilization at home in a full-body cast. The recovery period was characterized by repeated painful manipulations, muscle spasms requiring analgesic injections, and numerous sores over friction areas.

Symptoms documented in the records included disrupted sleep with frequent distress awakenings, fear of sleeping in her crib (where presumably the injury had occurred), panic at having her leg touched, and intense fear of male strangers, particularly during visits to the doctor's office (the doctors and physical therapists manipulating her leg had all been male). She also exhibited separation distress, startle distress reactions to loud noises and sudden movements, avoidance of physical positions which had been associated with pain, and emotional detachment punctuated with frequent temper outbursts. Over the next ten months her symptoms abated, although she consistently showed a resurgence of sleep difficulties immediately following checkup visits with her orthopedist.

Most compelling from a memory standpoint was Stephanie's reaction to a mild fall from a low stool eleven months after her original injury. Although unhurt, she immediately grabbed her leg, screaming, "My leg, my leg!" Her parents had commented that the fall must have jarred her memory, because for the first time she began to talk about being in the hospital and getting shots. There was a marked resurgence in her symptoms, including nightmares, fear of men, and repetitive play involving breaking the legs of all her dolls. She began walking around the house with her leg stiff, as she had walked right after the injury. These behaviors and the verbalization of her memories continued over the next several months and, interestingly, were accompanied by a significant improvement in her spontaneity and capacity for pleasure.

Stephanie entered therapy four months after her injury because of her posttraumatic symptoms and the stress they were placing on her parents. Unfortunately, her medical treatments were never discussed in the therapy. During the initial work-up, her very anxious parents were concerned about possible sexual abuse because of occasional touching of her vaginal area during diaper changes, and so the therapist had introduced anatomically correct dolls. Stephanie initially showed very little interest in the anatomical dolls. Six months later, at twenty-five months of age, after the birth of a baby sister and in the midst of her own toilet training, in her play Stephanie began to show age-expectable interest in issues of gender identity and genital awareness (Roiphe, 1968; Galenson and Roiphe 1971; Fagot and Leinbach, 1985). Her play at this time had what appeared to be a developmentally appropriate exploratory quality, such as undressing the anatomically correct dolls and examining the genitalia (particularly of the male doll) and play involving baths, bedtime, diaper changes, and going to the toilet (with the male dolls sitting on the toilet as the female dolls did).

After the fall from the stool at twenty-seven months, therapeutic notes documented a dramatic change in the character of her exploratory sexual play. Beginning with the first therapy session following her injury, in each of the next nine sessions she compulsively carried out a play sequence which involved tearing the leg off a doll, followed by undressing and aggressively grabbing the penis of the male doll. While sexual exploratory play continued, in contrast to the quiet curiosity which accompanied the earlier exploratory play, at this time it was accompanied by a great deal of anxiety. It was my interpretation that the heightened anxious preoccupation with her previously injured leg stimulated by her recent minor fall, combined with her developmentally prompted awareness of her lack of a penis, had caused her to conclude that she had lost her [male] genitalia as a result of her injury and treatments.

DISCUSSION

While each of the five cases has its unique aspects, I believe there is enough commonality to support tentative conclusions about the symptomatology, degree of memory, and enduring developmental effects of traumatic experiences occurring in the preverbal period.

The case material extends our understanding of the symptomatic effects of trauma in infancy. Not only do toddlers who have reached verbal fluency exhibit posttraumatic symptomatology similar in nature to that manifested by older children and adults (Drell et al., 1993; Scheeringa et al., in press), but it appears that such symptomatology can be observed in infants who have not achieved a level of language beyond isolated words. In the current diagnostic nomenclature, three major categories of response have been delineated for the diagnosis of posttraumatic stress disorder in children: (1) persistent reexperiencing of the trauma through intrusive recollections, nightmares, reenactment behavior, and/or emotional reliving when exposed to stimuli reminiscent of the trauma; (2) persistent avoidance of stimuli associated with the trauma and numbing of general responsiveness, manifested by a restricted range of affect, social withdrawal, and loss of interest in usual activities; and (3) persistent symptoms of increased arousal manifested by startle reactions, irritability, and sleep difficulties (DSM-IV, 1994). In the posttrauma period the infants showed multiple symptoms from every one of these categories. As would be expected from clinical experience with older children, the severity of the immediate posttraumatic reactions was correlated with the severity of the trauma: Tommy's symptoms were minor in comparison with Audrey's and Robert's quite severe reactions (Bloch et al., 1956; Pynoos et al., 1987).

The children not only demonstrated posttraumatic symptoms with a high degree of specificity but also showed evidence of retention of central elements of their traumatic experience over extended periods of time, as manifested in their various reenactments and associated communications. Such observations, if replicated, have important implications for our understanding of the nature of memory capacity in the preverbal period. The case examples support Terr's observations that memories of trauma are "burned in" to the brain in powerful ways. While visual memory appeared to be pivotal, as Terr has hypothesized, the children's symptoms and manner of communication suggested that the memories were not simply visual or photographic images of a fragment of the experience. Rather, within the bounds of the children's capacities to perceive, the representations appeared to involve multiple sensory modalities (visual, auditory, tactile, kinesthetic, and vestibular), a sense of temporal sequence, and compelling affective meaning.

The manner in which the memories were expressed would for the most part fit into the category of implicit or procedural memory, memories which are encoded automatically and expressed through images, behaviors, or emotions without conscious awareness. At the same time, the memory capacities exhibited did not appear to be completely encompassed within the boundaries of implicit memory but had characteristics associated with explicit, or declarative, memory as well. As noted, definitions of autobiographical memory have been limited by the emphasis on verbal communication. If autobiographical memory is defined as the capacity to describe personal events from the past, the purposeful way in which the children engaged in the play reenactments conveyed the strong impression that they were communicating what they felt had happened to them personally. In addition, in the children's communications, there did not appear to be an absolute disjuncture between nonverbal and verbal modes. As words became available, each of the children was able to superimpose verbal description on the nonverbal representations in ways which facilitated understanding and communication of the experience: Tommy in his exclamations of "Bad medicine" and "Daddy!" and his later description of "barfing," Beth in her warnings about trucks and reference to the car in the river, Audrey in various descriptions of her memories and intrusive images, and Stephanie in her ability to talk about the hospital and shots. Perhaps the most dramatic instance of verbal superimposition on nonverbal experience was the case of Robert, who, strikingly, appeared to have integrated verbalizations into the traumatic experience itself. The overlapping of features characteristic of both implicit and explicit memory would suggest that, developmentally at least, these two systems are not completely separate (Mandler, 1990).

Given current debate about the validity of early memories of trauma and the role of therapists in influencing the patient's memories, the manner in which these early memories were elicited is of great importance. I have tried to provide sufficient detail to allow readers to develop their own opinions regarding the context in which these memories emerged and the degree to which they were influenced by me or others. Children are able to convey their knowledge more effectively if they are allowed to communicate in both verbal and nonverbal ways (Mandler, 1990), and if cues are provided (Fivush, 1993). Cues may be purposeful, as in the provision of structured play settings (Levy, 1939), or accidental, as in the case of Robert's seeing an infant in the waiting room prior to his session. Providing appropriate cues is obviously a difficult task, fraught with the potential for leading the child. With the infants I worked with directly I attempted to provide cues, either in words or through structured situations, that created a general context within the bounds of what I knew about the trauma. I then encouraged the child to communicate what he or she knew from there, hopefully without the child feeling pressured. Questions about how actively to structure the therapeutic situation to help patients reexperience a trauma in the service of resolution are complicated and currently the subject of much controversy. I have recently discussed some of these issues as they pertain to therapeutic work with very young traumatized children (Gaensbauer, 1994).

Do traumatic memories operate according to different principles than ordinary memory? The markedly heightened tendency for traumatic memories to be retained has been well documented. The reasons for this are not understood, but may relate to the massive mobilization of stress-responsive neurohormones and neuroregulators occurring at the time of a traumatic event, in turn resulting in an overconsolidation of memory traces in a process termed "superconditioning" (Pitman, 1988, 1989). Based on these cases, it seems tenable to hypothesize that the neural substrates necessary for such "superconditioning" are present by seven to nine months of age. It is also likely that the physical nature of the traumas has contributed to the degree of retention seen in these cases. A most striking example of the permanence with which early experiences involving physical sensations of bodily injury can be encoded was reported to me by a colleague and his wife in an anecdote about their son. After his birth, he had required repeated heel pricks to monitor his bilirubin level to the point where his heels were macerated and raw. At age twenty-three, while talking with his parents about working under deadlines he commented with puzzlement, "Whenever I get really stressed, my heels ache!" At this point in time we do not know if memories for nonphysical trauma or for more ordinary experiences have the potential to be encoded with the same degree of permanence.

The fate of these early memories over time is also an important topic, particularly given current controversies about the reliability of reports of childhood trauma. As psychoanalysts have long understood (Freud, 1899; Kris, 1956), and as Terr (1988) has recently documented, memories of early experiences will undergo a variety of alterations over the course of development. Memories are not fixed in stone, but are reflections of a dynamic process, continuously subject to modification by both internal and external influences (Loftus, 1979). For the purposes of this paper I have emphasized the retention of core sensory and somatically based representations over time. Yet in each of the cases one can easily observe ways in which the children's internal representations have been expanded and modified, sometimes in the direction of increased organization and narrative coherence and sometimes in the direction of distortion and disorganization. Perhaps the most emotionally charged distortion incorporated into a traumatic reenactment was Robert's condensation of the traumatic experiences with his father and the frightening visits with his mother, where he reenacted that the woman Barbara protected him in both instances. One could also see illustrations of how early experiences are reworked at each developmental level and how subsequently gained knowledge can result in new interpretations carrying with them new forms of anxiety. Examples would be Stephanie's reinterpretation of the nature of her trauma in light of her new understanding about genital differences, and Audrey's increased anxiety during her Oedipal phase as she came to understand the nature of the relationship between her birth mother and the ex-boyfriend and developed the fantasy that the ex-boyfriend was her father.

It was my impression that the reenactments and verbalizations of the younger children had more direct connections in affect and content to the original experiences. As the children became older, their advanced cognitive development and increased defensiveness, and the influence of what they had been told made it difficult to know the extent to which they remained in touch with the original memories. Given the well-documented finding that most adolescents and adults do not have memories of their childhood prior to the ages of three (Freud, 1899; Pillemer and White, 1989), it is likely that specific memories of these early traumatic events will eventually be lost to conscious awareness, as they were in the case of Tommy by the age of seven.

Regardless of the fate of the actual memories, the traumatic experiences described here appear to have had significant and enduring detrimental effects on the children's development, not just in the form of posttraumatic symptoms, but in the ways they have interfered with the resolution of important developmental issues. These include interference not only in the accomplishment of developmental tasks relevant to the developmental period in which the trauma occurred—such as effects on physiological regulation, the children's basic sense of trust, and the development of their primary attachments—but in subsequent developmental issues as well, such as separation-individuation, the development of a sense of autonomy, and the regulation of aggression (Gaensbauer, 1994). Children who have experienced significant early physical traumas may be particularly vulnerable to disturbances in the areas of gender identity, the sense of bodily integrity, and Oedipal-phase development, as illustrated by the cases of Audrey, Robert, and Stephanie (Bloch, 1978; Coates, 1985; Meyer and Dupkin, 1985).

I believe the observations provide examples of the multiple ways in which preverbal traumas might "enter into the determination of evolving structure and function" (Meissner, 1989) in detrimental ways. In contrast to the presumption that such experiences are prerepresentational and "antedating the advent of conscious awareness," the observations suggest that memories in the preverbal period are neither prerepresentational in any absolute sense nor unavailable to conscious awareness. The children appeared not only able to develop internal representations of their traumas, but seemed capable of transforming and expressing these representations in symbolic terms. The dreams, play enactments, drawings, and thematic preoccupations of the children for whom follow-up material was available gave evidence of carryover of specific aspects of their traumas into metaphorical and symbolic forms. Evidence of such carry-over provides confirmatory data in regard to the multiple ways in which infantile experiences may be manifested at older ages, as documented in the psychoanalytic literature referenced earlier. At every age, traumatic memories and their associated affects can become powerful organizing elements within the psyche, coloring every aspect of a person's psychological functioning (Phillips, 1992). The more we can understand about the degree of representational organization available during the first eighteen months of life, the better we will understand the mechanisms by which long-term effects of early trauma may be produced.

In summary, the cases presented here suggest that capacities for the registration of meaningful internal representations of trauma and enduring trauma-specific symptomatology are present as early as the second half of the first year of life and do not depend on the achievement of language fluency. The developmental implications of early trauma, particularly if severe, appear to be profound. It is my hope that the clinical material will heighten awareness of the potential impacts of trauma in the preverbal period, perhaps contributing to a shift of focus back in the direction of Freud's early interests.

BIBLIOGRAPHY

AMERICAN PSYCHIATRIC ASSOCIATION. (1994). *DSM-IV.*

ANTHI, P. R. (1983). Reconstruction of preverbal experiences. *J. Am. Psychoanal. Assn.,* 31:33–58.

ANTHONY, E. J. (1962). A study of "screen sensations." *Psychoanal. Study Child,* 17:211–45.

BERNSTEIN, A. E. H., & BLACHER, R. S. (1967). The recovery of a memory from three months of age. *Psychoanal. Study Child,* 22:156–67.

BLOCH, D. (1978). Four children who insisted they belonged to the opposite sex. In *"So the Witch Won't Eat Me": Fantasy and the Child's Fear of Infanticide,* pp. 50–70. Boston: Houghton Mifflin.

BLOCH, D. A., SILBER, R., & PERRY, S. E. (1956). Some factors in the emotional reactions of children to disaster. *Am. J. Psychiat.,* 113:416–22.

BLUM, H. P. (1989). The value, use, and abuse of infant developmental research. In Dowling and Rothstein, 1989, 157–74.

CLYMAN, R. B. (1991). The procedural organization of emotions: A contribution from cognitive science to the psychoanalytic theory of therapeutic action. In *Affect: Psychoanalytic Perspectives,* ed. T. Shapiro & R. N. Emde, pp. 359–83. *Amer. Psychoanal. Assn.,* 39 (Supplement).

COATES, S. (1985). Extreme boyhood femininity: Overview and new research findings. In *Sexuality: New Perspectives,* ed. Z. Defries, R. Friedman, & R. Corn, pp. 101–24. Westport, Conn.: Greenwood.

COHEN, N. J. (1984). Preserved learning capacity in amnesia: Evidence for multiple memory systems. In *Neuropsychology of Memory,* ed. L. R. Squire & N. Butters, pp. 83–103. New York: Guilford.

DAEHLER, M. W., &GRECO, C. (1985). Memory in very young children. In *Cognitive Learning and Memory in Children,* ed. M. Pressley & C. J. Brainerd, pp. 49–79. New York: Springer-Verlag.

DEUTSCH, F. (1947). Analysis of postural behavior. *Psychoanal. Q.,* 16:195–243.

DOWLING, S. (1982). Dreams and dreaming in relation to trauma in childhood. *Int. J. Psychoanal.,* 63:157–66.

——— (1990). Fantasy formation: A child analyst's perspective. *J. Am. Psychoanal. Assn.,* 38:93–111.

DOWLING, S., & ROTHSTEIN, A., EDS. (1989). *The Significance of Infant Observational Research for Clinical Work with Children, Adolescents, and Adults.* Workshop Series of the American Psychoanalytic Association: Monograph 5. Madison, Conn.: Int. Univ. Press.

DRELL, M. J., SIEGEL, C. H., & GAENSBAUER, T. J. (1993). Post-traumatic stress disorder. In *Handbook of Infant Mental Health*, ed. C. H. Zeanah, pp. 291–304. New York: Guilford.

EMDE, R. N. (1981). Changing models of infancy and the nature of early development: Remodeling the foundations. *J. Am. Psychoanal. Assn.*, 29:179–219.

—— (1983). The prerepresentational self and its affective core. *Psychoanal. Study Child*, 38:165–92.

FAGOT, B. I., & LEINBACH, B. (1985). Gender identity: Some thoughts on an old concept. *J. Am. Acad. Child Psychiat.*, 24:684–88.

FIVUSH, R. (1993). Developmental perspectives on autobiographical recall. In *Child Victims, Child Witnesses: Understanding and Improving Testimony*, ed. G. S. Goodman & B. L. Bottoms, pp. 1–24. New York: Guilford.

FREUD, S. (1899). Screen memories. *S. E.*, 3:303–22.

—— (1918). From the history of an infantile neurosis. *S. E.*, 17:7–122.

GAENSBAUER, T. J. (1994). Therapeutic work with a traumatized toddler. *Psychoanal. Study Child*, 49:412–33.

GAENSBAUER, T. J., CHATOOR, I., DRELL, M. J., SIEGEL, D. J., & ZEANAH, C. H. (In press). Traumatic loss in a one-year-old girl. *J. Am. Acad. Child Adolesc. Psychiat.*

GALENSON, E., & ROIPHE, H. (1971). The impact of early sexual discovery on mood, defensive organization, and symbolization. *Psychoanal. Study Child*, 26:195–216.

ISAKOWER, O. (1938). A contribution to the patho-psychology of phenomena associated with falling asleep. *Int. J. Psycho-Anal.*, 19:331–45.

KRIS, E. (1956). The recovery of childhood memories in psychoanalysis. *Psychoanal. Study Child*, 11:54–88.

LEVY, D. (1939). Release therapy. *Am. J. Orthopsychiat.*, 9:713–36.

LEWIN, B. D. (1946). Sleep, the mouth, and the dream screen. *Psychoanal. Q.*, 15:419–34.

LICHTENBERG, J. (1983). *Psychoanalysis and Infant Research*, Hillsdale, N.J.: Analytic.

LOFTUS, E. (1979). *Eyewitness Testimony*. Cambridge, Mass.: Harvard Univ. Press.

MACK, J. E. (1965). Nightmares, conflict, and ego development in childhood. *Int. J. Psycho-Anal.*, 46:403–28.

MANDLER, J. M. (1990). Recall and its verbal expression. In *Knowing and Remembering in Young Children*, ed. R. Fivush & J. A. Hudson, pp. 317–30. New York: Cambridge Univ. Press.

McLAUGHLIN, J. T. (1989). The relevance of infant observational research for the analytic understanding of adult patients' nonverbal behaviors. In Dowling and Rothstein, 1989, pp. 109–22.

MEISSNER, W. W. (1989). The viewpoint of a devil's advocate. In Dowling and Rothstein, pp. 175–94. Madison, Conn.: Int. Univ. Press.

MEYER, J., & DUPKIN, S. (1985). Gender disturbance in children. *Bull. Menninger Clinic*, 49:236–69.

NELSON, K. (1990). Remembering, forgetting, and childhood amnesia. In

Knowing and Remembering in Young Children, ed. R. Fivush & J. A. Hudson, pp. 301–16. New York: Cambridge Univ. Press.

—— (1993). The psychological and social origins of autobiographical memory. *Psychol. Science,* 4:7–14.

NIEDERLAND, W. G. (1965). The ego in the recovery of early memories. *Psychoanal. Q.,* 34:564–71.

PERRIS, E. E., MYERS, N. A., & CLIFTON, R. K. (1990). Long-term memory for a single infancy experience. *Child Devel.,* 61:1796–1807.

PHILLIPS, S. H. (1992). Trauma and war: A fragment of an analysis with a vietnam veteran. *Psychoanal. Study Child,* 39:147–80.

PILLEMER, D. B., & WHITE, S. H. (1989). Childhood events recalled by children and adults. In *Advances in Child Development and Behavior,* ed. H. W. Reese, vol. 22, pp. 297–340. New York: Academic.

PITMAN, R. (1988). Post-traumatic stress disorder, conditioning, and network theory. *Psychiat. Ann.,* 18:182–89.

—— (1989). Post-traumatic stress disorder, hormones, and memory. *Biol. Psychiat.,* 26:221–23.

PULVER, S. (1987). The manifest dream in psychoanalysis: A clarification. *J. Am. Psychoanal. Assn.,* 35:99–118.

PYNOOS, R. S., FREDERICK, C., NADER, K. ET AL. (1987). Life threat and post-traumatic stress in school age children. *Arch. Gen. Psychiat.,* 44:1057–63.

ROIPHE, H. (1968). On an early genital phase. *Psychoanal. Study Child,* 23:348–65.

ROVEE-COLLIER, C., & HAYNE, H. (1987). Reactivation of Infant Memory: Implications for Cognitive Development. In *Advances in Child Development and Behavior,* ed. H. Reese, pp. 185–238. New York: Academic.

RYCROFT, C. (1951). A contribution to the study of the dream screen. *Int. J. Psycho-Anal.,* 32:178–84.

SCHACTER, D. L. (1987). Implicit memory: History and current status. *J. Exper. Psychol.: Learning, Memory, and Cognition,* 13:501–18.

SCHEERINGA, M. S., ZEANAH, C. H., DRELL, M. J., & LARRIEU, J. A. (In press). Two approaches to the diagnosis of post-traumatic stress disorder in infancy and early childhood. *J. Am. Acad. Child Adolesc. Psychiat.*

SIEGEL, D. J. (In press). Cognition and perception. In *Comprehensive Textbook of Psychiatry,* 6th ed., ed. B. Kaplan & W. Sadock. New York: Williams and Wilkins.

SPITZ, R. A. (1955). The primal cavity. *Psychoanal. Study Child,* 10:215–40.

SQUIRE, L. R. (1987). *Memory and Brain.* New York: Oxford Univ. Press.

STERN, D. (1985). *The Interpersonal World of the Infant: A View from Psychoanalysis and Developmental Psychology.* New York: Basic.

SUGAR, M. (1992). Toddlers' traumatic memories. *Infant Mental Health J.,* 13:245–51.

TERR, L. (1988). What happens to early memories of trauma: A study of twenty children under age five at the time of documented traumatic events. *J. Am. Acad. Child Adolesc. Psychiat.,* 27:96–104.

The Role of Free Movement in Separation-Individuation

A Study of Paralysis

PINI RABENU
TAMAR G. RABENU

This paper reevaluates the role of free movement in the separation-individuation process through the special case of its absence. We put forward some ideas, formulated gradually during the psychoanalytically oriented psychotherapy of a paralyzed adult suffering from a narcissistic personality disorder. By analyzing the transference and countertransference in this case, we realized that the patient's inability to regulate his distance from his mother by free movement impelled him to use an alternative mode of regulating his object loss and re-engulfment anxieties. We elaborate on two alternative mechanisms to cope with these anxieties: the motoric mode of approaching-distancing, and the mode of idealization-devaluation, inflating and deflating the inner significance of the object. We discuss the implications of these modes for the stability of self and object experiences, their different use of the Doing and Being experiential modalities, and their relation to pathological narcissism.

IT IS INTERESTING THAT WE HUMANS PUT SUCH GREAT EMPHASIS ON THE acquisition of the upright position and of free bipedal locomotion within human phylogenetic as well as ontogenetic development. The erect position is considered one of the most important characteris-

Pini Rabenu, formerly a neurobiolgist, is now working in Jerusalem in the field of psychoanalytic theoretization. Tamar G. Rabenu is a clinical psychologist and practicing and supervising psychotherapist at the Eitanim Mental Health Center and in private practice in Jerusalem.

The Psychoanalytic Study of the Child 50, ed. Albert J. Solnit, Peter B. Neubauer, Samuel Abrams, and A. Scott Dowling (Yale University Press, copyright © 1995 by Albert J. Solnit, Peter B. Neubauer, Samuel Abrams, and A. Scott Dowling).

tics distinguishing humans from other primates. The child's ability to stand and walk is experienced proudly by the parents and the child himself as a truly significant step toward his achievement of independence. These basic attitudes reflect the great symbolic value of this special form of mobility.

We would like to present some ideas concerning the regulatory role of free movement in self and object experience during the separation-individuation process. These ideas arose and were formulated during the psychoanalytically oriented psychotherapy of an adult patient who was paralyzed from the early age of eight months.

One can trace the importance of the motoric system to mental functioning to the fact that from the beginning of life, every muscle activity carries both an outward-directed function and an inward-directed function, the former by deflecting drive discharge toward the outside and the latter by eliciting centripetal proprioceptive sensations directed toward the inside. These two simultaneous functions shape the self experience, on the one hand, by avoiding the traumatic accumulation of drive energy and so stabilizing the self and, on the other hand, by providing direct stimulation on it, feeding and maintaining the self experience. From the start, these afferent-efferent aspects of the motor system are quickly mobilized by the ego to stabilize and maintain the self structure. The ego uses this double function to protect the self from being flooded by drive energy but also from being depleted of psychic energy. These two functions of the motor system are integrated during development with growing levels of complexity in highly coordinated self-induced behavioral activity, allowing more compound, adaptive, differentiated modes of drive discharge and experience.

The child begins to manifest these functions through his early affecto-motoric activity and continues to employ them in his behavioral interactions with the primary object and later with the extended world of objects. The dual role of the motor system in regulating and nurturing the self is maintained throughout life. Loss of the ability to move freely, whether due to illness, trauma, or confinement, threatens to shake the person's sense of vitality and self-esteem (Bernal, 1984).

The contribution of the motoric system to the process of identity formation has received increasing attention as psychoanalytic data on the early stages of development have been accumulating. Several authors refer to the importance of the erect position and of free upright locomotion for mental development (see Loewenstein, 1950; Greenacre, 1957). Yet it is not until the comprehensive work of Mahler and her colleagues on the separation-individuation process that they received their proper emphasis and documentation. Mahler frequently states that the significance of ego-directed locomotion for the separation-individuation process can hardly be overestimated. She notes that acquisition of the ability to move freely greatly enhances the child's sense of separateness and gives the self-object discrimination process considerable momentum, accelerating the ongoing separation-individuation process (Mahler et al., 1975; Mahler et al., 1982).

Mahler draws our attention to the invaluable contribution of free movement—first in the form of crawling, later walking—to three areas of development within the intricate process of self-object differentiation. She mentions its contribution to the body-self consolidation process, to the libidinal and aggressive investment in the autonomous ego functions, and to object relations:

Body-self consolidation. In the practicing subphase, the child starts to move by his own will. He propels himself in space and learns that his legs and arms are his own and that he can coordinate them into action. Encounters with inanimate objects in the environment help him to firm up and delineate his body-self boundaries. His frequent falls and knocks seem to augment his feeling of body-self boundaries. The child's free movement helps him to integrate his body image in conjunction with the vestibular and kinesthetic sensations elicited by his movements (Mahler et al. 1975). The repetitive voluntary movement of the child's body facilitates the process of body-part integration by the synthetic function of the ego (Lofgren, 1968; Mahler, 1968).

For the boy the upright position enables him to view his penis from more angles and positions. This facilitates the visual sensorimotor exploration of the penis in an effort to compensate for its not being subjected to ego mastery (Lofgren, 1968). During the rapprochement subphase the child's active movement helps him to protect his body against being handled as a passive object by the mother, affirming his possession of his own body (Mahler et al. 1975).

Investment in autonomous ego functions. The child's pleasurable exploration of the environment, made possible by the maturation of his locomotor apparatus, promotes a substantial shift in libidinal cathexis into the rapidly growing, autonomous ego functions. Free movement, especially walking, gives the toddler an enormous increase in reality discovery and testing of the world at his own control and magic mastery. It confronts the child with wider segments of reality and encourages him to exchange some of his magic omnipotence for pleasure in his own autonomy and developing self-esteem (Mahler et al., 1975).

Object relations. The widening of the child's interactional experiences gained by his free movement away from the mother expands the child's world of objects. The displacement of some interest from the mother to the environment, in ever-widening circles, serves a process of "spilling over" of his primary object onto the child's widened world of inanimate and animate objects. In this process the child adopts a whole new array of modes of aggressive and libidinal discharges, which are internalized as interactional patterns in his object relations.

The child's developing sense of self and object confronts him with the need to regulate and maintain the continuity and cohesiveness of these emerging structures. The child's self, which is motivated by the need to separate itself from the object but is still very dependent on the presence and availability of the actual primary object, is continuously threatened by either object loss or re-engulfment. The child's effort to maintain the optimal distance from the primary object, necessary for his individuation, may also serve to defend his self experience from these dangers. The child mobilizes his increasing motor skills and his growing capability to approach and distance his mother to cope with his object loss and re-engulfment anxieties. For example, in the practicing subphase, this regulatory function is achieved first by crawling and later by walking. The child's distancing from and short returns to his mother for what Mahler termed "emotional refueling" and the active peek-a-boo game, or the game of running and being swooped up by the mother, help him to master his fears by losing and regaining the need-gratifying object. As Mahler (Mahler et al., 1975) suggests: "We need not assume that such behavior is intended to serve these functions when it first emerges, but only that it produces these effects and can then be intentionally repeated" (p. 71).

These developmental roles of ego-directed motility begin to take effect in an impressive fashion in the practicing subphase. But we may assume that free movement keeps carrying these basic functions on some level, along with others, through the typical approaching and distancing behaviors of the rapprochement. It seems that motility plays a role throughout life in the constant readjustment of the self experience.

It is clear from what we have presented so far that the emergence of the child's "not me" experience and that of being separated from his mother is a genuine turning point in his progress toward a distinct consolidated identity. The development of the child's "not me" experience is greatly dependent on the quality of his relations with the primary object, on the father's functioning as a disidentifying agent (Abelin, 1971, 1972; Greenson, 1968), and on the child's growing cognitive, perceptive, and motor skills. Among the many areas involved in identity formation, we focus here on one aspect of the motor system's function in this process: the underlying mechanisms by which free movement, through its role in regulating the optimal distance between the child and his primary object, advances the process of separation-individuation and affects the child's self and object experiences.

An opportunity to penetrate the deeper layers of the child's psyche and gain some insight into the role of free movement in the stabilization and maintenance of the child's self-experience and representational world was offered to us by a paralyzed adult patient. This case gave us a unique possibility to unfold the role of free movement in the separation-individuation process through the special case of its unfortunate absence and to follow the implications of the patient's inability to regulate his distance from his mother by movement for the stability of his self and object representations, his sense of boundaries, and his object relations. The restraint inflicted by nature isolated the mobility variable in the second, third, and some of the fourth subphase of the separation-individuation process. However, we should note here that our lack of knowledge as to the traumatic impact of the disease on the child or his parents and the fact that we are dealing with one case only reduce the experimental value of the setting.

As the treatment of this patient progressed, a number of ideas referring to the connection between predominant features of the transference and countertransference and his early inability to move persistently forced themselves upon us. Through the analysis of the fluctuating nature of the patient's transference and the therapist's countertransference, and the synchronization between the two, reaffirmed by the impressive therapeutic impact of interpretations based on this analysis, it became possible to trace a nonmotoric mechanism put into action by the patient to regulate his object loss and re-engulfment anxieties. This provided us with a view of the psychodynamics that the normal child's developing ego tries to cope with and stabilize by the increased recruitment and use of his ascending free movement skills.

The clinical data produced by this case enable us to put forward two general propositions: (1) First under the conditions of an extreme and continuous restraint of free movement, the child's ability to regulate his object loss and re-engulfment fears by approaching and distancing his primary object is substantially impaired. We propose that under these conditions the child's ego compensates for the inability to regulate these fears motorically by fluctuating between idealized and devalued fused self-object inner images. (2) Second, we suggest that one of the main contributions of free movement to the identity-formation process lies in its strong integrative effect on the child's self and object experiences. Free movement, by enabling the child's ego to use approaching and distancing behaviors to defend against object loss and re-engulfment anxieties, protects the child from the need to use the less desirable nonmotoric mechanism, leading to the split of the self and the object into idealized and devalued representations. This stabilizing impact on the object and self experiences promotes the child's formation of object and self constancy and his anaclitic object choice. One may say, therefore, that free movement can serve as a protective shield against the formation of pathological narcissism.

CLINICAL DATA

David, a thirty-one-year-old man, came to me (T.G.R.) seeking therapy because he was worried and frightened by an anxiety attack following a violent argument with a driver who blocked him on the road. During the anxiety attack his feelings oscillated between grandiosity and helplessness.

David had been paralyzed by polio in both legs since the age of eight months. He reports that he did not move freely until the age of three years, when he received his first crutches; until then he moved only in his mother's arms and otherwise lay motionless on the floor.

A bachelor, David lives with his parents. He holds a steady job, but it is entirely unsuitable to his talents and education. He wishes, at the start, to understand the crisis he is experiencing. He also wishes to treat a problem he has in his unstable "relations with the world," as he calls it. David has social ties, but he has not succeeded in maintaining a long-lasting relationship with a woman. However, his main wish, which unfolds during the first few weeks of therapy, is to treat and deal with the unending pain and suffering caused by his incurable physical disability. There is no experience, no human contact, no failure or success that David does not connect with his disability. He feels worthless on account of his paralysis and hopes to be able to separate his physical condition from his self-esteem. He is seeking change. In his own words: "Until now I let my life lead me; now I want to lead my life." (David uses the Hebrew word for "lead," which is derived from the verb "to walk.")

From the beginning David gives me the feeling that I understand him well, as if I am the answer to all his needs, and at the end of the second session, he asks me, painfully: "Tell me, is it possible to become addicted to a therapist?" I am therefore quite surprised when he tells me at the next session: "I have no chemistry with you," at a moment when I feel close, understanding, and sympathetic toward him.

David attends therapy twice a week. After a short period of establishing a therapeutic alliance, the following pattern of work takes place.

He brings up different issues, always colored by rapidly alternating idealization-devaluation attitudes toward me, displaying a narcissistic feature of his personality disorder. At times he admires me and aggrandizes our union, granting it magical powers, for instance: "In the last few days I keep saying your name in order to strengthen myself and then I feel there is hope, and that you and I together are a great force." At other times he despises me; for instance, he looks at me disparagingly and says: "Sometimes I think that all this is too big for you." I interpret the issues brought up together with the transferential attitudes as deriving from a resistance to therapy in terms of contact with the pain, loss, disability; as deriving from envy, oral drives, feelings of entitlement, a wish for a miracle, aggressive drives toward "the woman who has done 'it' to him"; as deriving from wishes for merger and a resistance to change and to individuation, and so on. David reacts to my interpretations with some resistance but always accepts them eventually with admiration and cooperates, bringing more material that helps to restore his memories of painful experiences as a crippled child.

Over a year after the beginning of therapy, the treatment comes to a point of crisis. Although there have been many changes in David—he is more in contact with his pain, his unconscious wishes, his feelings of aggression and entitlement; he has moved into his own apartment, left his job, and begun independent, more creative work—and although he has become more and more attached to me and to his therapy and has increased his visits to three times weekly, the oscillations between idealization and devaluation in his relations with me not only have not subsided but have become more intense and disturbing to him. They increasingly have become the sole issue within the sessions. All my interpretations at this point are futile, not leading to any therapeutic progress. Moreover, the devaluation phases in these rapid oscillations are so severe as to threaten the therapeutic alliance. David experiences me as a phony, an unreliable person, someone he could not trust to treat him. At this point I feel that in order to get the therapy going again I must try to understand the meaning and function of the oscillations in David's experience of me. I realize that there must be a reason for this transferential phenomenon beyond its drive-oriented defensive role, that it might have some regulatory role in his relations with me.

In order to capture the meaning of these fluctuations, I turn to my own countertransference experiences with David from the beginning of the treatment. I could recognize that when he idealized me I would feel in a union with him, very empathic, helpful, and hopeful, and that following devaluation I would feel insignificant, impotent, detached, unattuned to him, and hardly existent for him. I also noticed that idealization consistently appeared following alienation, driving me back to a union with David, and that devaluation always appeared following intimacy, driving me away from him. For example: in a very delicate and sensitive conversation, in which David had shared with me the sensations in his legs, he suddenly had uttered: "You are unprofessional, you are too intrusive" and in that way drove me miles away from him, as if he were kicking me out of a close circle with him. These oscillations could be very frequent, often occuring a few times in a single session, rocking me from a position in which I was very significant for David to one in which I felt that I had hardly any value for him.

I then begin to realize that what I am experiencing may very well be related to the function of the idealization-devaluation fluctuations: that when David is threatened by our union he tends to devaluate me into practical nonexistence, reflecting his current experience of me, and that when he is threatened by our detachment he idealizes me back into union, reflecting the change in his experience of me. I can then imagine these fluctuations as very similar to acts of approaching and distancing. With this new understanding I start to interpret for David his devaluation of me as reflecting a need to get away from me, and his idealization of me as reflecting an urgent need to be close to me.

The consistent use of this new line of interpretation sets David's therapy in motion again, bringing up repressed memories, leading him to new and important insights, and changing his persistent transferential characteristics. The therapy soon concentrates on his difficulties, in the past and in the present, in regulating his object loss and re-engulfment fears and on the defensive strategies he has adopted to cope with them. In this phase David gains, rather painfully, insights as to the relation between his object loss and re-engulfment fears and his paralysis; his sense of separateness and individuality, being developed and constantly fed by the devaluation of others; and the function of idealization-devaluation oscillations in warding off these fears in his relations with me. The progress in therapy is accompanied by a gradual attenuation of the idealization-devaluation features of his transference and by exposure of the underlying object loss and re-engulfment fears. This is followed by David's increasing use of self-induced approaching-distancing behaviors, within the transference, to cope with these fears. This set of events suggests that the hypothesis introducing David's idealization-devaluation oscillations as a mechanism to reduce object loss and reengulfment fears was useful.

Let us now illustrate, in some detail, the main events following the change in emphasis in my interpretation.

David's most outstanding reaction to this change was a re-encounter with repressed, painful childhood memories, relating specifically to his inability to approach and distance his objects. He began to be preoccupied with photographs of his childhood, searching for a renewed contact with his early experiences. He said: "It is all there. It is as if they waited to be discovered by me, through what I am experiencing with you."

In the next session David came in with a set of photographs. He showed me a picture of himself without his special apparatus, the position he preferred throughout his childhood, and a picture with the whole apparatus; a picture with his "good kindergarten teacher" and a picture with "the bad one"; a picture of himself with his "good sister" and one with his mother, who seemed sad and reserved; and finally he showed me three pictures of himself aged three years, four years, and five years. In this set of pictures little David was standing by a tree, always the same tree, without his crutches, holding the lower branches so he wouldn't fall. Through these pictures, taken by his mother, David gained insight, revealed in a session that followed, to the very essence of his experience of being paralyzed. He described painfully, sobbing, the emotions of "the child by the tree." he said, "This boy is smiling, he is forced to smile, but he is so frightened, he cannot stand there alone. He wants to approach mother, but he is unable to. He wants to get away from her, but he cannot. He is terrified to stand there all alone, afraid to get angry at her, so she won't get farther away from him, or so she won't come closer and hurt him. He feels paralyzed. It seemed that being paralyzed for David was, in essence, not being able to distance and approach his mother according to his needs, an experience that exposed him to tremendous fears.

Some time later, David gained insights as to his active use of idealization and devaluation of others to regulate his fears of object loss and re-engulfment in the process of his development and in his relations with others and with me. For example, David pointed to his use of devaluation of family members in childhood as a means of maintaining his sense of separateness and individuality. He told me of the devaluing observational attitude, critical and arrogant, toward his parents and four older siblings that he developed while lying motionless on the floor. He said, "I think I had no choice. If I couldn't become one of them [tall, strong, rude, and violent], then I had to become very different from them." And he added, "I have a disturbing thought that my whole identity, my whole mental and spiritual development, of which I am so proud, is derived from my reaction to an inability to endure my passivity and weakness involved in being a cripple next to them." He then told me of the family occasions in which he felt lonely in his devaluing attitude and how he then changed his attitude to one of admiration and would have been willing to give up his individuality to become the same as they were.

David also became aware that he experienced my interpretations in accordance with his need to be close or far away from me—that he accepted them admiringly when he felt a need to be close, "and then I tell you whatever I think you want to hear, just so you won't leave me," and that at times he angrily devalued them, when "I need to be on guard, not to get too close, not to lose my sense of myself."

David's new understanding of the regulatory function of his idealization and devaluation of me was accompanied by a marked change in the principal manifestations of his transference. Its typical idealization-devaluation features gradually disappeared and were replaced by the underlying themes of object loss and re-engulfment fears, against which these oscillations had been defending. These themes were expressed in the transference in two ways: in accusations accompanied by rage and aggression, and in direct expression of these fears. Sometimes, for example, David accused me of forcing him to stay in therapy, not letting him go; and, alternatively, of becoming pregnant as a means of abandoning him. At other times he told me that when I helped him he felt close to me, and that confronted him with a fear of losing the sense of himself, or he told me that he was anxious over the thought that I would not be available when he desperately needed me.

The therapeutic exploration of these underlying fears revealed their association to David's motoric disability. David raised memories in which his inability to move left him exposed to intense fears of object loss and re-engulfment. In one session David expressed the fear of losing me. He came in a few minutes early and admitted that he did so because he wanted me to accept and enjoy him earlier. He talked about the rejection he experienced through the boundaries and rules of the therapy. I suggested that the fear of rejection was connected to my pregnancy and approaching absence and to his wish that I enjoy him, as I will enjoy my new baby. David told me that he had felt dizzy lately; ever since we began discussing our oncoming separation, he had not enjoyed anything, he could not find how and where to love and be creative. This object-loss anxiety experienced within the transference reminded David of a similar experience "from the time I was four or five years old. I probably annoyed my father. He hit me. I cried from under the table to call my mother. When mother did not come to me [and he, of course, was unable to approach her], I felt myself floating in space, and this is how I feel here and now."

In another session David was overwhelmed by re-engulfment fears. He talked of the wish that I would be with him, that he would be a part of me. Suddenly he turned to me in fear. "Why are you staring at me, testing me. I feel so small, and you are not saying anything." I suggested that his wish to be a part of me, when he experienced me as big and strong, frightened him. He replied: "Yes, it really frightens me to be passive and weak next to a woman." This activated re-engulfment dread reminded David of a childhood experience, "something I haven't told anyone, not even my mother. It reminds me of an Arab girl who blocked my way and threatened me when I was about six years old. She blocked me and didn't let me move away. I was so afraid, but I felt that I must hide my fears, that otherwise I am lost, I will disappear." This description supports Mahler's (1971) suggestion that children's anxieties about being blocked motorically by adults are associated with fears of re-engulfment.

With his increasing recognition of the connection between his idealization-devaluation oscillations, his re-engulfment and object-loss anxieties, and his paralysis, David began to be absent from sessions when he felt too great a burden; occasionally he left angrily in the middle of a session, and, more frequently than before, he came in early or late. He also found a way to meet me outside the therapeutic setting —on the street, or on the road. When David felt that he needed me he searched for me; he knew where he might find me, and often did. It seemed that David needed to be the one who determined the distance from and proximity to me, this time by free movement.

Finally, it might be added that, not without ambivalence, David eventually married a woman whose acquaintance he had made before the anxiety attack that brought him to treatment. We understood, in retrospect, that this relationship may have been the main trigger for his anxiety over the episode of being blocked, that his intimacy and growing attachment with her elicited fear of losing his individuality in the relationship and, alternatively, the fear of losing her.

DISCUSSION

This case illustrates the ego's desperate and endless struggle for existence and a sense of continuity, as it is constantly threatened within the child's primary object relations either by losing the object or by being re-engulfed by it. After all, as Mahler phrases it (Mahler, 1968): "The mother of our nurturance is also the mother of our frustration." Successful management of these two potentially traumatizing experiences appears to be a precondition for normal development and future mental health. But the child's developing ego is not alone in this unavoidable battle. If it is lucky, it receives tremendous help from the primary object, which continuously and with reasonable success (Winnicott, 1960) protects it from being shattered by such unendurable anxieties. Moreover, the ego is not unequipped in this battle. It has gradually maturing motor, affective, perceptive, and cognitive functions to assist it. It is only when one of these primary aid sources fails to function that the ego takes extreme measures, at the expense of its integrity, to fulfill this vital task.

This is exactly the case with the paralyzed child who wants to reach his mother to alleviate his emerging object-loss anxiety and cannot do so, or at other times, desperately tries to get away from his mother to reduce his re-engulfment fears but fails. This is the time when the child tries to compensate for his inability to approach and distance his mother, first, by cueing her to come and go according to his needs and, when that inevitably fails, by using less favorable mechanisms to cope with intensifying object loss and re-engulfment fears. Our main proposition is that under these conditions the child's defending ego reduces object loss and re-engulfment fears by actively changing the inner value of the external object, through fluctuations of idealization and devaluation, to increase and decrease the union experience between self and object. We propose that the child changes his experiences of union with the object by alternating between idealized and devalued fused self-object images, which he actively revives and attaches to his experience of the actual object: the child wards off object-loss anxiety by attaching his idealized, omnipotent, fused self-object image to his experience of the actual object, eliciting intense feelings of union and togetherness between the self and the object. The child defends against re-engulfment fears by coloring his experience of the actual object with his devalued, impotent, fused self-object image, reducing the union experience between the self and the object. This renders the object a shadowy, disparaged, insignificant figure and exposes the self to strong feelings of emptiness and boredom. The two fused self-object images are probably already shaped in the child's primary narcissistic phase and emerge out of two basic experiences of the child at that phase: omnipotent drive satisfaction and total attunement, on the one hand, and impotence, empathic failure and drive frustration, on the other.

It seems that we are explicitly claiming that idealization takes up an equivalent role to that of approaching and devaluation to that of distancing. But we often meet idealization as a psychic process with precisely the opposite experience, that of being distant from the unreachable idealized object. What, then, determines the closeness or distance of the experience accompanying idealization? Solan (1989) distinguishes between two different forms of idealization: the idealization of the object serving essentially as a defense against oral aggression, and the idealization of "togetherness" as being a mechanism of adaptation. She suggests that the idealization of the object involves projection of a great deal of aggression onto the object, which in turn is idealized as a defense against the loss of the good object. This type of idealization process is propelled by the anxiety arising from drive frustration and does not permit closeness or satisfaction. The idealized object carries with it projected aggression, making it the admired object that also despises and rejects the admirer. In the other type of idealization—serving adaptation—the idealization is not of the object alone but also of some pleasurable togetherness with the object, and it involves total withdrawal of aggression from this self-object union and its deflection out of this dyad.

It appears, then, that the close and distant experiential qualities attached to the idealization process are greatly dependent on the amount of aggression remaining within the idealized self and idealized object dyad: the more aggression remains, the greater the distance quality attached to idealization; the less the aggression, the greater the experiential quality of closeness attached to the idealization. Devaluation is a much more straightforward process which inherently serves as a barrier against closeness and dependency, especially in narcissistic personality disorders (Jacobson, 1964; Kernberg, 1975). But again, it is not its defensive function against envy and oral greed that we would like to emphasize. Devaluation is also a process of building an attitude on the part of the ego, reducing the object's attractiveness or value to maintain wellbeing. That is an aspect of object relations, a shading attached to the self's experience of the object, serving psychological homeostasis. Devaluation, as an active ego mechanism to reduce the inner significance of the object, is demonstrated within the narcissistic rage phenomenon typical of some types of narcissistic personalities. Kernberg (1975) recognizes that a characteristic function of the rage reaction is: "To angrily devalue the analyst in an effort to eliminate him as an important object who would otherwise be feared and envied" (p. 269).

We should note at this point that referring to the experiences elicited by idealization and devaluation as carrying closeness and distance features is somewhat misleading, and is done for purposes of clarity only. These experiences should be presented, more accurately, as being of "high" and "low" union, which differ in some respects, as we shall see, from that of closeness and distance.

The experiential registration of approaching and distancing in the ego as closeness or distance between self and object is dependent not only upon the actual distance between the self and the object but also, especially before object and self constancy are established, on the availability of the actual object to drive discharge and to participation in the child's self-regulation. The availability of the object is continuously being scanned by the ego through its various faculties, giving different self-object distances, positions, and interactions the subjective meaning of being close or far apart. This is probably why the child in the practicing period may receive emotional refueling just by establishing eye contact with the mother (Mahler et al., 1975). In behavior-induced closeness and distance experiences, the self-object boundaries seem to be well preserved, proximity is not replaced by oneness, and distance is not replaced by indifference, insignificance, and nonexistence. The self and object representations in these experiences are relatively protected from the damaging effects of excessive drive energy. This is most likely to be achieved by deflecting aggressive and libidinal discharges outward by muscle activity during these behavioral patterns.

The two alternative ego strategies for self-regulation—idealization-devaluation and approaching-distancing—differ substantially in their impact on the stability and continuity of self and object experiences. The idealization-devaluation regulatory mechanism impairs the continuity and cohesiveness of self and object experiences and promotes their split into two contrasting fused self-object images. This type of split is forced upon the ego by the idealization-devaluation oscillations, driving self and object experiences to fluctuate between pleasurable omnipotent self-object merger and devalued, detached, disharmonious coexistence.

The motoric regulatory mechanism, however, if it does not fail, enables the child to use closeness and distance experiences, instead of those induced by idealization-devaluation, in defending against object loss and re-engulfment fears. The closeness-distance experiences maintain better self-object discrimination and free the child's self and object experiences from the heavy burden of idealization-devaluation fluctuations. These effects, promoted by the motoric mechanism, shield the cohesiveness of self and object representations and facilitate the gradual adaptive split of self and object experiences into "me" and "not me" experiential poles, reducing their overlapping area gradually until the formation of two distinct and stable self and object representations is completed. This illustrates the developmental interdependency and mutual maintenance of self and object representations: the instability or stability of the one reflects the instability or stability of the other.

The overall pathogenic effect of the idealization-devaluation imposed split depends on the stability of ego boundaries formed by other sensory, perceptive, and cognitive mechanisms, and on the level of reality testing that has been established. It also depends on the intensity and frequency with which the child is forced to use the idealization-devaluation regulatory mechanism. The crucial factor in determining the frequency and intensity in which this mechanism is used seems to be the child's failure to neutralize excessive aggression in his relations with the primary object, whether because of a constitutionally strong aggressive drive, a deficiency of the neutralizing mechanism itself, or severe frustrations in primary object relations. For example, a constitutionally weak aggressive drive, a successfully cueing of the mother as to his need for being close to or far from her, the mother's adaptation to his needs, and the restoration of the approaching and distancing mechanism would all minimize the child's need to use the idealization-devaluation mode of regulation.

The patient whose case is presented in this paper had developed sufficient ego boundaries and reality testing to avoid psychotic disintegration, but he could not protect himself from pathological narcissism. He entered treatment with idealization and devaluation as a prominent feature of his object relations, enacted perpetually within his transference, unfolding the narcissistic nature of his personality disorder.

We may say that the ego uses its own subjective experiential productions as vital components of its self-regulatory devices. The exact nature of the experiences, however, is highly dependent on the specific ego function that elicits them. They appear with different shadings according to their perceptive, sensori-motor, or affective sources. So, impediment in any one of these functions would bring a change in the quality of the ego's subjective experiences toward the other two remaining sources. This change, if it occurs quite early in development, would impose on the ego to carry its self-regulatory functions through its own altered, imbalanced experiential productions. For instance, impairment in the perceptive-cognitive function would compel the ego to use its more motor-affective experiential constellations, or if an extreme restraint of motor actions occurs, as in the paralyzed patient presented, the ego would be more dependent, in its self-regulation, on perceptive-affective experiential organizations. This explains the more perceptive-affective nature of the "high" and "low" union experiences brought about by idealization and devaluation, as opposed to the more motoric active and interactional quality of the experiences induced by the approaching and distancing behaviors.

The differentiation drawn in this paper between two ego mechanisms for self-regulation reminds us of Erlich's model, differentiating between two basic experiential modalities, Doing and Being (Erlich, 1990; Erlich and Blatt, 1985). This model suggests two innate experiential modalities within the ego, which constantly scan and process the experiential field of the object relations. In the Doing modality, Erlich suggests, self and object are experienced primarily as separate entities, in some sort of doing or functional interaction, as acting upon or being acted upon, confined in time and place. This is the modality by which drive-related phenomena such as wish, anxiety, actual drive discharge, conflict, and defense are experienced. The boundaries in this modality are between self and object, granting the object a separate existence outside the self.

In the Being experiential modality, on the other hand, self and object are experienced as in a state of being together. Self and object are not separated by boundaries and appear to be in an experience free of time and place, rejecting boundaries as being strange and impeding. In this modality boundaries are drawn not between self and object but rather outside or around the self and the object. It is the modality in which empathic coexistence and omnipotence are experienced.

We propose that there could not be a Being experiential modality, colored with strong togetherness feelings with the object, unless there was this other type of being with the object in the background, tinged with detachment, alienation, and unattunement feelings, which serve as its contrast and give it meaning. If the Being modality is the one by which narcissistic object choice is facilitated, as Erlich suggests, then a child choosing his love object narcissistically should experience not only what he is, was, or would like to be (Freud, 1914), but also what he is not, was not, or would not like to be. It appears, then, that a child in narcissistic object choice scans his world of objects in accordance with two Being experiential representations, probably already shaped in his primary narcissistic fusion. The one represents an omnipotent, harmonious, empathic, united state of being with the object; the other represents an impotent, disharmonious, nonempathic, detached state of being. This compels a split of the child's self and world of objects into idealized omnipotent and devalued impotent entities.

The therapeutic effect of interpreting idealization-devaluation fluctuations within the transference as reflecting the patient's need for closeness to and distance from the therapist lies in its potential to set on the patient's gradual conversion of his Being-related regulatory mechanism to his more Doing-related one, promoting the stabilization and integration of his self and object experiences. This is achieved through the therapist's attunement to Being- as well as Doing- experiences within the countertransference and his reflecting them back to the patient by persistently naming his idealization and devaluation as approaching and distancing. As Fenichel has suggested (Fenichel, 1933), naming is one of the most powerful aspects of analytic work.

We may say, in conclusion, when there is a failure in regulating the distance from the primary object by free movement during development, whether it is due to paralysis or to the mother's failure to allow the child to come and go according to his needs, the child's ego is compelled to make use of the mechanism of idealization-devaluation to carry the vital task of lowering annihilation anxiety arising from object loss or re-engulfment. This compensatory mechanism exposes the child to unstable self and object experiences and contributes to the formation of pathological narcissism. An intact motor system, allowing free self-induced regulation of the distance between the child and his primary object, appears to be a powerful barrier against the formation of pathological narcissism and an important stabilizer of self and object experiences.

This case suggests that motor deficiencies and inadequacies are direct etiological factors in narcissistic pathology. It seems that the antipathological, narcissistic potential of free movement stems from its capacity to mobilize aggression in a more neutralized way to serve the formation of boundaries between self and object. But this is another story for another time.

BIBLIOGRAPHY

ABELIN, E. L. (1971). The role of the father in separation-individuation process. In *Separation-Individuation: Essays in Honor of Margaret S. Mahler,* ed. J. McDevitt & C. Settlage, pp. 229–52. New York: Int. Univ. Press.

ABELIN, E. L. (1975). Some further observations and comments on the earliest role of the father. *Int. J. Psychoanal.,* 56:293–302.

BERNAL, W. (1984). Immobility and the self. *J. Med. Philos.,* 9:75–91.

ERLICH, H. S. (1990). Boundaries, limitations, and the wish for fusion in the treatment of adolescents. *Psychoanal. Study Child,* 45:195–213.

ERLICH, H. S., & BLATT, S. J. (1985). Narcissism and object love. *Psychoanal. Study Child,* 40:57–79.

FENICHEL, O. (1933). Problems of psychoanalytic technique. In *The Evolution of Psychoanalytic Technique,* ed. M. Bergman & F. Hartman. New York: Basic, 1976.

FREUD, S. (1914). On narcissism. *S.E.,* 14:67–102.

GREENACRE, P. (1957). The childhood of the artist. *Psychoanal. Study Child,* 12:27–72.

GREENSON, R. R. (1968). Dis-identification. *Int. J. Psychoanal.*, 49:370–74.

JACOBSON, E. (1964). *The Self and the Object World.* New York: Int. Univ. Press.

KERNBERG, O. (1975). *Borderline Conditions and Pathological Narcissism,* New York: Jason Aronson, Inc.

KOHUT, H. (1966). Forms and transformations of narcissism. *J. Amer. Psychoanal. Assn.,* 14:243–72.

LOEWENSTEIN, R. M. (1950). Conflict and autonomous ego development during the phallic phases. *Psychoanal. Study Child,* 5:47–52.

LOFGREN, J. B. (1968). Castration anxiety and body ego. *Int. J. Psychoanal.,* 49:408–10.

MAHLER, M. S. (1968). Discussion of Borje Lofgren's paper "Castration anxiety and bodily ego." *Int. J. Psychoanal.,* 49:410–12.

——— (1968). *On Human Symbiosis and the Vicissitudes of Individuation.* Vol. 1: *Infantile Psychosis.* New York: Int. Univ. Press.

——— (1971). A study of the separation-individuation process and its possible application to borderline phenomena in the psychoanalytic situation. *Psychoanal. Study Child,* 26:403–24.

MAHLER, M. S., PINE, F., & BERGMAN, A. (1975). *The Psychological Birth of the Human Infant: Symbiosis and Individuation.* New York: Basic.

MAHLER, M. S., & MC DEVITT, J. B. (1982). Thoughts on the emergence of the sense of self, with particular emphasis on the body self. *J. Amer. Psychoanal. Assn.,* 30:827–48.

SANDLER, J. (1960). The background of safety. *Int. J. Psychoanal.,* 41:352–56.

SOLAN, R. (1989). Idealization and de-idealization. *Sihot,* 4:17–24.

WINNICOTT, D. W. (1960). The theory of the parent-infant relationship. In *The Maturational Processes of the Facilitating Environment,* pp. 37–55. New York: Int. Univ. Press.

CLINICAL CONTRIBUTIONS

Erotic Transference in the Male Adolescent-Female Analyst Dyad

SARAH ATKINSON, M.D.
GLEN O. GABBARD, M.D.

Erotic transference involving female analysts and adult male patients has received increased attention in the past ten years. Absent from the literature, however, are any clinical reports concerning erotic transferences of adolescent male patients with female therapists. This paper presents a fragment of a treatment involving an adolescent male patient who developed an erotic transference. The vicissitudes of the transference, as well as his relationship to his mother and father, are discussed from the perspective of developmental conflicts and tasks of adolescence. The countertransference dimensions of this particular gender constellation are also examined from the standpoint of intrapsychic and cultural factors.

THE PSYCHOANALYTIC LITERATURE ON EROTIC TRANSFERENCE TRADITION-ally has focused on a male analyst and a female patient. Indeed, Person (1985) noted that the absence of reports involving erotic transference between a female analyst and a male patient might convey the erroneous idea that erotic transference is essentially a problem of female psychology. Lester (1985) argued that reports of erotized transferences of male patients to female analysts were virtually absent from the literature because such transferences are rare in clinical practice. She

Sarah Atkinson is a staff psychiatrist, at Children's Hospital, the Menninger Clinic; and an adult and child candidate at the Topeka Institute for Psychoanalysis. Glen O. Gabbard is Bessie Walker Callaway Distinguished Professor of Psychoanalysis and Education at the Karl Menninger School of Psychiatry and Mental Health Sciences and a training and supervising analyst at the Topeka Institute for Psychoanalysis.

The Psychoanalytic Study of the Child 50, ed. Albert J. Solnit, Peter B. Neubauer, Samuel Abrams, and A. Scott Dowling (Yale University Press, copyright © 1995 by Albert J. Solnit, Peter B. Neubauer, Samuel Abrams, and A. Scott Dowling).

stressed that the emergence of transference fear of the powerful pre-oedipal phallic mother tended to overshadow and inhibit the full expression of sexualized impulses directed toward the oedipal mother. She felt that the destabilizing effect of such primitive anxieties on male gender identity contributed to the suppression of intense sexual fantasies in the female analyst–male patient dyad.

Following the appearance of Lester's contribution, a number of articles by female analysts (see Goldberger and Evans, 1985; Gornick, 1986; Myers, 1987) that presented a somewhat different view were published. These authors felt that erotic transferences were more common than Lester had suggested, but Myers (1987) and Goldberger and Evans (1985) acknowledged that resistances against the transferences are often powerful. Person (1985) suggested that male patients with female analysts often displace their erotic transferences to extra-transference figures, and she agreed with Myers and with Goldberger and Evans that resistance to the awareness of the erotic transference may be formidable.

Tyson (1986) and Russ (1993) observed that the female analyst's psychologically and culturally determined countertransference may inhibit the full development of erotic or erotized transference in the male patient. They suggested, moreover, that female clinicians may prefer to remain with early dyadic or preoedipal material not only because of the avoidance of genital sexuality but because of the powerful position associated with the preoedipal mother in the transference.

Much of this recent literature has emerged in concert with the demise of the classic view that the analyst's gender has minimal relevance in determining the nature of the transference. As analysts have become increasingly aware of the significance of the "real" person of the analyst, the gender configuration has come to be seen as a key element in the interaction between the members of the analytic dyad (Greenson, 1967; Lester, 1985; Ticho, 1975). As early as 1936, Bibring wrote that one of the most influential aspects of the "real" person of the analyst was her gender. The fact that the literature on erotic transference of male patients to female analysts has only recently come to the attention of clinicians may reflect a confluence of factors. As Russ (1993) noted: "Social convention says that an empowered man is unambivalently sexually desirable, but for a woman, the sex/power issue may cause conflict for herself and those around her" (p. 393). Ongoing societal changes may result in this perspective becoming less rigidly held. In the meantime, however, for many women, succumbing to a man's sexual advances, even psychologically, may conjure up a perception of loss of autonomy and authority, or even of a basic sense of safety (Benedek,

1973; Russ, 1993). These concerns may lead to a premature closure of the unfolding transference. The analytic relationship between a woman therapist and a male patient represents a reversal of traditional positions of power. The woman may be placed in a madonna/whore paradox of charging for the hour while simultaneously being viewed as the all-listening, all-giving mother (Russ, 1993). The analyst may collude with the patient, unwilling to see herself in both aspects of this paradox, and the transference may be viewed as only an asexual maternal one.

These difficulties are compounded when the patient is an adolescent. The literature is sparse with regard to erotic transference of male adolescent patients to their female analysts. There are several possible contributing factors to the silence on this topic. As both Russ (1993) and Lester (1985) point out, women are hesitant to reveal themselves in the academic literature as sexual beings, especially as they strive to establish themselves professionally. Society expects adolescent girls, budding into womanhood, to have "crushes" on older men, and these highly charged emotional attachments are viewed as benign. At worst, it is felt that the adolescent is creating a "scene," embarrassing herself and the recipient of her affections. In the reversed situation, with an admiring adolescent boy and an older woman (occasionally the mother), the woman may be condemned as a temptress. This theme is common in classic literature, such as the *Odyssey, Die Lorelei,* and the *Walkure,* and in popular films such as *The Graduate, Spanking the Monkey, Summer of '42,* and *What's Eating Gilbert Grape?*

Responsible parents have historically attempted to strike a balance between encouraging children toward adulthood and protecting them from the realities of the world. This dialectic has become even more strained as brutal, random violence and overt sexuality now permeate every level of our culture, creating a strong impetus for adults to simultaneously educate children about and shield them from the world. Child analysts, with or without the collusion of the child's parents, may seek to protect the child from worldly knowledge that would launch him or her into a genital sexual world of adulthood. This affords the child analyst and even the parents the illusion of working in a Neverland where boys remain playful, adoring, and asexual, which may serve to defend against awareness of any potential erotic transference or countertransference material. For the analyst, this stance guards against the psychological violation of incest taboos involving the transferential parent-analyst seducing the child-patient. If the adolescent agrees to maintain his station as a boy in Neverland, then the transference is thwarted and the potential for exploration and growth is constrained (Gornick, 1986). The exploration of all aspects of the transference, specifically any erotic components, within the analytic boundaries is frequently regarded by male analysts as benefiting their female patients' relationships through a flowering of their sense of femininity (see, e.g., S. Freud, 1915; Gorkin, 1985; Trop, 1988).

Acknowledging the erotic material in an adolescent's transference may create in the analyst a level of concern or even fear of parental retaliation should the parents become aware of the material. This potential is especially relevant in today's litigious climate in conjunction with the zealous pursuit of even the most remote adumbration of impropriety. An allegation of sexual misconduct could wreak havoc on the analyst's career. Even in the absence of fears of retribution by society and parents, the analyst may have concerns that he or she has manipulated the child's thoughts or actions into following a particular course. These concerns may lead the analyst to disregard or deny any emerging evidence of erotic transference rather than explore the material.

The subtle (and not so subtle) cognitive, physiological, psychological, and social development of the child as he or she matures may evoke strong countertransference reactions that may or may not be acknowledged. The analyst may wish, on a countertransferential basis, to maintain an internal sense of being the all-giving, benign, omnipotent, and asexual parent figure (Gabbard, 1994a, 1994b; Waksman, 1986). Over time both analyst and child may attempt to avoid the issue of what the child's maturation means relative to termination of therapy, graduation from school, attaining employment, and the child's becoming less receptive to the transferential parent-analyst. Some analysts may have qualms about their own aging process that influence how they experience their patients' maturation.

The process of normal and pathological development represents a cornerstone of psychoanalytic theory. Oral, anal, phallic, oedipal, and latency conflicts are integrated and subsumed under a final genital orientation during adolescence. In adolescence the oedipal conflicts come to the forefront once again, to be reexperienced not only with parents but with parent substitutes and older peers. The intensity of aggression shrouding the sexual aspect of relationships may determine the degree to which the manifestations of an erotic transference are consciously and unconsciously shunned (Russ, 1993).

The reawakening of pregenital urges with the newly acquired genital urges in conjunction with the cognitive and physical capabilities to fantasize and act on the fantasies enhances a sense of dangerous excitement in reexperiencing oedipal issues (A. Freud, 1958; Ritvo, 1971). The male adolescent is now focused on his body in a way not experienced or exhibited since infancy and toddlerhood (Ritvo, 1971). Adolescent boys are preoccupied with voyeuristic looking, not only at women's bodies but also at their own bodies and those of other young men (Blos, 1962). The actual experience of genital sexuality with a partner is preceded by a period of intense erotic looking, which culminates in the emergence of the adolescent's identity as a sexual male. These experiences serve to counteract "the ubiquitous fear that one's sense of maleness and masculinity are in danger and that one must build into character structure ever-vigilant defenses against succumbing to the pull of merging again with mother" (Stoller, 1975, p. 149). Russ (1993), Lester (1985), and Karme (1979) posit that the fear of regressive symbiosis with the mother may limit erotic expression in adult male patients, but for the adolescent patient the voyeuristic looking period that precedes physical genital expression may allow for the discussion of erotic transference issues. Overall, adolescent relationships are characterized by brief but ardent emotions. The intensity and exclusivity of analysis, without the brevity typical of adolescent relationships, may serve to enhance the development of an erotic transference in young adolescent boys as they struggle to consolidate their sense of sexual and personal identity. The analytic resolution of the erotic transference may be critical to the adolescent's developing a resolute sense of his own identity and not succumbing to a regressive fantasy of preoedipal merger with mother or mother-substitutes such as the analyst.

Here we report on a fragment of a treatment of an adolescent boy who developed an erotic transference. We review the evolution of the transference, the potential contributions of early mother-child/father-child relations and the developmental period of early adolescence, and the ramifications of an erotic transference on the treatment process.

CASE MATERIAL

At age thirteen Nicholas was a veteran of many forms of psychiatric intervention including brief hospitalization, pharmacotherapy, and a therapeutic boarding school. He was admitted to residential treatment with a litany of behavioral disturbances, including smoking marijuana, drinking alcohol, running away from boarding school, and spending large sums of money riding about in taxicabs. Despite his excellent intellect Nicholas had repeatedly failed his school classes. The immediate reason for his poor academic showing was Nicholas's refusal to do any work in school, although he attended class. To remedy this situation his parents transferred him from one private academic institution

to another. His first hospital admission occurred after a verbal altercation with his mother escalated to an exchange of blows.

Nicholas's father was from a frontier family of prospectors and
ranchers, in which formal education and conformity to social norms
were not valued; independence and a taste for adventure were prized.
His mother was from a prosperous intellectual and artistic family. She
herself was an artist of significant repute. The parental expectations
from treatment reflected their backgrounds. The father wanted to
have a better relationship with his son; the mother wanted Nicholas to
gain some "self-soothing for his inner fire." His father viewed Nicholas
as an emotionally distant child who was too dependent on his mother,
refused to "have any real discussions with me [father]," and was bullied
by his twenty-one-year-old brother. Nicholas had traveled extensively
with his mother during exhibitions of her works. The mother saw
Nicholas as an extraordinarily sensitive and talented child, but her
attempts to teach him to draw were unsuccessful. He seemed to "fly into
a rage whenever I [mother] corrected him. He tore up his drawings,
even wonderful, beautiful ones."

After a comprehensive psychiatric evaluation, Nicholas was referred
for three-times-weekly psychoanalytic psychotherapy. Despite years of
psychiatric intervention, he had never had a good trial of expressive
treatment, and the evaluating team felt that an in-depth exploration of
his internal conflicts was crucial.

Nicholas arrived in the therapist's office dressed as something between a conservative schoolboy and a punk rocker. His clothing was
immaculate, precisely coordinated, and costly. On the other hand, he
had nearly shoulder-length hair, with his head shaved on the top, and
he wore a small diamond earring. He stammered and stumbled when
the therapist, Dr. Z., asked what had brought him to the hospital.
Blushing and with his head bent so that his hair partially concealed his
eyes, he said he had run away from his latest school. His voice sounded
weary and sad, not defiant or angry. The unit staff had described him
as an angry, belligerent adolescent, a picture contrary to the young boy
who sat before Dr. Z. timidly asking if the cookie jar really contained
cookies. Nicholas's dress and presentation stood in sharp contrast to his
history as a stridently rebellious young teenager.

Over the next month, Nicholas carefully modeled clay roses complete with thorns. He was most concerned about the clay rubbing off
onto the table or bits falling onto the floor. After completing each
flower he meticulously tidied up, despite being reassured that he need
not be concerned about the mess. He was improbably fastidious. He
seemed nervous and anxious, like a small boy trying to please his

mother. As he carefully combined various colors to create magenta and coral, Dr. Z. commented on his choice of colors. Nicholas beamed, staring deeply into Dr. Z.'s eyes as he placed each new creation on her desk. His responses felt to her like those of a five- or six-year-old child, very warm and somehow sensual. Because he was thirteen, intelligent, and experienced as a patient, Dr. Z. had expected that Nicholas would be more verbally inclined, but each time she made an inquiry or remark about something other than his work he became sullen and mute. So he sat with her at a small table while he modeled with clay and drew sketches. Occasionally, a short note saying "hello," accompanied by a sketch, would arrive via interoffice mail. Dr. Z. felt uncomfortable with the way the treatment was proceeding and wondered if she should be interpreting more and confronting more of his behaviors. Yet she also felt that being more active would stifle the blossoming transference. The notes, sculptures, and drawings were like small tokens of affection. There was a flirtatious quality (bordering on seductive) to the single stems of roses and the surreptitiously sent messages.

Despite Dr. Z.'s comments the technique used in rendering the drawings and sculptures and the affects they evoked, Nicholas never destroyed his works until Dr. Z. asked how he felt about an upcoming prearranged phone call from his parents. He mumbled, "Fine," and abruptly destroyed a well-formed clay rose. Dr. Z. wondered aloud if she had intruded into his creation. He countered by saying how talented his mother was and offering to show Dr. Z. a photograph of her work. Dr. Z. remarked that her work was that of a mature artist with many years of experience, and Nicholas silently repaired the fractured rose. His art was a private affair between the members of the treatment dyad. He did not draw or paint on the unit or take an art course at the hospital school.

For the session following the destruction of the rose, he arrived scowling and pouting. Angrily he accused Dr. Z. of being "like all the others [adults], just like my parents." Perplexed, Dr. Z. asked him what had happened. He vehemently replied, "I didn't feel sorry about something I said to staff. What are they there for anyway? They are paid to take care of us. They told me I had to clean my room. I am not going to do it." Nicholas continued a long monologue of self-righteous indignation, relating how all adults treat children as if they have no feelings, no thoughts of their own, and no right to their own opinions. As the diatribe continued, his voice became pleading and soulful. Dr. Z. commented that she had been insensitive in introducing his parents into his treatment, disregarding how he might feel. Looking rather surprised and sad, he agreed. Play therapy was now over: the two had crossed the bridge from physical objects representing affects and wishes to verbal expression. Nicholas drew only once more during the treatment.

Rather than create objects to express himself, Nicholas began directly discussing how he felt and thought. Dr. Z.'s attire evolved into a central issue. Nicholas came in one day, sat down, and immediately noticed the length of her skirt; he said Dr. Z. looked better in short skirts. Dr. Z.'s initial response was dismay, as she pretended to ignore his comment. While attempting to recover her composure, she inquired about how he was getting on at school. Nicholas was a child, yet he was beginning to mature physically into a young man. His statements no longer had childishly innocent overtones. Nicholas fidgeted, made monosyllabic replies to her inquiries, and asked if they could go outside for a walk to a snack shop on the hospital grounds. Upon their leaving the office, the highly charged atmosphere in the office gave way to a more relaxed one. Nicholas walked quickly, too quickly for Dr. Z. to keep pace. She did not ask him to slow his pace, noting that she somehow felt safer with him a short distance ahead, and he too seemed in better control.

After several sessions with roughly this scenario, Dr. Z. commented that he was always observant about her style of clothing. She recognized a countertransference dread that Pandora's box might be opened by her acknowledgment of his comments and was afraid of what might be enacted in or out of the treatment. Would his feelings and wishes be confined to words? After all, it was only a few short months ago that he had left her roses. Dr. Z. now dealt with a more self-confident, handsome young man who demonstrated the air of someone wooing his first love. He was no longer a little boy playing with plasticine, worrying about a mother's reactions to a mess on the carpet. What would happen if the balance of power tilted, as it had done in his family? Dr. Z. had so far maintained the role of observing adult. Now she sensed that she might lose this position.

Nicholas and his mother had engaged in an exclusive, sensually intimate relationship long after his toddlerhood. Although there was no history of overt sexual abuse, Nicholas's every whim was catered to by his mother, but he also felt smothered by her and competitive with her. His tentative attempts to flirt with Dr. Z. appeared to parallel the flirtation with his mother that led to the physical altercation and his subsequent hospitalization. The sexual tension had become so intense that Nicholas was forced into physical action against his mother to ward off the sexual impulses. Furthermore, Nicholas's competence as an emerging young adult could not flourish in the competitive dance in which he and his mother were engaged. He viciously undermined his potential by refusing to discover his assets and weaknesses, as when he refused to do any schoolwork or to take an art class. By leaving his own competence undiscovered, Nicholas remained an infant, incapable of independent achievement.

Feeling that she was plunging into turbulent waters, while simultaneously wanting to remain in the relatively safe, serene world that had been previously created, Dr. Z. started keeping pace with Nicholas as they walked. As her pace increased, he slowed his and began to talk. He said that she was "really beautiful" and that he had not really noticed how pretty she was until six months into treatment. Actually, he said, he had first observed Dr. Z.'s earrings but he had felt too embarrassed to let her know how much he admired them. She commented that he had recently pierced his ear for a second earring, so that now both had two earrings. Nicholas grinned in agreement, flirtatiously adding that he bet she would not let him borrow the admired pair of earrings. Dr. Z. smiled and simply said no. He looked relieved, and she noted a parallel response in herself.

Sighing, he said how differently Dr. Z. dressed from girls his own age. She wondered aloud how he viewed the differences. His pace quickened, then he abruptly turned and said, "You're not like the others." Dr. Z. asked what he meant. Nicholas replied that she treated him like a person with something important to say. She commented that she frequently disagreed with his particular viewpoint on whatever subject they were discussing. He said that he knew Dr. Z. would sometimes disagree with him but that he did not feel devalued when she did so. He accurately perceived that she respected his opinions, even when she told him that they might be transient or that they were different from her own.

Nicholas rapidly shifted back and forth between discussing emotionally charged issues of his own competence and flirting. He commented that Dr. Z. now dressed better and that he like her shorter hair. His eye for detail was incredible. He noted every nuance of change in hairstyle, make-up, perfume, weight, and wardrobe that had occurred over eight months. Dr. Z. began to have a sense of being stalked. She said that it seemed to give him great pleasure to list her outfits. His initial response was flat denial, stated with a smirk. She felt stymied and rather undone, perhaps "undressed." He spent the next few sessions silently staring at Dr. Z. with a penetrating glare in which he periodically shifted his gaze from one part of her body to another. Simultaneously he would grin in apparent satisfaction.

Subsequent sessions were filled with unspoken tension. Dr. Z. did not feel angry, but she was anxious and unsure of what to do with this impasse. Finally, Nicholas made angry remarks to the effect that treatment was worthless and he did not understand how he could ever have wanted to become a psychiatrist. Dr. Z. commented that this type of relationship was incredibly close, maybe sometimes too close for comfort, and perhaps dangerous. Nicholas said she was completely wrong, that he never felt unsafe with her. He emphasized that he was larger than she. (Indeed, he was now taller than Dr. Z.) She agreed that he was growing up and would soon be moving into young adulthood. Pausing, he said that maybe he wanted more than just treatment. Dr. Z. asked what he had in mind. Tersely, he replied that he was fourteen, too young to get married. When she agreed, he visibly relaxed. (So did Dr. Z.)

He spent the next several sessions discussing dating and marriage. Then he had a dream about being forced into marrying an older women after impregnating her. He appeared extremely distraught when he first mentioned this dream. Then he walked rapidly away in silence. Later, he commented that he always went after the older girls on the unit and the ones who dressed right. Dr. Z. talked about how difficult relationships were to maintain over time, even between two mature adults. She also said that the task of adolescence was to find one's identity and purpose. She was letting him know that no boundaries would be crossed. He was very quiet.

Shortly after this conversation Nicholas's grades took a dramatic upturn, and he began talking about what he would like to do as a career. He said he could not imagine Dr. Z. not working. Dr. Z. asked what not working meant to him. He replied that his mother had always worked, even after she had children. Dr. Z. asked if he thought *she* would work even if she had children. He nodded his head affirmatively and moved closer. Dr. Z. did not move away. She commented that part of becoming professionally successful was knowing when to compromise. He agreed.

One day it was pouring rain, and Dr. Z. refused to go for a walk. Nicholas spent a few minutes pouting and then picked up the sketchpad to draw his dream of the previous night. He suddenly stopped and described what the dream was about: "I was hoping. I mean thinking. Dreaming that I could marry you." He recalled that when he was around five he had crept into his mother's studio where a nude male was modeling. He said how angry he felt, really envious, "like I wanted to kill him." Nicholas looked sad, confused, and frightened. Dr. Z. noted how very confusing that must have been for him. He replied that he did not have to share that part of his mother with his father. Dr. Z. asked what he meant. He said that his father was not an artist, unlike

Nicholas and his mother. As he spoke, Nicholas had sketched a nude male of seven or eight years. Dr. Z. pointed this out to him. Despite the obvious male genitalia, he insisted that it was a girl.

In the next session, he reexamined the drawing. He quietly stated that he had recognized himself in the picture and had become "too embarrassed to talk" to Dr. Z. any more: "I really thought about not coming here today, especially since I knew you keep all my drawings." Nicholas said he felt "like a tidal wave hit me." He realized that his mother used to draw nudes of him and that he had enjoyed being her special model. (This was confirmed by his mother in a family session with the social worker.) During his toddlerhood and early childhood Nicholas had traveled extensively and exclusively with his mother, despite the birth of a brother when Nicholas was three years old. He said that he had felt exposed in the previous session; Dr. Z. might reject him if she knew of his passionate feelings toward his mother. He elaborated that he thought about "being in bed with you, what it would be like." Dr. Z. commented that on some level he may have wondered also what it would be like to have his mother as his wife. Startled, he nodded his head affirmatively, but said that his feelings toward Dr. Z. were much stronger, "So strong that sometimes, well you know, I wake up really hard." Rapidly he added that he was too young to get married. Dr. Z. assured him that she had no intention of seducing him. But she wondered aloud if he had thought of being both the seducer and the seduced. She commented on how frightening and exciting it must be for him to think of being with her. Rather than changing the subject, sulking, or otherwise retreating, Nicholas agreed that his thoughts were all of the above and even more. He said that even when he had been little (ten months before!) and naive about what to do in therapy, he had thought about her "all the time."

Nicholas said that at first he had wondered if therapists ever adopted their patients. This picture rapidly took on sexual overtones, similar to his relationship with his mother. He said he was afraid that if Dr. Z. adopted him she would want him to model. When she asked a question or made an interpretation, he said, especially if it did not reflect favorably on him, he felt vulnerably exposed, as he had when he had modeled for his mother. At the same time, he felt extremely close to Dr. Z. and wanted to expand the relationship. He commented that he enjoyed making her feel uncomfortable and that he really liked her figure and her style of dressing. Dr. Z. noted that he had let her know how exposed he felt with his mother, despite being her favorite model and special child. He countered that his relationship with Dr. Z. was not directly parallel to the one with his mother and that Dr. Z. seemed to want him to "finish growing up." Asked to clarify what he meant, he said he wished for the relationship to mature into something even better than therapy. He liked therapy because he could express himself and "work out the problems inside myself," but, he said, "I want to sleep with you." Dr. Z. asked him what exactly he meant by "sleep with me." He said it depended on the day. Dr. Z. commented that it might depend on the minute.

He laughed, remarking that she was always clarifying adult time, adolescent time (a month is forever), and children's time (a day is divided into mealtimes) for him. He said it really depended on the day, the school day. If he was interested in school, then he thought that they should "just go off together to sculpt, draw, and write" in some ethereal manner. If school was not going well, then he wanted her to hold him and tell him that she would love him forever, even if he was not brilliant and creative. Dr. Z. said, "You want me to accept and love you for you, regardless of what your body looks like or how it changes with time or how you perform sexually, academically, or creatively." He said that he wanted this relationship to be "the one" and then added, "It feels like it should be the right one. You know me better than anyone else, and you know that you are attracted to me." He elaborated that the therapist had changed her perfume to one that he liked better (the perfume had in reality not been changed) and that she was now "dressing better" by wearing more colors and different types of fabric—like more silk (no new clothes had been bought). Dr. Z. commented that *he* was attracted to *her* and acknowledged that they did share some interests. He looked sad, angry, and embarrassed. Bitterly, he asked how much more he had to prove before she would let him get closer. She said that he had himself to face and nothing to prove to her. He seemed utterly defeated with this remark.

Before the next session real roses arrived in Dr. Z.'s office with a note from Nicholas expressing his love for her and hopes for a continued relationship. Dr. Z. was embarrassed, worried about how intense the acting out would become, and saddened by his desperation to win her over. When he arrived, he smiled at the sight of the roses and said he hoped they had arrived just before him; indeed, they had arrived less than five minutes earlier. Dr. Z. asked how he understood sending flowers and what he hoped for in her reaction. He looked angry and then started crying, asking how he could make her love him. Dr. Z. told him that the type of romantic, intimate relationship he kept attempting to create was not going to occur with her. He said he guessed he "had lost." Dr. Z. told him that she was never his to win. Again he looked defeated as he said that he had thought that maybe she was not his to win and wondered if maybe he could find someone like her. She reiterated her hope that he could find someone to share his life when he was "old enough." Nicholas said that he did not think that the time was right and that he was definitely not old enough. He added that maybe after graduate school would be a good time to find someone.

DISCUSSION

The foregoing clinical material raises a number of issues regarding the development of erotic transference in male adolescent patients with female analysts. Some features of the case appear to be specific to this particular patient, but others may be applied to treatment situations with adolescents that involve the same gender configuration.

Nicholas's presenting difficulties were remarkable only in their ubiquity as adolescent complaints. Like many children who are brought to therapy, he was not doing well at school despite more than adequate cognitive abilities. He had also failed to develop his artistic talents. There was intense conflict within his family relationships. Overall, he was rapidly turning toward a feeling of inferiority at the close of his latency years, rather than having a sense of industry and self-worth (Erikson, 1959). Initially, the transference wish for admiration from an adult woman was a maternal preoedipal transference. As he created precise clay sculptures, he sought and acquired praise for his talents from a maternal figure with whom he was not competitive, as he had been with his mother. Even within this transference there was a flirtatious, seductive quality—notes being sent and sculptures left on Dr. Z.'s desk. Her anxious wish to view this as a nonerotic maternal transference that would repair Erikson's industry versus inferiority conflict was evident in the absence of any interpretations that dealt with the sexual overtones that these tokens actually represented. Dr. Z. viewed sexualization of the transference as implying action rather than reflection. The vantage point of an asexual maternal transference preserves a perception of safety for the therapist and is highly promoted by our culture (Russ, 1993; Gornick, 1986).

The countertransference struggles Dr. Z. endured are not unusual. Her feelings of being stalked or "undressed" were highly disconcerting. Retrospectively, Dr. Z. recognized that Nicholas had turned the tables on her. As an artist, his mother had made him uncomfortable by having him pose nude for her and visually studying him. Nicholas had actively mastered this passively experienced trauma by looking at Dr. Z. in a way that made her just as uncomfortable as he had been as a model for his mother. Another aspect of Dr. Z.'s countertransference was to view the transference material as pregenital, which may have been experienced as castrating, in that the adolescent's identity as a phallic male was not confirmed. For this child, on the cusp of adolescence, failure to acknowledge the erotic component of the transference material would have consigned him to the role of a nonproductive, inferior person. Furthermore, failure to acknowledge his emerging sexuality would pull him toward a resumption of the symbiosis that he had experienced with his mother long after his infancy. His relationship with his mother led to violence just at the point at which Nicholas was physically maturing. This act may have represented Nicholas's perception that his sense of masculinity was endangered by his symbiotic yearnings toward his mother (see Stoller, 1975).

The role that looking played in the transference was striking. While the emerging genital sexuality of the young adolescent boy is always connected with voyeuristic activities, the particular nature of the mother-son relationship in this case (exemplified by his serving as a nude model for her) may have heightened the sexualization involved in looking and showing. The clinical material suggests that Nicholas's struggle to define his masculine identity was intimately related to visual themes of sexualized looking. He would look Dr. Z. up and down, studying the contours of her body and attempting to differentiate her anatomy from his own. His sketch of a young male nude with male genitalia was regarded by him as that of a little girl. While this misperception may reflect a way of handling his castration anxiety, it may also point to a wish to "have it all" (that is, both male and female features) and thus avoid dealing with envy of his mother's procreative capacities.

Jacobson (1951) noted that in male artists and other creative persons, analysis often reveals intensely cathected unconscious feminine reproductive fantasies. These men, according to Jacobson, may withdraw cathexis from their penis and displace it onto the wish for a baby or onto other creative pursuits. Nicholas' envy of his mother's ability to grow and produce children may have been heightened by the fact of her artistic profession and her seductive relationship with him in that context.

When little boys become aware of anatomical differences, they often seek to undo them in a variety of ways (Ross, 1977). The hermaphroditic fantasy that some boys harbor is often a derivative of the fantasy of the mother as a phallic woman (Bak, 1968; Greenacre, 1970). In discussing the analysis of adult males by female analysts, Karme (1979) has stressed that a man treated by a woman will very likely have to deal with his transference fear of the analyst as the phallic mother. He may worry that the analyst is more potent and phallic than he, and he may feel the need to "castrate" her by demonstrating that he is more potent than she. Similar issues may arise in the male adolescent patient, resulting in a counterphobic erotization of the transference.

In many cases of male adolescents treated by female analysts, the erotization is limited to looking. It is possible that the highly incestuous nature of Nicholas's relationship with his mother allowed him to be more forthright in verbalizing his sexual feelings toward Dr. Z. Many male adolescents are too ashamed of their feelings to address them directly with a female therapist. Similarly, some female analysts may deal with their countertransference distress by effectively "castrating" the young male's emerging sexuality and colluding in the resistance he experiences to discussing such feelings openly. The fact that male adolescents are often referred by female analysts to male analysts—with the rationalization that a strong identification figure is needed—may reflect female clinicians' countertransference anxiety at the potential for erotization of the transference.

While the intensity and sexualization of the mother-son relationship in Nicholas's family may be unusual, we speculate that similar factors may be at work in many other cases. Two major societal changes appear to contribute to such dynamics. First, the large number of broken homes with distant fathers may result in excessive closeness between mother and son, with an accompanying erotization on both sides of the dyad. Second, with more women in the workforce, boys increasingly may regard their mothers as objects of identification.

Psychoanalysis was born out of Freud's observation that the analytic setting was a fertile field for the emergence of symbolically incestuous erotic longings. Indeed, Freud believed the mechanism of cure was based on the patient's love for the analyst. Nevertheless, many forms of erotic transference are highly disconcerting to the analyst. Among these, the male adolescent's desire for his female analyst may represent a particularly unsettling situation. The age differences and gender constellation of the dyad appear to tap into highly charged intrapsychic and cultural incest taboos that present extraordinary challenges on the analyst's capacity to contain and interpret the analytic process.

BIBLIOGRAPHY

BAK, R. C. (1968). The phallic woman: The ubiquitous fantasy in perversions. *Psychoanal. Study Child*, 23:15–36.
BENEDEK, E. (1973). Training the woman resident to be a psychiatrist. *Amer. J. Psychiat.*, 130:1131–35.
BIBRING, G. (1936). A contribution to the subject of transference-resistence. *Int. J. Psycho-Anal.*, 17:181–89.
BLOS, P. (1962). *On Adolescence*. New York: Free Press.

ERIKSON, E. H. (1959). *Identity and the Life Cycle*. New York: W. W. Norton.

FREUD, A. (1958). Adolescence. *Psychoanal. Study Child*, 13:255–78.

FREUD, S. (1915). Observations on transference-love (Further recommendations on the technique of psycho-analysis, III). *S.E.*, 12:157–73.

GABBARD, G. O. (1994a). Commentary on Tansey, Hirsch, and Davies. *Psychoanal. Dialogues*, 4:203–13.

GABBARD, G. O. (1994b). Sexual excitement and countertransference love in the analyst. *J. Am. Psychoanal. Assoc.*, 42:91–114.

GOLDBERGER, M., & EVANS, D. (1985). On transference manifestations in male patients with female analysts. *Int. J. Psycho-Anal.*, 66:295–309.

GORKIN, M. (1985). Varieties of sexualized countertransference. *Psychoanal. Rev.*, 72:421–40.

GORNICK, L. K. (1986). Developing a new narrative: The women therapist and the male patient. *Psychoanal. Psychol.*, 3(4):299–325.

GREENACRE, P. (1970). The transitional object and the fetish: With special reference to the role of illusion. In *Emotional Growth: Psychoanalytic Studies of the Gifted and a Great Variety of Other Individuals*, 1:335–52. New York: Int. Univ. Press.

GREENSON, R. R. (1967). *The Technique and Practice of Psychoanalysis*. New York: Int. Univ. Press.

JACOBSON, E. (1951). Development of the wish for a child in boys. *Psychoanal. Study Child*, 5:139–52.

KARME, L. (1979). The analysis of the male patient by a female analyst: The problem of the negative oedipal transference. *Int. J. Psycho-Anal.*, 60:253–61.

LESTER, E. P. (1985). The female analyst and the erotized transference. *Int. J. Psycho-Anal.*, 66:283–93.

MYERS, H. (1987). How do women treat men? In *The Psychology of Men*, ed. G. Fogel, 262–75. New York: Basic.

PERSON, E. S. (1985). The erotic transference in women and in men: Differences and consequences. *J. Amer. Acad. Psychoanal.*, 13:159–80.

RITVO, S. (1971). Late adolescence: Development and clinical considerations. *Psychoanal. Study Child*, 26:241–63.

ROSS, J. M. (1977). Towards fatherhood: The epigenesis of paternal identity during a boy's first decade. *Int. Review Psycho-Anal.*, 4:327–47.

RUSS, H. (1993). Erotic transference through countertransference: The female therapist and the male patient. *Psychoanal. Psychol.*, 10:393–406.

STOLLER, R. (1975). *Perversion: The erotic form of hatred*. New York: Pantheon.

TICHO, E. A. (1975). The effects of the analyst's personality on psychoanalytic treatment. *Psychoanalytic Forum*, 4:137–51.

TROP. J. (1988). Erotic and erotized transference: A self psychological perspective. *Psychoanal. Psychol.*, 5:269–84.

TYSON, P. (1986). The female analyst and the male analysand. Presentation to the San Francisco Psychoanalytic Institute, 1986.

WAKSMAN, J. D. (1986). The countertransference of the child analyst. *Int. Rev. Psychoanal.*, 13:405–15.

Daughters and Mothers

Aspects of the Representational World During Adolescence

E. KIRSTEN DAHL, PH.D.

This paper explores the transformations of the girl's intrapsychic relationship to the mental representations of her mother and their contribution to mastery of the specifically female developmental milestones during adolescence and early adulthood. The vicissitudes of the girl's intrapsychic organization of the mental representations to the maternal object both reflect and characterize the psychological tasks of female adolescence: puberty, menarche, sexuality, and psychological independence. It is argued that the characteristic fantasies of this period can be understood not only as representing an intrapsychic developmental progression along object lines but as complex compromise formations which serve multiple structural functions as well. Clinical material is presented to illustrate typical fantasies of female adolescence.

JESSICA, A THIRD-YEAR LAW STUDENT, SOUGHT CONSULTATION FOR HER anxiety and transient depressive moods. Although she had performed brilliantly as an undergraduate and in law school, she found herself worrying excessively about her performance. She felt that she was too dependent on the approval of her faculty advisor: She would fall into what felt like a depressive abyss when she experienced him as critical of

---

Associate Clinical Professor of Child Psychoanalysis, Yale University Child Study Center, New Haven.

This paper reflects many conversations with Dr. Samuel Ritvo, whose thinking on female development has stimulated and shaped my own. I wish to express my appreciation for his teaching.

The Psychoanalytic Study of the Child 50, ed. Albert J. Solnit, Peter B. Neubauer, Samuel Abrams, and A. Scott Dowling (Yale University Press, copyright © 1995 by Albert J. Solnit, Peter B. Neubauer, Samuel Abrams, and A. Scott Dowling).

her intellect. During the consultative interviews, she spoke feelingly of her intense attachment to her father; she felt that her professional training was a tribute to his belief in her and her admiration of him. Jessica believed that her academic anxiety was somehow connected to her relationship with her father; she feared that she would in some indefinable way disappoint him. Just as with her advisor, Jessica felt, on reflection, that she was too desirous of her father's attention and admiration. She described with animation her childhood relationship with her father and how he had encouraged and supported her as she grew up. Her silence about her mother was a noteworthy contrast. When asked directly about her mother, she said dismissively that her mother never had achieved much of anything, adding more gently, "Oh, she's a very nice mother, but we really don't have much in common."

Within the first month of analysis, Jessica reported a dream in which she was standing in what she thought was a grade-school classroom facing her mother, who was a little distance away. She wanted desperately to catch her mother's eye, but her mother's face was "a mask": cold and unreadable. Jessica realized that her mother actually was wearing a mask, but as she reached to remove the mask, to her horror the furious and mocking face of a gargoyle was revealed. In association to the dream, Jessica suddenly recalled what she thought was a very early childhood memory. She thought she had been about three years old. She remembered sitting on the edge of her mother's bed. Her mother was turned away from her, asleep. Jessica wanted to reach out and touch her but knew she must not. Recalling this memory, Jessica began to weep. She said she thought her mother had often been quite depressed during Jessica's childhood. Jessica thought she had been "too much" for her mother—too loud, too wild, too demanding. Often her mother would sigh and turn away from Jessica, telling her to stop making so much noise.

Following the emergence of these memories, over the course of the next several months Jessica began to report feeling sad on the days between sessions. Frequently, during the first session after the weekend, she would speak in a nearly inaudible and somewhat abstracted voice. It became clear that she experienced the weekend interruption as very long and her analyst as very far away. Returning, she worried that her sadness and longing were "too much." These thoughts would frequently be followed by detailed recollections of her mother's criticisms of her, her mother's turning away, and efforts on Jessica's part to capture her mother's attention.

Six months into the analysis, Jessica anticipated with excitement a visit home over a weekend; she knew she would be welcomed and cosseted. During the session after the visit, Jessica reported with fury that the visit had been a disaster. Her mother wasn't really interested in her; all her interest had been focused on Jessica's father! Jessica had made a horrible scene, and the evening had been ruined. She had gone supperless to her room, sobbing and enraged. Later that night, she had crept out of her room and, finding her mother alone, reading in bed, had climbed into bed with her, where her mother had comforted her, stroking her hair.

Clinical material such as Jessica's is not unusual in the treatment of young women and adolescent girls, perhaps especially when the treating analyst is a woman. The preoccupation with the mother is startlingly intense, regardless of what the daughter's actual relationship with her mother is or has been. A ready-made transference resistance in which the analyst is experienced as harshly critical and angrily withdrawn is common in these young female analysands. Derivatives from unconscious fantasies of a fascinating, terrifying, omnipotent mother appear to color and shape the clinical material.

Such phenomena have led many psychoanalytic writers to emphasize the girl's preoedipal attachment to her mother and its subsequent "relinquishment" as central to feminine development. Beginning with the seminal papers of the 1920s and 1930s on femininity by Abraham (1922), Horney (1924, 1926), Deutsch (1925, 1930, 1932), Klein (1928, 1932), Lampl de Groot (1927), Jones (1927, 1935), Freud (1925, 1931, 1933), Fenichel (1934), and Brunswick (1940), psychoanalytic theory has struggled to understand the role of the girl's relationship to her mother in female development. These early writers explored the little girl's long dependency on her mother and the vicissitudes inherent in the turn from the mother to the father during the oedipal phase. Current literature emphasizes the reemergence during adolescence of the preoedipal object tie to the mother and a so-called second epoch of separation-individuation necessary to the attainment of adult femininity. Usually what is commented on is the tenacity of the daughter's attachment and the difficulty she seems to have in relinquishing it (Bernstein and Warner, 1984).

In marked contrast, recent developmental research (Offer and Shashin, 1984) suggests that for most girls, the psychological milestones of adolescence are achieved without dramatic behavioral manifestations. Although with menarche the girl confides less in her mother (Whisnant and Zegans, 1975; Whisnant et al., 1979), normative research suggests that during adolescence the relationship of the daughter to her mother is best characterized as one of strong attachment rather than of conflict and rejection (Apter, 1990). Such epidemiological and sociological data have been used to argue that a central task of adolescence for the girl is renegotiation of the relationship to her mother in reality in the service of psychic separation-individuation and adult independence; this is seen as a lifelong task, incomplete at the close of adolescence (Bergman, 1984; Dalsimer, 1986).

How can we best understand these apparently contradictory observations? As Solnit (1983) has argued, the confusion stems in part from a conflation between external reality and the psychic reality of the inner world. This conflation is mirrored in the adolescent girl, who frequently externalizes aspects of her inner world, especially those representations that pertain to the tie to the mother, to her mother-in-reality. Through the process of externalization and her subsequent actions to control external reality, the adolescent girl tries to avoid internal conflict.

Psychoanalytic theory distinguishes between the observable, external relationship between the adolescent girl and her mother and the daughter's intrapsychic relationship to mental representations of the mother. It is the organization within the inner world of these complex mental representations of the mother that undergoes substantive transformation during adolescence. The distinction psychoanalytic theory makes between external and intrapsychic reality provides a framework in which to understand the apparent contradictions between the normative data, which demonstrate a relatively unconflicted reworking of the daughter's attachment to her mother, and clinical data, which underscore the specific vulnerabilities the girl may experience in relation to her mother as the daughter strives for greater psychological differentiation. The difficulties involved in the girl's intrapsychic organization of the mental representations of her tie to the maternal object both reflect and characterize the psychological tasks of female adolescence. Some of the symptomatic phenomena characteristically manifested by girls during adolescence can best be understood as representing maladaptive attempts to transform the representations of the maternal object in the inner world (Dahl, 1989, 1993).

The transformations of the girl's intrapsychic relationship to the mental representations of her mother contribute to mastery of the specifically female developmental milestones during adolescence and early adulthood.[1] Characteristic fantasies can be understood not sim-

---

1. Because the emphasis in this paper is on the ways in which the adolescent girl utilizes intrapsychically fantasies of her relationship with her mother, the role of the father in the daughter's development is explored in only cursory fashion—that is, only as it finds representation in the tie to the mother. This should not be taken as an indication that the

ply as representing an intrapsychic developmental progression along object lines but also as complex compromise formations that serve multiple structural functions.

PUBERTY AND MENARCHE

Psychoanalytic theory concerning female puberty and menarche emphasizes that with the biologically based upsurge in drives comes an intensification of both sexual and aggressive urges, accompanied by a reawakening of incestuous fantasies and a more infantile tie to the parents (Blos, 1962; Burgner, 1988; Dahl, 1989; Deutsch, 1944). Menarche is frequently experienced as resonating with earlier anal conflicts and as stimulating anxieties about control of one's body. Concealment and secrecy become widespread as the pubescent girl attempts to defend against the regressive pull of these archaic fantasies (Ritvo, 1976; Whisnant et al., 1979).

Twelve-year-old Mary recounted to her therapist how she had gotten her period for the first time on a school field trip: "Ugh! It was *disgusting!* I was running, playing catch, and all of a sudden I felt, you know, something wet—I knew something was happening. I grabbed Sally and told her I had to get to the bathroom. We used all this toilet paper. I didn't want anyone to see what had happened. I felt so embarrassed, like people would think I was a baby or something!" Mary's next thoughts were of a fight she had had with her mother over how messy her room was. She didn't see what was such a big deal about having a clean room, she *liked* it messy! She looked momentarily sad, fell briefly silent, and then her thoughts turned again to getting her period. She said with visible disgust, "It was the worst moment in my life. I mean, I wanted to get my period but not on a field trip. I didn't want to get my clothes all dirty and everything. And my Mom wasn't even there." The associative links in Mary's thoughts seem almost transparent—the excitement, disgust, anxiety over making a mess, defiant messiness, and transient longing for her mother—as if at a nearly conscious level she momentarily experienced herself as a small girl needing her mother's bodily care and regulation.

The biologically based upsurge in the drives creates an internal climate of excitement that mirrors the primitive excitement of the girl's

daughter's intrapsychic relationship to representations of her father is insignificant to feminine development. Some of the clinical material presented here suggests that representations of the father play a crucial role in defending against regressive longings for the mother.

relationship to her mother during infancy and very early childhood. Then the mother was experienced as the regulator of affects, particularly excitement. Now, as the girl enters adolescence, the affect-regulating aspect of the remembered-in-fantasy mother of early childhood is simultaneously longed for, feared, and resented. The young adolescent struggles to free herself from this remembered mother of infancy and at the same time strives to keep these nostalgic memories of her mother as a part of the self forever.

The girl also moves toward a further psychological differentiation of her body from her mother's, while yearning for her mother's bodily care. This reawakening of longings for the active, care-giving mother of infancy arouses a fear of passive submission to the mother through the girl's unconscious wish to experience pleasure again at her mother's hands. The daughter is caught between her longing to surrender to her mother for gratification and her fear that she will be forced to submit, thereby losing her hard-won activity and sense of bodily integrity. She worries that her desires will result in engulfment by the mother. The newly awakened bodily excitement stimulates fears of an erotic attachment to the mother that is experienced as potentially homosexual.

These revived unconscious fantasies of infancy may be accompanied by a resurgence of preoedipally driven sadism, presenting yet another danger for the pubertal girl. If her defensive strategy is to externalize this sadism onto her mother—now linked internally to the imagined mother of infancy, for whom she regressively longs as a regulator of inner excitement—the daughter fears she is in danger from her mother's rage. In her attempt to strip the relationship of this valence of projected sadism, the daughter may reverse the direction of the sadism, thereby experiencing the tie to her mother as masochistic This masochistic strategy relieves the daughter of the conscious experience of hostile aggression, restoring the transient fantasy of harmony between mother and her "devoted" daughter. The masochistic valence, however, may awaken in the daughter the fear that she is now dangerously at risk of passively surrendering to this archaically powerful internalized mother.

In an attempt to ward off intolerable internal conflict, the young adolescent girl may insist, via externalization, on resurrecting a more infantile relationship to her mother in reality. The fantasy accompanying this more regressively organized relationship is of a magical, "always present" mother who will "make everything better." In the context of the girl's sexually maturing body this fantasy is now felt to be too dangerous, as it implies a homosexual tie to the mother. In her effort to control this reerotized infantile longing for the mother, the girl flees toward the oedipal tie to her father. However, this inner configuration of object relations at an oedipal level also leaves the girl feeling bereft of active maternal care, at a time when she experiences a heightened need for the excitement-soothing, pleasure-giving, and affect-regulating aspects of the archaic maternal representations. The girl may then tenaciously and defensively reactivate a clinging relationship with the mother, who is experienced as the source of conflict through her actions. The girl attempts to resolve the dilemmas of her inner world by fighting with her mother in reality (A. Freud, 1949). Externally directed hostility toward the mother may win for the girl some relief from inner conflict by regulating interpersonal distance. The daughter keeps her mother close and involved but is able to defend against her fears of being engulfed.

Twelve-year-old Janet was the daughter of parents who had divorced when she was six. She sought treatment for herself because of her concern that her worries made it hard for her to concentrate in school. Even though Janet got along well with the girls at school, she found herself preoccupied with what they were doing and thinking: she spent a lot of time thinking about who was fighting with whom. Frequently Janet found herself, somewhat mysteriously, in the middle of excited arguments and "fights." She also stimulated fights between her parents because she seemed unable to keep from telling tales about one parent to the other. When Janet was with her mother, she had trouble getting to sleep and often worried that her sleeping difficulties would make her sick. She demanded that her mother fix her special slumber drinks, and when this failed to settle her down, she liked to climb into her mother's bed and have her rub her back. She was calmer on the days she spent at her father's house, but there, too, she would sometimes wake during the night and feel that she had to call her mother to see how she was. She would think that her mother might be worried about her. With her mother, Janet was frequently argumentative and challenging, refusing to keep her room clean or do her homework consistently. Her mother felt quite sympathetic to Janet's sleep troubles, but her daughter's messiness and argumentiveness drove her to distraction, and she was appalled by how quickly their conflicts escalated into raging battles. In treatment, Janet insisted that "someone," preferably her mother, could make everything all right by telling her just what to do; Janet felt very angry that her mother expected so much of *her*. Following a session to which her father had brought her and during which she had talked about feeling calmer at school, she insisted that her mother accompany her to the next session. Janet began by saying angrily, "You say, Mom. *You* say!" Her mother explained that as they were driving to the session, Janet had announced that she didn't want to sleep at Daddy's any more; it was "too scary." Janet then said that she was angry because, when she had trouble sleeping, her father wouldn't help, and he wouldn't let her come into bed with him. At these times, she said, she felt she really needed Mommy. Janet then began to alternate between an anxious recitation of all her school worries, her sleep worries, her getting-sick worries, and angry attacks on her mother during which she insisted that her mother *did* know what was on Janet's mind and should just tell her what to do to feel better. At one point, after having berated her mother for refusing to tell the therapist what Janet was thinking, she said furiously, "You think you know everything, but you don't know anything!" Here, in the rapid shifts in Janet's material, we get glimpses of what appears to be an underlying fantasy in which she longs for her mother to care for her as if she were a much younger child, becomes frightened of surrendering to this archaic engulfing mother, and flees in fantasy to her father. However, the erotic longings for her father again awaken anxiety—this time apparently of maternal retaliation—and so she turns again insistently to her mother. Now in reality she demands that her mother behave omnipotently and simultaneously pushes away this externalized longed-for and feared mother of infancy.

This early adolescent phase in the girl is characterized by oscillations in her object relations between different developmental levels of organization that also reflect strong bisexual tendencies: in her inner world the girl wavers irresolutely between the desired and feared archaic omnipotent mother, the oedipal father, and the homosexually desired oedipal mother.

SEXUALITY

Early to middle adolescence is stamped by the girl's efforts to integrate her experience of her sexually maturing body with masturbatory fantasies as she moves toward a primarily genital and nonincestuous organization of her sexuality (Dahl, 1989). With the upsurge in drives and the hormonally induced physical maturation, the girl's attention is directed forcefully toward her body as she struggles to achieve psychic integration of these bodily changes. During this phase of adolescence, many girls develop an intense relationship with another girl—the best friend—an attempt via reality to relinquish the intrapsychic attachment to the mother of infancy. Psychically, the attachment to the best friend can be understood as a way station on the path to mature sexuality.

As noted in the preceding section, the biologically based increase in the drives that usher in the early pubertal period reawakens all the earlier sources of libidinal and aggressive modes of gratification. These earlier modes brought with them the valence of the infantile tie to the mother, which derived its intensity and strength from her bodily care. The preoedipal phase as it is reawakened in adolescence is especially significant in that it was during this infantile period, through the experience of the mother's bodily care, that the girl's relationship to her own body became established (Laufer, 1982). For the adolescent girl this is especially problematic and is experienced as dangerous, because these memories of bodily pleasure at the hands of the mother now take on a homosexual charge. For some girls, vulnerable to cultural pressures because of an insufficiently integrated superego, the danger of this regressive tie to the mother of infancy is warded off by a pathologically precocious turn to compulsive or delinquent heterosexuality (Blos, 1962; Dahl, 1993; Ritvo, 1984, 1989). For most girls, however, this attempt at a solution through a flight to reality is inhibited by superego disapproval.

In conflict about turning to reality to discharge her sexual urges, the girl experiences intensification of her attachment to her internalized mother and her relationship to her own body. Intense and painful internal conflict is generated as the girl struggles to integrate psychically the representation of her sexually maturing body into her developing personality. It is in this context that the girl turns her attention forcefully to her body as a source of representation and expression of internal conflict (Ritvo, 1984).

The associative pathway between representations of the mother and representations of the body forms because with the physical changes of puberty, the girl begins to possess a body that is identified with the mother's body (Dahl, 1989; Ritvo, 1984, 1989). This situation threatens to strengthen the closeness to the mother and to stimulate fantasies of merging and oneness, as well as fears of being overwhelmed (Ritvo, 1989). At the same time, relinquishing this infantile tie to the mother may be variously experienced by the daughter as liberating, or as necessitating a renunciation of future bodily pleasure, or as a dangerous and destructive surpassing of the mother (Laufer, 1986). Very gradually, during middle adolescence, the girl begins the intrapsychic turn toward the oedipal father. The earlier pregenital tie to the mother, now slowly being relinquished, is transformed into an oedipally tinged, erotized longing for the mother. The bisexual valence of this situation can be seen in the girl's continual intrapsychic oscillation between her mother and her father and their substitutes.

Nowhere is this bisexual "hovering" more clearly expressed than in the best friend, who, in fantasy, is simultaneously girlfriend and boyfriend. In actuality the best friend may also serve as a link to the first heterosexual encounters as well, her presence helping the girl to maintain an acceptable balance between impulse and inhibition and providing a safe haven when action becomes too exciting. Finally, the best friend is simultaneously an agent of the mother, a substitute for the mother, a companion on the way to relinquishing the tie to the mother, and a support for dawning heterosexual interests.

Another "solution" to relinquishing the tie to the mother that some daughters attempt via fantasy is *postponement* (Laufer, 1986), in which the preoedipal attachment to the mother is recast in an oedipal configuration, but a configuration that denies differences both between the sexes and between generations (Chasseguet-Smirgel, 1986). In this fantasy, the daughter's earlier experience of bodily pleasure through maternal care, her envy of the mother's capacity to provide gratification through her active ministrations, and the daughter's wish to provide such satisfactions to the mother spur her to take her mother as erotic object at the level of unconscious fantasy. In an effort to keep from awareness her inadequacy as mother's partner, she projects onto the mother the envious, hostile, jealous, and possessive aspects of her love, creating the image of the witch-mother who fascinates and imprisons the daughter. The primarily oedipal valence of the relationship to the "witch-mother" (Dahl, 1989) can be found in a characteristic unconscious fantasy configuration of this period. Elements of this fantasy structure include a secret excited longing for the mother and her body, which the daughter experiences as putting her at risk to be taken over by the mother for the mother's pleasure; projection onto the mother of the envious, hostile, jealous, and possessive aspects of the daughter's love; experience of the mother as malignantly destructive of the daughter's efforts to obtain genital pleasure from other sources; and oscillation between the wish to be the mother's erotic partner and fear that the mother would destroy the daughter if she knew the daughter had an alternative erotic object in the tie to the man. The latent fantasy configuration seems to be of a jealously possessive, envious, and malignantly destructive witch-mother whom the daughter cannot relinquish and who will not relinquish the daughter. The fascinating and terrifying witch-mother is seen by the daughter as the regulator, owner, or manipulator of the daughter's body and of her pleasure (Dahl, 1989).

In this fantasy it is now the *mother* who is experienced as malignantly destructive of the *daughter's* efforts to obtain pleasure from the man, as if the mother believed the daughter to be an adequate erotic partner and the man to be the mother's rival. This fantasy is rooted in denial of the generational difference as well as of the knowledge that the daughter's body is not adequate to the task of providing full genital satisfaction to the mother (Chasseguet-Smirgel, 1986). That the girl possesses this knowledge but denies it is revealed in her conscious preoccupation with feelings that her body is somehow lesser, lacking, and/or damaged in comparison to other female bodies. This stance allows her to postpone the feelings of loss and sadness she anticipates if she were to acknowledge the anatomical and generational differences and to accept that she cannot keep her mother's love to herself.

In addition, the creation of the internalized witch-mother and the anal-sadistic shading of the relationship function as a kind of preoedipal camouflage in the service of masking the daughter's secret—her erotic longing for the father. As she presents herself to her mother as a disgusting mess, unable to regulate her body and its sensations, the daughter's apparent preoedipal attachment conceals and protects the tie to the man from the jealous destructiveness of the internalized mother.

Fifteen-year-old Brenda began her analysis struggling with intense depressive affect and suicidal thoughts.[2] During the consultation, Brenda confessed her puzzlement over the fact that she frequently became so enraged with her mother that she felt as if she wanted to kill her, even though she recognized that her mother's demands in reality were not so unusual. During her second year of analysis, as her depression lifted, Brenda became actively involved with a popular crowd of boys and girls at school. During her sessions, allusions to one specific boy became increasingly frequent, although Brenda gave no outward sign that she was romantically interested in him. Nevertheless, she spoke with pleasure of the interests they shared and of his artistic talent, which she admired. During one session she mentioned in an offhand way that she and this boy had gone out together, emphasizing that they were simply attending a mutually appealing concert. Following this hour, his name dropped from her associations, and Brenda began to speak with great anxiety about what she experienced as dangerous behavior within her crowd. She thought there was a lot of drinking going on, "even though these are the kids that started SADD [Students

2. For further material on Brenda, see Dahl, 1989.

Against Drunk Driving] at my school!" "They are such hypocrites!" she added contemptuously. She was certain the drinking was really just a license for the sexual activity she was sure some of the kids engaged in. She described one Saturday night when she was hanging out with her crowd but very much on the periphery, feeling "out of it" because she certainly was not going to drink. At the next session she began describing feeling enraged with her mother because her mother just wouldn't "mind her own business." She continued, "I had arranged to go out with my friends just for a while in the evening. Just to hang out. I was getting ready to go, but I was just sitting down for a minute and my mother came and sat down right next to me, practically on top of me, and she wanted to know where I was going. And she didn't want me to go out. She made that clear with all her questions." As she spoke Brenda was in a fury again, accusing her mother of not wanting her to have any friends, of wanting to keep her a little girl "all to herself."

In this sequence we can see both Brenda's concealment and revelation of her new attachment to the boy, followed by increasing anxiety about things being out of control. By externalizing her own excitement onto her friends in her fantasy of their drinking and sexual activity, Brenda tries to walk away from the increasing pressure of her drives. When this is not altogether successful she calls forth for additional defense the fantasy of the intrusive controlling mother of infancy, which, via externalization, she projects onto her mother-in-reality. She rages against but simultaneously surrenders to her.

PSYCHOLOGICAL INDEPENDENCE

The central task of late adolescence is to bring the girl into a more definitive relationship with the wider world; it is at this point that decisions are made that foreshadow the shape of the adult woman's life. Characteristic approaches to work, to sexual intimacy, and to enduring values begin to crystallize (Dalsimer, 1986). Within the girl's inner world a more decisive disengagement from the earlier attachments, both preoedipal and oedipal, to the mother is begun as the daughter embarks on a search for the nonincestuous object of desire. The girl begins to relinquish her submission within her inner world to maternal authority and to experience authority as originating within herself (Bergman, 1984; Ritvo, 1989; Dalsimer, 1986).

The push of progressive development encourages a more sustained turn to external reality as a source of pleasure and satisfaction. Activity in the real world serves to ward off the threat of loss of the maternal object within the inner world as well. Feelings of being bereft, transient depressive moods, and conscious attempts to model herself on an admired adult woman are common during this period as the girl struggles to transform her object tie to her mother within her inner world. The dilemma for the girl at this point is to achieve a more integrated sense of herself as psychically differentiated from her mother without sacrificing those representations of the earlier object relationships to the mother that are employed in the service of self-soothing, self-esteem and affect regulation, and narcissistic valuation of the body and its capacity for genital pleasure. The resolution of this dilemma is gradual and continues to be felt as salient well into young adulthood (Dalsimer, 1992). As can be seen in the clinical vignette of Rebecca below, conflicts stemming from unsuccessful attempts at resolution of this dilemma are apparent in the analyses of adult women as well.

The hazards for the late adolescent girl attendant upon the consolidation of psychic structure as it reflects representations of the tie to the mother lie in the degree to which the daughter is unable to tolerate the conflict inherent in the internal oscillations between her attachments to the soothing, regulating mother of infancy and the rivalrous, erotic, law-giving mother of the oedipal phase. Fearing herself at the mercy of sexual excitement as she begins to relinquish more completely the tie to the infantile mother, the late adolescent daughter may organize her genital sexuality around the feared desire for maternal bodily care and the regulation of primitive excitement. At the level of the tie to the oedipal mother, fearing an inner world emptied of the erotically desired mother, the daughter may feel compelled to surrender to the unconscious fantasy of the tenaciously clinging "witch-mother" who can never be pleased. Although this defensive strategy allows her to retain the fascinatingly hateful mother as an aspect of herself, the result is a conscious preoccupation with a mother who must be warded off as endlessly frustrating. During this period of late adolescent psychological consolidation, the daughter reaches an accommodation within her inner world with the oscillating levels of the tie to the mother in which she integrates as aspects of herself a continuing intrapsychic dialogue with her mother. Premature closure to this process brought about by the daughter's need to strip her self representations of their resonance with the tie to the mother presents an obstacle to further development, including a brittle shallowness in which aspects of the self are treated as if lost.

Rebecca was an adult when she entered analysis because of recurrent depressive moods and an awareness of severe self-defeating tendencies. Although her mother was dead and she was estranged from her father, she continued to experience lingering anguish over her parents' frequently abusive and neglectful treatment of her as she was growing up. Much of her analytic work focused on memories of her mother, whom she came to view as a coldly self-involved woman who had preferred her other children to Rebecca. Rebecca felt that she had spent years trying to please her mother without success and that she had made enormous and self-damaging sacrifices in the hopes of winning her mother's love. In spite of this, Rebecca had managed to carve out a professional life for herself and had married a man she experienced as nurturing.

The hour reported below occurred during the fourth year of analysis. Rebecca began by announcing with pleasure that she had finally sold a painting she had inherited from her mother. She felt relief that she had finally done it and had gotten a good price for it, too. It was nice to have that money in the bank. Now she had enough money to fix up the back bedroom (a project associated in her mind with her conflicted wishes about having a baby). Rebecca then said she had had the thought that if her mother knew she'd sold the painting, she would be very angry. Rebecca herself hated the picture: all it meant to her was her mother's sense of entitlement, "my mother the queen." Rebecca sometimes thought it would have killed her to have any painting valued by her mother hanging in her own home. She then imagined her brother's finding out what she had done and becoming enraged. He had told her she was never to sell anything she had inherited from her mother, and anyway he had really wanted the painting himself. Suddenly Rebecca began to cry. She couldn't have kept the painting—she needed the money. She had *had* to sell it. Her thoughts quickly flooded with images of all the ways she felt she had failed in her life. In a fury she began to berate herself with how inadequate she was: "I've never amounted to anything! I just live this marginal life in my pathetic falling-down house." Her thoughts then turned to a recent fight with her husband in which she had experienced him as unjustly demanding that she sacrifice her own needs in favor of his.

In this hour, we can see the rapid associative shift as Rebecca moves from her momentary pleasure in having finally triumphed over her mother to representations of her mother as tenaciously retaliatory, forbidding Rebecca all pleasure except the masochistic pleasure of complete surrender to the omnipotent archaic infantile mother. This harsh, pleasure-forbidding mother is so dangerous that much of Rebecca's intrapsychic activity is of necessity devoted to preserving a modicum of space in which Rebecca herself can exist, but the result is an impoverished, brittle psychic organization stripped of all resonances with the tie to the mother, a condition that leaves Rebecca feeling depleted and numb.

DISCUSSION

A central task of female adolescence is reworking the tie to the mother in the service of psychic differentiation. Representations of the tie to the mother of infancy are employed by the adolescent girl in the resolution of internal conflict and in the construction of an integrated self. We can see a developmental unfolding in the organization of maternal object representations, their function in reemerging preoedipal and oedipal fantasy configurations, and their contribution to the resolution of internal conflicts associated with the developmental milestones of adolescence. Although these fantasy configurations appear to reflect a developmental progression in object relations along the line of increasing psychic differentiation of the daughter from her mother, to understand them solely at this level is to miss the complexity of their role within the inner world. First, it is important to remember that these fantasies are not simply brought forward or remembered from earlier epochs; they are constructed under the press of the intrapsychic demands of adolescence and represent transformations of memories and earlier fantasies in the light of current experience. Second, these fantasies are created in an effort to resolve the internal conflicts generated by the demands of the sexually maturing body, the biologically driven upsurge in the drives, the reawakened incestuous longings, superego constraints, and adaptations to external reality. As we have seen, these fantasies contain representations of the tie to the mother. The tie to the mother in turn is utilized in the service of representing the body, the drives, the desired object's body, and specific fears of retaliation and punishment. For these reasons, it is useful to view these complex fantasy configurations as compromise formations that may be employed in the service of multiple intrapsychic functions. In addition to representing the body and drive derivatives, these fantasies may be employed in the service of defense via externalizations, as we have seen with Janet and Brenda. And as we have seen in Rebecca's hour, representations of the tie to the mother may also give shape to aspects of the superego and can be used in the regulation of self-esteem.

The young girl discovers her body through her long dependence on maternal care. By this means she also learns to distinguish internal sensation from external stimuli and consolidates self-regulatory and self-soothing capacities. Through the experience of her mother's bodily care, the girl's relationship to her own body is established. In this context the body ego is formed. These infantile experiences with the mother and the associated fantasies are reworked and transformed with each new developmental epoch, becoming increasingly complex and densely layered. These complex fantasy configurations give representation to the girl's tie to her mother and also contain representations of the body and its demands, the parental bodies and their demands, and the drives. They therefore retain enormous creative potential as vehicles for self representation throughout development. They are employed intrapsychically in the service of structural differentiation and integration. It is for this reason that these fantasies are so ubiquitous and salient in the lives of women and not necessarily because the "relinquishment" of the tie to the mother is so fraught with difficulty. Rather, as I have suggested, the process of the psychic integration of the tie to the mother as an aspect of the self is never fully complete. The hallmark of adult female psychic organization lies in the daughter's capacity to permit continuing reverberations within herself of the representations of the tie to the mother in her ongoing intrapsychic dialogue with her mother.

BIBLIOGRAPHY

ABRAHAM, K. (1979[1922]). Manifestations of the female castration complex. In *Selected Papers*, pp. 338–69. New York: Brunner/Mazel.
APTER, T. (1990). *Altered Loves: Mothers and Daughters during Adolescence*. New York: Fawcett Columbine.
BERGMAN, A. (1984). On the development of female identity: Issues of mother-daughter interaction during the separation-individuation process. Paper presented at the symposium "The Many Faces of Eve," UCLA, February 1984.
BERNSTEIN, A. E., & WARNER, G. M. (1984). *Women Treating Women*, New York: Int. Univ. Press.
BLOS, P. (1962). *On Adolescence*. New York: Free Press.
BRUNSWICK, R. M. (1940). The preoedipal phase of the libido in development. In: Fleiss, (1948). pp. 261–284.
BURGNER, M. (1988). Analytic work with adolescents terminable and interminable. *Int. J. Psychoanal.*, 69:179–87.
CHASSEGUET-SMIRGEL, J. (1986). *Sexuality and Mind*. New York: New York Univ. Press.
DAHL, E. K. (1989). Daughters and mothers: Oedipal aspects of the witch mother. *Psychoanal. Study Child*, 44:267–80.
——— (1993). The impact of divorce on a preadolescent girl. *Psychoanal. Study Child*, 48:193–209.

DALSIMER, K. (1986). *Female Adolescence: Psychoanalytic Reflections on Literature.* New Haven: Yale Univ. Press.

—— (1992). Motherhood and mourning in Virginia Woolf's *To the Lighthouse.* Paper presented at the Gardiner Seminar in Psychoanalysis and the Humanities, Yale University, January 31, 1992.

DEUTSCH, H. (1925). The psychology of women in relation to the function of reproduction. In Fleiss, 1948. pp. 166–79.

—— (1930). The significance of masochism in the mental life of women. In Fleiss, 1948. pp. 223–36.

—— (1932). On female homosexuality. In Fleiss, 1948. pp. 237–60.

—— (1944). *The Psychology of Women: A Psychoanalytic Interpretation.* Vol. 1: Girlhood. New York: Grune and Stratton.

FENICHEL, O. (1934). Further light upon the preoedipal phase in girls. In *The Collected Papers of Otto Fenichel,* pp. 241–88. New York: W. W. Norton, 1953.

FLEISS, R., ED. (1948). *The Psychoanalytic Reader.* New York: Int. Univ. Press.

FREUD, A. (1949). On certain difficulties in the preadolescent's relation to his parents. In *The Writings of Anna Freud* 4:94–106. New York: Int. Univ. Press.

FREUD, S. (1925). Some psychical consequences of the anatomical distinction between the sexes. *S.E.,* 9:243–58.

—— (1931). Female sexuality. *S.E.,* 21:223–43.

—— (1933). Femininity. *S.E.,* 22:112–35.

HORNEY, K. (1924). On the genesis of the castration complex in women. In Horney, 1967, pp. 37–54.

—— (1926). The flight from womanhood. In Horney, 1967, pp. 54–71.

—— (1931). The dread of women. In Horney, 1967, pp. 133–48.

—— (1967). *Feminine Psychology.* New York: W. W. Norton.

JONES, E. (1927). The early development of female sexuality. In *Int. J. Psychoanal.,* 8(4):459–72.

—— (1935). Early female sexuality. In *Int. J. Psychoanal.,* 16(3):263–73.

LAMPL DE GROOT, J. (1927). The evolution of the oedipus complex in women. In Fleiss, 1948, pp. 207–22.

LAUFER, M. E. (1982). Female masturbation in adolescence and the development of the relationship to the body. *Int. J. Psychoanal.,* 63:295–301.

—— (1986). The female oedipus complex and the relationship to the body. *Psychoanal. Study Child,* 41:259–76.

KLEIN, M. (1975 [1928]). Early stages of the oedipus conflict. In *Love, Guilt and Reparation and Other Works: The Writings of Melanie Klein,* 1:186–98. London: Hogarth.

—— (1932). *The Psychoanalysis of Children.* New York: W. W. Norton.

OFFER, D., & SHASHIN, M. EDS. (1984). *Normality and the Life Cycle.* New York: Basic.

RITVO, S. (1976). Adolescent to woman. *J. Amer. Psychoanal. Assn.* (Suppl.) 24:127–37.

—— (1984). The image and uses of the body in psychic conflict. In *Psychoanal. Study of the Child,* 39:449–68.

—— (1989). Mothers, daughters and eating disorders. In *Fantasy, Myth and Reality: Essays in Honor of Jacob A. Arlow,* ed. Blum, Kramer, Richards, & Richards, pp. 371–80. Madison, Conn.: Int. Univ. Press.

SOLNIT, A. J. (1983). Obstacles and pathways in the journey from adolescence to parenthood. In *Adolescent Psychiatry: Developmental and Clinical Studies,* 11, ed. M. Sugar, S. C. Feinstein, J. G. Looney, A. Z. Schwartzberg, A. D. Sorosky, pp. 14–26. Chicago: Univ. Chicago Press.

WHISNANT, L., & ZEGANS, L. (1975). A study in attitudes toward menarche in white middle-class American adolescent girls. *Am. J. Psychiat.,* 132:809–14.

WHISNANT, L., BRETT, E., & ZEGANS, L. (1979). Adolescent girls and menstruation. *Adol. Psychiat.,* 7:157–70.

Termination in Child Analysis

A Child-Led Process?

JULIA FABRICIUS
VIVIANE GREEN

The paper begins by drawing attention to the disjunction between the theoretical conceptualizations of termination in child analysis and the process as it actually occurs. The central focus is on the process itself. Material is presented from four child analyses to illustrate the idiosyncratic ways in which the termination phase unfolded. The cases selected make it possible to consider termination in relation to each developmental phase. Our central argument is that, although the analyst should have certain criteria for termination in mind, termination in child analysis is essentially a child-led process.

MORE THAN THIRTY YEARS AGO, ANNA FREUD (1957) COMMENTED, "WE know more, no doubt, about the right time to begin a child's analysis than about the optimum moment for its termination" (p. 21). Today there are a significant number of publications on termination, but the numerous factors that come into play when deciding to terminate seem in many ways to make the decision as difficult as ever.

This paper was written after a series of meetings among the collaborators in which we discussed both our terminated child cases and the literature on termination. As we struggled to order our thoughts, we

Julia Fabricius is a member of the British Psycho-Analytical Society. Viviane Green is a senior staff member of the Anna Freud Centre, London.

This is an abridged version of a paper given to the International Colloquium of the Anna Freud Centre in November 1993. It was written in collaboration with Tessa Baradon, Jennifer Davids, and Hansi Kennedy. We are particularly grateful to T.B. and J.D. for contributed case material.

The Psychoanalytic Study of the Child 50, ed. Albert J. Solnit, Peter B. Neubauer, Samuel Abrams, and A. Scott Dowling (Yale University Press, copyright © 1995 by Albert J. Solnit, Peter B. Neubauer, Samuel Abrams, and A. Scott Dowling).

noticed a disjunction between the theoretical conceptualizations of termination and the actual process. We found that there was a difference between an analyst's objective assessment of criteria for termination (often made with the benefit of hindsight) and the experience of a given termination phase that unfolds idiosyncratically. We were more interested in the process as it unfolded than in whether our cases met the criteria for termination as defined in the literature. Although of course we realize that it is necessary for the analyst to distance herself from the process in order to appraise the overall progress of the analysis, the timing of the decision to terminate seems to be one of the most difficult situations in which to remain objective. It was from this position and a desire to be descriptive rather than prescriptive that we determined to present some of our work with terminated child patients. We have chosen to concentrate on the intrapsychic issues that arose rather than on the many external difficulties that can be involved in a child analysis, although of course these are frequently interrelated.

A recurrent, overarching theme in many of our discussions was the tension between allowing the developmental momentum to take over and encouraging the regression necessary for analytic work. In child analysis, where a main aim is to reestablish the child on the path of progressive development, achieving this goal may require accepting a reluctance on the child's part to pursue further analytic investigation. This is particularly so at the point of the move into latency, as a number of authors have noted (e.g., A. Freud, 1957; Panel of American Psychoanalytic Association, 1969).

More precise criteria for the termination of analysis have been put forward by Abrams (1978) in the form of four crucial questions:

> 1. **Are the dynamic issues engaged?** Have positive and negative oedipal matters been confronted and linked with specific references to the past? Are the preoedipal analgen delineated?
> 2. **Have specific drive derivatives become manifest?**
> 3. **What is the direction of restructuring?** Have more appropriate defenses evolved? Has emotional functioning showed signs of maturity?
> 4. **Has the resolution of past conflicts found a more fortunate pathway?**

To these Abrams adds that it is inadvisable to end a treatment without some conviction that a progressive push is present and continually imposing its influence. One way to test this, he notes, is to carry the treatment into the beginning of the next phase of development before electing to bring it to an end. Without the fulfillment of these criteria, Abrams would call the analysis "interrupted" rather than terminated.

However, formulations applicable to children who are able to work through the transference, let alone a transference neurosis, and to reach an oedipal level of organization presuppose that other, much earlier and fundamental developments have taken place. A significant number of children treated today have difficulties of a different order. The direction of work with such atypical children[1] is often toward helping the child carve out the internal contours for a whole range of experiences with affective meanings so that inchoate experiences can be represented and structured. The work is also geared toward stimulating the growth of a range of ego capacities. Criteria for termination would then be determined by these treatment goals.

The four cases described below cover a wide range of ages and pathologies. Determining the optimal time to terminate involved measuring the progressive movement of development against the regressive undertow of the therapeutic process. It was important to evaluate whether the thrust of development was preventing the necessary therapeutic regression and, conversely, whether the necessary therapeutic regression was in the service of overall development. These considerations were central in all the cases. However, each termination unfolded in a distinctive way.

CASE 1. JANE, A PRESCHOOLAGE CHILD

It was clear from the outset that Jane's problems, which were concerned with her difficulty in letting go of her clinging, controlling relationship with her mother, would be centrally confronted by the termination of her treatment. However, her analyst had not anticipated the brevity of her treatment. Jane started analysis at the age of four years, nine months and finished by mutual agreement fifteen months later, just before her sixth birthday. Such a short treatment must raise questions about whether the timing of termination was appropriate and whether her conflicts had been sufficiently worked through and integrated.

HISTORY AND PRESENTING PROBLEMS

Mr. and Mrs. A. sought help for Jane, their only child, because of her clinging and rather aggressively controlling behavior, particularly in relation to her mother. Jane had difficulty separating from her mother

---

1. Atypical children are nonneurotic children with pronounced developmental disorders as defined in Category 5 of A. Freud's (1966) Developmental Profile.

for nursery school or parties and ended up most nights in the parental bed. Her early development was apparently unremarkable, but two specific events may be significant. When she was three and a half, her mother was hospitalized for a few days to have a benign breast-lump excised. At about this time, as Jane had long pleaded for a dog, they bought a puppy. Jane adored Scamp, although she was openly rivalrous with her. Six months later the dog was run over and killed while out for an evening walk with Mr. A. After the loss of Scamp, Jane frequently asked if her family could have a baby. It was noted, both in the nursery-school report and by the social worker who took the social history, that Mrs. A. had a tendency to allow her own anxieties about Jane's ability to cope with progressive moves to interfere with her management of the child. Contact with the social worker during the course of the analysis helped her to modify this behavior considerably.

THE ANALYSIS

The central issue of the analysis was the working through of Jane's hostility to the oedipal mother and potential siblings. There seemed to be two layers of work in the transference. In the first, which mainly took place in play, Jane's vivid fantasies were explored. She took to this readily and in this way of working seemed able to use the analyst as a new object with whom she could move forward. In the second layer, which was much more arduous, she exhibited the difficult, controlling behavior of which her parents complained. Three key sessions can summarize the analytic work up to the termination period—one in the sixth week, one in the fourth month, and one in the eleventh month.

First Key Session. This session brought together Jane's preoccupation with babies and her oral aggression. She had played many games in which she became pregnant, with a doll crammed up her dress, and then went to the hospital, where she would "push and push and push" until the baby was born. She was also greatly preoccupied with fierce animals that eat people—crocodiles, or lions that prowled around saying things like, "I smell meat!" Often babies and baby animals were particularly under threat and had to be hidden. Work was done, in play and directly in the transference, which enabled Jane increasingly to tolerate her oral aggressive wishes toward babies.

In the session in the sixth week Jane played that she went to the hospital to have a baby. The analyst was assigned the role of proud father and had to visit her, bringing his dog with him. Then they drove home in the car, Jane sitting next to her husband with the doll in her arms. Suddenly she turned and said, "Do you think this baby might be

going to turn into a lion?" It instantly turned into a lion, and she threw
it into the rubbish bin, saying that she preferred the dog. The analyst
said Jane wanted to have a baby very much but grew worried that it was
a bad thing to want because it meant she would have to take the baby
from the analyst or from her mother; it then seemed that it might be a
fierce baby who could eat others and that it would be better thrown
away. Jane replied, "But let's pretend that it really is a lion, and it's going
to eat you up." Then she gave instructions that she be lifted onto a shelf
(at a safe height), "so that it won't get me." The analyst said that maybe
the baby felt like a lion because it was so cross that its mummy could
have other babies, and so cross with the babies she might have that it
would like to roar and eat them all up. She added that children often
felt like that and then became frightened that they might be punished.
It was the end of the session and Jane returned to the waiting room in a
relaxed and friendly way.

Second Key Session. This session, in the fourth month of treatment,
followed much work on Jane's oedipal concerns. She had expressed her
envy of and hostility to her analyst's grown-up clothes and body; she
said both that she was going to marry Daddy and that she was going to
have his willy when he was dead. She played many games in which her
sexual fantasies were elaborated. In this session she was clearly worried
about something. She meandered around the room, not settling onto
anything and chewing on a towel. She then spoke of another Jane at her
school. Some bad people had stolen this Jane's Mummy's car. She mentioned a dream of two crocodiles and a witch. The analyst said that she
was chewing that towel a bit like a crocodile and wondered what she
knew about witches. She said they rode on broomsticks. In gradual
stages the interpretation was made that the crocodiles were the crocodile parts of Jane that wanted to eat up Mummy's two titties (her word)
and have them for herself and that the witch was the witch part of Jane
that wanted to have Daddy's willy, taking it from both Daddy and
Mummy. Jane was quiet and thoughtful, saying at intervals, "All of
that's right." When her analyst added that perhaps when she wanted to
go into Mummy and Daddy's bed it was partly because she was frightened of the witch and crocodiles in her dream and partly to get close to
Mummy's and Daddy's bodies, especially the bits she was so interested
in, she replied again, "All of that's right."

A few days later, Jane reported that her teddy had a dream. It was
about two crocodiles and (after some thought) one rubbish-bin. The
dream was interpreted to Teddy, and when it came to the rubbish-bin
the analyst said that perhaps Teddy was worried that he might be

thrown away because of his thoughts. At first Jane was dismissive, saying no one would throw him away, but when the analyst said that of course no one would, but Teddy might have been frightened that they would, she turned to him and said with great intensity, "Your Mummy and Daddy wouldn't ever run away without you." The analyst said that Teddy really had been quite worried about this, and that, like a lot of children, he had been frightened sometimes of being away from his mummy and daddy for too long.

At about this time, Jane stopped visiting her parents at night and since then has slept the whole night in her own bed. She also became more able to separate and to start actively enjoying time spent with her friends.

Third Key Session. This session came after some months during which Jane was controlling and provocative. For some time she did her best to confine this aspect of things to play, which she did mainly by reversal—making the analyst play the role of a child, while she was a privileged grown-up. However, she was also very difficult in more direct ways and for a long time was deaf to any interpretation about this. She would boss the analyst about in a quite denigratory way, refuse to leave the waitingroom, and, in a giggly and irritating way, generally refuse to be cooperative. At the same time, she did her best to keep a firm overlay of friendliness between herself and the analyst and following a bout of the provocative behavior would suddenly want the two of them to play some nice and innocuous game together, as if they had been the best of friends all along. Slowly, as her fear of her hostility was tackled and ways found to talk about it, she became able to be more openly enraged.

This behavior reached a peak in the session in the eleventh month, and in it Jane made links with earlier work. Early in the session, she set up an argument with her analyst about whether she could take home a picture, the outline of which the analyst had drawn. The analyst suggested that it was because she had drawn it that Jane wanted it. A protracted period of pleading, raging, and provocation ensued, during which Jane would listen to no interpretation and the analyst became more or less silent. Finally, when the analyst tried again, saying that she would not give Jane the picture but would tell her why she thought she wanted it, Jane suddenly stopped the commotion, came over, and said, "You don't need to tell me. I think I know." At first the analyst was not sure if this was more defiance or was actually cooperation, but Jane went on, "It's because I want to steal your precious things." This sounded thoughtful and not as if she were parroting. After a little discussion Jane said pensively, "This is really just a piece of paper with a drawing on it, though." The analyst agreed that it was but said it had almost seemed as if it were one of her precious things. That was why it was important that she not let Jane take it. Jane responded, "You don't have any babies," and then asked if the analyst did have any babies and if she worked all day. The analyst said how much Jane would prefer it if she didn't have any babies; then there would be nothing for her to want to steal. It would be better if she just worked all day with grown-ups. "Except when you see me," Jane replied. At the end of the session she didn't even mention the picture, and she helped the analyst to clear up the mess.

TERMINATION

Some time during that month, Jane started to mention a time when she might not see her analyst any more. Although at times she also had shouted furiously that she did not want to come, this new remark had a more realistic and rather sad feel to it. Jane was quite sad in the week leading to the Christmas break, despite her pleasurable anticipation about Christmas. There was a sense in which she was exploring the feelings of separation, almost as a trial run, and child and analyst were able to talk about her mixed feelings of excitement about Christmas and sadness at the separation and relate them to the prospect of stopping analysis at some time in the future. They also made a connection to her mixed feelings over wanted to meet the challenges and pleasures of being a bigger child and wanting to stay little.

After the break these issues were still very much present, and Jane voiced the feeling that she wanted to stop, sometimes relating this to her sixth birthday in March. She reviewed her progress, listing the real improvements in her symptoms, and said that she wanted time to play after school. There was also quite a resurgence of the hostile, silly, controlling behavior. It seemed that this was to a large extent a defense against the pain of letting go and moving on—in fact, of course, the same conflict that had brought her into treatment. She had largely dealt with the problem outside treatment, doing well at a new school, being able to stay overnight with friends, and having a good relationship with both parents. During these final weeks, Jane also, on her own initiative, gave up the pacifier to which she had been very attached. She said that she didn't want to be seen with it when she stayed with other children and that, indeed, another child had laughed at her because of it. On balance, in the context of her overall progression, her wish to leave treatment appeared appropriate. It seemed important not to hold on to her unnecessarily, as her mother had tended to do, but at the same time not to allow her to stop before working sufficiently through the clinging hostility.

Her moves toward latency were also apparent in her play, which was at times less open than it had been and also seemed to show some new acceptance of her situation and her wish to move on. For example, there was one game in which the boy and girl went out to play while the baby stayed with the mother. Then the baby became a toddler whose pram could be thrown away and who wanted to join the others. The children then told the mother to go out to work. An agreement was finally reached that she would stop in about a month, at the Easter break before her birthday. She was not able to feel the sadness as much as she had before Christmas but was able sometimes to talk about the mixed feelings. On one occasion, after a bout of provocative behavior that had been interpreted as covering sadness, she suddenly asked the analyst if she knew about Super Glue, telling her that it would stick things together forever. After the analyst suggested that Jane half-wished they could be stuck together like that, Jane played that they were glued, laughing at the joke, but then said seriously and a little sadly that she did want to stop, though, by her birthday.

Since the termination, Mrs. A. has continued to be seen by the social worker, at first quite frequently. This has enabled her to be clearer about which anxieties are her own, rather than Jane's. Jane asked to see her analyst on two occasions, at three months and at six months after termination. Each time this seemed to be to confirm that she was able to do this if she wished, and the visit seemed mainly a social one. Near the end of the second visit, however, she said that her mummy's mummy had died and her mummy had been very sad. (The grandmother lived abroad, so that Jane did not know her well.) It was perhaps this that had led her to want to make sure that the analyst was all right, indicating a residual hostile transference.

The analyst's experience of the process was that Jane's analysis seemed to be carried forward on a wave of impetus created by the child. While, of course, any analysis is carried forward by the patient's unconscious, in this one there was a particular feeling of a momentum generated by the patient. This also led to some anxiety in the analyst, especially in regard to termination. She found herself wondering if, perhaps because of her inexperience, she were being railroaded into agreeing to a premature, defensive avoidance of further work. The supervisor's calm support of the plan to terminate greatly alleviated the analyst's anxiety. Although the analyst was aware of the mother's overanxious clinging to the child and was keen not to repeat it, she nevertheless felt anxious. The supervisor perhaps functioned here as a third object, a father, who could encourage and allow the letting go.

Anna Freud (1957) spoke of the unrealized hope of early child analysts that child treatment could be completed more quickly than adult treatment because the analyst would be confronted with a less firmly established superstructure. However, it seems possible that Jane was a case where the developmental hiccough was caught at a moment when there was also a great readiness to progress, with only a little help needed to disentangle the cause of the delay. It seemed that this short but intense intervention helped her to replace the regressive solution of her conflicts with a degree of repression, so that she could move on into latency. Kohrman (Panel of American Psychoanalytic Association, 1969) notes that frequently treatment in children results in more repression of conflictual sources, not less.

Jane's treatment finished eighteen months ago, and, from her mother's occasional contact with the social worker, the indications are that she continues to do well. Clearly, there was not a major working through of the conflicts, and her analyst's feeling is that further difficulties in the future are possible. If so, one must hope that the analytic experience was sufficiently helpful for Jane and her parents to feel able to seek further help.

CASES 2 AND 3

The next two cases are of latency-aged boys whose approaches to their terminations superficially showed remarkable similarities. Each took charge of the timing and pacing of the termination. Both brought up the wish to terminate and suggested a gradual weaning process. However, as will become apparent, the underlying psychodynamic reasons were rather different.

Both boys might be thought of as using a passive into active defense in order to control and manage a recapitulation of what, for Adam, had been a regular series of losses in early childhood and, for Max, a very early experience of being given up, to which he had attached several fantasies. It might be argued that they were attempting to provide their own "corrective emotional experiences" and that their analysts, by falling in with their patients' wishes, were ultimately stemming the flow of what might be analyzed. However, it was perhaps precisely because the boys had a degree of autonomy over their terminations that they felt safe enough to allow the ensuing material to occur. In the case of Max, it was only after he had reduced the frequency of his sessions that he allowed a fuller exploration of the transference concerns. Paradoxically, less meant more. In addition, the reduction in itself elicited material that was analyzable.

In both cases the analysts took their cue from the patient's wish to terminate. One can imagine cases in which there is a discrepancy between the patient's wish to stop and the analyst's assessment of how much work still needs to be done. However, we suggest that a completed analysis is not necessarily an exhaustive one, to the last dregs, as it were. Where a patient wishes to end in the face of some opposition, a distinction needs to be made between a resistance specific to a phase in the analysis and a more profound resistance to the very process, which perhaps rests on character. In the latter case, to carry on would be to invoke the law of diminishing returns.

CASE 2. ADAM, A LATENCY CHILD

HISTORY AND PRESENTING PROBLEMS

Adam was referred at the age of nine years, four months, due to difficulties in settling in London after a family move from a northern city a year previously. Adam pined for his previous home, school, and relationships. At the diagnostic stage he described how "everything changed at the same time." Although he was a bright boy, he was tearfully resistant to attending his new school, where, he complained, he was being bullied. His unwillingness to get dressed in the mornings, difficulty settling down at night (because he did not want tomorrow to come), and occasional refusal to eat led to battles with his parents. With his mother these were mainly verbal, but with his father Adam was sometimes physically aggressive.

Adam's parents were highly involved in their careers. The family had lived in South America for two years, from the time Adam was fifteen months old, and there employed a nanny who was important to him. There were other disruptions for Adam; a brother was born when he was two years, three months, and marked sibling rivalry was a feature from then on. When Adam was three, just after the family's return to England, his mother became depressed for a while after the unexpected death of her mother; and a stream of au pairs, with varied lengths of stay, exposed Adam to many unpredictable comings and goings.

Adam was small for his age. There had been concern that his penis was small and that he might have undescended testes; at the time of beginning treatment he had seen a doctor, and the family had been reassured that all was well.

For the first eight months of treatment, Adam did not engage in spontaneous play and, in an attempt to control his analyst, talked almost nonstop. He made extensive use of projection, externalization, and splitting of ambivalence. He described his previous home as a paradise lost in contrast to London, which was full of thieves and polluted by litter and dirt. His wish for his analyst to "magic" away his problems and his enemies was apparent and interpreted. It also became clear that his belief in his own omnipotence made him terrified of his hostile wishes. This was particularly evident in relation to separation. Breaks in treatment caused intense anxiety, which he was gradually able to verbalize. Some months into analysis he said, "Fridays are the worst. I think: 'I hope something horrible happens to Mrs. X' [his analyst]. On Saturday morning I wake up and think, 'I don't see you today.' If something has happened, I have to wait until Monday and look for your car, and when you come into the waitingroom I think 'Phew, she's still alive.'" Once he became more able to tolerate his anxiety, he was able to experience his affects of hurt and anger and his longing for a caring figure who would stay put and not leave. As his hostility and fear of object loss were interpreted, his positive feeling toward his analyst intensified, together with his anxiety that she, like the au pairs and his busy mother, would disappoint him by leaving. Trust was evidently a key issue for Adam.

From the beginning of the analysis, it was clear that Adam's poor self-esteem was closely linked to his body representation and his short stature. The family's concern about his genitalia considerably exacerbated his castration anxiety. On the day after a power struggle between Adam and a school friend, he reported the following dream:

> There's this lady in a flat high up. You have to climb some stairs to get to her. She's cross and she chucks me out of the window, and I land at the back in a rubbish-dump. But I don't get hurt. I'm a scarecrow made of straw. Then Harold and this magician appear and they start chucking cat-food tins at me.

In his associations, Adam said the scarecrow had no hands and he imagined that the birds had pecked them off. The cat-food tins were almost empty.

In the work on this dream and other related material, Adam's conflicts over masturbation and castration anxiety were analyzed, alongside his separation anxiety, and a shift occurred in the way he brought material. He began spontaneously to draw, paint, model, and play, and it became possible to address his concerns more directly. The analysis of the castration anxiety allowed the transference to become much more overtly oedipal, with the analyst placed in the role of either parent. For example, on the one hand, Adam battled with a powerful transference father by refusing to come to sessions. On the other, he tried to court the transference mother's favor by drawing her attention to his smart new clothes and athletic victories.

TERMINATION

The termination was ushered in when issues of autonomy versus control by the object reappeared, and Adam became unwilling to attend sessions. This was understood not only as a retreat from the dangers and pain of oedipal wishes and disappointment but as an appropriate move into preadolescence. Midway through the second year of analysis, Adam refused to return after the summer break. Eventually, he agreed to meet his analyst for a final interview. They were able to talk about the fact that, although he was much less troubled than when he first came, there were still some worries left. Adam then became less defensive, saying that he did want to leave on good terms. His analyst made the link for him between his feelings of distress at past losses and his fear of working through a planned separation from her. He agreed to return to treatment on a once-a-week basis, with the aim of completing unfinished work and moving toward termination at a date provisionally set for seven months hence. After eight weeks of this, Adam spontaneously asked to come twice a week. It seemed that he was experiencing a revival of his anxieties, was having difficulty sleeping, and was fearful that a fire might break out in his house. However, he showed insight in explaining that he thought his worry was about a fire inside him. His analyst recontracted to meet twice a week so that they could work on his fiery feelings and thoughts once more.

In the rich termination phase, despite the reduced sessions, Adam's play was characterized by a spontaneity and creativity previously less apparent. There was further work on issues of separation and loss and on his wish to leave rather than suffer again the pain of being left. There was an enormous intensification of his positive oedipal wishes, together with castration anxiety and fears for the safety of his temporarily absent father. As the final day drew near, he informed his analyst of his plan to arrive at the clinic one day to take her for a spin in his Porsche. But he was also gradually able to perceive his analyst as having a different role in life from that of his parents or that of Anna, his favorite of the (by-now twelve) au pairs: "One of the things I like about therapy is that you listen, and don't just say 'yes, yes' and make yourself a cup of tea." Nonetheless, the ending was awkward, and it was really only in a letter some months later that Adam said goodbye.

Adam's pacing of his own termination, although defensive against the risk and pain of abandonment, did seem important in allowing him to feel like a cooperating partner and not merely a helpless infant in the world of transitory adults. This control gave him a sufficient sense of safety to enable him to do further analytic work on his problems. Without this flexibility from his analyst, the opportunity might have been lost.

In summary, analysis seems to have facilitated a resumption of progressive development. However, Adam's self-esteem, although more soundly based, was still shaky in unpredictable situations and under stress. His analyst felt it not unlikely that he would need further help at a later date.

CASE 3. MAX, A LATENCY CHILD

Max was referred at the age of nine because of persistent soiling. He remained in treatment for two years. Max decided that symptomatic relief from soiling was an adequate termination criterion for him. His analyst was left wondering if his wish to terminate signified a progressive thrust, or whether it was a premature flight from psychic conflict within the transference.

HISTORY AND PRESENTING PROBLEMS

Max was adopted at birth into a caring family. The adoptive parents had a biological son who had already left home at the time of Max's adoption. From early on, Max showed curiosity about his origins. Upon realizing, at around age two years, that there were a birth mother and an adoptive mother he became very distressed, believing that his adoptive parents had taken him from his birth mother. Max was close to his father but regretted that he was not more available to modulate his more tempestuous relationship with his mother. His relationship to his mother was warm, with a tinge of aggression, although the aggression was largely encapsulated in his symptom of soiling. He was described as a charming, imaginative, intelligent and popular boy. Despite his intelligence he suffered from low self-esteem and was underachieving at school.

THE ANALYSIS

Max's analysis was characterized by an apparent charm and a veneer of compliance. However, upon entry into treatment his soiling was consciously nonconflictual, and there was little therapeutic alliance. He proved highly resistant to the entire analytic process, revealing that beneath the compliance was a markedly anal organization which manifested as a wish to control the object coupled with omnipotent and magical thinking. Max spoke openly of his wish to be psychic. His denial of affects (as well as his symptom) was striking. For the first few months, his play, mainly with water and paints, reflected his anal preoccupations and was filled with concerns about leaking, messing, and spoiling things and an unabashed pleasure in doing so. He seemed to enjoy the sense of the safety in being able to mess. Anal aggression also entered into play in the form of small plasticine "bombs" which he made and then threw at the analyst. As this was taken up in the analysis, he became more openly angry at home and began tentatively to report that, for instance, he had stormed off to his room and read a murder story after an argument with his mother. However, the anal aggression was overdetermined and imbued with fantasies about a profligate mother who gave her babies away. In one session Max made a large plasticine bomb surrounded by tiny bombs and the analyst was able to make the link between feces and babies.

As treatment progressed Max moved on from his anal concerns and entered into a distinctly phallic phase that was apparent to all and sundry as he made his descent from the treatment room to the waiting room holding the five-foot paper airplane he had made. He tried to consolidate his uncertain hold on his sense of phallic potency. At this point his soiling became a more conscious conflict. In one session, when his analyst, responding to Max's feeling that he was indeed getting older, had drawn a series of ever-larger boys, Max drew a balloon coming from the mouth of the biggest one with the words, "I am getting too big to soil." This developmental move, along with interpretations of his wish to control the analyst and of his aggressive wishes toward her, meant that Max was able to give up his symptom.

TERMINATION

A few weeks after his symptom had ceased Max began to ask when he could terminate and voiced a wish to reduce sessions from four times a week to two and then one. His analyst thought that, given the rigidity of his defenses, this schedule would not provide a chance for much work. In the end Max's sessions were reduced to three times a week and then, for a brief period, to twice a week. The termination phase took place over a ten-month period. Altogether, it was crucial for Max to take an active stance vis-à-vis his termination.

Throughout the earlier stages of his analysis Max experienced the analyst as an intrusive figure with whom he was engaged in a battle of submission and dominance. He perceived engagement in the analytic process as submission, against which he had to defend himself energetically. It was very hard for the analyst to make sense of the transference and for Max to elaborate on exploratory interpretations. It was only after the termination phase was under way that Max could elaborate (albeit to a limited extent) on the dynamics in the transference. Interestingly, once Max had made the decision to reduce his sessions and the end was in sight, it was as if the analysis proper could begin. Thus, rather than being a period of consolidation, the termination phase appeared to be an acceleration in his phase development in which Max's phallic concerns gave way to more oedipal sorts of preoccupations. The termination phase is usually a time for *reworking* issues around separation and loss. In Max's case these issues lay dormant until the termination phase, when they became readily available.

Max's wish to terminate was centered on his feeling that because his symptom had ceased he was better, but he voiced an anxiety that, in his words, while seventy percent of him wanted to stop, thirty percent was worried that once he had stopped he could never return. Max was very pleased to learn that if ever he wanted to come back to let his analyst know how he was getting on he could do so. It seemed important that the goodbye did not have the same irrevocability as being given up for adoption. His material now consistently touched on his fantasies about his adoption. The fact that termination was tied in with his adoption was symbolically expressed by his urgent wish to stop before March, the month in which he had been adopted. He demonstrated a wish to give up his analyst before she could get rid of him. His wish to be master of his termination was understood in the context of his adoption as well as of his continuing wish to control the analyst.

In the termination phase Max began to talk about his interest in a girl of his own age. He was competing for her interest with another boy and spent many hours trying to puzzle out which boy she might prefer. The analyst made links to his curiosity about his biological mother, to which Max replied, "Well, she must be on this earth somewhere. There are ten billion people, so I don't suppose I'll look."

In later stages Max began to express his feeling of uncertainty about libidinal ties. If he could woo the girl, would she continue to like him? Would he continue to like her? The uncertainty of the permanence of libidinal ties was taken up in the context of termination, links being made to fantasies about why his biological mother had given him up. There was also a level of concern about the fluctuations in object ties. However, these concerns could not be fully explored. As termination became imminent, Max began to seal himself up and understandably wanted to talk about his future plans and to review the forward strides he had made. This left the analyst wondering if, in the end, Max's analysis had been appropriately limited, or whether there was a flight from the transference ties. It was somewhat paradoxical that the transference issues relating to his tie to his adoptive mother and to his fantasies about his biological mother could become apparent only once the termination phase had set in.

On the whole, his analyst felt that although symptom relief had been achieved, there had been no great readjustment in his defenses. Withholding seemed to remain as a trait. Was the analysis circumscribed not simply because of latency or because Max might be taking a defensive flight, but because his underlying organization was not further analyzable?

CASE 4: ANN, AN ADOLESCENT

In the fourth case, like the first, it was clear from the outset that the presenting problem, entanglement with the mother, would be an issue in the termination. Unlike the first, however, there was in this case severe preoedipal pathology, which required considerable work before oedipal issues could start to be addressed. This case also serves as a reminder of the complexities involved in establishing an optimum length of treatment. Adolescence should be a period of progressive distancing from primary ties to the object. Analysis goes against the developmental grain. In some cases, as Burgner (1988) has pointed out, the protracted analysis of an adolescent can result in the adolescent's gaining gratification rather than doing psychic work. However, in this case the degree of early pathology seemed to necessitate a long analysis in order to try to prevent a perverse solution and foreclosure of the adolescent developmental process.

Ann was seventeen when she was referred by a perceptive teacher. Her situation at the time was precarious: she was failing at school, promiscuous with boys, and increasingly out of control in her rows with her mother and sister. This translation into action on all fronts increased her inner sense of chaos and despair. In the diagnostic assessment it was clear that Ann and her mother were bound by destructive and persecutory mutual projections and that a thin adolescent façade, helped by her beauty, camouflaged a breakdown of the adolescent process. The status of her oedipality/heterosexuality was questionable; her promiscuous engagements with boys seemed defensive against strong homosexual wishes to join in a sexualized merger with her mother but at the same time, father was an available and exciting figure. Thus, snuggling between mother and father in the parental bed, dancing naked with her sister, or sitting with her father in the bath represented in a figurative way her developmental entrapment between the breast and the penis.

THE ANALYSIS

Ann's wish for enmeshment, to stave off feelings of disintegration and madness, was immediately brought into play in relation to the analyst. For example, breaks in treatment, even from one day to the next, or witnessing the analyst with another young patient, brought frenzied and insatiable demands for more attention, availability, and concern. "If you cared," she said, "I would feel protected." Her fear was that she would fall to pieces if she could not capture the object on demand. Ann at first wondered how she would ever be able to survive without her analyst and later wondered how she would know if she were ready to leave. Getting better implied the danger of having to give up her analyst, so that a negative therapeutic reaction fed into the strong regressive pull.

As the six-year analysis progressed, it became apparent that Ann had never experienced a sense of safety from being held within the "maternal reverie," and that a disturbed mother-daughter relationship from infancy had led to an ongoing sadomasochistic sexualisation of family relationships. The sadomasochism in her analysis, particularly the pattern of blaming the object for her misery, reenacted the family pattern of closeness and was a defense against depletion and depression.

Over the period of the analysis, a number of separations were worked through. The first, early in treatment, was the ending of a sexual relationship with a boyfriend. This was a repetition of all the earlier separations in which Ann felt herself a victim of the object's rejection and attack. About a year later (three years into the analysis), Ann for the first time initiated a separation; after about six months of crisis, she moved out of her parental home into a college flat-share. Subsequently, she moved back to her parents' home during summer breaks and out again during the academic year. After a number of such moves she was more confident about her ability to leave home. Later she was able to initiate and work through a separation from a boyfriend of eighteen months' standing. In this instance, months of careful consideration preceded the separation, during which Ann went through a process of mourning.

These external moves were linked with work in her analysis in which she was increasingly able to differentiate between herself and her depressed mother/analyst. In terms of the infantile relationship, this entailed sorting out the confusion about who she was in contradistinction to who mother said she was ("she tells me I am evil . . . sometimes I think I'm evil")—that is, what she projected and what was projected onto her. In the transference, analyst and patient worked for years on the intensity of the ambivalence toward her mother and analyst, which seemed to interfere with her capacity to recognize and label her own feelings. For example, when talking about how confusing the ambivalence was for her, Ann burst out, "It doesn't happen only with you, it makes me not know who I am." Underlying the confusion was the initially unconflicted wish to be the unseparated and thus safely protected baby. As the wish to grow up strengthened, the regressive ideal of being looked after became split off as a scene of static, asexual gratification. It was only in working through the conflicts in the termination phase that Ann was able to acknowledge that the idealized image of dependency and gratification was only a fantasy.

For much of the analysis, Ann found the transference analyst difficult to relinquish as an object of narcissistic expectation and accusation (Anzieu, 1987). This was expressed in her ongoing demand to have "someone there for me" and her resentment at the analyst's perceived failure in this idealized protective role. Another function of the work, therefore, was to facilitate some internalization of the analyst's empathy for her pain, which would help build representations of both a good object and a good self. Without these, separation was experienced as severance, and Ann continued to fall into states of self-depletion and depression.

THE TERMINATION

As is to be expected in the treatment of an adolescent, the question of termination arose on a number of occasions, associated with such events as leaving school and choosing a college and with wanting to be like the rest of her peer group. At each point, although the pull to leave was strong, the fear of leaving and the conflicted recognition that she was not ready in terms of analytic work won. But in the fifth year, after some months of intense battling with her analyst, which seemed to repeat the kind of quarreling that had preceded separation from her mother, Ann raised the issue again. Now, on reviewing the situation, it seemed to the analyst that considering termination was more appropriate. Externally, whilst maintaining contact with home, Ann had achieved independent living arrangements, academic excellence, expansive peer relationships, and longer-term heterosexual relationships. She had an optimism and an ability to enjoy life and could speak realistically about finishing her degree, the possibility of traveling, and uncertainty about whether she wished to study further. Internally she had achieved a good degree of individuation and a stronger sense of self, with an increased, though fluctuating, ability to regulate her self-esteem. She had also, to an extent, developed an observing ego, had internalized the analyzing function to some degree, and could engage in an inner dialogue which offered some protection against the regressive pull. Oedipal issues were worked through as Ann figuratively moved from the breast to the penis, and heterosexuality became more firmly established despite unresolved conflicts about her female body.

A date was set for termination in the following summer. Initially, the thought of being able to stop made Ann feel that she was an adult taking charge of her life. However, the buoyancy rapidly declined, and there was a resurgence of sadomasochistic clinging, a regression to masturbation for self-comfort, and a loss of the observing, insightful ego capacities. Ann raged that her analyst did not appear upset at the thought of her leaving. The rage seemed to encompass the pain and humiliation of her dependency and a regressive attempt to use guilt to prompt the analyst to hold on to her. All this served to block any thinking about what ending meant for her. For Ann, the equation of letting someone go and rejecting them meant that she felt very guilty about the mutual annihilation that she imagined termination implied: she felt separation to be an act of aggression. After a while, the analyst realized that her own affective responses, which Ann was closely scanning, may have been adding to this. It seemed that Ann was picking up a rather stiff, constrained response on the analyst's part as she dealt with the termination of a highly cathected patient and that perhaps Ann needed the analyst to be less defended against her mourning in order to feel safe with her own. The following extract from the weekly reports illustrates how analyst and analysand worked through this:

Week 242
Ann described depression as something that is always there. She could give in to it if she did not fight it continuously. She described it as her mother's depression; in it she lives in a dome of inactivity, giving everything up so as to be looked after by her father. I thought I detected a yearning to be looked after, but Ann insisted that the price was too high. In a rather choked voice, she described the depression as part of her existence from the very beginning: in her mother's depression, her own depression since early childhood, and the experience of being bullied and feeling totally alone.

I felt that her descriptions and pain were authentic. Yet I was struggling throughout for an understanding that seemed just beyond my reach. Then I hit upon the distinction between depression and sadness and put to Ann the question of whether all sadness had to lead to depression. Slowly, she thought about and worked through this. We were able to identify that some of her feelings now are of sadness rather than depression: those feelings of grieving over the future loss of analysis and of college. She described the sense of being choked up much of the time, as though tears were there waiting to come out. She wanted to learn to say goodbye, and that was sad, but it was not depression. Ann seemed to experience mastery in exploring this issue; sadness is tolerable and the options are open for the future, whereas depression is intolerable and consumes all hope for the future.

This distinction highlighted the difference between the separation from the analyst as a transference object, which was felt to be intolerable, and the separation from the real object, which was sad. Ann's experience of her mother, repeated in the transference, was of someone who became unavailable (and therefore rejecting) because of her own depression and who clung because of her own narcissistic needs, so that separation may well have implied annihilation for the mother. Her question, then, about how her analyst felt, was a crucial one for the termination: was the analyst like her mother and therefore threatened by separation, or could the analyst cope?

In the final months of treatment, Ann could relinquish responsibility for her analyst/mother's wellbeing. Through the work in the transference the analyst had become the new object who could help her effect a "safe" separation. She then said that she knew she no longer needed analysis but would miss her analyst. She thought that her analyst might also miss her and that, when she felt settled after the termination, she would write to tell her how she was.

DISCUSSION

In this paper we have presented four cases, in which questions could be raised about the timing of the termination and the completeness of the analytic work. We have suggested that, in the decision to terminate an analysis, there is often a disjunction between theory and practice. While we acknowledge that this is, in part, because of the difficulty of making a clinical judgment of a child's state in relation to specified criteria, we also advance the view that the child analyst, although he or she has certain possible criteria in mind, is, and indeed should be, led by the child. By this we do not mean that the analyst should collude with overdefensive moves but rather that she should endeavor to be in touch, both directly and through the countertransference, with progressive and adaptive moves in the child as well as with factors that may necessarily limit change. Our central argument is that it is helpful for the analyst to have general criteria in mind, but specific criteria also have to be generated for each individual child. Thus the analyst's task is not only to assess the child against existing criteria but also to assess with the child what are the appropriate criteria for him, given his present stage of development, life circumstances, and psychological make-up. This may sometimes require the analyst to accept some limitations to the analytic work.

The analyst's countertransference, potentially useful as it is, requires careful monitoring. For example, the analyst may be colluding with a premature flight or opposing a progressive move. In the case of Jane, the analyst felt extremely anxious about allowing the child to leave, thus replaying a mother-child dynamic. In the case of Max, the analysis felt burdensome to his analyst. It is possible that the termination phase was unnecessarily protracted because of the analyst's need to compensate for her negative feelings about the case. It was almost as if the analyst feared being like the fantasied biological mother who gave Max away. Certainly, working with a child to find his criteria for termination requires an analyst with not too much unanalyzed omnipotence. On the other hand, an analyst with too little faith in the potential for change would also be unhelpful.

One also hopes that analytic work will continue after termination. The depth, range, and means are linked to the nature of the patient's internalization of the analyst and the analytic function. Adam, for instance, as he approached termination was rapidly able to make for himself the link between his fear of fire and his "fiery feelings." Similarly, Jane was able to formulate her own interpretation that she wanted to steal her analyst's precious things. The extent and depth to which internalization of the analytic function is integrated vary. The analytic function does not always become part of the child's own internal voice and may need to be summoned, as when the child says to himself, "Now, what would Ms. H. say about that?" With atypical children the question could be whether the acquisition of this previously lacking self-reflective function could be considered a criterion for termination.

One of the exciting aspects of work with young children is that their psychic structures are *in statu nascendi* or, in adolescents, in a new state of reorganizational fluidity, leaving open the possibility for an intervention to have a formative impact. For example, Jane's oedipal concerns could be addressed as they unfolded, and timely analytic work may have prevented an early difficulty from becoming entrenched. Thus in some cases the timing of termination may be related to the timing of the beginning of the analysis.

Finally, perhaps with all children, when we try to decide the optimal moment to terminate, we have to face the uncertainty involved in letting go of a patient. There is, after all, always another developmental phase into which we could lead the patient and where we might wish to see him safely ensconced. Weiss (1991) reminds us that with child patients we have to leave them long before their developmental story has fully unfolded but that they will have been well served if there is a certain adaptational flexibility that can enable them to meet the as yet unknown developmental tasks, stresses, and demands.

BIBLIOGRAPHY

ABRAMS, S. (1978). Termination in child analysis. In *Child Analysis and Therapy*, ed. J. Glenn, 451–69. New York: Aronson.
ANZIEU, D. (1987). Some alterations of the ego which make analyses interminable. *Int. J. Psychoanal*, 68: 9–19.
BURGNER, M. (1988). Analytic work with adolescents: Terminable and interminable. *Int. J. Psychoanal*, 69: 179–87.
FREUD, A. (1970 [1957]). Problems of termination in child analysis. In *Problems of Psycho-Analytic Technique and Therapy*, by A. Freud, pp. 3–21. London: Hogarth.
FREUD, A. (1966). *Normality and Pathology in Childhood*. London: Hogarth.
PANEL OF AMERICAN PSYCHOANALYTIC ASSOCIATION. (1969). (Reporter: R. Kohrman). Problems of termination in child analysis. *J. Amer. Psycho-Anal. Assn.*, 17: 191–205.
WEISS, S. (1991). Vicissitudes of termination: Transferences and countertransferences. In: *Saying Goodbye: A Casebook of Termination in Child and Adolescent Analysis and Therapy*, ed. A. Schmukler, pp. 265–84. Hillsdale, N.J.: Analytic.

The Analysis of an Overstimulated Child

AUDREY GAVSHON

This paper shows how environmental and medical overstimulation af-
fected a latency girl in all her developmental phases, leading to severe
impairment of object relationships. These factors are seen against the
background of an acrimonious parental divorce.
   Suzie's negative body image was inextricably interwoven with anxi-
eties about her masturbation activities and castration fantasies and this
was fueled by her physical condition (lichen sclerosis et atrophicis).
She was in a constant state either of withdrawnness or excitement. The
initial task of the treatment was to provide Suzie with a holding environ-
ment so that she could find alternative means of gratification and con-
trol in order to manage within a more organized secondary process mode.
When her difficulties around excitation abated, she could begin to make
analytic use of verbalization, clarification, and interpretations.

SUZIE WAS REFERRED TO THE ANNA FREUD CENTRE WHEN SHE WAS EIGHT
years old and was in analysis for three and a half years. The referral
followed an incident dramatically disturbing to the family. An anonymous report had been sent to the National Society for the Prevention
of Cruelty to Children (NSPCC) claiming that Suzie had possibly been
sexually abused. After a lengthy assessment the psychiatrist found the
allegation to be untrue but formed the opinion that Suzie was a deeply
unhappy child who might benefit from analysis.

   Senior child psychotherapist/psychoanalyst at the Anna Freud Centre, London; train-
ing and supervising analyst.
   The Psychoanalytic Study of the Child 50, ed. Albert J. Solnit, Peter B. Neubauer, Samuel
Abrams, and A. Scott Dowling (Yale University Press, copyright © 1995 by Albert J.
Solnit, Peter B. Neubauer, Samuel Abrams, and A. Scott Dowling).

BACKGROUND

The Centre's social worker found the mother physically and psychologically overpowering. Her ample body, clothed in scarlet, emphasized her theatrical presentation. She was impressively articulate, but when she was anxious or excited, that fluency was replaced by incoherence. Although her husband had left her nearly seven years before, her outrage and profound hurt at that unexpected event were still palpable.

The marital breakup was central to the family story. At the time she met her husband, Mrs. B. was a highly respected private secretary, widely traveled, multilingual, and with an organizing flair that allowed her to mount international conferences with confidence and efficiency.

Secure in these talents, she left her job and worked happily for her husband in the graphics company he owned. Mrs. B. found the atmosphere glamorous and exciting. Suzie was born three years later, and the mother was thrilled. But when Suzie was fifteen months old the father announced without any apparent warning that he was leaving to live with another woman, with whom he'd been having an affair for some time. The mother's deep involvement with her baby had kept her unaware of her husband's growing alienation, and she was shattered when brought face to face with his infidelity and deception. Her mortification was intensified by the fact that she had been displaced by an internationally known woman of beauty and talent. The humiliation was compounded further, since, following his defection, her husband continued to work with her in their shared office until, when Suzie was twenty-one months old, he finally made the break complete by finding new premises for himself and taking most of his clients with him. During these six months, the mother's relationship with Suzie, initially so tranquil, had become fraught and laden with anxiety. These difficulties persisted, changing perhaps in form but not in substance. For this reason, the mother welcomed the referral. She had felt increasingly helpless in dealing with Suzie's urinary and defecatory problems which manifested when Suzie was four years old. She was unable to offer her comfort or containment effectively.

The incident which triggered the child abuse allegation was based on Suzie's excited and inappropriate behavior. Some of the mother's relatives played a significant contributing role in the story. Her parents, who had given her and Suzie so much support during and after the marital breakup, emigrated to Portugal when Suzie was three years old.

This intensified the mother's feelings of loneliness and near-panic. But both she and her daughter repeatedly visited them and spent holidays with them. The mother's younger brother, Peter, divorced and also moved to Portugal. His two daughters remained in England, and Suzie has always regarded them as her best friends. With them she shared bodily excitement and elated chatter. The three girls often bathed together with Peter, and Suzie bathed with the maternal grandfather even at the age of seven. The close extended family embraced two generations. During treatment it emerged that Suzie was sometimes invited by aunts or great-aunts to join in watching unsuitable late-night movies.

The mother and maternal grandmother feared that the social worker would be too readily influenced by the father, whom they viewed as a persuasive and manipulative liar. In his one interview, the father professed deep interest in his daughter, but he refused invitations to participate further in the proceedings. He was highly intelligent but brash and overconfident. He said that at twenty-eight he had "not felt ready to be a father" but still had been delighted when his wife became pregnant. He showed neither guilt nor distress over his defection, divorce, and subsequent remarriage. On reflection, he said he felt that he and his first wife were incompatible.

From the time she was fifteen months old until she was six years old, Suzie had had virtually no contact with her father. Then, suddenly, he had appeared in Portugal where she was staying at her maternal grandparents' house, and had taken her out for what the mother described as a "wonderful treat." Subsequently (without consulting any of the adults) he phoned Suzie and asked if she would like to live with him and his new family. He explained to the interviewer that his fondness for Suzie had grown and that he had come to admire and take pride in her intelligence. He felt he could offer her routine and discipline, although he was well aware how exhausting she was for her mother and would be for her stepmother. He described her eating habits at six as atrocious, messy and wasteful.

From all that has been learned since this interview, it seems clear that father's offer to care for Suzie had little meaning. When she did spend weekends with his family (which for a long time she idealized) her father was often absent, and she spent most of her time with the nanny. Both her mother and father regarded the paternal grandparents as difficult and disturbed, though Suzie herself seldom discussed them. As treatment progressed, Suzie's visits to her father became increasingly rare.

HISTORY

Her mother found Suzie's birth "terrific." She was a "wonderful baby"—"sweet and totally happy." The mother worked from home and breast-fed Suzie for nine months. Weaning was easy. Suzie sat up early but walked "late." At fifteen months, with the father's traumatizing revelations to the mother, the relationship changed: the mother was overwhelmed with anxiety, distracted, and unable to set limits; she expressed a suffocating love for Suzie with possessive embraces. The mother said that from that time on, she "had felt a real *need* for her [Suzie]." She became anxiously concerned with her daughter's development and repeatedly arranged for medical check-ups, sometimes with good reason: the lateness in walking led to the discovery that Suzie was double-jointed in hips and knees (though she was walking well by eighteen months), and the mother correctly detected a squint, for which she sought ophthalmic advice.

Following weaning, Suzie's attitude toward food became problematic. She ate less and less frequently and then only in small quantities. After the father finally left, the mother had to work full-time to maintain an expensive house. She no longer could work at home, and she employed "an excellent nanny who stayed for two years." The mother gave an inconsistent account of Suzie's life between the ages of two and four: on the one hand, "she slept well, and her play was wonderful"; on the other, "she was very nervy and cried a lot."

While the mother said that toilet training was "great, no problems at all," she could not in fact remember much about it and supposed that Nanny had taken care of it. But she was sure that Suzie had been clean and dry by two-and-a-half, when she joined a morning playgroup. One of Suzie's beloved cousins attended the same school, the mother said, and acted highly excited and unrestrained; she sometimes stripped off her clothes in the classroom and involved Suzie in these hilarities.

At about the age of four, Suzie began to feel a soreness in her genital region, and there were signs of bleeding. Tests for bladder infection were negative, and a course of antibiotics failed to improve the condition. Thrush was ruled out. As the irritation continued, Suzie would urinate only over a bowl of warm water. A scan for a possible foreign body was negative. When Suzie was five, she went to stay with her maternal grandparents in Portugal where "the combination of hot sun, salt water and no pants" gave her some respite, but when she returned to England the condition again flared up. The skin around the vulva looked pink and began to shrivel. Repeated scratching once more caused bleeding. The mother consulted a pediatrician, who advised against the GP's suggested referral to a child psychiatrist. Instead he sought the opinion of a dermatologist, Dr. S., who diagnosed *Lichen sclerosis et atrophicus*.[1] He prescribed steroid cream and advised scrupulous attention to cleanliness. Her mother said that all of Suzie's medical examinations were done gently and considerately: the doctors paid attention to her whole body and not simply to the local affliction.

At about this time Suzie began to avoid wiping her bottom, insisting that it hurt her to do so. Further irritation resulted, now around the anus. The repeated contact of the skin with urine and with the remains of excrement, day and night, exacerbated the pain. Suzie and her mother were now entrenched in frequent battles: Her mother insisted that Suzie wipe herself, and Suzie refused. Her mother needed to apply steroid cream to Suzie's vulva, but Suzie begged her mother not to touch her.

When Suzie was five-and-a-half she and her mother moved. Suzie changed schools, and her nanny, who had been present from the onset of the problem, was replaced. The mother was now working away from home for the first time. Suzie began to withhold her feces, which her mother thought was due to the lichen sclerosis. As business demanded that the mother work long hours, the new nanny was left to cope with Suzie's excretory difficulties and hygiene, including her persistence in returning from school with wet pants. Her mother reported that she was "hit by a bombshell" when Suzie was six years old. Suzie was reported to the NSPCC as a possible child-abuse case. As the report had been made anonymously and implicated Suzie's paternal grandfather, the mother said that she entered a period of "dreadful doubt and fear" which only cleared when she discovered through an aunt that her cousin was the anonymous reporter. Two years previously, the same cousin had urged the mother to have Suzie tested for sexually transmitted diseases at the onset of her urinary infections.

Suzie's mother reported to the Centre's social worker her view of the episode that precipitated the abuse allegation. Mother and Suzie had visited one of the mother's cousins (the maternal grandfather's sister's daughter). This woman's children, younger than Suzie, were looked after by a nurse who had previously worked at a renowned children's hospital. Everyone was in the very large living room, adults at one end of the room, children milling around. A plumber was working on some pipes at the far end of the room, watched by his young apprentice, who

---

1. This condition is usually found in postmenopausal women, but the incidence in children is growing. White patches of rough, thickened skin appear around the genital area. If steroidal cream treatment fails, surgery may be recommended.

was bent over, standing legs apart, holding a tool out horizontally at the ready. Suzie came running behind him, and either took the tool or picked up another and thrust it forward and back between the lad's legs. Nothing was said to Suzie's mother, but it was this occasion which gave the impetus to the cousin, influenced by the zealous nanny, to telephone Social Services anonymously. At some point during the Local Authority's investigation, allegations against the paternal grandfather seem to have been around, but they were also dismissed. Suzie did not have a medical examination. She did have to undergo questioning and observation over some months. The psychiatrist and social workers agreed that she should not be on the child abuse register. The police were not involved, and there was no confrontation with the paternal grandfather. Neither mother nor Suzie could furnish any details about the procedure. Mother expressed relief about the gentle handling of the case and about the outcome, which led to Suzie's referral for analysis. The incident and its consequences highlighted Suzie's ongoing exposure by innuendo or action to sexual excitement from the paternal and maternal extended families.

At the time of referral, Suzie's disordered eating, of which both her mother and her father complained, had become a "fraught issue" between mother and child. The mother also said that she despaired of Suzie's slowness with everything she did—for example, dressing for school, even while Suzie herself was worried she would be late. Suzie was considered a "superb reader" at school, yet at home she rarely picked up a book (although she adored being read to). She had no friends. When, on occasion, another child came to tea, Suzie's demanding, excitable behavior would ensure that the visit was never repeated.

Suzie's full-scale IQ was 120, but given her neurotic problems, the test result may have been an underestimate. Her teachers noted a lack of concentration that interfered with her work. They also commented on her inability to form peer relationships.

TREATMENT

MANAGING BODILY FUNCTIONS

When treatment started, Suzie was underweight, pale, gaunt, and tense. She smelt of urine. Her physical condition pointed to our immediate therapeutic task. We had to mobilize the wish to be clean and help her to relinquish her dependent and aggressive use of elimination. Only in this way could secondary infection be controlled and social acceptability fostered. It seemed evident from the history alone that

Suzie's resistance to taking responsibility for her body management was multiply determined; her aggressively clinging relationship to her mother, the consequences of her father's abandonment for both her mother and herself, and her exposure to environmental and physical (medical) overstimulation must all have played a part.

In her first session, Suzie cheerfully listed all the things she did not like about her mother—her overweight, her unpunctuality, her forgetfulness. During the second session, she talked about her "wet pants and sore bum" problem. She claimed she wet her pants at school only because her teacher wouldn't let pupils leave the class. She explained that she was constipated and couldn't get the pooh out unless she pushed, and that hurt her. She said she knew she should eat lots of fruit, but her mother never gave her any.

Suzie regarded the problem of wet pants as a "simple" one. When she was bored, she went to the loo and didn't wet herself. But if she was having fun or watching a TV program she liked, she didn't want to miss anything, so she wet her pants. One day the mother, who was rarely able to bring Suzie to sessions, came with her and on arrival whispered to me theatrically that she had to go back to the car to fetch clean pants for Suzie. I asked Suzie whether wetting her pants that day was connected with mother's bringing her, adding that maybe it felt exciting to hold her wee in until it was too late. "How did you know *that?*" was her astonished reply. But before the session was over, she said defiantly, "I told a lie. I wet my pants at school because I didn't want to miss the fun."

Suzie's fecal withholding was related to a period in her life when she had lost her home, her beloved nanny, and her mother's presence, and these events were followed by a series of painful infections during which she attacked her mother as she herself felt to be bodily attacked. She wished—omnipotently—to destroy her mother for failing to protect her. She said she liked the feel of the soft pooh round her and didn't like sitting on the cold, dark loo, which I understood as her way of holding on to, and angrily hurting, her mother. My interpretations were focused on Baby Suzie's fear that, if she could look after her toileting herself, no one would trouble to care for her. She longed for the idyllic state of her baby half-sister, Ruth, who had no responsibility for her actions and still got all the admiration she desired. In the course of the analysis that wish became unacceptable, and Suzie said, "Please don't talk about Baby Suzie any more. Big Suzie doesn't like it." The shame of her infantile, messy behavior was now conflictual and therefore accessible to analysis.

Suzie had liked the diagnostician, Mrs. M., who had taken charge of the initial assessment, and her quizzical responses to glimpses of this woman in the corridor provided an opening for interpretations. I said that she felt discarded because she was just a dirty, smelly, no-good pooh. For the same reasons, she felt, her father had abandoned her, and she feared that I might do the same thing. Perhaps I too would prefer a helpless baby as sweet as Ruth, or a beautiful, clean girl who could grow up to be as glamorous as her stepmother.

In her fifth week of treatment, Suzie complained about a sore on her lip. As she did she chewed on her hair, tugging the long strands so it cut into the sides of her mouth. This incident made it possible to draw a distinction between the conditions she brought on herself and the lichen sclerosis, which was not of her doing. As she lay on the couch restlessly fiddling with her tights and picking her nose, she said, "I want to see Dr. S. forever." I related her fear of being boss of her body to the concern that she would lose mother, Dr. S., and me forever, and she replied, "I want to come here for four hundred years," demonstrating that her anxiety about loss of object was as uncontained as her impulses.

At the end of our first term of treatment, Suzie went to spend the Easter holiday with her grandparents. On returning, she announced that her "pants worry" was over because Grandma had given her Bran Flakes every morning. It was easy to pooh, so her pants didn't get dirty, and she did not wet them any more. She asserted that therapy had nothing to do with this development—rejecting my analytic endeavors just as she had rejected her mother's help. Her improvement was maintained and, writing some weeks later, her dermatologist said that, although the lichen sclerosis was still present, "there were no signs of the blisters or secondary infection that have been a problem. She seemed less active and calmer in Outpatients."

BODY DAMAGE AND SEDUCTIVE BEHAVIOR

Suzie's negative body image was inextricably bound up with her anxieties about her masturbatory activities and castration fantasies, and these fears were fed by her physical condition. As a way of engaging me and resisting analytic work, she sometimes would perform ungainly exercises. One day, as she was flamboyantly displaying her underpants and throwing her hair over her face, I commented on her showing off of her body. "I'm not showing off," she responded, "I'm showing *you*." She then struggled to do the splits and asked: "If I do the splits, will I crack my bottom and my ninny?" Physical activity and the excitement that accompanied it brought a memory. When she had been riding bicycles with her cousins she had fallen off, and she had crawled along the grass until she realized she wasn't injured. I linked this recollection to her concerns about doing the splits and her fear that she had cracked her willie. Suzie replied that girls didn't have willies, ever. But she was thoughtful when I suggested that, she might believe that if she were a boy or a perfect girl, with no need for a therapist or for Dr. S., her father might never have left.

When Suzie was told that she had to wear glasses all day for a squint and shortsightedness, she was vehemently resistant. "Everyone," she said, would know about her "fanny troubles." She was convinced that her masturbation and fantasies were responsible, not only for the lichen sclerosis, but for her eye damage. I suggested that the shame she felt over her damaged body was given away by the imperfection of her eyes. Subsequently, if she arrived without her glasses, she would blame her mother for not reminding her to wear them or for failing to fix them if they had been broken. In the same way, she blamed her mother for her "broken" female body and believed that, if it had been whole and more beautiful, her father would still be with them.

One day Suzie broke a biscuit, then joined it together and asked me to find the crack. I commented on her wish that I could magically repair her cracked body, and her rejoinder was: "But I did damage my fanny!" When she had a "wiggly" tooth, she begged me to tell her at what hour, what day, what week, what month it would fall out. These demanding entreaties reflected her unsafe and unpredictable past, and I linked them to her craving for certainty. Suzie became enraged with me, as she had hoped that I, unlike mother, had the omnipotent power to control and protect her from every source of harm.

Suzie's traumatic experience of being abandoned was organized around a distressing episode before treatment started, when her mother had forgotten to fetch her from school and she said she had waited for six hours. (She did wait a long time. The pupils and most teachers had left. Suzie believes she was all alone. Her mother remembers forgetting to fetch her and coming very late—but not six hours late.) Once, following a violent row between her parents at the weekend about who was to be responsible for taking her and collecting her, Suzie was late for an analytic session. Her mother told her not to wait while she parked the car but to go straight inside. Suzie panicked and was inconsolable. She sobbed, begging the receptionist to tell her the minute her mother arrived. She was convinced that her mother had, again, forgotten her forever. Under the impact of overwhelming anxiety, her capacity for reality testing disappeared.

Suzie despised her mother for being overweight and unglamorous, but these hostile feelings caused her concern, and she dealt with them by giving her mother devouring embraces. In a similar way her mother had clung effusively to Suzie after the father had abandoned her. Suzie's behavior spilt over into other relationships. She kissed and pawed the au pair, Lena, who had been with them a few months and who brought her to treatment four times a week. (Later, when Lena was replaced, Suzie omnipotently thought that if she were nasty to the replacement, Lena would magically return. I linked this fantasy to fears about her mother and to her belief that, if she did not hang on by sexualized envelopment, Suzie would lose her female caretakers just as she had lost her father. Suzie argued: "But Lena was so-o-o nice, and what's wrong with kissing and hugging? She tasted like lovely roast chicken. Anyway, you taught me that thing about thoughts not coming true just because you think them!" She shamefacedly confessed that, in a row with Lena's successor, she had called her "cow muck." I related this to her earlier shame about her own degrading muck. Suzie responded with denigrating acceptance: "Are you sick? Aren't you feeling well? Because now you're talking sense.")

When her mother went to the United States for a week, Suzie was looked after by Lena. During this time, in one of her sessions, she walked on the wooden edge of the couch in slippery socks. I suggested that she wanted me to protect her from hurting herself by her risky balancing act and that she *could* look after herself a little in spite of her hostile concern for Mummy, far away in another country. She asked if she could kiss me, pleaded provocatively to be allowed to, and tried to make the issue into a battle. I related this to her fights with her mummy over body management—brushing her hair, fastening her safety belt in the car—and her need for a truce through devouring kisses. "But please—can't I give you one little kiss?" she persisted. At the end of the session, after her usual dawdling routine of collecting herself, her shoes, plate, and glass, she quickly and triumphantly planted a kiss on my cheek.

During the week her mother returned, Suzie proudly showed me her American shoes. Then, in a flash, she lifted her dress to show me her new Calvin Klein underpants. She was enraged by my unresponsive silence, my failure to be seduced, and said, with an air of theatrical shock, "Calvin Klein means all things to all people, and you don't say anything about my new pants." I pointed out her wish to excite me and interest me in her sexual body, as if without it I could not value her. When, some months later, a temporary helper brought Suzie to her sessions, she defended against her insecurity with an upsurge of giggling and a cajoling request for physical contact with me. She gave me a surprise by at first hiding her new short hairstyle, hastily sneaking a kiss on my cheek, and saying, "Don't be angry, my cream pie, my little pepperoni."

Later in this session Suzie reconfirmed her belief that the path to safety was through seduction and disarming exhibitionistic behavior. A school friend urgently asked Suzie's advice about an anxiety. The girl was terrified that someone would come to the front door intent on murdering her. Suzie's advice was immediate: "Don't be frightened," she said. "This is what you have to do. Make friends with him and invite him in and put on a tape and dance. He will enjoy himself so much he'll forget about murdering you." She gyrated in front of me to the imaginary pop music, oblivious of my presence. This autoerotic activity was at times replaced by exhibitionistic actions that Suzie hoped would magically increase my investment in her. When themes of castration and bodily inferiority were uppermost, Suzie defended against her concerns by showing me all she had.

Suzie thought that, as an unattractive female, her only offerings were her sexual displays. This feeling was exacerbated by her stepmother's glamor, a glamor that had won her father. Suzie's despair about her appearance matched her yearning for beauty. She believed that if her own mother had been responsible for her bad looks, a good-looking analyst/mother would be a positive influence. She urged me to improve my appearance—"Well, you could try using a little mascara or blush"—and asked with polite abuse if I knew my bottom teeth were uneven. Once, when she was particularly angry, she said viciously: "You look like a gray blob. Couldn't you at least try to look like a pink blob?" She tried to make me as disgusting as she felt herself to be. But almost at once she feared I would seek revenge for this assault by withdrawing love and attention, and she spent the remainder of the session complimenting me on my clothes and the brilliant way I shuffled cards to play "Snap." She thought compliments, however feeble, would make amends for her attack.

Suzie had controlled most of our first eighteen months of treatment either by daydreaming or by verbal or physical excitement. She would gaze out of the window or flop on the couch transfixed by her fantasies, making no response to my words or actions. Or, alternatively, she flooded the sessions with sexual stories, and the slightest reaction from me—a remark, a movement, a silence—brought more excitement. She complained that I didn't smile enough, demanding to know, "Why can't you be more like Mrs. M.?" As early as her third session she had dramatically related how she and her cousin had pretended they were making love to a boy and had kissed their pillow so much that the fabric was too wet to sleep on. More than a year later, she reported that another cousin had told her what a French kiss was and proceeded to demonstrate. "You put your whole mouth into the person," she said, and after some passionate miming she sat down, fidgeted in her chair, picked at her fingers and then at her toe, which she put into her mouth. (For Suzie, the thought could all too quickly become the deed.) On another occasion she asked whether I'd seen a late night TV film on sexual abuse that she had watched with her great-aunt. It was about a man who had forced a boy to kiss his willie even though the boy didn't want to. Suzie would not elaborate on this, so we focused on the boy's— and her own—feeling of confusion, shame, and excitement, as well as on their condemnation of the unsafe adult world.

FIGHTING FEAR

In her sessions, Suzie often complained of boredom. "I hate feeling bored," she said. "Feeling sad is more exciting than feeling bored." In this connection, when I suggested that masturbation made her feel "terribly nice," she thought for a moment, then asked, "Do you mean like hollow inside?" Her sense of emptiness reflected states in which there were profound disturbances of affect, object relations, and bodily experience. It was not only bodily and object loss that terrified Suzie but loss of her own fragile sense of self. It was better to feel *anything* than *nothing*. Precisely this fear prompted her search for the excitement that alone could pull her back from the verge of annihilation. The fear was pervasive. "I'm frightened I'm going to die," she said: "That I'll just stop breathing and then I'll die." She reported dreams of drowning. In one, the waves were sending a message, "In Memory of Suzie." In an attempt to master the anxiety, she tried to draw the dream-scene with a crayon and became so absorbed in her activity that she could not hear me speak. She wanted oceanic harmony and at the same time feared that her self-boundaries would crumble and that she would be groundless, drowned, and dead. At the end of the session I commented on her resistance, reminding her that therapy was meant to help her, not make her feel worse. She became frightened that I too might withdraw a lifeline, and she said with compliant thoughtfulness: "I think I've got a therapy clue. When my friends are very nasty to me, I'm down in the dumps. Perhaps I'm so far down I'm frightened of dying."

Suzie's failure to understand why she had no friends and why she experienced her peers as "nasty" was closely linked with a general difficulty in understanding the relation of cause and effect. This was an important contributing factor to her ignorance of the rules of simple board games. Her shame about this ignorance compounded it and intensified her aggressive defensiveness. She lied and was spiteful. Her humiliation at losing was altogether striking. Concentrating on watching me so that I didn't cheat enabled her to feel she was controlling her fate, but it also interfered with her capacity to learn. When I finally insisted on reciprocity, on strictly taking turns and maintaining the same rules for both of us, she slowly understood that her difficulty in peer relationships was rooted in her frantic demands for immediate gratification and her anxiety that if she shared with others or waited for what she wanted she would get nothing and be nothing: if she did not insure her survival by wielding this grabbing, snatching, vicious power, she would be annihilated.

Suzie then became much more aware that her unpopularity was a result of internal problems. Instead of resorting to projection and externalization, she became more in touch with her defenses. After a year of treatment she said one day that she had spent playtime resting on a bench. In response to my silence, she asked, "Well, what's wrong with being tired and resting?" But we both knew that she was rationalizing her withdrawal, that her behavior was at last becoming conflictual, and that, with time, therapy could help her find another solution for her pain.

Suzie's fear of failure restricted her functioning in work as well as play. In a session to which she brought arithmetic homework, she began to recognize that the idea of failure was so humiliating to her that fear of failure itself interfered with her concentration and prevented her from mastering the task. We had learned this lesson from board and card games, and it was repeated with her violin and piano lessons. Despite having a beautiful singing voice she refused, when given the choice, to join a choir rather than to play a musical instrument. But, in the treatment room, she showed no sign of conflict over sitting naked from the waist up after she had spilled juice on her dress and vest and had spontaneously taken them off. Nor was she self-conscious about singing during sessions. Yet she was terrified that she would make a "boo-boo" in the school play. Suzie's uncoordinated gymnastic displays at school were in sharp contrast to her agility in spontaneous movement. At one point a gang of girls excluded her because she could not pass a ball test. She had been unable to throw or catch, let alone to clap her hands while the ball was in the air and catch it before it hit the ground. She brought a ball to her sessions and practiced, while I tried to point out that her anxiety and excitement interfered with the concentration necessary for these maneuvers. Again, her thoughts were invested in prospective acceptance or rejection rather than in the task itself. Her special sensitivity to bodily injury also interfered with her performance.

SLOW CHANGES

Almost two years after treatment started there was a major external change in Suzie's life. She moved from a local state school to a small private school near the Anna Freud Centre with excellent and perceptive teachers. She remained there for a year and a half. This experience, together with her mother's growing conviction about the need to set limits, fostered Suzie's slow movement toward gaining autonomy from her primary objects and control over her own body.

Her first term at the new school coincided with another change of location. My office had temporarily moved to another, very much smaller treatment room in a building across the street. At first, Suzie expressed delight with the new school and the new room. She busied herself making a doll's house from a cardboard box. But almost daily there was some confusion about the arrangements for bringing her to treatment. One day she arrived late, in tears because the helper had lost her way. While she had been waiting, her teacher had said sympathetically: "Now, two things. One: put on your coat, and two: would you like a chocolate biscuit?" Suzie had said no to the biscuit, explaining to me, "You know, when you're worried you can't eat. Now I'm sorry I didn't say yes, because I'm not worried any more." We talked about her earlier unhappy and aggressive eating, so often related to worries about getting too fat like Mummy, whose overweight had repelled Suzie's father. Suzie said thoughtfully: "I knew I didn't feel happy, but I didn't know I was worried." She was beginning to show a capacity for self-reflection. But Suzie's pleasure in these external changes didn't last long. At school, friendships initially begun were crushed by her characteristic modes of behavior. In treatment, her defenses shifted from daydreaming and attempts at seduction to fierce anger and hostile silence, expressive of her terror of her murderous wish to destroy the analyst/ mother for failing to shield her from her hopelessly frustrating life.

Suzie insisted on leaving her schoolbag in the clinic's waiting room which was in the same building as our original meeting room and where there was always a friendly atmosphere, but as soon as her session started she would need a book, or her calculator, and would order me to fetch the schoolbag. Her resistance to staying in the small room in such close proximity to me made her think of innumerable ways of separating us and wasting time. Thus she fought her developing trust, and the anger too served a defensive function. She had to reject me before I engulfed or abandoned her. She would taunt me with threats: "If you don't do it at once, I'll run across the street and not look where I'm going." She spent many sessions reading a book with her knees raised to hide her face. Any attempt I made to describe what I thought she was feeling, or any interpretation, would make her stop reading—or whatever else she was doing at the time—vindictively and at once. During her sessions Suzie would play computer games, fiddle aimlessly with felt pens, or look out of the window into the dark street. In all this she continued to put distance between us with the same motivations (avoiding both rejection and annihilation). Her oral withholding was a way of punishing mother and me for her vulnerabilities. When, at one session, I interpreted this, Suzie replied that she had not been to the loo for two days; she knew she should eat more fruit but had forgotten. Significantly, this time she did not blame her mother.

During one session Suzie joined some pens together with cellophane tape and discovered she had created a teachers' ruler. She used it as a pointer to an imaginary blackboard and became absorbed in writing on the board, planning a program of activities and enjoying her exclusive game. She would not include me in this play, fearing the exposure that object-related imagination might produce. I talked about how her inability to share or take turns affected me as well as her peers. I insisted on having turns as the teacher or the pupil and tried to inject some fun into the action, so that Suzie could experience some pleasure in playing with another. Eventually, as the teacher, I asked the class where they were going for their holidays. Suzie, as a pupil with a different name, gave a garbled account of travels around the world with different members of her family. In displacement I interpreted the pupil's anxiety about not knowing where she would be and with whom—she felt she was passed like a parcel from one adult to another, with no control or choice. She commented, "If you do therapy when you're supposed to be a teacher, I won't play anymore."

Suzie's tenuous friendships were briefly shored up when her mother acquired four guinea pigs. Suzie took them to school in a box. The children crowded round her, wanting to touch the furry creatures and asking to go to her house to play with them. She became the center of attention. At the same time, Suzie herself developed a "squeak." The birth of this symptom was related to her acquisition of the needy, helpless, nonverbal, squeaking animals. But when I pointed this out she either denied having a squeak at all or else said she had a tickle in her throat. She was adamant that it had nothing to do with the guinea pigs. I referred to Suzie's longing to be cosseted, admired, and held like the baby animals and related this to her infancy, when her needs were met.

Similarly, she longed for the life of baby Ruth, who was never reprimanded, never had to do homework or worry about her peer group.
She was like her famous mother, a star, unburdened by physical defects
or an overweight and unpunctual mother. The squeak persisted even
as Suzie angrily denied it was happening. Suzie nagged at me to let her
bring the animals, and I used this demand to make her fully conscious
of her characteristic behavior, to give her a choice between being a
squeaky, dependent, fondled baby or a more appropriately behaved
10-year-old who could responsibly look after pets and bring them to
her session. I insisted that I could not have *five* babies in the room! The
squeaking stopped, and Suzie brought in the guinea pigs. When on
occasion squeaking returned, Suzie weakly protested her ignorance,
and the symptom soon stopped altogether.

As the guinea pigs grew, they were no longer a source of interest to
the other girls. Suzie again felt diminished and insecure, and new
symptoms appeared. After a weekend with her exciting cousins, Suzie
arrived for her session with the area between her bottom lip and chin
very sore and inflamed. She gave as the cause the fact that her pillow
got very wet at night and made her skin sore, she accused me of lying
when I reminded her that she had once told me that they used to kiss
the pillow until it was wet. Suzie put cream on during the session,
blaming her mother for not giving her the right cream. She complained also about a sore foot, predicting surgery, perhaps amputa-
tion. Suzie touched her sore skin repeatedly, reviving a regressive need
to soothe her own irritation. I suggested that this felt terribly necessary
when work and play at school were so difficult. Suzie understood this,
and completed an interpretation about displacement upwards, saying,
"And next week I have to go to the dentist." At about this time she
became insufferable in her sessions, rude, demanding and bossy, insisting on having me fetch articles from her schoolbag in the building
across the road. I spoke to her sharply on one occasion, showing her
how she provoked this kind of response from her mother and her
peers. She thoughtlessly treated people as though they were
commodities—like her microwave oven, which could be switched on,
used to provide instant gratification, and then ignored.

Suzie's low self-esteem took a turn for the worse when she learned
she had been given only a minor part in the school play. This was "the
unkindest cut of all." She would tell the teacher she wouldn't be in the
play, she shouted in helpless rage and frustration. The next day she did
complain to the teacher, who patiently counted Suzie's lines and demonstrated that she had as much to say as most of the other children.
Suzie brought the script to each session asking me to prompt her. When

I did, she criticized me for being too loud, too soft, too quick, too slow, or too stupid. Her fear that her father was only interested in leading ladies was heightened when he said that it was doubtful he would come because he had to go abroad. She added, "And don't talk therapy because I'll walk straight out of here if you do." By the time the play was performed, however, Suzie had become happy with her role. Her father did attend and sat next to her mother but left as soon as the play ended. She accepted this, saying, "I love my Daddy and that's all there is to it."

Parts in school plays were never again an overt issue. When the school was performing *The Wizard of Oz* Suzie cheerfully sang the songs in our sessions and discussed without rancor which pupil had which part. Her father couldn't be present at this concert as he was out of England watching her stepmother perform. Suzie rejected my interpretation that, if she were as beautiful, talented, and famous as the stepmother, her father would have made *her* performance his priority: Father, like the therapist, didn't find the time to go to her concert because she was not valued or loved—a messy, ugly girl.

The fact that Suzie really did have a good voice brought her into direct competition with her acclaimed stepmother. She consistently dismissed interpretations about this rivalry, but when I suggested that perhaps she feared her stepmother's anger if she, Suzie, excelled, she exclaimed: "That's more like it—she'd murder me!"

With much help from the social worker and much protestation from Suzie, however, her mother finally persuaded her to join a local youth choir. She was able to enjoy it because she was singing in a group, but when she was asked to audition for a part in *The Secret Garden* she was terrified. What might come out of her mouth? How would it be received? Still, she arrived one day for her session saying, "I've got some therapy news that you'll really like!" She not only had gotten a part, but the show would be performed at the National Theater and televised. It was striking that, during this period, she managed to get to school on time each morning in spite of rehearsals and performances that finished late at night. She was fetched to and from these events by a special bus and seemed unconcerned that she was without her mother.

When the play started, Suzie begged me to come and see her: I would be so proud of her! She continued to nag me: had I been yet and, if so, when? This wish for my approval reflected her belief that exhibiting herself was the way to get her father's love and mine. We talked about her certainty that "showing" equaled "admiration," and I made links between this conviction and her earlier material about her body. (Two terms later, when Suzie asked me to attend her farewell concert at school, the invitation was significantly different in both form and content. "I want you to come," she said, "because I think you'd be very interested in seeing all the pupils and teachers I've been telling you about for so long.") On her opening night at the National Theatre Suzie's father sent her flowers, and she reported delightedly that he "was very pleased" with her. She wanted to know which flower was my favorite and said without resentment that Dad had sent her carnations, which were lovely but not her favorite. She could tolerate disappointments from her father as long as she had his approval: that was what really mattered.

Suzie's relationship to her father underwent a change once she had faced her disappointment in his hitherto idealized family. When she visited he was always busy, and she was left with the nanny and children. She no longer looked forward to weekends in the country. But she feared that if—omnipotently—he knew what she was thinking, he would retaliate and abandon her for another five years. She seemed to have given up the fantasy that her parents would come together again and just hoped that, if they were to meet, they would be nice to each other. On one occasion, when I linked her present feelings to her past experiences, she said, with a certain offended hauteur, "Mrs. Gavshon! How long have I been coming here? How long have you been telling me that? Don't you think we've done that therapy by now?"

Suzie's last insulting remarks about my appearance came in our penultimate term of treatment. She asked if the beads I was wearing were real silver. She paused, then said, "They can't be real, because if they were you'd be rich, and if you were rich you'd have a nose job." Later, she returned to the subject. "My father's brilliant," she averred. "He isn't handsome, but *I* think he is. He's got a big nose like mine and he's promised me a nose job when I'm eighteen." Her father, unlike her mother and me, was capable of repairing her imperfections. But, when she stated (accurately, I believe) that her paternal grandmother was difficult and nobody liked her, she was able to add, "The only person she's a little bit frightened of is my father, because he can be slimy and cruel."

Suzie, then, was more at peace with her criticisms of her father—with his neglect, selfishness, and unreliability. But the occasional times she spent with him (often engineered by her mother) were golden times for her. She was aware of how little attention he paid her half-siblings and of her role as the grown-up daughter, saying: "He seems more interested in me now." Suzie and her father spent much time competing happily over video games. This made her special, since she was the only member of the family who enjoyed them as much as he did.

At the end of her first term at her new school, Suzie's teachers remarked on her manipulative, distracting behavior and on her failure to concentrate, which interfered so much with the proper use of her intelligence. But when she returned from her Christmas holiday in Portugal she was calmer and more contented. Her holiday homework essay was cheerful in style and spirit, free from the doom and disaster that had pervaded previous stories.

Suzie started to walk to the Centre by herself, accepting responsibility for her punctuality. On her first trial walk she was shadowed by her mother, whose behavior she later criticized. She was, said Suzie, so busy chatting to other mothers that she was setting a pretty poor example of how to be serious about responsibility. After a second day of being followed by her mother, Suzie came alone, and she continued to do so, delighted with her independence. Furthermore, she gave no sign of panic or anxiety if whoever was meant to collect her came late. This did not prevent her from condemning her mother's unreliability on the frequent occasions when she was overwhelmed by business demands. Suzie derided her mother's "scattiness" and couldn't stand it when she was "hypo" (meaning "hyper"): she mimed her mother's states of uncontained anxiety—forgetting her bag, mislaying her keys, needing to be reminded of appointments. She contrasted her with a friend's mother who worked full time but always found two hours for her daughter after school. Suzie's account of these maternal shortcomings and her suggestions of ways in which mother could improve took no heed of her own contributions to the difficulties, of her provocations and expressions of dependency, for instance, refusing to wear a watch or keep a schedule book, and leaving her clothes lying where she dropped them. On the other hand, in treatment Suzie took her own plate and glass to the waiting room and made no fuss about tidying up, and she took similar responsibilities when staying with her father. Her defiance over chores at home in part expressed her unresolved rage over her mother's early neglect. She punitively tried to ensure that her mother would pay for this for the rest of her life, transforming every maternal request into a mammoth demand.

In her sessions, Suzie no longer discharged anxiety through sexual behavior. Like her dictatorial manner, this was replaced by attempts to overwhelm me with verbal avalanches of argumentative discourse. Interpretations referring to her low self-esteem and fear of criticism revived her fear of shame, but she was able to accept the idea that she tried to fend this off by shooting me down with a verbal gun going rat-a-tat-tat. If she thought she was losing in a game, she bombarded me in just this manner. On one occasion, when I unexpectedly won a game, she felt psychologically depleted and refused to have a return match. She had to be the "star" every time, or she was nothing but a stupid, ugly, damaged female, as my interpretations tried to make clear. This went on through endless, dreary games of tic-tac-toe and hangman. When Suzie began games testing categories of general knowledge, I told her that, if she wanted to play such games, we would have to put them to some therapeutic purpose because that, after all, was why she was coming. So we introduced a category called "Feelings," in which initial letters were used to suggest a particular feeling state. Most of Suzie's spontaneous responses were negative: H suggested *hate*, for example, and C *cry*, emphasizing her loneliness. But when we played this game in the closing terms of treatment, she wrote *happy* for H and *calm* for C. For G, *greedy* was replaced by *grateful*. Reparative feelings were at work.

ENDING TREATMENT

As treatment progressed, Suzie displayed an increasing capacity for adaptive object relations. This was evident at school as well as during the sessions. She described a film she had watched called *Problem Child*. The story of the ghastly child and the equally dreadful adults led us to talking about adoption and family romance. We related these issues to her own life situation and the choices she would have made if these had been possible. Since, in a slip of the tongue, Suzie had called me "Grandma," I asked where I would fit into her fantasized family. She exclaimed, "Mrs. Gavshon, that's mental. That's real sick. It's all right for a child to like a therapist, but to like them as much as that would be mental. You'd *really* need therapy if you loved your therapist."

Suzie's relationship with her peer group was changing. She could apologize when convinced she was in the wrong. She no longer fluttered from one "best friend" to another. In keeping with the others, she wore "trendy" clothes and shoes. And, like some of her classmates, she even had her ears pierced: a move that reflected a new capacity for reality testing in terms of bodily damage. During a severe attack of measles she had lost a good deal of weight. She hated her thinness and wanted to look feminine. This was indeed a change: hitherto, she would have welcomed the demonstration that she was not at all like her mother, whose excessive weight was, in Suzie's view, partly responsible for father's desertion.

Suzie's sexual excitement appeared when she described plotting and maneuvers over Jack, the best-looking boy in the school, with whom she was "madly in love." She spent hours on the phone talking to her cousins, whose advice was to play hard to get. "What do you think?" she asked me. I said that her need for excitement was met not only by her fantasies of winning Jack but by involving her cousins. I wondered why it was still so important for her to be associated with the "best looks" and, in this connection, reminded her of the work we had done in the past. Suzie discussed the dangerous liaisons between the boys and girls in her sessions and recommended that certain children should have therapy because they got too excited! She asked, "How does therapy work? You didn't give me advice or tell me what to do. They have to have therapy to know why they are doing it."

As her work at school steadily improved, Suzie was gaining recognition and "merits." On one occasion she had a setback in science: she had forgotten to take home a book she needed to review for an exam. She gave me a rambling story, blaming both the layout of her desk and the teacher for her forgetfulness. She shouted me down when I pointed out that she was doing, to her own detriment, just what she accused her mother of doing—being disorganized and unreliable. Then she calmed down and, after a long silence, found her own solution. "My class work is very good, and next time I'll concentrate hard on science," which she did, thereby winning the praise of her (male) teacher. Suzie won the school essay prize on the topic: *What It Feels Like to Be Blind*. On her headmaster's recommendation she took the entrance exam for a competitive girls' boarding school and was thrilled to gain a place, although she expected to be "lost and miserable" at first on going there.

She defended against any sense of loss or misery over leaving me. This was in keeping with her singular and significant lack of curiosity about my personal life. She never asked about my family, my holidays, the color of my car—despite interpretations and the fact that I did not discourage her from doing so. As her confidence at school grew, she demanded to know, "When can I stop coming?" She tried, with everything from manipulation to unadorned reasoning, to persuade me to agree to terminate. When Suzie said, "I've got good therapy news that you will really like," she was sometimes bringing some fresh insight or evidence of progress, but frequently her assertion was simply defensive or seductive. She arrived for one session with tidy, shiny hair. I said, "Hooray! At last Suzie likes her hair." She replied, "You should say, 'Hooray! At last Suzie likes all her body!'" She was frustrated but relieved when I recognized the device, assuring her that bluffing me as well as herself did nothing to help: it would not make her feel any happier. And when, as often, she was resistant and defiant, angrily refusing to participate, I would interpret her wish and fear that this behavior would precipitate the end of therapy but add that the duration of treatment was largely her responsibility. She knew, I pointed out, that I would not agree with her until she was well enough inside: the infantile, provocative way of relating that still stamped her behavior toward her mother was no way of achieving an agreed termination. Suzie also tried to persuade me to drop one session a week by saying, reasonably enough, "You know, most kids *would* have wanted to have worked out their worries enough to want to stop having therapy. There's so much to do after school." When we did enter the closing period of therapy it was possible to reduce her attendance to three times weekly.

Two days after she left treatment, Suzie wrote the following letter. It was the height of summer, and her allergy to pollen was intense.

> Dear Mrs. Gavshon,
>   I miss you already. It is quite funny because as soon as I left you, all these therapy problems came to my head that I had carelessly brushed aside while having sessions with you.
>   ANYWAY! I have an awful cold and I am going to Portugal in two days and I had to go to the doctors because I had rather a loud wheeze and GUESS WHAT! I got a ventilator from the chemist.
>   PLEASE WRITE BACK!
>   I am looking forward to your letter.
>   Love Suzie

I did not hear from her again until two terms later, when she telephoned half an hour before she was due to leave for her Easter holiday in Portugal. She said she had dyed her hair and that she liked school very much, except for one girl who was nasty.

After early on begging her mother to take her away Suzie settled into boarding school. Her term reports comment on her very good work and her pleasure in her achievements, although she still cannot enjoy competitive sports. One report notes that "her sense of fun and natural enthusiasm are proving delightful."

From age fifteen months, when her father left the family, Suzie's development seems to have been in jeopardy. Her mother—narcissistically shattered, overwhelmed, and preoccupied—could no longer respond to Suzie's basic needs and provide an appropriate protective shield against internal and external stimuli. Without that auxiliary ego support, Suzie was unable to tolerate frustration in the face of mounting excitation; the resulting lack of sense of safety intensified Suzie's global distress, and undifferentiated affective states could not be contained. Suzie's inability to differentiate adequately between different parts of her body was exacerbated by physical disturbances, and their investigation and treatment brought further confusion. Preoedipal oral and anal organizations could not be integrated into an oedipal phase which would, in any event, have been problematic in the absence of a father. (Suzie's father was not available to her until she was six.) Furthermore, since the necessary conditions for that integration had not been met, the repression barrier was poorly established and had never been consolidated, so that fantasy far too readily gave way to action (Kennedy et al., 1985). Indeed, thought and action could not always be clearly distinguished (Mayes and Cohen, 1992). Suzie tried to deal with these psychological and physical deficits by maintaining her body as the focus of attention, especially the erogenous zones and their functions—in particular, eating, wetting, anal withholding, lonely masturbation, and public exhibitionism.

Medical intervention for urinary infections and lichen sclerosis reinforced Suzie's belief that she was damaged, unworthy, and unvalued; such a self-valuation was seemingly endorsed by her father's desertion and neglect. Her shame and humiliation fueled her low self-esteem, and her psychosexual development was distorted in the interest of bolstering her self-image and regard for her damaged body (see Yorke, 1990). Exposure to inconsistent and frequently excessive stimulation by others, whether from medical necessity or during social interchange, offered her little opportunity to develop internal controls. Ego development suffered early interference, leading to a poorly established sense of self and object and restriction in the growth of object relations (Solnit, 1982). Since she could not distinguish cause and effect or postpone gratification in the service of the reality principle, she used her objects for instinctual discharge, and her resulting mounting excitement was reinforced from all available fronts, including, above all, by aggression. Unavoidably, her relationships were disastrous.

Certainly, her mother's verbal communication with Suzie was intellectually stimulating, but it often had an excited and agitated quality that was inappropriate. Despite her precocious vocabulary, Suzie had no means of mastering her chaotic feelings through verbalization (Katan, 1961), and this deficiency brought her into conflict with her environment. Analysis provided a holding environment that helped Suzie find alternative means of gratification and control. It supplied the words to help her identify and recognize her feelings so that they could be managed in a more organized way, with less intrusion of primary process thinking and behavior. Suzie's capacity to develop a reflective self brought structural change, enabling her to move away from need-satisfying limitations to the level of emotional object constancy. It is possible that her mother's initial attunement to her infant daughter, together with the presence of a reliable nanny, provided some sense of safety and well-being; without this, mother and child might have been unable to respond to the therapeutic help that was offered.

Although Suzie's analyst was a real person—a special adult, as well as an object for transference—the psychoanalytic technique was classical in terms of interpreting resistance and defense, utilizing constructions and reconstructions in an interpretative modality, and summoning appropriate means to maintain analytic conditions of abstinence. The analyst adapted the technique to take into account and clarify Suzie's symptoms, specifically those she brought on herself, as distinct from the lichen sclerosis et atrophicus. In this way she could learn to master the management of her body.

Whether or not Suzie will be able to remain on a path of relatively normal development is still somewhat questionable; when she reaches puberty, the impact of adolescent sexual and genital strivings and the revival of unresolved conflicts may cause her to regress to inappropriate and less restrained behavior. It is not possible to predict how she will manage her body care when she starts menstruating or how the lichen sclerosis will contribute to the fantasies that accompany these bodily changes. Since there was a period when Suzie was unable to distinguish clearly between urethral, anal, and genital zones and their functions, the inability to control the flow of blood may reactivate the despairing anxieties around her low self-esteem linked with failure of bladder and bowel control. The physical characteristics of the lichen sclerosis and the ongoing treatment may once again encourage, stimulate, and reinforce exciting but conflictual fantasies about the nature of her femininity, which may exacerbate her difficulty in negotiating her entry into adolescence. The "sense of fun and natural enthusiasm" her teachers applaud may be a step toward appropriate restriction of emotional overflow. Suzie's experience in analysis will, I hope, also make it possible for her to recognize the need for further treatment when she is older.

BIBLIOGRAPHY

KATAN, A. (1961). Some thoughts on the role of verbalization in early childhood. *Psychoanal. Study Child*, 16: 184–88.
KENNEDY, H., MORAN, G., WISEBERG, S., & YORKE, C. (1985). Both sides of the barrier: Some reflections on childhood fantasy. *Psychoanal. Study Child*, 40: 275–83.
MAYES, L. C., & COHEN, D. J. (1992). The development of a capacity for imagination in early childhood. *Psychoanal. Study Child*, 47: 23–47.

SOLNIT, A. (1982). Developmental perspectives on self and object constancy. *Psychoanal. Study Child*, 37: 201–18.

YORKE, C. (1990). The development and functioning of the sense of shame. *Psychoanal. Study Child*, 45: 377–409.

Enactment and Play Following Medical Trauma

An Analytic Case Study

MARIANNE GOLDBERGER, M.D.

This paper on the four-year analysis of a five-year-old girl with a school phobia details the playroom enactments of medical trauma and its sequelae. Early in the analysis the patient expressed herself almost exclusively through play. Gradually she connected her conflicts, including those over her compulsive masturbation, to her hospital experiences. Only after the traumatic medical experiences were no longer the major issue did other important conflicts become available for analytic work. Physical activity remained prominent in the analysis and generated pressure for mutual enactment. This case again draws our attention to the complex overlap of play, enactments, and verbalization in child analysis.

THIS CASE STUDY OF THE FOUR-YEAR PSYCHOANALYTIC TREATMENT OF A five-year-old girl demonstrates yet again the therapeutic usefulness of repetitive enactment, with appropriate affective discharge, in the treatment of a child for medical trauma and its sequelae. Much of her repetitive play during the course of her analysis did not reflect the medical trauma directly, although connections to the trauma were often discernible. These latter play themes reflected conflicts from every developmental level, including those preceding the trauma. The clini-

Training and supervising analyst at the Psychoanalytic Institute at New York University; clinical professor of psychiatry at the New York University Medical Center.

This paper was presented in an earlier version as the Anna Freud Memorial Lecture to the Freudian Society, New York; November 9, 1993.

cal picture with respect to the medical trauma resembled what Yorke (1986) has called the "posttraumatic neuroticlike state" and Kennedy's (1986) description of the "organizing experience of trauma" in the analysis of an adolescent boy. Only after major analytic work regarding the traumatic medical experiences had been accomplished could the patient's enactments and play reveal the ever-present fragility of her self-esteem, her pervasive fears of separation, and her conflicted feelings toward each parent.

Maria was five-and-a-half years old when she was referred to me for analysis because of her intense fears of going to school, leading finally to complete school refusal. It was October of her kindergarten year. Her anxiety about school had begun about a year earlier in nursery school at the same private school, on "picture-taking day." Maria had said it was because the teacher was angry at her. Her parents had a hard time getting her back to school. Every morning she vomited before school and often had a fit of anger, but Maria always seemed to have a good time once she got there. Field trips were so upsetting to her that eventually her mother kept her home on those days. Her nursery school year had also been characterized by one infection after another, so that she was out of school as many days as she attended. These infections included several episodes of cystitis.

Maria had begun full-day kindergarten two months before referral, and for the first six weeks there seemed to be no problem. Suddenly one day she burst into tears on the school playground, refused to eat lunch, and insisted on going home. "I know it isn't true," she said to her mother, "but I get the feeling that you won't ever come back—won't come to get me." During her two consultations with the referring analyst, Maria's symptoms improved, so that by the time she began analysis with me she was going to school each morning. But she was calling to be taken home before lunch.

Maria was the only child of white, Catholic, upper-class parents. She was an active baby from the beginning, with marked colic for her first few months. There were no feeding problems. She became, and remained, the emotional center of her family. Mr. and Mrs. A. were both much involved with all aspects of her life. They were largely permissive, feared their daughter's anger, and in general seemed to fear intense emotional expression. At the same time they were a rapt audience for whatever she might choose to do. They indeed believed she was the brightest and most gifted of children.

Mrs. A had married in her thirties and had given birth to Maria after several years of marriage. She was reserved, intelligent, and honest. She blushed easily. She clearly enjoyed talking about her child in great detail and was forthcoming most of the time. The strength and extent of Mrs. A.'s fearfulness emerged only gradually, as she overcame her embarrassment and shame in my presence. To give one example among many, she said that she had overcome her lifelong fear of driving a car only when Maria's analysis began, because treatment would not otherwise have been possible. Mrs. A. actually became more firm with Maria as the analysis went on, though I never directly advised her to that effect.

Mr. A. was a soft-spoken, seemingly passive man who was successful in business. He had been considered a gifted child and had been educated at first-rate schools. He was an avid reader but did not show much interest in social life. Initially, it seemed that he largely deferred to his wife in childrearing, but Maria's involvement with him increased over the course of the analysis.

When Maria was eighteen months old, it had been noted that "one eye turned out," and she was under the continuous care of an eye doctor, with periods of patching, until the age of four, when the strabismus was corrected surgically. During the first two years of life, she was left with babysitters only twice. At five, she was still afraid and upset when her parents went out, but she would settle down once they had left. Bowel-training was accomplished without difficulty; she never became fully bladder-trained. She was "always wet," her mother said, and around the age of three there had been considerable struggle with her mother about urinating. Her mother frequently reminded her to use the toilet and Maria ignored her. She improved somewhat during her fourth year.

Shortly after the onset of her school phobia at four and a half, Maria began to complain of dysuria and refused to urinate. Cystitis was diagnosed and recurred intermittently throughout the nursery school year. During the winter she had a severe case of chicken pox, with involvement of the vulva, so that again she had marked dysuria. She continued to have urinary symptoms during the summer after nursery school—being wet "constantly," unable to urinate on the toilet and wetting in her pants shortly thereafter. Maria's genitals were irritated, consequently, much of the time, leading her mother to use frequent applications of an ointment. She was finally referred to a urologist by her pediatrician, and a cystoscopy was done under anesthesia. According to her mother, the urologist had said Maria had an "extremely short" urethra, the "smallest [he] had ever seen." He dilated it. Following this cystoscopy and dilatation Maria had bright red blood in her urine and intense pain for three days, which frightened her very much. Then the urinary symptoms subsided. A week after this hospital experience, the family moved to a new house.

Let me digress to discuss "small and short" urethras. In the early 1970s, I was consulted several times about girls with an almost identical history of urinary symptoms, including traumatic cystoscopy. Many urologists had a tendency to do cystoscopies for so-called recurrent cystitis, which might be as few as three episodes. This situation led me to explore the literature in this area. I found several excellent radiological studies showing that girls' urethras are *normally* very small and short. That is how females are made, and it is why they are more susceptible to cystitis than males. Girls and women are also prone to urethritis, which causes painful urination but is not necessarily the result of cystitis. Remarkably, during each consultation I had about these other girls with histories of urinary symptoms, it was mentioned that the urologist had said that the child had an unusually short urethra. On the other hand, some pediatricians, even at that time, maintained that most cases of dysuria in girls could be managed conservatively (personal communication, George Cohen, M.D.). While preparing this manuscript, I surveyed the literature once again and was relieved to find that the era of invasive urological procedures is largely past, mainly because of the rapid advances in medical technology. Nowadays, noninvasive techniques such as sonography, are available for cases of recurrent cystitis or urethritis to rule out serious urinary-tract pathology.[1]

When we began our work together, Mrs. A. reported that Maria wet her bed at night and still tended to be damp during the day. When I asked about masturbation, she said there had been a great deal of it openly during the previous summer. She had discouraged it— "perhaps too harshly," she thought—and now Maria did it alone in her room but told her mother about it. Aside from the problems I have described, Maria functioned well and loved school. Her parents had always considered her behavior mature and were able to take her everywhere with them. She showed unusually advanced intellectual and motor skills.

When I first met Maria her intelligence and giftedness were evident, but her behavior was different from what her parents had described. She was a cute, round-faced, dark, and well-built little girl, who clung to

---

1. However, immediately after I gave this paper at the Freudian Society in New York City, several women therapists spoke with me both about their own similar experiences in the past and about those of girl patients.

her mother in the waiting room, burying her face in her mother's lap. When I invited both of them to come in Maria came quite readily and looked at the playthings with interest.

Her initial weeks of analysis involved teasing and testing limits. At the same time, I felt Maria trusted me easily and readily made a connection. She behaved as if she owned everything in the office. However, she delayed beginning her sessions and had great difficulty ending them. She often left the door to the waiting room open and made repeated trips out to her mother. My comments about this were at best ignored and at worst exacerbated the behavior. For example, she sometimes would leave both the entrance and exit doors to my office open and would run wildly around the circle she had created.

At first Maria used the puppets in the room only to make significant-sounding remarks such as, "You need to go to the hospital" and did not respond to any comment of mine or sustain the play.[2] One day, during the fourth month of the analysis, she said, "Let's play puppets. You be the doctor, and then I'll be the biter." With this, she picked up a dragon puppet, gave me the doctor and the nurse puppets, started to bite my puppets with hers, and then told me to have them run away and hide. There followed a lot of hiding, finding, chasing, and killing. Once the nurse got kidnapped, was tied to a chair, and had her mouth taped. At times the doctor and nurse kissed each other, and Maria's behavior would get more excited. Once the dragon cried when doctor and nurse kissed, saying, "I wanna be kissed," whereupon the nurse alternately hit and kissed the dragon many times. When I commented that Maria had mixed feelings about the dragon—"she likes and doesn't like the dragon"—Maria mimicked me over and over, "I do, I don't, I do, I don't." At one point she pretended to swallow the dragon and then told me to talk as if I had something in my mouth. She also made sporadic comments such as "You have blood all over you" or "Open your mouth" but then would immediately change the subject.

Over time Maria increasingly gave me the dragon and took the doctor and nurse herself. She told me to make the dragon talk in a scary voice, and when I complied, the doctor and nurse jumped with fright. The nurse knew why the dragon was so mad: he didn't want to be a dragon. The nurse and doctor hid for a long time, and the dragon couldn't find them. Then the doctor looked at the dragon's mouth and eyes and declared, "They're ugly; there's something wrong." After

---

2. Description of the first two years of the analysis is taken from the process notes, and I summarize the rest of the treatment.

hiding again for a while, the nurse and doctor came back and said they were "gonna fix him up."

"How?"

"Give blood in his mouth. His mouth is all dry. He's not to eat for a week." Then, addressing the dragon, "That's to make you better."

After this sequence Maria hid the puppets for the next day and asked me not to let anyone else use them. She left the session easily for the first time!

The next day, she took the dragon and told me to make the doctor and nurse hide. The dragon searched for them in vain, and this was repeated many times. Then she told me to make the doctor and nurse kiss, and she said, "Don't make him cry," and then to the dragon, "They won't kiss you! You're all wet!" Then she started to whisper new directions to me, telling me that the dragon couldn't see or hear, and that he could tell what I was saying from my lips. There ensued a sequence in which she said the doctor and nurse had gone to heaven, at first denying they had died, but then agreeing and having them go up, up, up together. This ended with her abruptly going out to the waiting room to get something from her mother. When she came back, she went to the shelves to look for something else. I said maybe the dragon had got worried, with all the talk about heaven and dying. She denied this but muttered something about not seeing someone again. So I said, "Oh, the idea of not seeing a person again is the hard part." She said, "Let's play cars" and started lining up cars. I said, "I guess you didn't like that part of our game."

After a little desultory play she picked up the dragon again, saying, "He has to get fixed up, there's something wrong with him. He's gonna go to the hospital. He'll get shots and blood. He's gonna get blood mixed with water to drink." During this sequence she put a rubber band around the dragon's mouth and, while administering shots and drinks, involved his eyes and teeth in the procedures. The dragon became unable to talk, getting "hoarser and hoarser."

"He has laryngitis," she announced. She mouthed the words "thank you" when he got a drink of blood and was delighted that I was able to read her lips.

"I want more," she mouthed, and when I understood that also, she played it over and over. Dragon wanted more and more, and Maria directed me to also give shots and to "doctor him." Dragon then died and was brought back to life dozens of times.

"He has to get twenty-five shots," she said.

As this play went on, Maria showed increasing excitement, continually putting her legs up on the chair as she sat or lay on the floor and wriggling her pelvis. She touched her genitals intermittently. I commented that the dragon seemed to get excited feelings when he got doctored. Her response was, "Let's play checkers." I said she really had to get away from these feelings, and after first denying it, she came back to the dragon and said that he likes and doesn't like doctoring. She wanted me to go on doing things to Dragon. When Dragon woke up from a long period of being "dead," the doctor and nurse were so happy they kissed each other. But Dragon was angry and attacked them viciously. I asked, "He's not happy the way they are?"

"No. He's angry."

"About what was done to him?" There was no reply, but Maria indicated that Dragon was to be tied up to the arm of a chair.

"Tie him tighter," she urged, as she made him struggle strenuously to get loose. "Tie up his mouth, too, *very tight.*"

When our time was up, Maria carefully hid the puppets and left easily.

In my next session with Mrs. A., I learned that within the previous month there had been a funeral at the family's church, and that she had explained to Maria about people dying when they are very old, about burial, and about heaven. After this Maria had resisted going to bed for a week, saying, laughingly, that she would die. Later, a custodian at her school had died, and Maria had become more apprehensive.

During that session, I was able to ask Mrs. A. about Maria's first and second teeth, and she told me her development in this area had been normal. At the age of three, however, Maria had fallen and cut her mouth and gums "a lot" so that blood was "spurting out of her mouth." She was taken to the dentist for treatment and there was no permanent injury. Her mother then commented that Maria looked like her father, "but she acts like me." She went on, "She has my temperament, so much so that I can feel just exactly how Maria feels. I remember very vividly having all the same feelings as a child."

In early sessions Maria's conflicts over masturbation were expressed in her behavior, but she was unable to talk about it for a long time. One day, she said that the excited feelings had to do with the "operation on my bottom," but then didn't say anything about it again.

Our first summer break was clearly hard for Maria, and before vacation she kept saying, "I should tell you everything. I'd feel better and it would be easier, but it's hard, and I don't want to." Once she said it had to do with the hospital and getting tied up: "Then I get that feeling, the funny, tickly feeling. And it also has to do with going to the doctor's office." I said that being tied up seemed to be important, and she replied, "Thinking about that gives me the tickly feeling . . . Now I *did* tell and it's easier . . . Was that the right answer?" When I said that it sounded as if she thought she was supposed to say the right thing in here, she readily agreed. She mentioned that she had washed her bottom yesterday and hadn't touched it except once today. In another session, she said that she was scared to talk about her worries, "because I don't know you very well. . . . I've come lots of times but you take lots of vacations."

After that summer break, Maria's conflicts about masturbation became clearer. Certain kinds of play made her feel excited, which she revealed through her behavior, since she still had great difficulty talking about masturbation. She would roll around on the floor, wiggle her pelvis, spread her legs and touch her genital area surreptitiously with whatever object she was playing with, or with her hand. There were many hours in which she crawled under my couch and lay on her stomach with both hands under her, masturbating and largely unresponsive to me.

The doctor game with the puppets made her excited, particularly when there were forcible procedures, such as shots, or when a puppet was struggling against restraints. Very often she also got the "tickly feeling" from spooky thoughts. She would ask me to make monster noises by strumming on the springs under the seat of a chair, because they "went well" with the excited feeling in her bottom. She occasionally elaborated verbally on the game, so that slowly some details of her picture of the medical procedures emerged. But there was one kind of repetitive play that she never spoke about. While I held and played the dragon-patient, she would vigorously shove an object down the dragon's throat (a flashlight, the handle of the reflex hammer, or a bunch of pencils).

In another very frequent sequence she told me, as the dragon, to go to sleep, or had me put to sleep by some adult puppet. The adult would go far away for a very long time, and the dragon would search and search but wouldn't be able to find the adult. This was repeated innumerable times within the same session. Sometimes, when the adult finally returned, the dragon was enraged and fought with the adult. In another version the tied-up puppet was kidnapped by monsters, then was abandoned, and when the kidnapper was found, a fight ensued. The fighting, especially if it was physical, would make Maria writhe on the floor as we played. If she became absorbed with masturbating she tried to hide it. Once, while playing the dragon I whispered to another puppet, "When I play like this I get excited feelings and I have to hide them." "You're too young," she told me sharply, and that was all she would say.

In the middle of the second year of analysis, Maria began to talk directly about herself. She confided that she always "itched" in her bottom and that she often put her hands there. Her mother made her have an operation because she wasn't made right there, "and neither are some other people." The operation fixed her, she said, but she knew she would have trouble again because she would keep putting her hand there; she couldn't help it. Her mother told her there was no connection between touching herself and having to have an operation, but she knew her mother didn't want her to do it because she would irritate herself there, so now she did it when her mother couldn't see her. She remembered having two operations, one on her eye and one on her bottom. She saw her red eye in the mirror afterwards. She talked about "breathing to go to sleep"—how she didn't want to, and how the doctor had said she had to. She demonstrated, with the doctor-puppet putting a hand around the puppet's neck to make her go to sleep. Then, with the puppet looking in the mirror, Maria said, "She doesn't want to know it's blood." She said, "With the bottom operation it was the same, with anesthesia . . . I don't know what happened . . . I don't know what happened." And she went on, "I had to have the operation because I couldn't go to the bathroom . . . it hurt to go . . . it hurt after the operation, and then it was okay." She denied that there was blood after the operation, though she had once before told me there was. Now she complained only about the pain.

In our puppet game, Maria, as the (male) doctor, got angry and said *he'd* had the same operation lots of times, and *he* would just go to the bathroom. He then did go to the bathroom and "had blood," and then started to hit the girl puppet with intense anger. "Go to sleep!" Maria yelled, and then turned off all the lights and started making spooky noises in the dark. This was at the end of a session, and she wrote a note for us to remember this for tomorrow.

The next day, Maria picked right up from before, with the doctor hitting a girl puppet and telling her to go to sleep. (Her parents had told me that there were almost nightly battles about going to sleep, involving both parents. Maria frequently woke up in the night and crept into her parents' bed. Her father was critical of his wife's inability to be firmer about Maria's bedtime.)

"He hates her," she explained. As the doctor and two girl puppets went to sleep, they heard scary noises. This whole sequence was re-peated many times, with Maria reassuring the scared girl that "as long as we're all together, you don't need to be scared." When I tried to use the game to figure out what makes a girl scared at night, Maria said firmly that she had *no* idea and abruptly ended this long repetitive sequence.

Maria went on to build a house under my desk (a very frequent activity). She hid herself in the house and instructed me to keep making a strumming noise on the chair. It was clear that she was masturbating in her hiding place, and while she denied that she was touching herself, she said, "The noise goes good with rubbing myself." Then, from under the desk, she said, "That's how I got to go to the hospital—I rubbed myself and got sore there, so I had to go." She became impatient with my attempts to talk about worries connected with soreness. She insisted that she loved rubbing herself, that her bottom tickled, and that I should just keep making the monster noise because "it goes good with it."

After this session, Maria had a nightmare from which she awoke crying because in the dream she "didn't have a mother." Her mother in the dream was someone from a TV family; she had lost her real parents. After telling her own mother the dream, she asked about the origin of babies. Mrs. A. had never told her about the father's role.

The next day was Christmas Eve. In her session Maria played a story about a girl who did not want to sleep, because she was scared, because she had bad dreams, and because "she had no fun." All the puppets performed Christmas songs. Maria animated a man and woman dancing together, and then one was on top of the other. There was a long sequence of puppets fighting with swords (we used pens), and Maria directed my girl puppet to be very pleased to have a sword. As Maria repeatedly jammed a sword down the dragon's throat, she became increasingly wiggly and ended up lying on her tummy with her hands under her.

Early in the second year of analysis, Mrs. A. supplied some details of the cystoscopy that she had never mentioned before. Both parents had been present for the induction of anesthesia, but they were not allowed to stand close to Maria (in contrast to her eye surgery, when both parents had been able to be near her). The anesthesiologist for the eye surgery had held the mask away from Maria's face and had given her "laughing gas." But on the occasion of the cystoscopy, the doctor put the mask close to her face, and Maria began to gag and make gurgling noises, as if she were choking on her own saliva.

"Then they shoved a tube down her throat rapidly, while she was still awake," the mother went on. "She struggled and was held down by two or three nurses. Her body was twitching and fighting for some time after the doctor said she was asleep." Mrs. A. said that afterwards she had avoided thinking about this horrifying experience.

Maria had had a difficult time in the recovery room as well. She had to be catheterized and she bled heavily, which was considered unusual. She was very upset, with nausea, pain, and a great deal of urinary urgency. At home the next day, she was afraid to void for twelve hours.

Mrs. A. also described how upsetting the intravenous pyelogram prior to surgery had been. Maria had spent two hours in the X-ray room without her mother. Finally, when her mother was allowed to come in, she found Maria lying on the table and crying, "Please get me my clothes, please let me leave." The nurses had wanted her to void on a towel on the table but she could not do it; despite her distended bladder, it took another half an hour before she could void.

The school fears subsided gradually and were gone after about two years of treatment. Both day- and night-time wetting also stopped. Maria remained fearful of monsters, however, especially at night. She was afraid of going upstairs to the bathroom alone and often had trouble going to sleep. In the analysis, Maria continued to communicate mostly through dramatic play, but the major themes in her play began to change. She still found it difficult to relate thoughts and feelings directly to herself.

The doctor game diminished in importance, reappearing mostly in connection with the issue of going to sleep. The girl puppet was supposed to go to sleep so that others could sleep, and a great deal of anger was displayed toward the puppet when she would not comply. The dramatization of spooks and monsters remained important. The spook games were accompanied by signs of excitement, and Maria and I were able to connect this with masturbation, with her thoughts about her own and her parents' bodies, with being tied up, and with things that went on in bed. The spook game increasingly took the form of two children, often boys, who were camping out together. One of the boys (usually the figure assigned to me) was afraid of the dark and of spooky noises, and Maria's puppet alternately reassured him and strictly told him to be quiet and go to sleep.

Maria made up a sleeping game in which she hid in a cozy nest, and there ensued all kinds of hidden movements which were meant to puzzle me. The camping game finally culminated in a session in which Maria enacted in pantomime what was obviously a primal scene, saying she was a boy who was having a dream. She was unable to relate this to any experience of her own and insisted that the boy had remained fast asleep the whole time.

The new themes developing were about being a boy, the idea of being ugly, and the abandonment of a child for being bad. Maria described in play, and even discussed directly at times, that it was better to be a boy than a girl: boys could be the boss and boys could be stronger. But often it seemed best to be both a boy *and* a girl, and Maria made some drawings of bisexual figures. In her puppet play, she made girls change into boys, and vice versa.

The idea of being ugly arose mostly in connection with repeated dramatizations of getting married. She wondered whether the girl puppet was pretty enough to marry, or was too ugly. One part of her ugliness was that she was dirty. The girl puppet was often afraid of marriage, and both her wish for and fear of the big father puppet were clear. In one sequence, the fantasied marriage led to the tying-up game formerly associated with masturbation. There were hints at family romance fantasies, but Maria was clearly fearful of them, especially since they led to thoughts of parents being dead and of a girl living alone. In her striving to be a very good child, she had the greatest difficulty owning her hostile thoughts and feelings. Her fear of her aggression turned up in stories about a child who was abandoned for being bad. It was hard to learn more about the "badness," but some of it involved attacking her mother and being messy. Earlier in the analysis, through drawings we had made together, Maria had invented an "opposite girl" named Lucy, and she told me to "make her very bad." Lucy yelled a lot and shouted "No!" to everything.

Maria's competitiveness with me, only hinted at before, emerged in her play about differences between adult and child. Role reversal predominated in the play. As the adult, she directed long fighting dramas between puppets, with an abundance of physical and verbal attacks, and finally allowed more direct portrayal of strife between mother and child. These reversals of child and adult were expressed with the most intense feeling in a game in which she was the queen and I was "the little boy who wants the world." The game was played innumerable times, with long, loud arguments between us.

On beginning the fourth year of analysis we talked about plans to terminate during the coming year. Maria was now intensely involved with doing well at school and in fact was an outstanding student in every area. Her sleep problems were largely gone, although she still feared going upstairs alone. The teasing, provocative behavior in the analysis had mostly disappeared. She continued to stall at the end of her analytic hours and had trouble bringing them to a close. I hoped that the separation issues could be worked on during the termination period.

The game that predominated during the final months had to do with school. Maria was usually the very bossy, strict, and often punitive teacher. I was alternately the good child and the bad child. The good child never complained and got all her work right. A theme of being the best and favorite child came to the foreground. Unless Maria felt she was the best she felt worthless, and this was one reason school was a strain on her. The "boss" aspect of the game elaborated Maria's wish to be completely in charge. Although the school game gave us valuable information, it was also used a good deal as defense—defense against oedipal fantasies and against fantasies related to her old concerns about bodily injury. The picture was of a girl struggling to get into latency. At this time, her parents reported cessation of signs of masturbation. She displayed more adaptive compulsive defenses as she was more and more invested in her school activities.

Maria increasingly viewed analysis as an interference in her school day, and she often said she wanted to stop, since she had no more worries. At the same time she was fearful about stopping and sometimes said she would stop in twenty years. When, in January of our last year, I suggested setting a date for termination, she insisted she wanted to stop but shrugged off all attempts at concrete planning. She expressed the wish that her mother and I decide for her, so that then she could be angry about our plans. She was greatly relieved when she finally realized she could help decide the issue, and this led to our discussing her strong feelings about being controlled by adults. After this work of several weeks, she fairly easily chose the following May 15 as the day to stop. The meaning of that particular date? She said, "Because in fifteen years I'll have a baby, and I'll tell you about it." She went on to say that in about ten years' time she would get married, and she would let me know about that, too. She wanted reassurance that if I changed my address, she would be notified.

Discussion

The relatively brief analysis of this five-year-old girl was more therapeutically effective in relieving the anxieties resulting from traumatic experiences than in helping her find better solutions to her characterological problems. Even at this age the alterations in her ego were apparent but not sufficiently accessible to analysis, at least not in the time available. During the first two years of analysis, dramatic play centered mainly on the repercussions of the medical trauma. Once the anxiety generated by the traumatic experiences began to subside, other conflicts, from all developmental levels, emerged more clearly.[3]

---

3. This discussion includes contributions by colleagues who have helped to clarify my thinking about this case.

Freud consistently maintained his basic, economic view of trauma as an experience of helplessness on the part of the ego in the face of an accumulation of excitation, whether of external or internal origin, which cannot be dealt with. Several symposia on psychic trauma in the past twenty years have pointed to the difficulty of restricting the definition of trauma to a serviceable concept that meets clinical needs and experience (see A. Freud, 1967; Yorke, 1986; and many others).

Clifford Yorke (1986) pointed out the necessity of distinguishing among *traumatic neurosis, traumatic anxiety,* and the *posttraumatic neuroticlike state.* He elaborated on the third of these conditions, illustrating it with a case that demonstrated how later significant events, conflicts, and experiences were drawn into his patient's trauma. He demonstrated that every developmental phase, and every part instinct or its derivatives, achieved some form of expression in the context of the trauma (p. 229). In his view, the trauma had a decisive effect on all later development, and served to incorporate all antecedent conflicts.

Hansi Kennedy (1986) described the analysis of an adolescent boy whose phimosis in early life was the subject of his mother's intrusive ministrations and led to surgical treatment at the age of two-and-a-half. She described her case—similar in many features to Maria's—in terms of the organizing effect of the traumatic experience.

In Maria's life the traumatic events can be seen as organizers, incorporating all of her antecedent conflicts. We know that from an early age Maria was quite vulnerable to separation anxieties and that her fears of school preceded the urinary problems. Her dramatic play repeatedly linked all her earliest anxieties to her hospital experiences—for example, the repetition of scenes of abandonment in connection with derivatives of hospital scenarios. The hallmarks of trauma were apparent in her strong impetus to turn passive into active and the incessant need to repeat.

The medical trauma had also had a decisive effect with regard to later development. For the first two years of treatment, oedipal themes that did appear were heavily colored by the same violent battles present in the enactments derived from the hospital experiences. The fusion of doctor and father images was clear. The vicissitudes of aggression were often played out in terms of doctoring. Maria's states of bodily excitement, particularly genital excitement, were frequently at the center of her enactments. It is significant that as we understood her masturbation conflicts and her perceptions of her medical experiences, the doctor game became gradually less important. I have wondered if, slowly, subsequent conflicts became less affected by the trauma due to the analysis. Also her oedipal development had an impetus of its own, and the beginning of latency facilitated her increased mastery of her impulses.

A persistent enactment in the transference demonstrated Maria's imperative wish to be in control of the situation, at the same time that her behavior frequently invited interference from me. This enactment can be seen as reflecting the trauma, but it also expressed her most basic conflicts. For a long time my attempts to put this enactment into words were completely ineffective and often detrimental; only during the termination phase did this change. Maria usually communicated with me in the "language of transference" (as Eugene Mahon [1986] has put it),[4] and when I stopped being so attached to verbal expression, we both gained a great deal. She made me feel helpless, frustrated, stupid, and angry, and I often had the desire to control her. The relentless, innumerable repetitions gave me a sense of the urgency under which she lived, and I felt what Herzog (1993) has called the "press for interactive or mutual enactment" (p. 262). My experience in acceding to the interaction (up to a point) confirms what Herzog has said about acquiescence in such situations: that it "facilitated the subsequent playing out of material—not only deepening it but also elaborating the modes by which it could be expressed and thus become accessible to consciousness and to analysis" (p. 259). In other words, as Chused (1991) said in her landmark paper, *Enactments occur when an attempt to actualize a transference fantasy elicits a countertransference reaction* (p. 629, original emphasis).

An example of mutual enactment was a game in which Maria directed the expression on my face. She evinced endless delight in watching the various facial expressions she had told me to assume and then making me do them over and over and over again. This made me realize how hard she was struggling to master her affects and that one of her major defenses was denial of feeling in herself. I also thought she may always have had a strong sensitivity to facial expressions. (She had attributed the onset of her school phobia to her teacher looking angry.)

One area in which Maria could not help expressing her own strong feeling was her genital excitement. For a long time she manifested this feeling in our sessions while hiding under my couch or in one of the

---

4. At the Seventh International Scientific Colloquium held at the Anna Freud Centre in 1985, Mahon suggested that, in addition to the themes of the meeting—enactment and verbalization—"we have two other kinds of languages, the language of play and the language of transference, and that these really straddle the gap between enactment and verbalization" (Report of the Seventh International Scientific Colloquium, 1986, p. 96).

"nests" she had built. My initial discomfort in "going along" with this activity—at least to the extent that I did not interfere with it—led me to wonder about the therapeutic usefulness of having a child masturbate in my presence.

In an effort to maintain "reasonable scientific rigor," Solnit (1993) delimited the concept of play. He said, "If the activity (such as masturbation) and its mental content become primary . . . [and] the 'pretend function' is replaced by direct pleasurable gratification it no longer is play." However, he also said, "If the activity is not pleasurable but is tension-relieving, we can still consider it play, accompanied by a sense of relief—the avoidance of unpleasure" (p. 39). In other words, the line is hard to draw. Steven Marans (1993) distinguished enactment from play by characterizing the former as "direct action and immediate gratification" (p. 193). Many of his descriptions of analytic sessions with a certain girl patient are reminiscent of Maria: "In a child who cannot play we need first to understand why not and then to facilitate a move from enactment to pretend" (p. 184). Maria's inability to play was particularly apparent in the sessions she spent hiding while masturbating.

Maria's compulsive masturbation condensed multiple functions and meanings. Her repeated, intense experiences with urethral and bladder sensations surely played a central role. Since spasms of the smooth muscles of the urethra in particular are a source of strong stimulation, they can lead to a powerful combination of pain and pleasure. Her mother had become involved with the external urethral irritation by salving Maria's irritated vulva. Maria's bout with chicken pox at age three involved her vulva too. Eventually, she herself connected her "sore bottom" to masturbation.

The chronic mother-daughter battle about urination had been present even before the episodes of cystitis. Mrs. A. had unhappily told me that despite her efforts not to get angry about the wetting, her anger erupted at times. Perhaps even more significant, she could not stop herself from hovering over Maria to persuade her to use the toilet. The function of urination had become involved in a sadomasochistic interaction, and that was the background against which the stimulation of urinary infections was played out and later intensified by the invasive cystoscopy.

In 1985, in a colloquium at the Anna Freud Centre entitled "Repeating: Enactment and Verbalization in Different Stages of Development," Anne-Marie Sandler said, "If a disturbance of great magnitude occurs to one's body in early childhood. . . something very special will happen, not only from the point of view of the child's instinctual wishes, but also from the side of the relationship between the child and the primary care-taking object, namely the mother. The mother will be forced by events to centre a lot of her caring attention on the ailing organ or the ailing area of the child's body. . . . [T]his would create something very special in the child's representations, something which is feared but also looked to have repeated. What develops is a privileged way of having a relationship with a meaningful object" (Report of the Seventh International Scientific Colloquium, 1986, p. 106).

In the instance of Maria, one can see how the attachment to painful experience was built into a gratifying object relationship. For her to change anything about her relationship with her mother would mean significant loss. Maria's enactments in the transference can be partly understood as her attempts to recreate with me this aspect of her relationship with her mother.

But what about Maria's masturbation in a prolonged state of incommunicado, while hiding under my couch or in one of her "nests"? Samuel Ritvo has stated that a child's body and its functions are always available as an *alternative object*. In a child who has had early experiences of somatic illness and pain, certain early alterations of the ego can take place that provide the individual with a structured mode of repeating and enacting. Ritvo went on to say, "This feature of having a function of the body which can be manipulated, so to speak, through which anxiety, pain, and tension can be heightened and relieved, provides the individual with what Phyllis Greenacre called 'a gradient' of pain to pleasure, of anxiety to relief" (Report of the Seventh International Scientific Colloquium, 1986, pp. 97–98). Maria's compulsive masturbation illustrates this phenomenon. It gave her the ability to master internal tensions which otherwise left her feeling helpless.

Maria's aversion to my attempts to put things into words made sense to me when I realized that simply listening to me talk meant, for her, having to passively endure a dangerous stimulus. Words could so readily stir up her internal world of impulses and fantasies. Her main complaint about the analysis to her mother was, "She's always making me talk about my *feelings!*" Activity was a major line of defense: it made her feel in charge of both her internal and external world at the same time that it helped to discharge some of her tensions.

How can we understand why this child had a good analytic result, despite the fact that she preferred to communicate by means of enactment or displacement in dramatic play, with limited use of verbalization? Enactment often leads to therapeutic results in children. The repetitive reliving of traumatic experiences—reliving with vivid affects—is generally accepted as a major road to mastery of those experiences. In a much more general way, child analysts have supported the view that rich expression in play helps a child to rework and find new, more adaptive solutions for conflicts of all kinds and from all developmental levels. And such expression produces beneficial results even when the enactment always remains displaced. This describes what we all know happens but does not provide a theoretical basis for it. Such a basis is important in view of analysts' explicit goal of eventual verbalization.

Neubauer (1993) has discussed the importance of a child's use of displacement, emphasizing that one should not interfere with the displacement: "A one-sided approach that leans on the technical aim to link the displaced content of play to the primary experience neglects those elements of play that search for solutions in an arena in which it can succeed" (p. 45). He also mentioned that in certain forms of play the displacement is *not* unconscious and that "children use an acceptable disguise that is distant from the original intent" (p. 50). Perhaps it is specifically in the therapeutic setting, in the presence of the analyst, that the displacement becomes *more* conscious, and yet it must not be undone by the analyst. Landau (In press) has used common clinical examples to demonstrate that "being in consciousness" is a *relative concept*.

Maria's traumatic memories, which emerged through her puppet play, can be seen as the kind of play remembering that Piaget referred to as *psychomotor memory* (see Solnit, 1987, p. 213). I believe that her gradual recall of major parts of the medical trauma was convincing and that she was able slowly to connect many feelings directly to herself, in the case of the medical experiences, even through words.

The situation is different when we consider her more general conflicts. Maria's play was often relentlessly repetitive, with little elaboration and without her seeming to find any new integration. Waelder (1933) suggested that mental and emotional "assimilation" can result from repetition little by little over a long period of time. He mentioned the constant repetition involved in mourning as a process analogous to assimilation by means of play. But if we take Maria's school game, for example, in which she was the superior, bossy teacher and I was the child, the issue was more complex. How could she use this enactment to ultimately become less vulnerable to feeling foolish, helpless, and enraged about being a child? Without relating any of this directly to herself, how could she find better ways of dealing with the frustrations of her wish for omnipotence? My guess is that the most important work we did in these games was to steadily lessen her defenses against affect. She could bear some of her painful feelings, especially the many hurts to her self-esteem, when they were affectively verbalized by me, playing the part of the vulnerable child, with Maria in the part of the controller of events. She was able to reach a better adaptation when she did not have to work constantly at warding off feelings. But I do not think she was able to rework her deeper character problems.

Waelder (1932) stressed that *"play is . . . a leave of absence from reality, as well as from the superego"* (p. 222, original emphasis).[5] The various changes in the compromise the child makes with her superego must have particular importance and complexity in the presence of her analyst. In the case of Maria, the pull into latency made her increasingly defended against continuing to take a "leave of absence" from her superego in her analytic sessions. In addition, my impression was that she increasingly used reality both as a defense and as part of a suitable developmental adaptation.

The concept of trauma as organizer, as described by Yorke (1986) and Kennedy (1986), was useful in understanding the clinical findings in Maria's analysis. As expected, repetition with strong affect was helpful therapeutically with the sequelae of the trauma, but repetition was also helpful for many other painful experiences, presumably by permitting their very gradual assimilation. Play enactment in displacement was the only route by which Maria could reach more successful solutions in many areas. Thus, the use of displacement did not change in the course of analysis, but the displacements became more and more conscious. At the same time, Maria's frequent refusal to use displacement and insistence on direct enactment leading to gratification put her in the difficult gray area between play and direct impulse expression. The role of physical activity remained prominent, and a strong pressure for mutual enactment was often present during our sessions. My imagination and understanding were frequently challenged to try to find an acceptable, "analytic" way to accede to Maria's demands so that she could keep on elaborating what she was feeling and thinking. As she was able to expand and deepen the expression of the sources of her tensions, it was possible to understand the complex ways in which she was attached to her primary object relationships, as well as the ways in which she used her own body as an alternative object.

The case of Maria illustrates some of the problems in analyzing a child with a posttraumatic neuroticlike state who also had marked narcissistic vulnerabilities. The latter were insufficiently analyzed because the improvement in her symptoms as well as the momentum of

---

5. Waelder attributed this formulation to Ernst Kris.

her progressive development hastened the termination of the analysis. I hope that the experiences detailed here will be useful to others attempting to understand the area in which play, enactments, and verbalization overlap in child analysis.

BIBLIOGRAPHY

CHUSED, J. F. (1991). The evocative power of enactments. *J. Amer. Psychoanal. Assn.*, 39: 615–39.
FREUD, A. (1967). Comments on trauma. In *Psychic Trauma,* ed. S. S. Furst, pp. 235–45. New York: Basic.
HERZOG, J. M. (1993). Play modes in child analysis. In Solnit et al., (1993), pp. 252–65.
KENNEDY, H. (1986). Trauma in childhood: Signs and sequelae as seen in the analysis of an adolescent. *Psychoanal. Study Child,* 41: 209–19.
LANDAU, B. (In press). Consciousness as a "beacon light." In *Defense Analysis: Developments in Psychoanalytic Technique,* ed. M. Goldberger. Northvale, N.J.: Aronson.
MARANS, S. (1993). From enactment to play to discussion: The analysis of a young girl. In Solnit et al. (1993), pp. 183–200.
NEUBAUER, P. B. (1993). Playing: Technical implications. In Solnit et al. (1993), pp. 44–53.
Report of the Seventh International Scientific Colloquium at the Anna Freud Centre, Nov. 8–9, 1985, published in *Bltn. of the Anna Freud Cntr.,* 9: 79–152, 1986.
SOLNIT, A. J. (1987). A psychoanalytic view of play. *Psychoanal. Study Child,* 42:205–19.
——— (1993). From play to playfulness in children and adults. In Solnit et al., (1993), pp. 29–43.
SOLNIT, A. J., COHEN, D. J., & NEUBAUER, P. B., EDS. (1993). *The Many Meanings of Play.* New Haven: Yale Univ. Press.
YORKE, C. (1986). Reflections on the problem of psychic trauma. *Psychoanal. Study Child,* 41:221–36.
WAELDER, R. (1933). The psychoanalytic theory of play. *Psychoanal. Q.,* 2:208–24, trans., Sara A. Bonnett. This paper originally appeared in German in the "Games and Play" number of the *Zeitschrift für psychoanalytische Pädagogik* 6 (1932).

Post-Traumatic Stress and Coping in an Inner-City Child

Traumatogenic Witnessing of Interparental Violence and Murder

ERWIN RANDOLPH PARSON, Ph.D.

Violence today appears to be ubiquitous: it even enters the clinical session, deeply internalized within child victims who were exposed to often unspeakable horror. Violence and its pernicious, horrific effects are observed in the streets, schools, parks, playgrounds, and homes of some inner-city communities. This article introduces the use of Anna Freud's Diagnostic Profile system with an inner-city child who, at the age of four, witnessed his mother fatally stab his father with a kitchen knife and at age eleven was assessed and treated by the author. Clinicians may wonder whether any kind of therapy could ever undo the serious fixations, regressions, developmental arrests, and integrate trauma-shattered ego functions observed in children exposed to visual horror and affective terror. Application of the Profile may offer some direction with these children: a panoramic view of their painful mood, their hypervigilance and distrust, fears, separation and annihilation anxieties, nightmares (with murder imagery), developmental anomalies and arrests is presented with clarity and force. The therapist uses countertransference responses to monitor the affect tolerance in the child and to determine the

Clinical psychologist, supervising psychologist, and consultant in the area of post-traumatic stress disorder (PTSD) at the Department of Veterans Affairs Medical Center at Perry Point, Maryland; chief investigator of the U.S.-Vietnam Full Circle Research Trauma Project at the University of Massachusetts at Boston.

The Psychoanalytic Study of the Child 50, ed. Albert J. Solnit, Peter B. Neubauer, Samuel Abrams, and A. Scott Dowling (Yale University Press, copyright © 1995 by Albert J. Solnit, Peter B. Neubauer, Samuel Abrams, and A. Scott Dowling).

*appropriate dosages of awareness the child can integrate from one mo-
ment to the next. The therapist also serves as the child's external stimulus
barrier and explores feelings about media-driven portrayals of violence,
stereotypes, and inner-city children and youths. The unsurpassed utility
of the Profile as a diagnostic system that documents vital economic,
dynamic, structural, genetic and adaptive-coping information about the
child is discussed in detail as is the Profile's added benefit of possibly
guarding against misdiagnosis and charting a course for psychotherapy
in difficult city-violence trauma cases.*

BIOPSYCHIC TRAUMA

THE QUESTION OF THE PATHOGENICITY OF PSYCHOLOGICAL TRAUMA HAS
had an important history in the annals of psychoanalysis and in the
etiology of mental disorders (Breuer and Freud, 1893–1895; Freud,
Ferenczi, Abraham et al., 1921; S. Freud, 1918, 1919, 1920). Freud
found traumatic neurosis to be a most interesting and perplexing area,
and early in his career had understood the trauma response as a problem of memory; he wrote that the victim suffered "mainly from reminiscences" (Breuer and Freud, 1893–1895). The precipitous decline in
the capacity of contemporary culture to neutralize and regulate the
aggressive drive has led many to paint a bleak picture of children's lives
in the inner city. Though American inner cities are not officially desig-
nated as military theaters of war, the violence and carnage that exist in
some inner-city communities today can be equated to the devastation
and tragedy of loss and death on the battlefield. These "killing fields"
or "combat zones" expose children to painful losses, unspeakable terror, and violence—in the streets, parks, playgrounds, in the school,
and in the home. Paradoxically, these potentially traumatic locations
are the very places society once viewed as bastions of tradition, safety,
and values. Traumatic harm to children's minds and bodies from random violence (Timnick, 1989) and from witnessing parental murder
(Malmquist, 1986) is expected to increase (Bell and Jenkins, 1991).

Child victims of intrafamilial and community violence who suffer
traumatic ego anomalies in many ways resemble those who suffer the
traumatic neurosis of wartime (Parson, 1994a). Over two decades ago,
Meers (1970, 1972, 1973a, 1973b) spoke about violence and its contributions to cultural distortion and psychopathology in children of the
inner city. He thus noted that "since traumatization is endemic in the
ghetto [that is, the inner city communities]. . . *this might produce in the*

child some equivalent of 'combat fatigue,' i.e., a further overloading of the ego because of the *constancy* of dangers" (Meers and Gordon, 1975, p. 586, italics added).

Child victims of trauma represent an area of great interest to clinicians, the criminal justice system, and policymakers (Fish-Murray, Koby, and van der Kolk, 1986; Furman, 1986; Terr, 1984; Green, 1983; Gislason and Call, 1982; Newman, 1979; Pynoos and Eth, 1986; Thompson and Kennedy, 1987; and Yorke, 1986).

Albert Solnit and Marianne Kris (1967) defined psychological trauma as "phenomena that reflects a reaction of the individual to an inner or outer demand or stimulus that is experienced as overwhelming the mediating functions of the ego to a significant degree" (p. 123). These buffer functions of the ego are literally knocked out of operation after trauma. Like adults suffering from "traumatic neurosis," children overwhelmed by "violence neurosis" show a particular pattern of traumatic symptomatology. "Biopsychic trauma" (literally, "wound to the body and mind") refers to the ego psychological state in which there is a rupturing of normal mental protective shielding as a consequence of an overwhelming event that overtaxes the victim's psychic and biologic capacities. Freud (1920) called this shielding function the "stimulus barrier" or *Reizschultz,* which is understood to be a biological structure that regulates internal and external stimulation (Parson, in press a; van der Kolk, 1987). For Freud (1916–1917) the term *traumatic* referred to "an experience that within a short period of time presents the mind with an increase of stimulus too powerful to be dealt with or worked off in the usual way, and this must result in permanent disturbances in the manner in which energy operates" (p. 175). Traumatogenic disturbances alter a wide range of immunologic functions, nervous system (CNS) changes, and endocrine activities that produce restlessness, irritability, sleep disturbance, hypervigilance, and hyperarousal in the child.

The clinical utility of Anna Freud's Diagnostic Profile (A. Freud, 1962; Nagera, 1963; Thomas, 1966) has been demonstrated for many years in providing conceptual clarity, diagnostic accuracy, and informational guidance to planning psychotherapy for a variety of neurotic developmental manifestations (A. Freud, 1965), borderline, psychotic, and "traumatic psychotic" disorders in children (Thomas, 1966), convulsive disorder (Meers, 1966), and organic dysfunction (Burlingham, 1972). The Profile also has been used in the clinical descriptions of babies (W. E. Freud, 1967, 1971), blind infants (Burlingham, 1972), adolescent disturbances (Laufer, 1965), psychopathic personality disorder (Michaels and Stiver, 1965), adult psychopathology (Nagera, 1963), and in description of deaf children (Brinich, 1987).

THE POST-TRAUMATIC CHILD PROFILE

Anna Freud's Diagnostic Profile advances a method that employs "a structured consideration of the ubiquitous processes of biology and psychology . . . in all infants" (Meers, 1966, p. 484), representing Anna Freud's attempt to capture and clarify the problems intrinsic to self functioning in childhood disorders (A. Freud, 1962, 1965). The Profile originated from the Hampstead Child-Therapy Clinic where it was used in studies by the Well-Baby Research Group.

Although in applications the Profile has generated as descendants a number of specific profiles—for example, the Baby Profile, the Blind Infant Profile, the Adolescent Profile, and the Adult Profile—it has not to date been used to describe the inner-city child's traumatopathology and developmental, defensive, and adaptive functioning.

The objective of this article is to formulate and develop a Post-Traumatic Child Profile that systematically details and documents a child victim's spectrum of symptoms, defenses, developmental anomalies, and coping as conceptualized from economic, structural, genetic, and adaptive metapsychological perspectives. The psychological and biological focus of the post-traumatic child profile goes beyond the *DSM-IV* descriptive criteria for post-traumatic stress disorder, for, though these criteria are useful, they lack the ability to make the child come alive, and they fail to state the neurosogenic aspects of post-traumatic responses in children.

Since the Profile has not been applied to the study of inner-city ethnic minority children before, at least one modification is essential: a formulation on culture and coping in the *nonaverage, precarious, and catastrophe-generating environment* (in contrast to Heinz Hartmann's [1939] concept of the "average expectable environment"). Since many inner-city children come from ethnic minority and lower SES groups (Powell, 1983), the therapist understands that having a knowledge of ethnocultural issues and how they interact with traumatized ego functioning in therapy is very important to the child. Recognizing the need to extend psychoanalytic therapy to underserved populations, Freud (1925) expressed a willingness to modify psychoanalytic clinical theory to accommodate the psychological conflicts of the poor, the addicted, and the impulsive. He wrote that "we shall need to find the simplest and most natural expression of our theoretical doctrines" (p. 402) to make psychoanalysis useful to the largest number of people in need of assistance. While psychoanalysis is a general theory of psychopathology that focuses on etiological and dynamic assessment of the personality irrespective of culture, "the need for research on black [and other ethnocultural] norms . . . and psychopathology has been stressed for over three decades" (Meers, 1973b, p. 37; see also Kardiner and Ovesey's [1962] psychoanalytic study of the black personality). Despite Freud's position "some contemporary analysts still view the poor and socially traumatized . . . as posing problems that are incompatible with the procedures and requirements of psychoanalysis" (Parson and Gochman, 1994, p. 145). Other writers have made modifications of the Profile's original format in the past (for example, Brinich's [1987] modification for deaf children).

This writer's many years of assessment, psychotherapy, consultation, and supervision of cases of inner-city children in New York City, Baltimore, and other parts of the country indicate that the Profile can be meaningfully applied to this population. Most of these children and adolescents with traumatic ego pathology are "biopsychologically traumatized [and] suffer secondary conditions like sleep disturbance, disturbed attachment behavior, conduct disturbance, hyperactivity, concentration and attending deficits, cognitive and academic dysfunctions (e.g., learning disabilities, pseudoimbecility, and pseudolearning disability), self-doubts, phobias, helplessness, depression, and low self-esteem" (Parson, 1994a, p. 240). The Profile can facilitate a panoramic unfolding of a synergistic blending of personality, cultural, and trauma elements that are always present in these children. When the diagnostician does not recognize these elements, diagnostic inexactitude and ineffective treatment planning may result.

I. Sources of Information

Psychiatric Interview Date: current (Dr. P.) and two years ago (Dr. T.)
Psychological Diagnostic Assessment Date: current and six years ago (Dr. W.)
Medical History Date: current (Dr. S.) and two years ago (Mr. O.)
Social and Family History Date: current (Dr. F. and Ms. Q.), and three dates over past eight years (Dr. A.)
Neurological Examination Report Date: current (Dr. E.) and three years ago (Dr. U.)
School History Date: current (Dr. L.), and three years ago (Ms. Y.)
Therapy, Assessment, and Notes from Interviews (of Significant Others): Author's Records

II. Reasons and Circumstances of Referral and Case Presentation

The ubiquitous rise in intrafamily and community violence in the presence of children and the increase in child sexual and physical victimization makes the development of better diagnostic methods imperative. Children affected by overwhelming events are now being referred in large numbers by parents, school guidance counselors, the courts, the churches, and protective child services. Such methods could conceivably increase early detection and diagnostic accuracy, as well as guide effective treatment planning.

The name of the child discussed in this article is Eric Smith. He is an eleven-year-old inner-city boy who witnessed the fatal stabbing of his father by his mother. The writer interviewed the boy in a series of diagnostic-evaluative sessions and consulted with many health-care professionals who had seen the child for psychological, psychiatric, medical, and psychosocial evaluations over some years.

After the traumatic event at age four, of watching his mother fatally stab his father, Eric underwent sudden changes in his mood and general behavior which were baffling to those who knew him, including his foster parents, who had known him from birth. From a relatively positive and contented child (despite his early deprivations) he changed to a jittery and irritable boy who had crying spells and could not easily be consoled when distressed. He was extremely nervous, had trouble sleeping, and suffered troubling nightmares. He developed a generalized negative attitude toward himself, his family, friends, school, and people in general. Eric also regressed in development; for example, he lost bowel and bladder control. Though the child and his siblings had been given some medical and mental-health care immediately after the tragic event, when Eric was seen initially by this writer his traumatopathology seemed imbedded in his personality structure. The chronicity of ego pathology seen in the child may have been averted had he been offered secondary preventive services in the aftermath of the murder.

Eric's foster mother, Mrs. Eva Thomas, encouraged by child protective agency and social services personnel, brought the child to me for assessment and possible treatment. Together with her aged husband, she had been caring for the child since the stabbing. She outlined the following symptoms and complaints: aggressive behavior in the home, school, and larger community; hyperactivity; and inability or unwillingness to accept and benefit from adult guidance. Mrs. Thomas also reported enuresis, encopresis, and poor social and academic functioning. Having known the child and his family before the tragic event, Mrs. Thomas felt she could state with confidence that Eric's traumatic experience at the age of four was largely responsible for his current problems. This writer both conducted the diagnostic evaluation sessions and treated the child. The treatment approach was psychoanalytically oriented in nature, with two sessions per week.

III. Description of Child

At the time of assessment Eric was eleven years old, a light-complexioned black boy, who appeared jovial, carefree, and behaviorally spontaneous. He smiled "almost" constantly. Though shorter in physical stature than most boys of his age, Eric was sturdily built and physically agile. He liked to play and did so regardless of place or occasion. Thus, in the therapy sessions he would take any inanimate object within his reach, or leave his chair to get one, then speedily transform it into a toy with which he would play in a self-absorbed scenario. He seemed to experience autistic enthrallment with the sounds and sensations he would generate. At such times, he was involved only with himself and the toy—with no one else and no other object. Almost every spontaneous activity was directed toward play. For example, he would pick up a pencil from the desk or table and suddenly it would become a jet bomber or a violent projectile, jutting through space at high velocity. He opened and closed my desk drawers in a rapidly alternating pattern, accompanied by sounds of a truck, train, or jet. According to Eric's foster mother, he had wet his bed "just about every night" and soiled his pants twice a day since the time of the trauma.

IV. Family Background and Personal History

Mother. She was thirty-seven years old when she gave birth to Eric, her last child. Most of the information about Eric's relationship with his mother was provided by his foster mother. Mrs. Thomas reported that Eric's mother wanted him but was emotionally unprepared for a new child. She was emotionally unavailable and behaviorally inconsistent and would abandon the child for hours or days at a time. A confused, disorganized, and self-destructive person, she used alcohol excessively and was violent with members of her family. Thus she was unable to provide the child with the emotional holding and consistent care essential to promote his psychological growth and social development.

Eric's earliest feeding was by bottle and breast, and both were reportedly harshly and inconsistently provided. His feeding came from many persons. Though the presence of multiple nurturing persons is a characteristic of African-American families, in Eric's home extended-family transactions were chaotic and confusing to the child.

Eric's mother killed his father with a kitchen knife. Each of her five children was deeply affected by this event. She was sent to prison for several years for the crime.

Upon discharge, Mrs. Smith got a job and lived in an apartment very close to where Eric lived with his foster parents. This created a very difficult problem for Eric: he was torn between wanting to be with his biological mother and, at the same time, wanting the love and stability his foster parents provided for him. There was some evidence that Eric had begun to get close to his mother emotionally but, after suffering from an unspecified illness, Mrs. Smith died suddenly and unexpectedly. Eric's symptoms were reportedly exacerbated by his mother's death, which occurred a few months prior to the assessment and the beginning of his treatment.

Father. He was thirty-eight when Eric was born and was described as a wanderer, a lost person with no sense of direction in his life who had very little to give his son. Like the mother, he drank heavily, and he would disappear for weeks at a time, his whereabouts often unknown to his family. Eric still idealized his father and intensely missed him, as though he had died just a few days or weeks before.

Siblings. Eric's eldest sister, Toni, was twenty-three. She was described by the Thomases and two professionals who had worked with Eric as lacking in motivation and drive to improve her life and as having a penchant for a good time. At fourteen, she had given birth to a son, whose care was taken over by Eric's foster parents, then in their late sixties and seventies. Recently she had had a second child. Eric's second eldest sibling, Natasha, four years before, at age thirteen had begun to refuse to leave the apartment because, she said, she feared "getting into trouble with some man" or having people "accuse her of something bad" were she to be seen "in the streets." Natasha's phobic avoidance appeared to be related to pathological fears of either killing a man, as her mother (with whom she was symbiotically merged) had done, or being killed by a man, in retaliation for her mother's crime. She was later hospitalized on two occasions in state psychiatric institutions.

Norman, Eric's eldest brother, was in a residential home for boys. Eric idealized this seventeen-year-old brother and displaced upon him feelings he had had for his father. At the age of thirteen Norman had been expelled from school after he severely beat a woman teacher who he claimed had spit on him while she reprimanded him for inappropriate behaviors. He seemed to be the most disturbed of the five children, with a history of severe ego disturbance that included fire setting. He had set the homes of both his mother and his cousin on fire after the traumatic murder of his father by "a woman," his mother. Like his other siblings, he was impulsive and hyperactive and acted out violently. He made a serious homicidal attempt against his younger brother, Michael.

Michael, fourteen months older than Eric, was on tranquilizers at the time of Eric's referral and appeared to be more disturbed than Eric. Both children had been considered for placement in psychiatric residential treatment settings. Michael and "Tookie," the older of Toni's children, lived with Eric at the Thomases.

Friends. Eric reported that he wanted friends "to play with me," but he didn't have friends. In a diagnosticotherapy interview, Eric verbalized his loneliness in a series of hypothetical scenarios. For example, he asked the therapist, "How would you like it if no one wanted to play with you?" To this the writer replied, "I would feel very hurt, upset, and maybe even angry about the whole thing. How would you feel, Eric?" He replied, "I don't care if nobody wants to play with me; I won't force them. I like playing by myself, anyhow." Much of his difficulty in making even one friend was due to his hyperaggressive demeanor and to his problems with sharing and the give-and-take of age-appropriate play.

Personal History. According to historical and current medical and psychological records, Mrs. Smith reported that her pregnancy with Eric was a planned one, and that he was a wanted baby. She stated that she "didn't believe in abortions." She was reportedly happy during the pregnancy because she was separated from Eric's father at the time.

Eric's foster parents also reported that he had been wetting his bed since the age of four, "just about every night," and the boy also soiled his pants two times every day even up to the current age of 11. Familial and medical reports show no evidence of disturbance prior to the age of four, and his enuresis and encopresis were not found to have underlying organic causes.

V. Possible Significant Environmental Factors

TRAUMATOGENIC WITNESSING OF INTERPARENTAL VIOLENCE

The child who is an eyewitness to murder experiences the event as too shocking to be truly felt and comprehended. The bits of traumatic data are too internally fragmenting and disorganizing to be managed by the child's ego. This single event may produce a loss of a sense of self, while setting up a pathologic response paradigm in all areas of personality functioning.

The witnessing of parental murder and the responses to that event are the cardinal environmental factors in profiling this child. Consistent with Laufer's (1965) recommendations, this section of the Profile deals with "external factors [which] may have had a special impact on the child's . . . life (e.g., . . . events which may have been traumatic, crises in the history of the family" (p. 103). The current posttraumatic child profile documents the impact of Eric's traumatic witnessing in shaping symptoms and organizing coping capacities.

The significant environmental influences in Eric's life were as follows: (1) maternal and paternal deprivation and abandonment; (2) the stabbing of his father by his mother; (3) the breakup of his family and dispersal of his siblings and his awareness of his siblings' instability and psychiatric illness; (4) ridicule and humiliation from peers at school and in the community due to bowel and bladder dyscontrol; and (5) loss of his mother for a second and final time, following a brief period of positive contact with her.

Even prior to the age of four, Eric lived in a home that was unstable and lacking in predictability. His parents were incapable of nurturing and promoting healthy, adaptive developmental experiences in their children. Eric's mother interacted with him in ways that were deeply hurtful and damaging: she seemed unable to give her son the love he needed and failed to protect him from being overstimulated by exposure to the sounds of sexual activity with her male friends.

His father's murder produced pathological internalizations depicting all men as women's prey: men are always vulnerable and passive; women are always dangerous victimizers.

Eric's school performance was very poor, and he did not have familial models to instill in him the importance and value of learning. Most members of his family were chronic underachievers—low in motivation, angry, and full of feelings of deep deprivation.

VI. Possibly Significant Non-Environmental Factors

In order to correct a deviant orthopedic problem in both legs that his pediatrician had discovered, at age two Eric underwent an elective therapeutic fracture. This experience may have produced an engram predisposing him to certain vulnerabilities, such as castration anxiety. When Eric would speak of the many enuretic episodes he had experienced at home and at school, he gave the impression that he had lost total control of his emotions, his thoughts, and of the very contents of his being. These enuretic loss-of-control experiences left him with an empty feeling and were in part symbolic of a broken cistern that was incapable of containing water; that is, lacking in capacity to contain what is inside—powerful traumatic affectivity. From the age of four, Eric suffered from nightmares that featured a knife and images of "someone being killed and needing to be saved." The diagnostic-evaluative process revealed that he was troubled several times per month by traumatic dreams involving his "father's ghost" which frightened him and kept him fearful of going back to sleep. Testing also indicated significant learning disabilities associated with neurological deficits.

VII. Possibly Significant Stabilizing Environmental Factors

Despite Eric's early exposure to intergenerational familial disruption, poverty, and pathology, his foster parents did provide him with some "good-enough" (Winnicott, 1975) parenting and opportunities for some viable "transmuting internalizations" (Tolphin, 1971; Kohut, 1977). Eric was very fortunate to have had the Thomases in his life. They were the only stable and reliable people he had ever known. They gave him a home, and they provided him with guidance, discipline, and love. Another significant stabilizing factor was the therapeutic relationship with the author, which provided the child with a sense of safety and the experience of security from intrapsychic and extrapsychic threats to his self-esteem and sense of well-being.

VIII. Assessment of Development
  A. Drive Development
    1. Libido
      a. Phase Development
      In traumatized children, excessive levels of excitement pour in through the breach in the young ego's stimulus barrier, thus "putting the pleasure principle out of action" (Furman, 1986, p. 193). Psychosexually, Eric was developmentally arrested at the oral phase, though he manifested a veneer of "phallic" dynamics, interests, and behavior. For example, despite his oral dependency, in one posttraumatic play therapy session, Eric spontaneously wrote "p———" on the blackboard. He said, "If you were not married and you took a girl into bed. . . . What is the thing you take a pee out of?" In this instance, he tried hard to avoid the use of street vulgarity; after a year in therapy he had gained knowledge of what was appropriate in the presence of an adult.

b. Libidinal Distribution
   i. Cathexis of Self
   Clinical and scientific studies have revealed that children
   with traumatic stress demonstrate deficits in taking the perspective of others. For example, Fish-Murray, Koby, and
   van der Kolk (1986) report that children like Eric use pre-
   operational cognitive schemas (a basic narcissistic tendency
   referred to by Piaget [1970] as "egocentrism"). Narcissistic
   investment in the bodily self was very evident in Eric's behavior. He found pleasure in physical performance: it
   seemed to increase his sense of competence. Eric focused
   on his physical self and tended to use his body as a defensive
   armamentarium against intrusive ideas, emotions, and
   people and environmental situations of danger. Like many
   deprived, traumatized children, when it came to investing
   libidinal nurturance in self Eric appeared to show a kind of
   libidinal bankruptcy. For example, though he dressed himself very well, basic hygienic practices had to be consistently
   monitored. Eric's avoidance of body management appears
   to be rooted in his lack of self-caring skills and in a feeling
   that he does not deserve to be cared for—either by himself
   or by others.

   In addition to psychic trauma, Eric had experienced the
   uneven emotional investments of his parents and a pattern
   of shifting investments in self- and object-representations.
   Eric's early lack of mirroring experiences may have resulted
   in a sense of narcissistic vulnerability. To counter this, he
   used "grandiose-self" defenses: in one of his spontaneous
   fantasies during a session, for instance, he visualized himself orbiting in space around the Earth, far above the ba-
   nalities to which ordinary mortals are subjected.

   ii. Cathexis of Significant Figures
   Eric was very attached to his oldest brother, Norman, who
   lived in a residential home for disturbed, violent boys. He
   also had cathected Natasha, his second eldest sibling, whom
   he experienced as a surrogate mother, especially after his
   mother's death. Later, Eric was able to become emotionally
   attached to his aged foster parents, who provided him with
   healthy models of caring and control.

   iii. Cathexis of Self-Representations and Object-Representations

Eric's self-representations were inferred from psycho-diagnostic testing results and from therapeutic observation over the span of several months. One aspect of his self-representation was that of a boy playing a guitar with a crippled, broken leg, which shows the fragility of fleeting moments of inner peace, creativity, and freedom for the child. Another aspect of his general self-image was noted on a TAT story, reflecting a depressogenic character of this child's experience—of sadness, object loss, profound oral deprivation, and abject squalor and physical and emotional hunger. He stated, "This boy is sad. He has no food nor nothin'. He lives in a shacked-up house. He has to eat dirt and wood for food. He takes a big bucket of mud to drink water. Then he makes mud pies for supper, then he eats them."

For Eric, images of self and others ranged from magical to reality-congruent. His developmental image of others is one of rejection, abandonment, and tremendous threat of annihilating him. Though Eric's restless, jittery physical movements and expressions were in part associated with CNS deregulation aggravated by the trauma, these movements were also determined by unconscious relational re-enactments. For Eric, hyperaroused physical movements were unconsciously motivated to serve several functions. First, they warded off "toxic objects"—people whom he feared would overwhelm, harm, or even kill him. Second, they served counterphobic ends to keep potentially re-traumatizing "agents of aggression" from overwhelming him by himself becoming a threat to would-be aggressors. Thus, his "violent motor discharge" is undergirded by primitive paranoid and splitting ego defenses. For example, during the fourth diagnostic-evaluative session, he was unable to put into words his anxiety-laden thoughts and fears about being attacked by "people inside the house." Instead, he got up from his seat and in a furious, speedy, agitated manner, he ran across the therapy room, as a pro-jectile. He returned to his seat and said, "Whew! I feel safer now."

There were times Eric was able to cathect the world of people, but this was usually done in a sporadic, random fashion that spans the entire dynamic gamut from "total objectal avoidance" to "total object addiction." Stability in perception and in relating to others was a later therapeutic achievement for the child. For the most part, people were experienced as needs-satisfiers and as "stimuli buffers" (protecting him against a profound sense of vulnerability, against intrapsychic overstimulation and environmental dangers).

2. Aggression

Eric was an aggressive boy who got into fights frequently, even though he was reprimanded or punished for these behaviors. He was put off the bus several times for starting fights: his fantasy life was characterized by violent and aggressive preoccupations. After several months of treatment with the author on a two-times-per-week basis, Eric reported the following aggressive fantasy: "A man came up to me and my girlfriend and kissed her. I was beating up this man for kissing my girl: I knocked him into the water, beat him in the water, dragged him out, and beat him some more." The fantasy was delivered with excited affect and violent gesticulations and jerky body movements in demonstrating how he discomfited a man—an adult, someone bigger than he. This fantasy illustrates Eric's basic aggressive tendency toward adults who betrayed him and would potentially retraumatize him by separating him from love. These issues formed aspects of complex transference configurations in the therapeutic enterprise.

After the sixth month in therapy, on two occasions after speaking about very painful interactions with adults, Eric raised his voice loudly (as if to block out intrusive ideas, affects, and memories), and suddenly went off on a tangential subject. On both occasions he became increasingly agitated and hyperactive as he got out of his seat and launched himself into the surrounding space like a projectile, his entire body becoming a symbolic representation of "the deadly knife" (the fatal weapon).

During the course of the analytic therapy Eric expressed hostility toward his age-peers from whom he felt estranged and isolated: he didn't understand them; they didn't understand him. He experienced them as threatening (in terms of their ability to inflict upon him self-esteem-destroying humiliation and ridicule). On many occasions during the treatment Eric discussed this and described a number of preemptive counterphobic attacks against "the enemies": he hit them first, while using a hyperaggressive street demeanor replete with expletives.

It often seemed that Eric did not give in to depressive feelings, that little or no aggression was directed toward his self. This appeared to be due to manic motoric defense against depression, which complicated the process of bereavement over the many significant losses in his life. There were times, however, when Eric did show depressive feelings in therapy. For example, at age twelve, one year after beginning therapy, he said, "I don't want to talk about my feelings; I can't. They hurt me too much." On a previous occasion in therapy, Eric had promised the writer, "I'll give you only one feeling." He then lowered his head and spoke of his depression and suicidal ideation, and his deeply felt sense of rejection by members of his family and his peers. After ten months of therapy, he expressed at length his concerns about one of his sister's criminal activity in an all-girls' gang. Psychodiagnostic testing had revealed strong depressogenic feelings associated with suicidal thoughts and wishes as a way of being reunited with his dead parents. Thus, on an Incomplete Sentences item, beginning with the stem, "IF I HAD A GUN," Eric completed the sentence by stating, "I would kill myself!" As he spoke his voice fell, and a somber spirit captured his countenance, and he hung his head in depressed, almost lifeless silence.

The quality of Eric's aggressive impulses reflects the relative absence of the modulating effect of libidinal self- and object-investments. In this regard, Furman (1986) notes that "the damaging effect of trauma on drive fusion and integration is . . . particularly severe. The clinical manifestations of defusion and impaired integration are especially prominent in the personality functioning of traumatized children" (p. 197).

B. Ego and Superego Development
  1. Ego Development
    a. Basic Apparatus
    Eric's biogenic endowment appeared to be relatively intact, except for some neurological difficulties in visual-motor coordination reported in psychoneurological test reports. Organic and language problems reportedly were associated with lead poisoning from the projects where Eric's family lived. He suffered from learning disabilities as well. Neurological soft

signs were also associated with biopsychic disruption and alterations in the aftermath of psychological trauma (Parson, 1994b; van der Kolk, 1987). As Fish-Murray, Koby, and van der Kolk (1986) pointed out, "The memory of the trauma is registered in the CNS, but not as yet digestible by the existing structures of logic . . . [and] adaptive thinking processes" (p. 101). Eric's level of intellectual functioning was in the low-average range on the WISC-R, an instrument that measures verbal and nonverbal intelligence. On a test measuring ego functions involved in perceptual organization and planning he performed at the level expected of an older child.

b. Ego Functions
The causative link between psychic trauma and severe ego regression is well documented (e.g., Furman, 1986; Parson, 1994b; Wexler, 1972). Children with traumatic stress often show significant deficits in the executive functions of the ego (Parson, 1994a). Schaer's (1991) observation of traumatized inner-city children led him to the conclusion that "the occurrence of the actual (traumatic) event . . . fundamentally skews ego formation, and distorts affective growth while casting a pall over object relations development" (p. 15). Formal assessment with psychological instruments (Bender-Gestalt Test, House-Tree-Person, the Peabody, the WAIS-R, WRAT-R, the Rorschach, TAT, Incomplete Sentences, and a structured clinical interview) was conducted prior to the therapy to assess Eric's psychological functioning. As noted before, results revealed that the child's intellectual capacity was in the low-average range of measured intellectual abilities, while specific deficits in Eric's ego were noted in realistic perception; regulation of affects, impulses, and drives; language and communication; thought organization; control over motor behavior; frustration tolerance; and defensive organization. He showed problems in reading, spelling, handwriting, composition, arithmetic, small motor coordination, and grapho-motor competence.

Eric, like most children of violence, showed the phenomenon of developmentally advanced ego functions juxtaposed with regressed ones. Because the ego is "the central victim in the traumatic event" (A. Freud, 1967, p. 236), its functions may become arrested or regressively enfeebled. As a result of the trauma, Eric's ego was "knocked out by a flood of excitation" (Yorke, 1986), which was, as Freud put it, "too powerful to be worked off [i.e., mastered] in a normal way" (p. 75).

This "knocking out of the ego" is associated with a traumatic shattering and developmental incapacity of the synthetic-integrative functions of the ego. The deficit in this function was implied in the ego's poor binding of the drives. The traumatic splitting asunder of the drives (libidinal from aggressive) after the inciting violent event exerted a primitivizing effect on Eric's integrative ego functions, resulting in ego weakness that made the portent of encountering potentially disintegrative stimuli symbolic of the trauma very problematic. Other ego-psychological consequences of trauma included severe difficulties in keeping track of time (which Terr [1981] called "time skew") and incapacity to shift sets and employ cognitive flexibility. Ego functions associated with symbol-using were also adversely affected in this child (Hoffman-Plotkin and Twentyman, 1984; Parson, 1994a). Eric also showed problems in the area of conflict-free information processing, as in the ability to contrast, compare, and find causal connections. Thus, ego functions involved in post-traumatic mastery show anomalous vulnerability; but also noteworthy are the child's adaptive ego operations.

From a culturopsychoanalytic perspective, Meers' (1970) research studies that explored the dynamics of African American culture led him to conclude that inner-city children showed much less neurotic symptomatology than middle-class white children with the same degree of familial pathology. He found, however, that the inner-city children he studied had more problems than the middle-class children in intellectual ego functions. Borrowing from the works of Fenichel, Mahler, and other psychoanalytic writers on pseudoimbecility, pseudodebility, and pseudodefect, Meers theorized that the high incidence of intellectual deficits among African American children may be understood as symptomatic.

c. Ego Reaction to Danger Situations:
Post-Traumatic Defensive Organization
Child victims of trauma have been overwhelmed by threats to their lives or threats in their presence to the lives of others. After the trauma the emotional climate of danger persists internally, and an "enduring vigilance" (Kardiner, 1941) per-

sists toward the environment, an adaptive hypersensitivity to external reality. Basically, the defensive organization of traumatized children develops out of the need to manage intrusive-repetitive mental phenomena—aggressivized split-off, dissociated mental processes and associated primordial anxieties and fears, which persistently threaten to overrun intrapsychic defenses. Thus, the organization is primarily geared to ward off danger. The associated state of hypervigilance is costly to the child's well-being and may result in patterned regressive changes in the child's personality.

To regulate the sense of pervasive danger that comes from the compulsion to repeat the anxiety-provoking, terrorizing images and memories of the original traumatic situation of violence, Eric employed the defenses of psychic numbing, avoidance, denial, projection, reversal, identification with the aggressor, regression and, as mentioned before, hyperaggressivized motility—a counterphobic-paranoid defense against would-be attackers or intruders. This defense also served Eric's need to transform menacing passive-repetitive play into grandiose actional-adaptive play that empowers through ego control rather than debilitating through the sense of dyscontrol. Eric often used denial to cope with narcissistic mortification and disappointments. For example, during one therapy session, he told the therapist that he was hurt because his sister had not kept a promise to take him to the movies. He then stated that he preferred to remain at home after all and play alone. Here is the pertinent exchange.

> Eric: "How would you like it if you was left alone and had to play by yourself. And how would you like to be turned down and no one to take you to the movies because they say you stink because you pee yourself?"
> Therapist: "I would feel very upset, hurt, sad, maybe even angry. That's how I would feel. How would you feel if these things happened to you, Eric?"
> Eric: "I would feel bad, too, and angry."

When he was directly asked whether he had had such experiences, he categorically denied that he had. In another therapy session, Eric complained that his sister did not give him money. He later stated that he preferred play money anyhow because it could buy him more things.

Early in therapy Eric was observed to manage inner torment through immersion in constant play, daydreaming, and "reorganizing fantasies" in which he reconstructed or remade a more benevolent world for himself and those whom he loved. Thus, his world of loss and pain was often magically transformed from the situation of parental deaths, family dissolution, isolation, and abandonment to a happier time and place. According to his foster mother, Eric was able to accomplish various chores around the house. However, these chores would turn into "reenactment play" motivated by defensive and adaptive fantasies involving feats of extraordinary strength and prowess, courageous exploits, great wealth, and being "super cool." He often used this capacity adaptively and it has served him well in therapy.

In an ego defense paradox, Eric demonstrated both traumatophobic-avoidance and traumatophilic-reexposure tendencies. Freud (1920) himself was fascinated by the tendency of trauma patients to reexpose themselves to traumatic stimuli. An example of Eric's "voluntary" reexposure to trauma is his tendency to get into hostile exchanges with older girls. Prior to the beginning of a therapy session during the first six months of treatment, Eric's foster mother informed the author that the child had told her that an older girl in his neighborhood had threatened him the day before. Eric had run back to the apartment, entered the kitchen, opened the drawer, pulled out a large kitchen knife (the weapon his mother had used to kill his father), clenched it tightly in his left hand with a fierce, determined, murderously rageful look on his face, and rushed through the door. When confronted by his foster mother, he said, "She's not going to mess me up; I am going to protect myself from her!" Confronting a girl much older and stronger than himself was an unconscious "invitation" to her to stab him with a knife, thus an identification of himself as victim with his slain father and as victimizer with his decreased mother.

d. Secondary Interference of Defense Activity
Eric's developmental arrest in ego defensive organization interfered with successful age-appropriate play, adaptation to school, and self-control. The child's reactive hyperaggressivized motor behaviors also undercut opportunities for vital internalization. As Alpert, Neubauer, and Weil (1956) pointed out, "Surplus discharge in motility makes neutralization diffi-

cult since it does not lend itself to modification through object relations" (p. 45).

As is true in traumatized children in general, Eric's hypervigilant and traumatophobic-avoidant defenses prevented the exposure to increasingly complex environmental stimuli so essential for the evolution of psychological complexity, defense integration, and personality cohesion. Avoiding persons, places, things, and situations because of fear of the return of the dissociated (Parson, 1984) is a real threat to the child's future maturation and well-being. Eric's affective constriction also robbed him of experiencing a full range of human emotions.

e. Affective States and Regulation
Post-Traumatic Affective Stress Response
Failure in posttraumatic mastery also was seen in the ego's relative incapacity to use signal anxiety and to produce neutralized energy for its use. Eric's traumatized ego structures were unable to modulate strong affective tensions, making him vulnerable to a complex state of posttraumatic affective syndrome, consisting of inner tension states, anxieties, fears, sadness, shame, guilt, rage, and violent feelings (Parson, 1994a), poor impulse control, physiological arousal, and persistent catastrophic expectations that either he or someone close to him would be killed *again.*

Numbing is a dose of "anesthesia" injected into the child's affective response repertoire to control revivifications of traumatic imagery and associated affective responses. An example of this response was observed during the sixth month of therapy when he would state, "I have no feeling" or "I can't have a feeling now: it hurts too much." Eric's difficulties in processing feelings were also manifested in his use of denial and negation, as noted during the testing and in therapy. During a psychological testing session, for example, Eric gave a typical "affect-disavowing" response to every Rorschach chromatic Card (color), and to TAT Cards with affect-laden contents. He said, "This is not a feeling; I don't feel anything!" The general problem of affect intolerance made mourning for his many losses difficult to achieve.

Eric also utilized projection to handle feelings of sadness, guilt, and rage. For example, in his response to the Incomplete Sentence stem, "MY MOTHER IS," he stated, "Sad in

Heaven; she's sad because she died." During the same session, with significant transference implications, he insisted, "I don't want to kill him; he wants to kill me!" Anna Freud, in *The Ego and the Mechanisms of Defense* (1936), described the ego defense mechanism of *reversal,* by which the child inverts from a passive, acquiescent victim to an active participant to control the sense of inner danger. In reversal, Eric turned vulnerability into brutal force, dependency into self-sufficiency, while his helplessness was transformed into feats of magical rescue.

Identification with the aggressor protected the child from experiencing persecutory feelings associated with his basic traumatophobic orientation. This defense was noted in Eric's behavior when, after producing a projective drawing of a female figure in the shape of a large knife (identification with his mother as aggressor), he explained, "This is me; I am a boxer. I am boxing." When confronted by powerful trauma-related imagery (here, a knife), Eric may identify not only with the aggressor but also with the victim. For a TAT story he stated, "She stabbed herself with a pair of scissors like this" (demonstrating).

2. Superego Development and Characteristics

Eric's superego functions are varied and are at differing levels of maturity and integration. His superego operations are based upon fear of losing people who are close to him and upon whom he depends for survival and fear of immediate retaliatory measures from adults or people in authority. Children and adolescents who have witnessed violence and are traumatized by it suffer conflicts between the id—in the form of split-off, dissociated impulses—and external reality and, to a lesser degree, between id and superego. This is in part because the ego of the child who has been an eyewitness to violence is unable to master intrusive traumatic imagery and affects.

Eric's superego operations were assessed by analysis of his dreams and nightmares, spontaneous verbal and nonverbal behavior, and transference and countertransference materials and of the results of psychological testing. The superego's relationship to the ego was marked by harsh criticism, and his ego ideal was exemplified in a fragmented, incongruous image of a narcissistically wounded and profoundly deprived figure—a "tough, fierce, wealthy dude who spends all his money in feeding himself, so he don't starve." Diagnostic-evaluative procedures and psychotherapy notes, comparing the situation before and after a year of therapy, showed that Eric's superego, which initially lacked the positive elements of the "loving and beloved superego" (Schafer, 1960), later acquired a sense of internalized benevolence and increased self-esteem.

IX. Assessment of Fixation Points and Regressions

This section of the Profile deals with the persistence of earlier modes of psychic organization and expression in instinctual and object relations domains. As noted earlier, Eric's pathology was related to developmental arrest and ego disorganization (Lachmann and Stolorow, 1980; Kardiner, 1941). Thus, at age four certain maturational mechanisms were "frozen in time," reducing Eric's later capacity for empathy (oral), generosity (anal), healthy assertiveness (phallic stage), and ambition and values (genitality). Eric was constantly reminded of his painful past through "traumatic reminders" (Pynoos and Eth, 1986) when he interacts with certain people, under certain environmental conditions, and in traumatic dreaming or nightmares.

X. Assessment of Conflicts

Post-Traumatic Character Traits

Anna Freud's (1965) concept of "internalized conflict" refers to the taking into the child's self of drive-conflict experiences that originally occurred in relationships with people in the external world. Eric's internalized conflicts were maintained independently of environmental influences until the effects of therapy provided sufficient structuralization and ego autonomy. Character is the supraordinate structure and organization of the psyche that coordinates and consolidates the simultaneous influences of id, ego, and superego operations. It is "an *organizational principle* applied to psychic functions" (Steingart, 1969, p. 282). Eric's style of relating or character pathology represented a convergence of internalized conflicts and traumatic experiences. His post-traumatic defensive organization was based on turning passive acquiescence as victim into active-oppositional demeanor as victimizer, on identification with the aggressor, and on ego-syntonic intrusive-repetitive dynamics in relating to others, numbing of feelings, avoidance of stimuli that trigger traumatic reminiscences, and hypermotor movements to ward off depressive affect, grief, and internalized images of terror.

From a very young age, Eric internalized adult models of violence and sadistic impulse expressions in human relationships. His distrust of adults was based upon a deeply internalized principle: "Adults kill, they murder; they cannot be trusted to offer me safety. They may kill me, too. Sometimes I feel I have to kill them first before they kill me." Internalized violence-organized models of this kind offered Eric no protection against inner persecutory "presences," and made him fearful of his own potential for violence and murder.

Eric's traumatic experiences were within the context of relationships between people. He had witnessed intense conflict between his parents and had learned that people kill each other when they disagree, that people close to him could harm and kill each other, and that losses are apt to occur from any human encounter. Though a part of him was fearful of violent consequences from being with people, his anticipation was that other people will "do me in,"—that is, harm or even kill him.

As a consequence of violent expectations, Eric maintains a "strike-first" personal policy: he feels he cannot take a chance. He seeks this strike-first advantage after any threat. In Eric's mind, a threat is the same as an actual violent assault. He also has learned that when violent impulses are unleashed they cannot be retrieved. People disappear, never to return, and if they do return, they are dramatically changed, and return only to disappear again. He was aware of two kinds of objects, both to be found in the context of violent conflict: the aggressor and the victim. He avoided becoming a victim and eschewed passivity in the face of violence and threat. If given a choice, he preferred to be the (defensive but protected) aggressor, one who defends himself from violence by becoming violent. Generally, Eric's personality was organized around the dynamic themes of horror, danger, paranoid anxieties and distrust, and profound vulnerabilities, and it featured primitive anxiolytic defenses and protection against dysphoric feelings.

XI. Assessment of Some General Characteristics
Implications for Post-Traumatic Child Psychotherapy
This section of the Profile creates forecasting scenarios "to assist the diagnostician to predict the chances for spontaneous recovery and reaction to treatment" (Laufer, 1965, p. 119) and "long-term prognosis" (Nagera, 1963, p. 531). In predicting Eric's possible response to posttraumatic play therapy, the clinician evaluated (1) the child's bicultural self-organization (which Erikson [(1950) 1993], Halpern [1964], and Parson [1985] believed to be important in clinical work with African American and other minority and lower SES children); (2) his psy-

chic trauma and associated ego distortions and problematic object relations; (3) the nature of his developmental arrests, regressions, and points of fixations; (4) his bonding capabilities; and (5) the course of initial contacts with the child and his foster parent (Mrs. Thomas), which included psychological and socioecological explorations.

After the assessment, an interdisciplinary team agreed that Eric's prognosis both for therapy and for spontaneous recovery were poor to guarded. Despite this bleak early picture, therapy ultimately proved to be very beneficial for the child.

Culture and coping

Culture in the psychotherapeutic process is important. Its importance, however, may vary from child to child, from a patient in one socio-economic group to one in another, and from one therapist to another; it may even vary in importance from one session to next. If therapists working with inner-city children, youths, and families experience undue fear over the child's potential for violence due to personal conflicts or to media portrayals of inner-city people as violent, the therapist takes responsibility and explores any potential impediment to the therapy.

Coping refers to a highly individualized strategy employed during states of crisis. During these states, people are typically unable to fall back on ordinary skills they have found of value in the past. Highlighting the coping capabilities of inner-city children who live in a non-average, precarious, and catastrophe-generating environment, Schaer (1991) writes that "despite the existence of overwhelming, frightening events in the lives of inner-city children, they do not become marasmic, literally withering on the vine due to their submission to hostile environments" (p. 14). The concepts of "psychological hardiness" and post-violence adaptivity (Parson, 1993) are relevant here. They serve as moderating variables (or "stress buffers") between traumatic stress and illness.

Meers' (1970, 1972, 1973a) work in the area of culture and coping also is germane to the current discussion. He reported on the unique characteristics of inner-city-reared children and held that psychoanalytic research offered a rich source of data unobtainable through any other method of observation. He believed that longitudinal research explorations would provide valuable documentation of black children's adaptive as well as dysfunctional ego processes and that professional ignorance and social indifference were responsible for the virtual absence of psychoanalytic data on inner-city children. The current posttraumatic child profile could make a contribution here.

Several writers have highlighted the coping capabilities of black children in crisis (Coles, 1967; David, 1975; Meers, 1972, 1973a, 1973b; Parson, 1985). These strengths need to be identified and then incorporated into diagnostic and psychotherapeutic processes used with these children. Meers (1970) found that the unique ego strengths of black inner-city children made it possible for some of them to tolerate noise, confusion, and isolation but, as mentioned earlier, at the high price of impeding learning, curiosity, and other essential capacities.

The Nonaverage, Catastrophe-Generating, and Precarious Environment
As a general theory of human behavior and of therapy, psychoanalysis extends its methods and healing processes to accommodate the psychological and biological responses to catastrophe-making hyperaggressive environs. Unlike the hypothesized "average expectable environment" advanced by Heinz Hartmann ([1939] 1958), in which order and regularity are key variables, the inner city is a place of patterned unpredictability and catastrophe for many children and their families.

Myers and King (1983) propound the idea that the stress-coping processes of inner-city children should be analyzed as an aspect of the assessment. They point out that "very little work has been done in this area." These writers advance an "urban stress model," which consists of five basic elements: (1) the *antecedent stress state,* the basal level of stress for a person or group; (2) the *eliciting stressor,* the objective external stressful stimuli that force the individual into states of disequilibrium and adaptational struggles to regain the usual level of functioning; (3) the *mediating factors,* intrapsychic ego capacities, and persons, structures, and situations that alleviate or exacerbate the effects of the stressful situation; (4) the *adaptation process,* the physiological, cognitive, affective, and behavioral elements of coping; and (5) the *health outcome,* the positive product of the coping effort.

Eric's world was one of high basal rates of stress, with an eliciting stressor that did not produce merely an ordinary stress response but a catastrophically stressful one, witnessing the homicide of a parent (Eth & Pynoos, 1994). The mediating factors—both intrapsychic and environmental—were overwhelmed by the deprivations and traumatic experiences Eric had endured, and the adaptational and health-outcome processes were assisted by the psychotherapeutic process, and the benevolent and caring integrity of Eric's foster parents.

XII. Diagnosis

A. Categorical-Descriptive Diagnosis
Eric's level of ego disturbance described in the Profile combines Anna Freud's (1965) third, fourth, and fifth diagnostic categories.

Thus, the child showed pervasive developmental damage due to both early deprivations and neglect and exposure to traumatic violence. Eric's fixations and regressions and his acquired destructive psychic processes had interfered markedly with his overall development and structuralization of personality.

B. Diagnostic Statement and Formulation

Many clinicians may find assessing posttraumatic stress disorder (PTSD) in inner-city children as unnecessary and so avoid differentiating posttraumatic stress from other psychological disorders. In a thematic issue on trauma that appeared in the *Psychoanalytic Study of the Child*, Erna Furman (1986) advanced the view that assessing for PTSD was essential even though "professionals find it hard to differentiate post-traumatic stress from other disturbances" (p. 193).

As noted before, Freud (1920) was intrigued by the problems posed by the traumatic neuroses and wrote that in these conditions "there really does exist in the mind a compulsion to repeat [as in traumatic neurosis] which overrides the pleasure principle [implied to be operative in the hysterical neurosis]" (Freud, 1920, p. 340). He saw recollections experienced by the victim as "factually disturbing" and with an "intensity of stubborn persistence." This involuntary tendency to persistently repeat aspects of the original trauma in life and in therapy was clearly demonstrated in Eric's personality operations. Structurally, compulsion to repeat (trauma) represents an archaic functional organization that "gives the appearance of some 'demonic' force at work" (Freud, 1920, p. 340). In order to understand Eric's traumatodynamics, and the process by which an external event (such as murder) is tranduced into ego psychological conflicts and physical symptoms, it was necessary to integrate psychoanalytic theory of trauma (Freud, 1918, 1920; Freud, Ferenczi, Abraham et al., 1921; A. Freud and Burlingham, 1943) and the descriptive criteria for the diagnosis of posttraumatic stress disorder (PTSD; *DSM-IV*) which reflect recent clinical and scientific developments in the assessment of psychological responses to trauma in children (e.g., DSM-IV; Frederick, 1985; Nader, Pynoos, Fairbanks et al., 1993; Parson, 1994a; Pynoos and Eth, 1986; Terr, 1979, 1981).

Posttraumatic stress disorder is a psychiatric disorder characterized by significant biopsychological disturbances that are reflected in problematic cognitive, affective, physiological, and social functioning. Its descriptive criteria involve a *history of trauma* (for example, episodes of rape, incest, car accidents, aggravated criminal assaults, or, as in Eric's case, eyewitnessing unspeakable violence by a parent to another parent). It is a history in which (1) "the person experienced, witnessed, or was confronted with an event . . . that involved actual or threatened death or serious injury"; and (2) "the person's response involved intense fear, helplessness, or horror. In children, this may be expressed instead by disorganized or agitated behavior" (*DSM-IV*, p. 428). Moreover, the diagnosis constitutes *reexperiencing the trauma* (in Eric's case, he experienced intrusive ideas, memories, and feelings associated to the original event in the form of nightmares, spontaneous feelings and thoughts, and traumatic play rituals); persistent *avoidance of stimuli*, resulting in reduced responsiveness to and interaction with the external world (Eric's numbing and avoidance, denial, and negations, noted earlier, were observed in direct verbal contents and in the symptomatic hypermotility and traumatic hyperplay); and (4) *psychophysiological arousal* (Eric showed irritability, hypervigilance, startle reactions, and difficulty going to sleep and remaining asleep). Eric's symptomatology reached *DSM-IV* criteria for posttraumatic stress disorder.

XIII. Recommendations and Disposition of the Case
A. Posttraumatic Child Psychotherapy
For Freud (1900) the latent contents of dreams constituted the royal road to the unconscious in adults. He found that dream-analysis tended to increase understanding of unconscious communication. For the child, however, play-analysis is a royal road to understanding the child's unconscious, while "trauma-analysis" is a path to understanding the patient's dissociated traumatic repetitions—in memory and in frightening and painful affects and nightmares, as well as in human relationships.

Posttraumatic child therapy in this case utilized biopsychoanalytic data derived from formal assessment, verbal and nonverbal behavior, transference behavior, countertransference responses, affective expressions, associations, play-analysis, traumatic-dream-analyses, disturbed sleep patterns, general physiological reactivity, startle reaction, disturbed capacity to modulate alarm and hyperarousal, irritability, aggressive explosiveness, separation and annihilation anxiety, guilt, shame, hypochondriasis, somatization, panic, flashback "twilight" phenomena, affect constriction, numbing, and fixation on trauma themes and repetitive-compulsive phenomena.

During the initial phase of the treatment, attachment to and trust in the therapist were tenuously organized and very fragile. The child found play to be ungratifying, conflicted, dysphoric, anxiety-provoking, and affectively turbulent. For him, play was not a pleasurable or even neutral event: it was charged with potential dangers that threatened the reactivation of dissociated affects and memories around loss, murder, and death.

The goals of the treatment were (1) to establish the therapeutic alliance and basic trust; (2) to increase the child's sense of control over inner turmoil and chaos and over the unpredictability of the environment; (3) to create a climate of safety and predictability in the therapeutic setting; (4) to assist the child in making connections between feelings and behavior; (5) to reconstruct traumatic childhood events (to integrate trauma elements, losses, and actual and symbolic forms of violence within the self and in relation to others) and to increase capacity to organize events and experiences into stable inner representations; (6) to work through the child's pathologic defenses and character distortions; and (7) to facilitate the recovery of a progressive development.

In order to achieve these goals, techniques and procedures governing the building of the therapeutic alliance, treatment climate control, and phase-specific operations were employed. The emphasis in the early phase of the treatment was on communicating safety and providing the child with reassurance in a here-and-now process that emphasized holding rather than transference interpretative activity. This is in part because this kind of interpretation would have required a higher level of ego integration than the child yet possessed, due to his developmental ego anomalies. By the *holding* function of the therapist is meant active fostering of a child-sensitive therapeutic attitude accepting the child as he is; it means that the therapist actively supported the child's feelings, thoughts, and behaviors and affirmed his sense of self.

The therapist's functions also included monitoring countertransference feelings while listening with third-ear acuity to derivatives from the child's trauma story-telling rituals as they unfolded over time. The power of listening to horror, tragedy, and experiencing the child's internalized affective terror may induce images, cognitions, and psychophysiological changes in the therapist, countertransference management through increased awareness is imperative. As Eric's posttrauma needs-satisfying object, the therapist provided an essential "affect-buffering function"—an auxiliary stimulus barrier, providing posttraumatic guardianship that protected him while respecting "the child as a person in his own right" (A. Freud, 1972). Protecting Eric from overstimulation in therapy and outside the physical setting of the treatment was a constant challenge.

The therapist's technical stance modeled nonviolence in a relationship that could be experienced as empathic, predictable, reliable, nonimpinging, and facilitatingly maturational. This stance made it possible for the therapeutic relationship to be experienced by the child as a model of the safe, nonviolent world (Parson, 1994a).

Early interpretations were geared primarily to assist Eric gain insight into how split-off, terror-driven affects, drives, and impulses were being kept in check by behaviors that constantly got him into trouble with other people—at home, on the school bus, and during the school day. Later phases utilized transference interpretative activity to foster integration of the child's traumatopsychic fragments.

The physical setting selected to treat Eric had its own "holding features," which promoted an essential emotional holding environment. Physical holding included a room that was warm, inviting, and nonintrusive (or nonimpinging, in Winnicott's [1975] sense). Thus, stimuli such as lights, sounds, and color of the walls and carpet were subdued. Stability and predictability were integral factors in site planning. That is, it was important that each session be conducted in the same room, same location, and during the same time of the day, as much as possible.

In the mid phase of the treatment, explorations were geared to help Eric face "the unrememberable and unforgettable" (Frank, 1969), through periodic systematic reconstruction of trauma elements and analysis of transference feelings. Frank maintained that regaining memories lost after traumatic situations required "understanding and communicating the nature of the experience, reconstructing the nature of the trauma, and supplying the missing events" and that when this was done "crucial change soon occurred" (p. 103).

Freud (1914) believed that remembering and repeating in therapy were not enough. In his essay, "Remembering, Repeating, and Working Through," he spoke about the difficulty patients have in remembering. He felt that in order to ensure integration and long-term resolution, *working through* was essential. Working through with Eric empowered him to alter rigid, defensive psychological armaments against feelings generated by intrusive thinking and memories, grief states, and dissociative ego defenses, such as numbing. This was facilitated by the therapist, who provided the child with object constancy, "an illusion through which children maintain a delicate balance between a past that offered safety and a future yet to be discovered" (Kaplan in Cohen and Sherwood, 1991, p. 13). The therapeutic setting is "a kind of emotional home base from which children venture forth to confront the larger world" and "an emotional bridge for children" (ibid.).

In terms of changes in Eric's behavior and attitude, his internalizations had matured beyond vendetta rage, narcissistic rage, and other narcissistic vulnerabilities. No longer was violence an instrument for conflict resolution, self-esteem-building, and hyperarousal management. He had gained a sense of greater autonomy and a strategy for mastery. He also achieved some capacity to be alone and made important strides toward an ethics of caring and concern for others. Moreover, he was able to grieve his losses and began to construct a new nonviolence paradigm within himself.

B. Clinical Learning Laboratory

Eric also was referred for a specialized training program to address his learning disabilities, one that integrated didactic with experiential learning, like the programs outlined in *Children with Special Needs: Case Studies in the Clinical Teaching Process* (Sapir and Cort, 1982) and in "I Ain't Nobody": A Study of Black Male Identity Formation" (Beiser, 1988). In "Cognitive Ego Psychology and the Psychotherapy of Learning Disorders," Herman and Lane (In press) present a contemporary psychoanalytic view of cognitive functioning and learning which has tremendous relevance to the theoretical integration of organic, sensory, ego, drive, and superego maturational factors in children with learning disorders. The authors note that despite the need to understand the child's internal world, positive parental attitudes and behavior are essential to move the child toward ego psychological maturation. Thus, they mention that "on the parental side, the presence of positive responses to every forward step" (A. Freud in Herman and Lane, in press, p. 3) offers the child opportunities for integrative inspiration. These programs recognize the child's unique personality dynamics, cultural, and academic and remedial needs.

C. Family Support and Conferencing

The tragedy to which Eric's family was subjected is categorized as "catastrophic" (Mc Cubbin and Figley, 1983), as opposed to a normative, expectable occurrence. Meeting with Eric's foster parents and siblings and his extended family members for mutual information sharing proved helpful to the child and the treatment experience.

D. Follow-up and Aftercare

After eighteen months of intensive analytic psychotherapy with Eric, the author terminated the treatment in order to fulfill time-commitments elsewhere. At follow-up with his new therapist, the child was still progressing toward psychological integration, while achieving freedom from internal psychotraumatic conflicts and symptoms.

VALUE OF THE PROFILE IN CLINICAL WORK WITH MULTIPLY VIOLENCE-TRAUMATIZED INNER-CITY CHILDREN

Assessment with the Profile and posttraumatic analytic child psychotherapy may be useful forms of intervention for many inner-city children. This Profile-therapy combination works for the child and is therefore recommended to clinicians. For while the Profile structures the details of in-depth information about every significant dimension of the child's personality and functioning, the therapy uses this information to structure the most meaningful intervention possible for a specific child.

This author's experience and the experience of others (e.g., Thompson and Kennedy, 1987) indicate that integration of general psychoanalytic principles of treatment with the special characteristics of inner-city children is very important if meaningful change is to occur. For clinicians who desire to help these children, introspective surveys into countertransference feelings about specific traumatic experiences (e.g., rape, mugging, incest), class, ethnicity, and race are imperative (Nader, 1994; Parson, 1994; Schaer, 1991; Schowalter, 1985).

Many practitioners seem reluctant to apply psychoanalytic principles and methods in treating these children. This reluctance is often rooted in countransference-based feelings and distortions of the true nature of the child's self and its conflicts (Parson, 1988, 1994a). These feelings then lead to a consciously formulated set of "reasons" why dynamic formulations and approaches should not be applied to these children. For example, a therapist may "fear" that analytic approaches may harm the child, may "create" acting-out of violent impulses, or may be ineffectual because the child's intellectual functioning may be "too low." The child may be perceived as "too damaged," or as "unmotivated, unanalyzable, or untreatable." Others may view this approach as too time-consuming and "not cost-effective enough" for such a child.

Of course, it is clear by now that the consequences of not finding effective preventive methods will also continue to prove very costly to children, families, communities, and society in general. Not only does the Profile provide a structured, systematic means of studying the child's traumatodynamics and culture, but it offers the clinician, the child, the family, and the school the opportunity for both intervention and prevention (including primary, but especially secondary and tertiary).

The specific findings derived from profiling the inner-city child in this article are that: (1) inner-city children do benefit from and change as a result of psychoanalytic psychotherapy; (2) even a child with less than average measured intelligence may benefit from this kind of intervention; (3) management of internalized violence is possible with careful assessment and "good-enough therapeutic holding"; and (4) therapists' management of feelings about violence and about media-formulated images of inner-city children and youths is imperative.

The psychoanalytic study of the inner-city child, because of its profound commitment to a true discovery of the child's internal models of conflicts, desires, internalized terror, and defenses, can play an important role in creating the possibility of a new paradigm of a nonviolent world.

BIBLIOGRAPHY

ALPERT, A., NEUBAUER, P., & WEIL, A. (1956). Unusual variations in drive endowment. *Psychoanal. Study Child,* 11:125–63.

AMERICAN PSYCHIATRIC ASSOCIATION (APA) (1994). *DSM-IV.*

BEISER, H. (1988). "I Ain't Nobody": A Study of Black Male Identity Formation. *Psychoanal. Study Child,* 43:307–18.

BELL, C., & JENKINS, E. (1991). Traumatic stress and children. *J. Health Care Poor and Underserved,* 2:175–88.

BREUER, U., & FREUD, S. (1893–1895). Studies in hysteria. *S.E.,* 2.

BRINICH, P. (1987). Application of the Metapsychological Profile to the assessment of deaf children. *Psychoanal. Study Child,* 42:3–32.

BURLINGHAM, D. ([1964] 1972). Hearing and its role in the development of the blind. *Psychoanal. Study Child,* 19:95–112.

COHEN, C., & SHERWOOD, V. (1991). *Becoming a Constant Object in Psychotherapy with the Borderline Patient.* Northvale, N.J.: Jason Aronson.

COLES, R. (1967). *Children of Crisis.* Boston: Atlantic Little.

DAVID, J. (1975). *Growing Up Black.* New York: Pocket Books.

ERIKSON, E. ([1950] 1993). *Childhood and Society.* New York: Norton.

ETH, S., & PYNOOS, R. (1994). Children who witness the homicide of a parent. *Psychiat.,* 57:287–306.

FISH-MURRAY, C., KOBY, E., & VAN DER KOLK, B. (1986). Evolving ideas: The effect of abuse on children's thought. In *Psychological Trauma,* ed. B. van der Kolk, pp. 89–110. Washington, D.C.: American Psychiatric Press.

FRANK, A. (1969). The unrememberable and the unforgettable: Passive primal repression. *Psychoanal. Study Child,* 24:48–77.

FREDERICK, C. (1985). Children traumatized by catastrophic situations. In *Post-Traumatic Stress Disorder in Children*, ed. S. Eth and R. Pynoos, pp. 73–99. Washington, D.C.: American Psychiatric Press.

FREUD, A. (1936). *The Ego and Mechanisms of Defense*. New York: Int. Univ. Press.

—— (1962). Assessment of childhood disturbances. *Psychoanal. Study Child*, 17:149–58.

—— (1965). *Normality and Pathology in Childhood*. New York: Int. Univ. Press.

—— (1967). About losing and being lost. *Psychoanal. Study Child*, 22:9–19.

—— (1968). Indications and contraindications for child analysis. *Psychoanal. Study Child*, 23:37–46.

—— (1972). The child as a person in his own right. *Psychoanal. Study Child*, 27:621–25.

FREUD, A., & BURLINGHAM, D. (1943). *War and Children*. New York Medical War Books.

FREUD, S. (1900). The interpretation of dreams. *S.E.*, 4 and 5.

—— (1914). Remembering, repeating, and working through (Further recommendations on the technique of psychoanalysis). *S.E.*, 12:145–56.

—— (1916–17). Introductory lectures on psychoanalysis. *S.E.*, 16:347.

—— (1917). Introductory lectures on psychoanalysis. *S.E.*, 16:431–63.

—— (1918). From the history of an infantile neurosis. *S.E.*, 17:7–79.

—— (1919). Psychoanalysis and the war neurosis. *S.E.*, 17:207.

—— (1920). Beyond the pleasure principle. *S.E.*, 20:7–66.

—— (1925). The question of lay analysis. *S.E.*, 2.

FREUD, S., FERENCZI, S., ABRAHAM, K., SIMMEL, E., & JONES, E. (1921). *Psychoanalysis and War Neurosis*. London: Int. Psychoanal. Press.

FREUD, W. E. (1967). Assessment of early infancy: Problems and considerations. *Psychoanal. Study Child*, 22:216–38.

—— (1971). The baby profile, Part II. *Psychoanal. Study Child*, 26:172–94.

FURMAN, E. (1986). On trauma: When is the death of a parent traumatic? *Psychoanal. Study Child*, 41:191–208.

FURST, S., ed. (1967). *Psychic Trauma*. New York: Basic.

GREEN, A. (1983). Dimensions of psychological trauma in abused children. *J. Amer. Acad. Child Psychiat.*, 22:231–37.

GISLASON, L., & CALL, J. (1982). Dog-bite in infancy: Trauma and personality development. *J. Amer. Acad. Child Psychiat.*, 21:203–07.

HALPERN, F. (1964). Psychodynamic and cultural determinants of work inhibition in children and adolescents. *Psychoanal. Rev.*, 51:173–89.

HARTMANN, H. ([1939] 1958). *Ego Psychology and the Problem of Adaptation*. New York: Int. Univ. Press.

HAUSER, S. (1982). *Black and White Identity Formation: Studies in Psychosocial Development in Lower Socioeconomic Adolescent Boys*. New York. Wiley-Interscience.

HERMAN, J., & LANE, R. (In press). Cognitive ego psychology and the psychotherapy of learning disorders. *J. Contemp. Psychother.*, 25(1).

HOFFMAN-PLOTKIN, D., & TWENTYMAN, J. (1984). A multidimensional assessment of behavior and cognitive deficits in abused and neglected children. *Child Devel.*, 55:794–802.

KARDINER, A. (1941). *The Traumatic Neurosis of War.* New York: Hoeber.

KARDINER, A., & OVESEY, L. (1962). *The Mark of Oppression: The Psychoanalytic Study of the Black Personality.* Cleveland, Ohio: World Publishing Company.

KENNEDY, H. (1986). Trauma in childhood: Signs and sequelae as seen in the analysis of an adolescent. *Psychoanal. Study Child,* 41:209–20.

KOHUT, H. (1977). *The Restoration of the Self.* New York: Int. Univ. Press.

LACHMANN, F., & STOLOROW, R. (1980). *Psychoanalysis and Developmental Arrests.* New York: Int. Univ. Press.

LAUFER, M. (1965). Assessment of adolescent disturbances. *Psychoanal. Study Child,* 20:99–123.

MALMQUIST, C. (1986). Children who witness parental murder: Post-traumatic aspects. *J. Amer. Acad. Child Psychiat.,* 25:320–25.

MCCUBBIN, H., & FIGLEY, C. R. (1983). Bridging normative and catastrophic family stress. In *Stress and the Family.* Vol. I: *Coping with Normative Transitions* ed. C. R. Figley and H. McCubbin, pp. 218–28. New York: Brunner/Mazel.

MEERS, D. (1966). A diagnostic profile of psychopathology in a latency child. *Psychoanal. Study Child,* 21:483–526.

———— (1970). Contributions of a ghetto culture to symptom formation: Psychoanalytic studies of ego anomalies in childhood. *Psychoanal. Study Child,* 25:209–30.

———— (1972). Crucible of ambivalence: Sexual identity in the ghetto. *Psychoanal. Study Child,* 27:40–61.

———— (1973a). Psychoanalytic research and intellectual functioning of ghetto-reared, black children. *Psychoanal. Study Child,* 28:230–46.

———— (1973b). *Definitions, Perceptions and Accommodations to Mental Illness of Low Income, Ghetto Resident Black Families.* Ann Arbor: Xerox University Microfilms.

MEERS, D., & GORDON, F. (1975). Traumatic and cultural distortions of psychoneurotic symptoms in a black ghetto. *Ann. Psychoanal.,* 20:580–92.

MICHAELS, J., & STIVER, I. (1965). The impulsive psychopathic character according to the Diagnostic Profile. *Psychoanal. Study Child,* 20:124–41.

MYERS, H., & KING, L. (1983). Mental health issues in the development of the black American child. In *The Psychosocial Development of Minority Group Children,* ed. G. Powell, pp. 275–306. New York: Brunner/Mazel.

NADER, KATHLEEN. (1994). Countertransference in the treatment of acutely traumatized children. In *Countertransference in the Treatment of Post-Traumatic Stress Disorder,* eds. J. Wilson and J. Lindy, pp. 179–209. New York: Guilford.

NADER, K., PYNOOS, R., FAIRBANKS, L., AL-AJEEL, & AL-ASFOUR, A. (1993). A preliminary study of PTSD and grief among the children of Kuwait following the Gulf crisis. *Brit. J. Clinical Psych.,* 32:407–16.

NAGERA, H. (1963). The Developmental Profile: Notes on some practical considerations regarding its use. *Psychoanal. Study Child,* 18:511–40.

NEWMAN, C. (1976). Children of disasters: Clinical observations at Buffalo Creek. *Amer. J. of Psychiat.,* 133:306–12.

PARSON, E. R. (1984). The reparation of the self. *J. Contemp. Psychother.,* 14:4–54.

———— (1985). The black Vietnam veteran: His representational world in post-traumatic stress disorder. In *Post-Traumatic Stress Disorder and the War Veteran Patient,* ed. W. Kelly, pp. 170–92. New York: Brunner/Mazel.

———— (1986). Ethnicity and traumatic stress: The intersecting point in psychotherapy. *Trauma and Its Wake: The Study and Treatment of Post-Traumatic Stress Disorder,* ed. C. R. Figley. New York: Brunner/Mazel.

———— (1988). Notes from the Editor. *The difficult patient: Psychotherapeutic strategies.* Special Issue of the *J. Contemp. Psychother.,* 18:77–81.

———— (1993). Violent realities, post-violence adaptivity: Protective factors governing response patterns in violence-traumatized inner city children. Paper presented at Ninth Annual Meeting of the International Society for Traumatic Stress Studies, San Antonio, Texas, October 1993.

———— (1994a). Inner city children of trauma: Urban violence, traumatic stress response syndrome, and therapist's responses. In *Countertransference in the Treatment of Post-Traumatic Stress Disorder,* ed. J. Wilson and J. Lindy, pp. 151–78. New York: Guilford Press.

———— (1994b). Post-traumatic stress disorder: Its biopsychobehavioral aspects and management. In *Anxiety and Related Disorders: A Handbook,* ed. B. Wolman and G. Stricker, pp. 226–85. New York: Wiley and Sons, Inc. (Interscience).

———— (In press a). *Inner City Children and Violence: Assessment and Treatment. Innovations in Clinical Practice: A Source Book.* Vol. 14. Sarasota, Fla.: Professional Resource Press.

———— (In press b). The effects of the violent socioecology on inner city children: Stress, symptoms, and post-traumatic child therapy. In *Trauma, Loss, Dissociation: Foundations for the 21st Century Traumatology.*

PARSON, E. R., & GOCHMAN, S. I. (1994). Psychoanalytic psychology: Its place in identifying social issues and guiding solutions through humane public policy. In *A History of the Division of Psychoanalysis of the American Psychological Association.,* ed. R. C. Lane and M. Meisels. Hillsdale, N.J.: Lawrence Erlbaum.

PIAGET, J. (1970). *Structuralism.* New York: Basic.

POWELL, G. (1983). *The Psychosocial Development of Minority Group Children.* New York: Brunner/Mazel.

PYNOOS, R., & ETH, S. (1986). Witness to violence: The child interview. *J. Amer. Child Psychiat.,* 2:306–16.

SANDLER, J. (1967). Trauma, strain, and development. In *Psychic Trauma,* ed. S. S. Furst, pp. 44–66. New York: Basic.

SAPIR, S., & CORT, R. (1982). *Children with Special Needs: Case Studies in the Clinical Teaching Process.* New York: Brunner/Mazel.

SCHAER, I. (1991). A theoretical conceptualization of the multiply traumatized inner city child of poverty. *Section on Childhood and Adolescence (Division 39) Newsletter,* 1 (August 1991):12–22.

SCHAFER, R. (1960). The loving and beloved superego in Freud's structural theory. *Psychoanal. Study Child,* 15:163–88.

SCHOWALTER, J. (1985). Countertransference in the work with children: Review of a neglected concept, *J. Amer. Acad. Child Psychiat.*, 25:40–45.

SHAPIRO, S. (1973). Preventive analysis following a trauma. *Psychoanal. Study Child*, 28:249–85.

SOLNIT, A., & KRIS, M. (1967). Trauma and infantile experiences. In *Psychic Trauma*, ed. S. S. Furst, pp. 175–220. New York: Int. Univ. Press.

STEINGART, I. (1969). On self, character, and the development of a psychic apparatus. *Psychoanal. Study Child*, 24.

SYLVESTER, E. (1952). Discussion of techniques used to prepare children for analysis. *Psychoanal. Study Child*, 7:306–21.

TERR, L. (1979). Children of Chowchilla: A study of psychic trauma. *Psychoanal. Study Child*, 34:547–623.

——— (1981). "Forbidden": Post-traumatic child's play. *J. Amer. Acad. Child Psychiat.*, 20:741–60.

——— (1984). Time and trauma. *Psychoanal. Study Child*, 39:633–65.

THOMAS, R. (1966). Comments on some aspects of self and object representation in a group of psychotic children: An application of Anna Freud's Diagnostic Profile. *Psychoanal. Study Child*, 11:527–80.

THOMPSON, C., & KENNEDY, P. (1987). Healing the betrayed: Issues in psychotherapy with child victims of trauma. *J. Contemp. Psychother.*, 17:195–202.

TIMNICK, L. (1989). Children of violence. *Los Angeles Times Magazine*, Sept. 3, 1989, pp. 6–15.

TOLPIN, M. (1971). On the beginnings of a cohesive self: An application of the concept of transmuting internalization of the study of transitional object and signal anxiety. *Psychoanal. Study Child*, 26:316–54.

TRAD, P. V., RAINE, M., CHAZAN, S., & GREENBLATT, E. (1992). Working through conflict with self-destructive preschool children. *Amer. J. Psychother.*, 46:640–62.

VAN DER KOLK, B. (1987). *Psychological Trauma*. Washington, DC: American Psychiatric Press.

WEXLER, H. (1972). The life master: A case of severe ego regression induced by combat experience in World War II. *Psychoanal. Study Child*, 27:565–97.

WINNICOTT, D. W. (1975). *Through Pediatrics to Psychoanalysis*. New York: Basic.

YORKE, C. (1986). Reflections on the problems of psychic trauma. *Psychoanal. Study Child*, 41:222–36.

Helping Foster Children to
Mourn Past Relationships

SHIRLEY C. SAMUELS, Ed. D.

*In spite of the increasing number of foster children who have had patho-
logical relationships with their biological parents, there are relatively
few reports of intensive therapy with these children. This paper focuses
on the psychoanalytic psychotherapy of two young foster children whose
treatment began shortly after placement. The paper describes the children's developmental problems, their conflicts and defenses, and the
therapeutic process utilized to enable them to resume progressive development. The children were helped to mourn their past objects and to form
more appropriate attachments to their foster parents.*

THE ADEQUACY OF A CHILD'S OBJECT RELATIONS STARTING FROM THE
early months of life determines how the child will cope with and defend
against separation from primary caretakers and early object loss
(Provence, 1987). Even if object constancy has been reached, it can be
weakened or destroyed in the child whose primary object is absent
(Solnit, 1982). Recent infant research has demonstrated that the newborn can detect tactile, vestibular, olfactory, auditory, gustatory, and
visual stimuli (Haith, 1986) and that the infant can discriminate between self and other in the first few weeks of life (Stern, 1985; Pine,
1985; Mayes and Cohen, 1992; Flashman, 1992). These studies support the view that very young infants are able to form early representations of experiences with others (Mayes and Cohen, 1992).

Assistant clinic director and supervisor, Center for Preventive Psychiatry, White
Plains, New York.

The author expresses her appreciation to Gilbert W. Kliman, M.D., and Thomas
Lopex, Ph.D., for their support with these cases.

The Psychoanalytic Study of the Child 50, ed. Albert J. Solnit, Peter B. Neubauer, Samuel
Abrams, and A. Scott Dowling (Yale University Press, copyright © 1995 by Albert J.
Solnit, Peter B. Neubauer, Samuel Abrams, and A. Scott Dowling).

Foster children are especially vulnerable to severe pathology and unresolved mourning because of the likelihood of pathological object relations early in life resulting from unfavorable life conditions preexistent to the children's placement. Birth parents' pathology and psychosocial problems predispose them to faulty parenting (Burland, et al., 1981; Kliman et al., 1982; Samuels, 1990). A study of children entering foster care found that three-quarters of them were not living with their biological parents because of abuse and neglect. (National Committee for Adoption, 1985). Festinger (1986) reported that 23.6 percent of foster children had been abandoned by their biological parents.

The crack epidemic, AIDS, and homelessness have led to recent increases in the number of foster children who have been abandoned or have families unable to rear them (Barden, 1990). In the United States in 1988, there were 323,000 children in foster care (U.S. Senate, Committee on Finance, 1990). By January 1990, the number had increased to 360,000 (Barden, 1990).

The pathological memories and attendant emotions related to earlier-life caretakers are recreated in subsequent relationships (Bowlby, 1980). Unresolved preoedipal issues give rise to maladaptive symptoms to defend against ambivalence, depression, and anger. These symptoms can lead to a reoccurrence of rejection, this time by foster parents. This makes it even more difficult for the child to develop a representation of himself as a wanted child (Brinich, 1980). With each new loss and reattachment, aggression increasingly tends to dominate the earlier libidinal attachments, and the stabilization of object constancy is threatened (Solnit, 1982).

Without appropriate interventions for the increasing number of severely disturbed young children placed in foster care, the negative consequences for them and for society will become substantial. There are relatively few studies reported in the literature on the trauma of loss for foster children. In some of the studies, the children discussed were later adopted by their foster parents and, in several of them, the therapeutic process was short-term (Kliman et al., 1982; Schaeffer et al., 1981; Clifton and Ransom, 1975; Ament, 1972; Defries et al., 1964; Fraiberg, 1962; Warfield, 1972; Reeves, 1971; High, 1982; Kaplan and Turitz, 1957; Kaplan, 1982; Lush et al., 1991; Frankel, 1991; Brandell, 1992; Auestad, 1992).

Since 1965 the Center for Preventive Psychiatry (CPP) in White Plains, New York, has been a pioneer in utilizing intensive psychotherapy for severely disturbed foster and adopted children (Kliman et al., 1982). This paper focuses on psychoanalytic psychotherapy with two children treated by the author at the Center. The aim is to illustrate that long-term psychoanalytic psychotherapy can be effective in helping foster children who have had pathological attachments to their biological parents to resolve preoedipal conflicts with those parents and move on to form healthy new attachments. In the therapeutic process described here, the children worked through their memories and attendant feelings related to their birth mothers and were able to form new attachments to their adoptive homes.

CASE 1

Five-year-old Frances started therapy within a month after she and her two brothers, aged four and three, entered a foster home. Her foster parents were in their forties and had a daughter in high school. Frances had lived with her birth parents for the first five years of her life. Both parents had grown up in multiproblem homes. A case worker reported that much of Frances' early life was stormy, chaotic, and traumatic. Her parents' marriage had many problems. The family first came to the attention of Westchester Child Protective Services when Frances was three years old because of her regressive behavior on entering a Head Start program. Both parents had been unemployed for many years, and her father was physically ill during most of Frances' early childhood. Both parents had mental breakdowns during her early life. According to a report by a social worker, the child's day was characterized by emptiness and a lack of stimulation.

Westchester Social Services, the parent agency of Child Protective Services, monitored the family situation for two years after it came to their attention. When Frances was five years old, her mother had an acute psychotic attack, and her father abandoned the family. The children and their mother were found by neighbors in a dirty, roach-infested house. The mother was catatonic, and the younger children were being cared for by Frances. The mother was admitted to a psychiatric hospital, and the children were placed together in the same foster home.

At the time of referral to the clinic, Frances' speech was about 60 percent unclear and her play was repetitive and compulsive. Her behavior varied from rigid overcontrol to a complete breakdown of control with acute anxiety attacks. In kindergarten, she hit other children and was unable to sustain cognitive work with the teacher, although she appeared to have the capacity to do so. Her foster mother reported that Frances bossed her younger brothers and teased them when they did not obey her. She did not respond to her foster mother and spent long periods of time staring into space and talking to herself. She was terrified of the dark and screamed and wet her bed at night.

The child saw the therapist for four sessions a week over three and a half years. At the same time, the foster parents were seen weekly for parent guidance, and there was frequent contact with the social worker in charge of the case. The younger siblings were seen by other clinicians at our agency.

Frances spent many sessions in early therapy either starving or overfeeding the dolls. She would whip the female dolls after feeding them and then put them to bed. She tested the therapist at every turn by destructive or dangerous behavior, such as breaking toys deliberately and jumping off furniture. She sought acceptance by cleaning up the room but then dirtied it to see if she would be rejected. Early in therapy, the child "fed" the therapist (in play) and verbalized a wish to go home with the therapist and take care of her. During this time, the therapist had to address developmental deficits, setting safety limits firmly and consistently. At the same time, a therapeutic alliance developed as the therapist empathized with and respected the child's internal world as the material revealing it was played out.

Frances' mother was released from the psychiatric facility to a community home after three months. She was deemed incapable of taking care of the children but saw them monthly in the clinic. A clinician present during the meetings noted that the child's mother held Frances on her lap against her will and tried to force-feed her. She would also ask Frances to come home to take care of her. During the early months, Frances was very depressed after these visits and said she wanted to leave with her mother. Afterwards, she was uncontrollable in her foster home and at school. After a few months of therapy, she began to establish a trusting relationship with the therapist. Much of the anger and sadness were expressed during the therapeutic sessions, and the rages at home subsided considerably.

In the second six months of therapy, Frances spent a great deal of time taking care of the dolls. At the end of each session during this period, she went into a rage, destroyed materials, and threw toys on the floor. She would beat the dolls, call them dirty, and dump them out of bed. Clarification and interpretation focused on the child's early and continuing relationship with her mother and the anger and sadness related to their interactions.

A primary theme was Frances' need for closeness with the therapist, along with her fear of it. She would sit on the therapist's lap and demand to be fed and hugged. Almost immediately, she would flee in panic. The regression was not discouraged, and her conflict related to ambivalence and anxiety was clarified by the therapist. During one session, she shared a dream about a hungry witch becoming a spider. She said, "If I swallow the spider, I die." This material clearly described the fear of incorporation related to what seemed to have occurred between mother and child early in life. This fear was noted directly in the interaction between mother and child and was repeated monthly when they were observed together.

Gradually, Frances' speech improved and there were fewer times when she rambled on incomprehensibly, both in and outside therapy. She showed a growing capacity to tolerate her depression and to verbalize her positive and negative feelings to the therapist.

At the end of the first year of therapy, the children's social worker felt it was not in the best interests of the children to return them to their biological mother, and they were released for adoption. After being told that her foster parents wanted to adopt her, Frances began to test her foster mother. She had temper tantrums and urinated on the floor. The child told the therapist sadly one day, "My mommy has no one." This guilt was expressed over and over again in therapy as she obsessively cleaned the therapy room and its contents. She made food for the therapist in play and kissed and stroked her.

Before the therapist's first annual vacation, Frances talked about food, tried to feed the therapist, and attempted to control her every move. Two days before the separation, she wet the floor, tore up a calendar that the therapist used to count off the days before the vacation, and scattered the pieces all over the room. The interpretations during that time focused on her feeling that she was bad, dirty, and lonely, as she had felt when her mother left her. She regressed perceptively in her adoptive home during the separation and tore up the postcards the therapist sent to her.

During the next six months, as she began to separate more and more from her birthmother, she was able to allow herself to experience and deal with depression. She expressed her sadness verbally to both the therapist and her foster mother. She continued to reenact her earlier life experiences with her biological mother. Her conflict between wanting to be taken care of and the necessity in early life of being the one to take care of her mother and her baby brothers was expressed over and over again. There was loving behavior toward a doll alternating with hitting and pulling her own hair. This behavior frequently ended with her throwing the doll in the garbage. There were times when she threw things and screamed and alternated this with self-punitive behavior, such as head banging. She teased and provoked the therapist to the point of having to be stopped physically. The therapist continued to verbalize Frances' guilt about her anger and to clarify for her its meaning in her life. As therapy progressed, Frances was able to express her wish to be the baby more directly. She began to put the doll into the therapist's lap and to tell her to feed it. At the same time, outside of therapy she allowed her adoptive mother to take greater care of her. She let her hug her and told her that she wanted to be her little girl. Her language improved perceptibly, and her anxiety decreased radically.

After the second year of therapy, before the therapist's vacation, Frances was able to verbalize her anticipation that she would miss the therapist. She admitted to being afraid that the therapist would leave her and not come back. She followed this by first demanding food and then drawing a picture showing both sadness and anger.

During the third year, Frances' early relationship with her biological parents continued to be played out. In one session, she took a Barbie doll and said to the therapist, "I cook for you and take care of you and all your children." The therapist reflected on how Frances had taken care of her mother and her two little brothers when her mother got sick. Following this, the child got on the therapist's lap and said, "I'm sad" and pressed her head against the therapist's breast. She brought up her biological father during one session and recounted a memory of his buying her ice cream. For a few weeks thereafter, with a sad expression on her face, she talked about how she was loved and taken care of by her daddy. After having difficulty ending in a subsequent session, in which memories of her interactions with her father were revived, she asked where her daddy was. The therapist reflected on how her daddy, whom she loved and who had taken care of her, had left her and not come back and how maybe she worried that the therapist, who also took care of her, would not come back either.

As therapy progressed and the child's relationships with her parents were interpreted, she became less and less terrified about closeness. There was a reworking of the narcissistic developmental process. The therapist relived the child's infancy with her, becoming a new mirror for the child. She would walk around like a toddler, returning to the therapist's lap for "refueling," and then moving out again, saying, "I walk around furniture alone." As she reworked the rapprochement subphase of the separation-individuation process (Mahler et al., 1975), her speech steadily improved. At the end of this period, she began to make remarkable progress in school and in her adoptive home. Her adoptive parents found her to be helpful and friendly and to be behaving age-appropriately. Termination was felt to be indicated at this time. The termination phase was filled with upheaval and confusion.

Frances tried to hurt the therapist physically. She threw toys and trash at her. These rages alternated with periods of depression, when she did such things as putting both feet in the toilet and drinking urine. All these actions were interpreted as a revival of feelings of anger and sadness related to her biological parents. Clarification and interpretation of transferential reactions continued to be linked to earlier life interactions and feelings to make the disorder of her earlier life into an understandable order.

At that time Frances expressed a wish to go home with her birth mother to take care of her. She was helped to see that it was not her fault that she was not living with this mother and that it was Frances who needed to be taken care of. The therapist further helped her to gain insight into her mother's difficulties in taking care of the children without faulting her mother. This was linked, when appropriate, to the therapist's knowledge of their interactions. In one session, after seeing her birth mother, she commented sadly that her mother acted "funny" and described her tuned-out behavior (not talking, staring into space, ignoring Frances), noting that her other mommy was not like that. As she continued to work through her anger and sadness related to the impending loss of the therapist, her birth mother's inability to care for her was becoming more evident to Frances. The worker present at one visit with her birth mother observed that the mother once again had told Frances she wanted to take her home with her. Frances told her she couldn't go because her mommy was still sick. About a week before termination, she told the therapist that she wanted to be grown up like the therapist and later she wrote a card saying she loved and would miss her. At the same time, Frances' attachment to her adoptive parents became stronger. She began to identify with the mother, saying that she wanted to be like her as well when she grew up. Except for occasional stormy times, which usually followed a visit with her birth mother, she did not act out outside of therapy.

A few months after termination, Frances was seen by the psychiatrist who had done the initial intake on the child. He stated that her pathological object relations were reversed. He saw real empathy. Her speech, learning, attention span, frustration tolerance, impulse control, secondary process thinking, and reality testing were all appropriate for her age.

The adoption was finalized within a year after termination. All three siblings were adopted by the same family. A follow-up five years later, when Frances was almost fourteen, found her to be sociable and doing well academically in a regular classroom. Projective testing showed good interpersonal functioning, reality orientation and ego integration, and age-appropriate adolescent concerns and anxieties that she appeared to be managing in an appropriate autonomous manner. While early conflict issues over the loss of her mother were stirred up by seeing her therapist again, she showed good perspective of this event and an ability and desire to continue to function independently. The severity of her early pathology was totally absent at that time.

CASE 2

Larry was released for adoption at the age of two. His mother, who was white, had a history of drug addiction. His father, who was black, had been in prison for most of the child's early life. His mother relinquished Larry when she became totally unable to care for him and could no longer leave him with friends, as she had done sporadically during his earlier life. Her extended family would not help in any way. A black couple in their forties became Larry's parents with the intention of ultimately adopting him. Larry was brought to the clinic at three years of age because of anxiety, depression, and too-compliant behavior. He had a short attention span and severe nightmares and sucked his thumb almost constantly while he lovingly stroked a blanket. He cried immediately if reprimanded.

In the first therapy session, it was noted that Larry appeared younger than his stated age. Although his speech and comprehension were age-appropriate, his gait, mannerisms, attention span, and questions were those of a two-year-old. He had a mildly depressed face, voice, and posture. He took one toy off the shelf and asked what it was. Then he went on to another toy and another without waiting for an answer. The therapist suggested to Larry that he really knew what those toys were but that there might be other questions he wanted to ask that he was afraid to ask. At that point, Larry asked the therapist to put him into the play crib. As soon as he was put into it, he anxiously asked to be taken out. The therapist suggested that he seemed to be telling her something about what worried him and that he seemed to want to know about when he was a littler boy. She said she was going to try to help him with those worries. This introduction to therapy relaxed him a bit, and he became engaged and enthusiastic about a play house. He spent the next two and a half years in psychoanalytic psychotherapy, being seen three times a week. His adoptive parents were seen biweekly.

During the first six months of therapy, Larry appeared subdued, gloomy, and serious much of the time. Most of his play was repetitious, monotonous, and constricted. He was anxious and generally wary, but there were moments when he could definitely enjoy the activity he was engaged in and his interactions with the therapist. He spent many sessions being a little baby. He would climb into the crib, ask to be given a bottle, and suck on it. As he lay there sadly, the therapist would ask him if he was having a dream. Stroking his blanket, he would talk about the ghosts, monsters, lions, and tigers that scared him. When the anxiety became too great, he jumped up, threw toys around, hit the dolls, and said he was a lion or a ghost. Changing from passive into active enabled him to keep his anxiety from overwhelming him. He was very dependent at this time on the teacher in his prekindergarten classroom and had difficulty playing with other children. Although he was inhibited intellectually, the teacher found him to have good verbal ability and a great fund of information. His parents reported that he seemed too good, as he didn't complain about anything, but he cried at night because of nightmares.

The therapist's annual month-long summer vacation was approaching and Larry reacted to the news first by hitting the therapist and saying she was bad. He said that he was Superman and that nothing hurt him. He then demanded to end the session immediately. The therapist related his behavior to his past abandonment and his anger and pain about it. She added that he was telling her he was going to be in charge and was leaving her before she left him. From the time he was told about the impending temporary break from therapy until the vacation began, at the end of every session, he would throw the black doll into the garbage can. At the last session before the therapist's departure, Larry said he knew she was not coming back. Even though the therapist sent him weekly postcards during her absence, he regressed during the summer and had a very difficult time in daycamp. He soiled, disobeyed the teachers, and sucked his thumb almost constantly. At home, he had frequent tantrums. He withdrew to his bed with his blanket and slept a lot.

Upon the therapist's return, he was able to say he was sad that he had not seen her for a lot of days. For a few days, he tried to control her every move. He screamed at her and called her a "poo-poo." The therapist reflected on his anger at her for leaving him for so many weeks. She made the link between his earlier life feelings, when he was abandoned and the revival of those feelings when he was separated from the therapist.

In the second half of the year, he was able to verbalize his feelings more directly. During one session, he threw the black doll away but took care of the white one. He said, "I like white babies." At the very next session, as he looked into a full-length mirror in the treatment room, he said, "I hate myself." He then climbed into the crib and asked for a bottle of water. The therapist suggested that he seemed to be telling her about a feeling he had about his life with his birth mommy. Maybe he felt she liked white babies more than black babies and that was why she had given him to another mommy to take care of him. He nodded in affirmation.

At about this time, Larry began to show more anger with his adoptive parents. He tested limits with them and tried to control them by not eating. He had bowel movements in his pants several times after they made demands on him to obey them. This behavior was interpreted to the parents. They apparently handled it well, since the eating and elimination problems stopped. However, he continued trying to control them verbally when he was upset. During this time in therapy, he alternated in play between being an omnipotent figure, such as Superman, and being a helpless, defeated, scared little baby. As Superman, he was totally in charge and always came out on top. As the little baby he sucked his thumb, looked very depressed, and sometimes fell asleep during the session. Whenever there was stress—especially related to loss and separation in his life, such as when a grandparent died—depression was quite overt outside of therapy.

In the middle of the second year, when Larry was almost five, the therapist decided to begin a book with him to try to reconstruct his earlier life experiences. She felt, that if his experiences were organized, he might be able to remember and to sort out his memories of earlier life.

There were two parts to the book. One part was for things he could remember; the other was for things he couldn't remember. The first few pictures he drew of what he remembered showed a baby in a crib under a blanket, a baby on a swing covered in a blanket, and a teddy bear he had had as a baby. In the next session he went over these pictures. He said the baby was a bad black baby. When asked why the black baby was bad, he refused to continue the book. He threw the book up into the air and didn't go back to it for three weeks.

When he went back to the book, he drew a face that he called a monster. He said he couldn't remember any more, left the drawing, and played out with the dolls a scene about a bad baby whose mother did not feed him. For the remainder of therapy, he would go to the book from time to time and embellish his story about the baby's feelings. For months, when the material would get to be too much for him, he would throw something. Later in therapy, he would more frequently look sad and put his finger in his mouth.

When it was time for the therapist to go on vacation in the second summer, Larry was able to say directly that he did not want her to be away for a month, although he also said he knew she would be back. In the next few sessions he regressed and isolated himself in the playroom crib. During the separation, he regressed only for the first few days.

In a session soon after the therapist's return from vacation, the crib Larry used became a rocket, and he said, with very positive affect, that his first mommy was in the rocket with him. He then said, "I wish this rocket would go up." The therapist verbalized his wish to be a little boy again and to have his biological mother with him to make him feel good. His last reported fantasy in the crib was, "Once, I really mean it, I was in prison. It was dark and there was no toilet. I could not get out, and I had to go in my pants. I was scared; no one else was there." The therapist again reconstructed for him his early emotional reactions to being left alone. His "I really mean it" was said as if to convince both himself and the therapist that the experience had great meaning for him and that he wanted the therapist to know it.

At the end of the second year of therapy, Larry's cognitive performance at school was above average. He revealed an IQ of 117 in an intelligence test. He had many friends, and his creative ideas in play made him a leader among his peers. Once, when he was angry at his adoptive mother, he told her he wished he were white and back with his birth mother. His adoptive mother was very upset about this. The therapist helped her understand its meaning in terms of the child's pain in relating to his earlier feelings of rejection and not as indicating that she was an inadequate mother. The next time he said the same thing, she was able to tell him she loved him as he was.

About the same time that he told his adoptive mother he wished he were with his biological mother, he told the therapist he wanted to be *her* little boy. After saying this, he threw the black doll into the garbage can and said that black boys were stupid. The therapist related this to his possible feeling that he was not with his first mommy anymore because he was not white, as she was, and that now his white therapist didn't want him for the same reason. His vigorous response of "That's right!" was a very strong affirmation of that feeling.

During the termination phase of therapy, Larry began to play checkers and cards with the therapist and relished beating her. His competitiveness manifested itself further when he told the therapist he was the best boy she saw. He asked about her family and said again that he wanted to be her white child. He told her he would miss her, and verbalized his sadness frequently. She became more of a real person to him. He appeared to have internalized the object relationship with the therapist as a result of reworking earlier life conflicts (Chused, 1982).

He continued to do well socially and cognitively in school and in his adoptive home. All his initial symptoms were gone, except that when there was stress, he needed to order his parents around.

DISCUSSION

The long-term goal of therapy with these children was to help them work through the conflicts related to their earlier relationships with their biological parents and to mourn the loss of these relationships. They clearly had abnormal attachments to their biological parents. Self-other differentiation was pathological in both children, and neither had attained object constancy (Mahler et al., 1975). Therefore, they defended against separation anxiety and ambivalent libidinal and aggressive feelings with maladaptive symptoms. They recreated in their subsequent relationships their versions of their early life-experiences. Their therapists felt that the gradual working through of their conflicts and feelings in the therapeutic arena, was critical to the children's ability to move on developmentally and to invest in their new parents.

Frances demonstrated widespread developmental arrest and unmanageable impulsive behavior after her separation from her mother. The memories and enactments during therapy revealed the confusion and upheaval of her early life and her lack of higher-level ego functioning. Early in therapy, separation activated the feelings of emptiness, anxiety, despair, and grief experienced with an unpredictable mother. There was evidence of confusion of self and object, an immature ego, and weak ego defenses. There were conflicts between her aggressive feelings and wishes and her strong wish for regressive libidinal gratification. Her ambivalence in the relationship with her mother was manifested in behavior indicating anxiety, anger, and guilt, for example, getting on the therapist's lap and then anxiously running away from being too close, rages when she tore things up, and her expressions of wanting to go home with her mother to take care of her.

It appeared that Larry had had somewhat better mothering than Frances, but he was abandoned by his mother at eighteen months, at the height of the separation-individuation stage (Mahler et al., 1975). Depression was the predominant symptom, with a serious impairment of affect and cognition. He appeared to be expressing helplessness and resignation in the face of pain (Sandler and Joffee, 1965). He alternated between despair and protest throughout therapy (see Bowlby, 1969, 1973, 1980). Early in therapy and to a lesser extent later on, he replayed over and over again the life of a little baby who had been left alone in the crib with his blanket for comfort. In other sessions, he would attempt to ward off his feelings of emptiness and helplessness by controlling the therapist and throwing toys in the air. Larry was an attractive child and was able to relate to others in a positive way, again suggesting that there had been a primary object attachment in his early life. This enabled him to benefit from the positive rearing of his adoptive parents as he worked through in intensive therapy the depression resulting from the pain of rejection and abandonment by his primary caretaker.

The children's self-denigration indicated that they were identifying with the internalized bad object representations of their biological parents (Sandler and Rosenblatt, 1962). The lack of good internal objects resulted in self-esteem problems (Tyson, 1983) and their abandonment and feelings of rejection related to it also had had a profoundly negative effect on the children's self-acceptance and self-esteem (Samuels, 1990). They showed feelings of worthlessness, of being unloved and unappreciated (Bibring, 1953). There was intolerable injury to their fantasized omnipotence (Wolfenstein, 1969). Both children seemed to express fears of further abandonment related to their feelings of badness, inadequacy, and guilt for not being good enough. Frances did not feel she did a good enough job in taking care of her birth mother. Larry felt that his black skin was not acceptable to his biological mother.

Both children employed the defense of omnipotence. For example, Larry played the invulnerable Superman in order to counter his feelings of helplessness. He attempted to control and manipulate the powerful adults in his life to assure himself that he was not weak, inadequate, or helpless. Frances got great pleasure in using the therapist as a mirror for her every action (Kohut, 1971) as she reworked the separation-individuation stages.

These children also showed as symptoms destructiveness, guilt, anxiety, and narcissistic depletion. These symptoms were reactions to their pain, confirming reports in other studies (Frankel, 1991; Nickman, 1985; Kliman et al., 1982; Tyson, 1983; Burland et al., 1981; Brinich, 1980; Smith, 1979). Both children had internalized threats of punishment in a harsh superego directed against the self (Kennedy and Yorke, 1982). Frances expressed narcissistic rage when faced with the risk of another abandonment. This behavior on being abandoned and made to feel helpless was an attempt to get away from the helpless and passive feelings of rejection and low self-esteem. It is common for an individual to attempt mastery, turning passive into active, when such feelings become overwhelming. After being told that she was going to be adopted, Frances tried to gain mastery by acting out so that she could feel in charge of the expected new rejection.

The children seemed to have a fear of their mothers' anger. Frances was afraid that the "hungry spider" would kill her, and Larry remembered a monster face from when he was a baby. It is suggested that their fears represented a premature superego identification with the angry, avenging mother, reinforced by earlier deprivations and narcissistic rage.

Anxiety in Frances was intense and dominated her behavior after she was separated from her mother. Frances destroyed and threw things. She was afraid to get too close to the therapist, and she tuned out and stared into space when she was with her foster mother. Anxiety about closeness indicated that she could not predict how others would react to her (Kennedy and Moran, 1991). Larry threw the black doll (representing himself) into the garbage can. His frightening dreams, constriction, and early repetition of questions to which he knew the answers were other indications of his anxiety. Anxiety about being abandoned again was easily stimulated by any possibility of rejection. Both children regressed before any separation from the therapist. Early in therapy, for Frances this included the separation from the therapist at the end of each session.

The inhibition of ego functions in both children supports the literature on loss (Milrod, 1988; Kliman et al., 1982; Bowlby, 1980; Sorosky et al., 1975; Furman, 1974; Warfield, 1972; Wolfenstein, 1973, 1966, 1969). As their conflicts were uncovered in therapy, they mourned appropriately the loss of their previous caretakers, reworked the narcissistic developmental process, and reached higher levels of ego integration (Loewald, 1971). Their regressive behaviors and symptoms decreased, and their ego functions became more appropriate for their ages.

In the therapy room, the children replayed the traumata that needed to be worked through. The therapist had as a goal providing unity and meaning to the fragments of material the children gave her. She helped them sort out and organize their experiences before, during, and after their painful separations, by empathic reconstruction of these experiences and the attendant feelings. Reconstruction led to a reorganization of memories and the associated affect with a beneficial change in both object and self representation (Chused, 1982). Additionally, it was important that their strengths and adaptive capacities were recognized and supported. Frances needed more structure and ego-supportive measures, especially early in therapy (Kennedy and

Moran, 1991). Interpretation became more valuable for her as she was able to tolerate more pain. Ultimately, both children were less impulsive and reached higher levels of play. They found it easier than it had been to verbalize their feelings, instead of defending against them by acting out. They dealt with their pain by using symbolic, creative, and cognitive materials. The therapist, as a "real person" in play, removed obstacles to more normative development (Cohen and Solnit, 1993).

Transferential manifestations and interpretations also allowed the children to view themselves and their experiences in new and more adaptive ways. Sometimes they experienced intense negative countertransference feelings. This was true especially of Frances, who would usually throw things and destroy toys at times of separation from significant others, including the therapist. It was essential that the therapist stop the destructive behavior without rejecting the children, recognizing that each time separation occurred there was a reworking of the separation-individuation process with the therapist. She could not be effective if she was overwhelmed by a child's negative actions or words and acted as a punitive parent because of intense countertransferential feelings.

As termination of therapy was approaching, it appeared that the children had internalized the object relationship with the therapist (Chused, 1982) and used the therapist more as a real object with whom they could identify (Chused, 1988; Cohen and Solnit, 1993; Novick, 1990). Larry played board games with the therapist, and Frances told the therapist she would like to be grown up like her, indicating identification. The regression and rage relating to the loss of biological parents were more intense in Frances during the termination phase. Larry was able to verbalize the pain of the loss. Frances used the therapist to help her catch up on developmental deficits due to her tuned-out mother. At termination, the therapist's role was turned over to her adoptive mother, who was helped to assume that position.

Without therapeutic help, the children would probably irrationally and constantly have repeated negative, regressive behavior in order to gain mastery (Freud, 1920). Unfortunately, this repetition frequently leads to further abandonment (Kliman et al., 1982). Parent guidance by the therapist prevented this from occurring in these cases. The therapist met regularly with the future adopting parents, reassuring them that they were important partners with the professionals in helping the children deal with their problems.

The therapist helped the parents to express their feelings early in placement, when the children were especially difficult to handle, and empathized with their emotional reactions to the children's behavior.

She assisted them in utilizing appropriate fair, firm, and warm management techniques, in recognizing that they did not have to be perfect, and in understanding the children's overidealization of their biological parents. The goal was to enable them to see that the children's negative reactions were not necessarily directed personally against them but could become so if the parents reacted in kind. They learned to listen to the children's questions, to empathize with their feelings, and to allow the children to talk about their biological families at their own pace without criticizing their original families. Both children told their adoptive parents they wanted to be back with their birth families. Both sets of parents needed the therapist to help them deal with their reactions to these statements. She helped them to understand the children's feelings and not to react defensively. The adoptive parents were helped to communicate to the children that they belonged in the family. Of course, these parents were carefully chosen in the first place, so that they were well-equipped to accomplish these tasks.

Another significant reason for the success of these cases can be attributed to the cooperation of the Westchester County Department of Social Services. A therapeutic alliance with foster parents is difficult to maintain, and it is common to have inconsistent attendance as a result. The social workers in these cases were instrumental in helping with whatever resistance there was against continuing therapy. They also arranged all the meetings and communications between the therapist and the significant others in the children's lives and obtained transportation to the clinic for the children when the parents were unable to do so. The social workers honestly told the parents all they knew about the children's earlier lives. Social workers were available when the parents had problems or when the children became symptomatic after visits with and/or rejections by their biological mothers. They helped the new families to deal with maladaptive intrusions of the biological parents into their lives. Their interventions prevented the adoptive parents from reacting inappropriately. For example, Frances' mentally ill mother showed up at the adoptive mother's house once and wanted to take Frances away with her. This was very upsetting for the adoptive parents. The social workers were available to keep them from reacting inappropriately. The therapist supported the positive interactions of social services and kept in close contact with them to keep the lines of communication open. At the same time, the social workers urged Frances' adoptive parents not to discourage appropriate maternal contact. Frances met with her biological mother while she was in therapy and for a short time after she was officially adopted. Although the visits early in therapy led to regressive behavior, with the help of the therapist, they eventually enabled her to see more objectively why it was not a good idea for her to live with her mother.

Psychoanalytic psychotherapy at a critical time, shortly after separation, aimed at helping these children to develop enough inner stability to cope adequately with future loss and stress. They may have not have mourned completely the loss of their biological parents. Furman (1974) has suggested that the process of decathexis is more difficult for children who have been given up by mothers who are still alive. It is possible that in these two cases, the children are still vulnerable to stress later in life despite what appeared to be excellent placements. Difficulties may occur, particularly in adolescence, when identity concerns are likely to become problems. Larry did not yet accept his racial inheritance, and this could cause considerable difficulties for him during adolescence, when a positive sense of identity is essential for healthy development (Erikson, 1968). However, the children made significant gains in ego functioning. They had moved into latency and resumed progressive development, an important criterion for therapeutic success (A. Freud, 1970; Ablon, 1988; Novick, 1990). Five years after the termination of therapy the adolescent Frances was found to be free of observable pathology.

BIBLIOGRAPHY

ABLON, S. L. (1988). Developmental forces and termination in child analysis. *Int. J. Psycho-Anal.*, 69:97–104.
AMENT, A. (1972). The boy who did not cry. *Child Welfare*, 51:104–09.
AUESTAD, A. M. (1992). "I am father's baby—you can have the turtle": Psychotherapy in a family context. *J. Child Psychoth.*, 18:57–74.
BARDEN, J. C. (1990). Foster care system reeling, despite law meant to help. *New York Times*, Sept. 21, A1:18–19.
BIBRING, E. (1953). The mechanism of depression. In *Affective Disorders*, ed. P. Greenacre, 13–48. New York: Int. Univ. Press.
BOWLBY, J. (1969). *Attachment: Attachment and Loss.* New York: Basic.
——— (1973). *Separation: Anxiety and Anger.* New York: Basic.
——— (1980). *Loss: Sadness and Depression.* New York: Basic.
BRANDELL, J. R. (1992). Psychotherapy of a traumatized ten-year-old boy: Theoretical issues and clinical considerations. *Smith College Studies Social Wk.*, 62:123–38.
BRINICH, P. M. (1980). Some potential effects of adoption on self and object representations. *Psychoanal. Study Child*, 35:107–33.
BURLAND, J. A., KLIMAN, G. W., & MEERS, D. (1981). Psychoanalytic observations of foster care. *J. Prev. Psychiat.*, 1:37–45.

CHUSED, J. F. (1982). The role of analytic neutrality in the use of the child analyst as a new object. *J. Amer. Psychoanal. Assn.*, 30:3–28.
——— (1988). The transference neurosis in child analysis. *Psychoanal. Study Child*, 43:51–82.
CLIFTON, P. M., & RANSOM, J. W. (1975). An approach to working with the "placed child." *Child Psychiat. and Human Development*, 6:107–17.
COHEN, P. M., & SOLNIT, A. J. (1993). Play and therapeutic action. *Psychoanal. Study Child*, 48:49–63.
COMMITTEE ON FINANCE, U.S. SENATE. (1990). *Foster Care Adoption Assistance and Child Welfare Services*. Washington, D. C., G.P.O.
DEFRIES, Z., JENKINS, S. & WILLIAMS, E. C. (1964). Treatment of disturbed children in foster care. *Amer. J. Ortho.*, 34:615–24.
ERIKSON, E. (1968). *Identity: Youth and Crisis*, New York: W. W. Norton.
FESTINGER, T. (1986). *Necessary Risks: A Study of Adoptions and Disrupted Adoption Placements*. Washington, D.C.: Child Welfare League of America.
FLASHMAN, A. J. (1992). The moment of recognition. *Psychoanal. Study Child*, 47:351–69.
FRAIBERG, S. (1962). A therapeutic approach to reactive ego disturbances in children in placement. *Amer. J. Orth.*, 32:18–31.
FRANKEL, S. A. (1991). Pathogenic factors in the experience of early and late adopted children. *Psychoanal. Study Child*, 46:91–108.
FREUD, A. (1970). Problems of termination in child analysis. *Writings*, 8:96–109.
FREUD, S. (1920). Beyond the pleasure principle. *S.E.*, 18:3–64.
FURMAN, E. (1974). *A Child's Parent Dies: Studies in Childhood Bereavement*. New Haven: Yale University Press.
HAITH, M. M. (1986). Sensory and perceptual processes in early childhood. *J. Ped.*, 109:158–71.
HIGH, H. (1982). The consequences of severe deprivation as they emerged in the psychotherapy of a girl in foster care. *J. Child Psychoth.*, 8:37–55.
KAPLAN, A. (1982). Growing up in foster care: One boy's struggles. *J. Child Psychoth.*, 8:57–66.
KAPLAN, L. K., & TURITZ, L. L. (1957). Treatment of severely traumatized young children in a foster home setting. *Amer. J. Ortho.*, 27:271–85.
KENNEDY, H., & MORAN, G. (1991). Reflections on the aim of child analysis. *Psychoanal. Study Child*, 46:181–98.
KENNEDY, H., & YORKE, C. (1982). Steps from outer to inner conflict viewed as superego precursors. *Psychoanal. Study Child*, 37:221–44.
KLIMAN, G. W., SCHAEFFER, M. H., & FRIEDMAN, M. J. (1982). *Preventive Mental Health Services for Children Entering Foster Home Care: An Assessment*. White Plains, New York: Center for Preventive Psychiatry, Inc.
KOHUT, H. (1971). *The Analysis of the Self*. New York: Int. Univ. Press.
LOEWALD, H. W. (1971). The transference neurosis. In Loewald, *Papers on Psychoanalysis*. 221–56. New Haven, Conn.: Yale Univ. Press, 1980.
LUSH, D., BOSTON, M., & GRAINGER, E. (1991). Evaluation of psychoanalytic psychotherapy with children: Therapists' assessments and predictions. *Psychoanal. Psychoth.*, 5:191–234.

MAHLER, M., PINE, A., & BERGMAN, A. (1975). *The Psychological Birth of the Infant.* New York: Basic.

MAYES, L. C., & COHEN, D. J. (1992). The development of a capacity for imagination in early childhood. *Psychoanal. Study Child,* 47:23–47.

MILROD, D. (1988). A current view of the psychoanalytic theory of depression. *Psychoanal. Study Child,* 43:83–99.

NATIONAL COMMITTEE FOR ADOPTION. (1985). *Adoption Factbook: U.S. Data, Issues, Regulations, and Resources.* Washington, D.C., National Committee for Adoption.

NICKMAN, S. L. (1985). Losses in adoption: The need for dialogue. *Psychoanal. Study Child,* 40:365–98.

NOVICK, J. (1990). Comments on termination in child, adolescent, and adult analysis. *Psychoanal. Study Child,* 45:419–36.

PINE, F. (1985). *Developmental Theory and Clinical Process.* New Haven, Conn.: Yale Univ. Press.

PROVENCE, S. (1987). Psychoanalytic views of separation in infancy and early childhood. In *The Psychology of Separation and Loss,* ed. J. Bloom-Feshbach and S. Bloom-Feshbach, 87–108. San Francisco: Jossey Bass.

REEVES, A. C. (1971). Children with surrogate parents: Cases seen in analytic therapy and an aetiological hypothesis. *Brit. J. Med. Psychol.,* 44:155–71.

SAMUELS, S. C. (1990). *Ideal Adoption: A Comprehensive Guide to Forming an Adoptive Family.* New York: Plenum.

SANDLER, J., & JOFFEE, W. G. (1965). Notes on childhood depression. *Int. J. Psycho-Anal.,* 46:88–96.

SANDLER, J., & ROSENBLATT, B. (1962). The concept of the representational world. *Psychoanal. Study Child,* 17:128–45.

SCHAEFFER, M. H., KLIMAN, G. W., FRIEDMAN, M. J., & PASQUARIELLA, B. G. (1981). Children in foster care: A preventive service and research program for a high risk population. *J. Prev. Psychiat,* 1:47–56.

SMITH, W. R., JR. (1979). The foster child. In *Basic Handbook of Child Psychiatry,* Vol. 1: *Development,* ed. J. D. Noshpitz, 348–56. New York: Basic.

SOLNIT, A. J. (1982). Developmental perspectives on self and object constancy. *Psychoanal. Study Child,* 37:201–18.

SOROSKY, A. D., BARAN, A., & PANNOR, R. (1975). Identity conflicts in adoptees. *Amer. J. Ortho.,* 45:18–27.

STERN, D. M. (1985). *The Interpersonal World of the Infant.* New York: Basic.

TYSON, R. L. (1983). Some narcissistic consequences of object loss: A developmental view. *Psychoanal. Q.,* 52:205–24.

WARFIELD, M. J. (1972). Treatment of a two-year-old in preparation for adoption. *Social Casework,* 53:341–47.

WOLFENSTEIN, M. (1966). How is mourning possible? *Psychoanal. Study Child,* 21:93–123.

——— (1969). Loss, rage and repetition. *Psychoanal. Study Child,* 24:432–60.

——— (1973). The image of the lost parent. *Psychoanal. Study Child,* 28:433–56.

Silent Eulogy

Elective Mutism in a Six-Year-Old Hispanic Girl

JESSICA VALNER, Ph.D.
MARC NEMIROFF, Ph.D.

A case of elective mutism in a six-year-old Hispanic girl treated in a public mental health setting is presented. The central feature of the case was the facilitation of a delayed grieving process in a little girl who had witnessed her father's death. The presentation stresses the critical need to integrate the unfolding clinical material with the realities of the stresses of parental distress and resistance. An attempt is made to understand this "resistance" in the context of cultural and social realities, while attending to the possible underlying psychodynamic meaning.

CHILDREN SPEAK IN WAYS THAT HAVE THEIR OWN LOGIC; THEIR PLAY HAS the power to unite seemingly disjointed objects and points of view to create meaning. The "magical realism" of certain Latin American writers captures this expressive quality of a child's mental life. The Chilean author Isabel Allende's use of life's inherent metaphors is particularly expressive of the core of psychoanalytically oriented play therapy. Clara, in Allende's *House of the Spirits* (1986), became mute upon

Jessica Valner is a clinical psychologist in residence, currently working at the Northwest Family Center, Washington, D.C. Marc Nemiroff is coordinator of youth and family clinical programs at the Woodburn Center for Community Mental Health in Annandale, Virginia. He is an affiliate member of the Baltimore-Washington Society for Psychoanalysis.

This paper is adapted from a case presentation to the Instituto de Psicología Clínica y Social, Mexico City, June 1993.

The Psychoanalytic Study of the Child 50, ed. Albert J. Solnit, Peter B. Neubauer, Samuel Abrams, and A. Scott Dowling (Yale University Press, copyright © 1995 by Albert J. Solnit, Peter B. Neubauer, Samuel Abrams, and A. Scott Dowling).

witnessing the tragic destiny of her magnificent and precious sister Rosa—to be "stripped of her insides" as her body was embalmed following her death. The following passage, which describes the world Clara inhabited thereafter, captures important aspects of the case to be presented in this paper: "Clara lived in a universe of her own invention, protected from life's inclement weather, where the prosaic truth of material objects mingled with the tumultuous reality of dreams and the laws of physics and logic did not always apply" (p. 82).

The patient, Lucero, was a six-year-old electively mute girl from Nicaragua. The phase of her treatment to be described in this paper represented the continuation of play therapy begun by a previous therapist. Treatment occurred at a comprehensive community mental health center within a large metropolitan area with significant immigrant population.

The treatment proceeded under the following clinical and therapeutic assumptions: (1) that unconscious motivation is operational in symptom formation, (2) that intrapsychic conflicts and concerns are symbolically expressed in a child's play, (3) that the transformation of unconscious content to enable its expression in an interpretable form is critical and can be facilitated through both play and language, (4) that the nature of the conflict is "betrayed" by the presenting problem, (5) that it is necessary to pay close attention to a child's affective environment and to determine whether this environment might be exacerbating the conflict, and (6) that the primary symptom is an apparently acceptable compromise for the child's family—thus, the direct expression of what the primary symptom *represents* is more threatening than the symptom itself. Theoretically, we are assuming (1) that play has significance, (2) that transference can become evident in the course of treatment, (3) that attention to the vicissitudes of psychotherapy (including countertransference aspects) is essential both for the therapist's understanding of the psychodynamic process and contents and for the interpretation to be meaningful to the child, and (4) that free (nonstructured) play is the child's equivalent of free association (Goldblatt, 1972; Segal, 1972).

Lucero was an appealing, somewhat chunky little girl with olive skin, dark hair, and captivating brown eyes. She was the only child of a Nicaraguan woman and her African-American husband. Lucero's mother described her pregnancy as "horrible," complaining of unrelenting nausea and the sudden development of repugnance toward her husband. Although she was somewhat unclear, she reported having a "heart attack" as a result of childbirth. The birth was vaginal and described by the mother as extremely difficult. Lucero was in an incubator for five days. Toilet training was reported to be normal, and language development was unremarkable until age three. The mother reported that Lucero was her father's "treasure" and that she (mother) "did not exist" in the child's eyes. Lucero and her father would spend hours together playing. When the father would invite the mother to join in the play, Lucero would push her away and slam the door. "She couldn't tolerate seeing her father and myself together." Lucero spoke Spanish to her mother and English to her father.

When Lucero was three years old, she accompanied her mother and father to the supermarket. She stayed with her father in the car while her mother went into the store. During that time her father suffered a fatal heart attack, falling on the horn and causing a great deal of commotion as he stepped on the brakes and the accelerator. Lucero stopped speaking to everyone but her mother on that day. When her mother tried to improve her own English, Lucero would dispose of her study books.

Before seeking treatment, the mother had attempted to influence what she called Lucero's "tantrum" (her mutism) in numerous ways. Her attempts remind again of *The House of the Spirits*. Clara, the character who became mute, had a traditional Hispanic *nana* (nanny) who tried to scare her out of her mutism, as if it were a bad case of hiccups. In the novel, as in Lucero's case, the result of this strategy was a worsening of the situation. The mother with the assistance of teachers, relatives, and friends, adopted commonly used behavioral strategies. She reinforced every word Lucero spoke at home and she used a combination of punishment and negative reinforcement when Lucero refused to speak. As a consequence, the symptom became exacerbated, and conflict within the family was aggravated. At this point, her mother presented Lucero for treatment.

Lucero was first seen for one year by a play therapist under psychoanalytically oriented supervision. This therapist was an American woman who worked with Lucero in English. During that year, the foundations of her treatment were sufficiently established that the current therapist (J. V.) could readily build upon them. The youngster had begun to establish some verbal communication with her therapist, and the therapist had encouraged the mother to disengage from the power struggle over Lucero's speech. The mother was also in treatment during that year, with particular attention being paid to unresolved grieving.

Lucero's continuing treatment, as well as conferences with the mother, were conducted in Spanish. (The current therapist is Hispanic and bilingual.) The psychoanalytically oriented supervision was provided by the same person (M. N.) who had supervised the initial phase of treatment. During the treatment, Lucero lived at home with her mother, two maternal uncles, and the wife of one of the uncles (the other was single). Lucero and her mother were American citizens. The mother's extended family, including Lucero's maternal grandmother, lived in Nicaragua, and she and Lucero went to visit them about once a year for a month. When the current therapist began seeing Lucero, she was speaking only at home. She continued to be virtually mute in school, with friends, and with others. The initial treatment plan called for weekly individual play therapy with twice-monthly parent conferences. This was later intensified to twice-weekly play therapy.

We will discuss the evolution of Lucero's internal processes, as manifested in her play, as well as the external changes that transpired in her life, as these unfolded in the parent conferences. In this way, we hope to reflect the interaction of Lucero's internal and external worlds. All discussion pertains to Lucero's treatment with her second therapist.

Lucero began her relationship with her new therapist in silence. She manifested continuous defensive attempts, particularly by compulsive behavior (washing, or continuously issuing nonverbal orders e.g., pointing, grunting, gesturing). The therapist viewed this as a response to anxiety elicited by the change in therapeutic conditions. Early in this treatment, Lucero selected a dinosaur and a blonde doll—the current therapist has light hair—which she pleasurably suffocated. Initial interventions consisted of narrating Lucero's actions and asking for her permission to let the therapist join her in play. We assumed that her play with the dinosaur and the doll was her way of gaining access to the lost therapist and, by implication, to other significant losses. Perhaps she was trying to suffocate or annihilate the new therapist in the hope that this process might magically restore the former therapist. The therapist wondered aloud if the former therapist's absence was difficult for Lucero. In a subsequent session, once Lucero's confidence had grown and the intensity of her defenses had lessened, she shifted her play: she gestured to the toy telephones and indicated the possibility of verbal communication.

In the early parent conferences, the therapist helped to establish with the mother their primary goal, which was understanding the child's difficulties, rather than eliminating problem behaviors (Freud, 1965). The therapist suggested that Lucero's symptoms had communicative meaning. Once we could understand what she was trying to convey, she would not have such need of her symptoms, and they should abate. Concurrently, the therapist worked at attempting to understand the interaction between Lucero's internal world as expressed in her play and the external environment as described and demonstrated by mother. Mother appeared to be so immersed in her own mourning process and feelings of abandonment that she was having significant difficulty handling Lucero's questions about her father's death.

Lucero had been told that her father had gone with Jesus. Her Nicaraguan grandmother was also named Jesus. In addition, Lucero's mother told her that God decided these things, and the mother would add, "I'm also going to leave one day." This information suggested to us the probable confusion with which Lucero was experiencing the internal representation of her father. She informed us, in her subsequent play, that she did not know where to place him, where to find him, and thus where (in fantasy) to re-find him.

The mother complained about Lucero's behavior toward her unmarried uncle Jaime: "She's unbearable when the three of us are together; when the two of them are alone, everything is okay." The replication of the earlier intact (and early oedipal) family constellation hinted at the potential for conflicted triangulation among mother, Jaime, and Lucero. The mother also expressed her ambivalence about this situation. She felt "locked out" by her daughter when she was with the uncle, yet she also was less burdened then by Lucero's powerful need for attention and affection, which her mother saw as agonizing and perpetual. Her own incomplete mourning for her husband also affected her ability to listen to Lucero. It relieved her that Lucero would sit on Jaime's lap "so that he reads to her, just like she did with her daddy."

Shortly thereafter, there was a striking shift in Lucero's playroom behavior. She began to talk. The themes that were to dominate her treatment began to be expressed. Lucero oscillated between expressing her yearning and hunger and expressing her need to project in order to expel her bad, sometimes murderous, feelings. Oscillation between the poles of this ambivalence kept her in a continuous state of confusion. This was regularly manifested in her play material.

Lucero's yearning and confusion were symbolized by *panzota* (a huge "tummy"). This became a poignant example of the detective work a therapist must sometimes do. Lucero would often speak about the huge tummy, the tummy with a baby inside it, the tummy full of chocolates, the tummy full of gas. Was the *panzota* a metaphor for Lucero's yearning for a brother? her yearning to bring her father back? her longing for mother's nurturing? her wish to have a baby of her own who could function magically as a father whom she could also care for and protect? or her introjection of her rage, located at a site of frustrated internal contentment? (Almond, 1990). Eventually, we developed the understanding that Lucero had condensed uncle Jaime's imagined big tummy and the therapist's imaginary *panzota*, and had become perplexed by their fusion. A big tummy—which Lucero would draw, touch, and then disguise—may have represented the yearning for a brother, her mother, and her father in wishful restoration. Jaime's *panzota*, when perceived individually, appeared to represent the sought-after availability of nurturant supplies in a father-as-maternal-object. Lucero's longing for the restoration of her dead father had become joined with her longing for a generous mother to feed and care for her.

As the complexity of Lucero's image of the *panzota* became clearer, therapeutic work increasingly attended to the possible meanings of other symbols in her play. Lucero began symbolically to evoke the yearning for her (maternal) father with food and particularly sugar. Lucero's use of sand as "sugar" came to take on an almost ritual, sacred importance. The sugar was understood as serving to evoke the father. Lucero sought to communicate with him in sweet silence. She behaved in play as if she were starving. She played with sand, vigorously making numerous tortillas. In addition, she repeatedly acted out the drama of packing and traveling to Nicaragua, where grandmother Jesus lived and where, according to her mother, her father was. ("Your father has gone to be with Jesus.") Preparations for these "trips to Nicaragua" invariably required the strenuous preparation of food.

Symbolization of Lucero's rage and confusion emerged in the following manner: after a period of several weeks, she began to play hide-and-seek, manifesting her worry regarding object permanence. The manifest content of her play was, for the first time, directly associated to the relationship between children and parents. One day, for example, while playing with dolls, Lucero narrated: "Lucero is angry because her father doesn't take care of her; he doesn't feed her." Thus she began expressing her rage regarding her abandonment by her father. The projection, the expulsion, of this rage, raised to "assassin" status, was manifested symbolically. Lucero would fart (both genuine farts and verbally produced pretend-farts) forcefully and powerfully. She would then yell "PIG!!" and play with dolls' pretend-urine. On one occasion, when she needed to go to the bathroom and move her bowels, she demanded that the therapist wait outside the bathroom door. Given her magical thinking, we hypothesized that Lucero was probably experiencing her assassin-rage literally, believing that in some way her rage had killed her father. It seemed that a pivotal therapeutic element during this stage was for Lucero to see that her rage did not destroy her therapist (Klein, 1975).

This case provided evidence that it is important for the same therapist to see both the child patient and the parents. Lucero's mother was struggling with her own withholding nature and sadistic impulses, traits that, internalized by her daughter, entered into the formation of Lucero's character. The mother also reported some background information about the father that came to be important in understanding the little girl. Lucero's father had worked as a cook, preparing food and supervising other Hispanic workers in this activity. Lucero had taken great pleasure in accompanying her father to his work. Her play thus combined attempts to identify with her father through the preparation of food and to retain his image through the almost ritualized repetition of behavior seen as characteristic of him.

After the father died, the mother had explained to Lucero that he would not come back, that God had taken him away and that He "could take anyone away." Subsequently, when she would become angry with her daughter, she would threaten to leave if Lucero couldn't behave herself. Thus it seemed likely that Lucero was learning from her mother the connection between expressed rage and the possibility, even likelihood, of her mother's being taken away from her by God. During this phase of treatment, the therapist worked to help the mother to feel less threatened by her daughter's grieving. She wanted to help the mother to feel strong enough to give Lucero permission to feel sad. She observed, "Lucero wants to take care of you. Part of her wish for her father to return is a wish for you to be happy."

During the middle part of this treatment, the therapist had to be away for two weeks. Lucero experienced this prospect as an abandonment and became anxiously confused and, as a defense, more rigid, although eventually her confusion yielded to continued grief work. When she had first learned of the expected two-week absence, sadistic orders dominated her play. The quality of her activity at first evoked her mother, but in time it became informed by the image of her father supervising the Hispanic food preparers. Lucero's manic defenses dramatically escalated: she would become frantically busy, play with striking expansive energy, inundate the room with words (many of which were incomprehensible in either English or Spanish), yell, and emit forced exaggerated laughter. In the sandbox, she would play with making the sand "disappear," probably attempting to manage the anxiety the two-week vacation was eliciting. Lucero would not allow the therapist to talk directly about her feelings. She ignored the therapist or cursed at her if she offered a clarification of feelings. During the last session prior to the two-week interruption, in an attempt to alleviate the immediacy of Lucero's distress, the therapist suggested that she and

Lucero put the baby dolls to sleep, singing to them to soothe them. With her fear of abandonment thus displaced onto the dolls, Lucero began to calm somewhat. Therapist and child then each drew a picture and signed it. They exchanged pictures before the session's end, and the therapist's absence began.

Upon the therapist's return, close to Christmas, Lucero played with the play-dough, making elongated figures. Her mother reported during this time that Lucero's father had used to dress up as Santa Claus. The following is an excerpt from a session just after Christmas. Lucero wordlessly had evoked her father in play, and then had paused, half-distractedly.

Therapist: Do you miss someone at Christmas?
Lucero: But my mommy bought me gifts, not Santa.
Therapist: Santa didn't bring anything?
Lucero: No, because Santa doesn't have toys.
Therapist: Do you miss Santa?
Lucero: A little, yes. Santa is poor.
Therapist: How do you know?
Lucero: My mommy told me. He doesn't have gifts: doesn't have toys.
Therapist: How did it go without daddy?
Lucero: My daddy was with God.

During the sessions that followed, Lucero manifested her yearning and perplexity with particular force. She showed marked confusion in her play; she would ask to play with board games but insisted that no rule be followed. This invariably led to chaos. She frequently and fragmentarily invoked sugar, the big tummy (*panzota*), food, and Thanksgiving during sessions. She wrote "Jesus" on the blackboard, her grandmother's name and the place where she believed her father to be. Her manic defenses, use of rigid orders to control the therapist, and the sadistic content of her play and demeanor all escalated dramatically. There was almost an element of frenzy—of this youngster working as hard as she could to express what she needed to understand, but having too little time. At that point the therapist added another session per week. With this increased frequency of sessions, Lucero was better able to gain functional access to her sadness and emptiness. The therapist viewed her manic defenses as a safeguard against utter despair. When these defenses began to yield, she came closer to the abyss but bravely continued on (Hoffman, 1989).

In one of the next sessions, Lucero began to gather crayons, chalk and markers rapidly and energetically, while laughing in a strikingly exaggerated manner. She wrote, "who, why."

Therapist: Are you asking who and why?
Lucero: (Continues to draw expansively and feigns a loud belch)
Therapist: Are you thinking about your daddy?
Lucero: Yes, and mommy too. My daddy is here!
Therapist: Where?
Lucero: In my home.
Therapist: Are you missing daddy?
Lucero: Yes. (Her energy decreases and she appears sad for the first time
   in the session.) My daddy likes red. (She writes random letters and says,
   "Daddy.") Is that how you write daddy?
Therapist: No.
Lucero: Show me how.
Therapist: (Writes *daddy*)
Lucero: (Writes *daddy*)

It was around this time that a series of events transpired within the
parent conferences which had a significant impact on the evolution of
Lucero's treatment and eventually facilitated Lucero's mourning process proper. Jaime, the mother's brother, agreed to come to a parent
session in which we discussed Lucero's behavior and its possible meaning within the family constellation. Shortly afterward, her mother
agreed to encourage Lucero's interaction with her peers. She enrolled
her in swimming lessons and invited friends over to their home. But
most important, the mother began to speak of her own (incomplete)
mourning for her husband. She was visiting the cemetery. Lucero was
protesting that she wanted to go, too; her mother, feeling overwhelmed,
insisted on going alone.

   In the Hispanic Catholic culture, offering flowers to the dead is a
tradition that is usually adhered to meticulously. The therapist and
supervisor struggled over how to manage this situation, taking into
account both the clinical considerations and the need to respect the
relevant cultural and religious values (Shorris, 1992). The therapist
suggested that the mother invite Lucero to the cemetery and explain
that her father was resting there and indicated that Lucero might want
to offer her own flowers at her father's grave. The therapist hoped that
this intervention could clarify Lucero's confusion regarding where her
father was and what had happened to him, thus facilitating her mourning process. The mother, feeling therapeutically supported, agreed to
this suggestion.

   The impact of these interventions was quickly and vividly reflected
in the sessions that followed. From the confusion in the playroom and
the continuous invoking of the almost talismanic "sugar," Lucero's

grieving process at last began to blossom. She used the play telephone to answer the pretend caller's question: "Daddy? Yeah, he's here, but he's resting . . . he's dead . . . but there is a mommy." In another session, the therapist sneezed repeatedly. Lucero responded to this and incorporated it into her play with the dollhouse: "Mommy [indicating doll] is sick!" Asked whether it scared her to think about mommy getting sick and maybe leaving her, she responded "Yes . . . but Jaime also cooks."

Lucero began to reenact her father's death, using dolls in the service of working through. She added flowers to her play, began to build cemeteries and graves, and, as she did so, became silent again in the playroom. Therapeutic interventions included validating the importance of thinking about her daddy. The therapist understood Lucero's silence as her way to connect with and retain her internalization of her father. Numerous symbolic affective expressions, including sadness, rage, and joy characterized the treatment sessions (see Pine, 1990). The therapist's role consisted of labeling and clarifying Lucero's ambivalence regarding her father's death—her mournful pain for her once-sick-but-now-"resting" father and her anger at his abandonment of her.

During the later stages of treatment, Lucero's improvement was having an impact on the family constellation. Meetings of the therapist with her mother and her school teachers helped to consolidate Lucero's therapeutic gains. The school had considered transferring Lucero to an ESL (English as a Second Language) class. The therapist suggested, despite concerns about Lucero's limited classroom verbalizations, that she be kept with her classmates provisionally. Lucero was talking with her friends in school (though not in the classroom) and becoming increasingly socially involved. One of the most difficult tasks in working with multicultural populations is to negotiate the thin line between the therapist's potential to normalize pathology and to pathologize normality. A normal behavior in one cultural context may be "different" in another context yet not pathological. On the other hand, a *truly* pathological process does not cease to be pathological even amidst cultural differences. This struggle was especially difficult during this stage of treatment. The current extended family unit consisted of persons who had left their native country in search of personal and financial security. What they were facing now was the ensuing identity conflict, the struggle between assimilating into the new culture and retaining their native, formative identity. Her mother's resistance to Lucero's treatment began to escalate notably. She would cancel sessions and refer to multiple financial obstacles (which were inconsistent with the information we had about family income), and she made plans to take Lucero to Nicaragua for their annual month-long visit despite recommendations from both school and therapist to the contrary. The therapist needed to understand this "resistance" in the context of her cultural and social realities, yet attend to the possible underlying psychodynamic meaning. On the one hand, the mother was a single Hispanic woman attempting to raise a daughter in a "foreign world." She came from a culture where the empowerment of women is achieved primarily vis-à-vis her roles as wife-of-a-provider and as mother. On the other hand, she had not worked through her own mourning process and she was refusing to continue treatment for herself. Lucero's improvement, occurring in the midst of her mother's unresolved mourning process, seemed to accentuate her mother's tendency to feel persecuted, and envious of what she could not receive for herself. Lucero's improvement, the therapist believed, also threatened her self-image as an adequate mother, one able to meet her daughter's needs. Considering these factors along with Lucero's clinical needs, the therapist scaled back sessions to once weekly.

Mother and Lucero did go back to Nicaragua for the annual visit. Lucero understood this as an abandonment by her therapist. In response to this anticipated abandonment, her sessions immediately before her trip were characterized by confusion, the return of anal preoccupation (withholdingness and farts), and sadism. Lucero gave the therapist orders, increasingly found fault, and appeared to entertain fantasies of harming the therapist.

After several sessions characterized by this pattern, the therapist had a countertransference experience that guided an interpretation. On that day, Lucero "caught her" eating a mint, noted that the therapist had lost weight, and when she saw the sandbox commented that there was less sand than usual. Prior to conceptualizing these events as expressions of the anticipation and experience of abandonment (withholding of food; there being "less of" the therapist—less sugar), the therapist associated to a period in her own life when she felt remarkably frightened and utterly alone. Although she had not consciously established the framework, she told Lucero: "It's really yucky to feel that there is not enough of me, right?" Lucero nodded and, as if by "magic," her defenses notably de-escalated.

Close attention to the process of countertransference had permitted the therapist to understand just how frightened and alone Lucero felt. She seemed to believe that not only her therapist but also her mother—and even the availability of all necessary nourishment in the world—were slipping away, as sand slips through one's fingers. As this was interpreted to Lucero, her defenses de-escalated significantly. She used her remaining previsit sessions with much less distress and with a restored range of relatedness. Upon her return from Nicaragua, she was able to reenter the playroom in a productive manner.

The termination of Lucero's treatment had an almost textbook quality of recapitulation and reenactment of her therapy experience. Themes of loss, yearning, expulsion, destruction, and confusion predominated. The following segment provides a glimpse of the quality of these sessions. Lucero had been told about the impending termination, and several sessions had been devoted to her concerns about it. Her play in this particular session began as chaotic, lacking structure and order. She was holding a dog puppet.

Therapist: Do you think I'm leaving because I'm angry?
Lucero: No!
Therapist: Because you've been bad?
Lucero: (Long silence, whose character shifts to a softly mournful contemplation)
Therapist: Are you thinking about daddy?
Lucero: Yes (softly, a bit of yearning).
Therapist: He loved you, even if he's no longer here. It's okay to be silent.
Lucero: (Uses dog puppet, suddenly makes him bark)
Therapist: Is he angry?
Lucero: No, he's a dog. He's only a little angry.
Therapist: Yes?
Lucero: Yes, he's hungry.
Therapist: Do you want to feed him?
Lucero: He's hungry because mommy and daddy won't feed him and he doesn't have a tummy (*panzota*) . . . Mommy is taking away his teeth because he's not eating (concerned tone).
Therapist: How can we help him?
Lucero: Feed him and don't pull teeth out. (She feeds the dog and then has the dog feed the therapist.)
Therapist: Do you think the dog will get a *panzota?*
Lucero: No. (Continues to feed dog)
Therapist: Is the *panzota* getting a little bit bigger?
Lucero: Yes, because he's eating.
Therapist: Because we love him a lot.
Lucero: Should we tuck him in?
Therapist: Where do you think we could do that?
Lucero: (Looks at empty bedroom in dollhouse, tucks dog in the dollhouse bed, and pretends to put play food inside the dog's tummy)
Therapist: (Gives dog a goodnight kiss)
Lucero: (Takes a woman puppet and has it kiss the dog, too) She sleeps with him. She wants to because she doesn't have a mommy or a daddy.

Therapist: She wants to be very close to him?
Lucero: Yes.
Therapist: (Nods head to convey understanding)
Lucero: (Becomes sad, silent, looks longingly at therapist)
Therapist: (Playing a hunch) Were you thinking about giving a hug?
Lucero: (Rushes over to therapist, gives her a long hug)
Therapist: You're working so hard . . . and doing so well!

During the last session, having previously discussed this with the mother and having gotten her approval, the therapist gave Lucero a (real) tortilla maker (Talan, 1989). Lucero instructed the therapist to write her name on it, and Lucero then wrote her own name. Lucero also gave the therapist a card. On the upper left-hand corner was the therapist's name, and on the bottom right-hand corner she had written "is mom," bounded by a large smiling face on one side and a smaller one on the other.

This case study highlights the importance of plunging into exploration of the patient's process, to navigate and discover along the journey the intricacies and dynamics of her internal and external worlds. It is essential to juxtapose understanding of unconscious contents with understanding of external realities.

What, then, was the meaning of silence for Lucero? Clinically, elective mutism is a very dramatic symptom. For Lucero, this symptom appears to have been a compelling way to retain her attachment to her father, simultaneously to offer silent tribute while being withholdingly angry. As her play with sugar indicated, her yearning—her hunger for the retention of his sweet affection—was instrumental in developing and sustaining her mutism and its associated symptomatology. Thus, even though the silence originated in indescribable, wordless pain, the metaphors in her play poignantly suggested its inherent sweetness—the sweet need to connect to a lost father and to struggle never to lose him fully.

In a recent discussion of her work, Isabel Allende was asked whether she considered magical realism an expression of her love for life, or an escape from reality. She suggested a third alternative: magical realism *is* reality, a way of embracing what we are otherwise unable to control or grasp, a way that transcends what we can sense or perceive. She elaborated her response, citing examples of the symbols and metaphors that prevail in the world and in our lives. This is one of the reasons that working with children is so enchanting. Children do not need to dichotomize reality and fantasy. For them, that distinction simply does not exist in its rigid adult totality. Thus, the internalization of external reality takes place through a series of rich, complex, and interactive metaphors. Working with these metaphors allows us to understand the internal world of children, in the service of helping them to resolve conflict and integrate the diverse aspects of their world.

BIBLIOGRAPHY

ALLENDE, I. (1986). *The House of the Spirits*. New York: Bantam.
ALMOND, B. R. (1990). The secret garden: A therapeutic metaphor. *Psychoanal. Study Child*, 45:477–94.
FREUD, A. (1965). *Normality and Pathology in Childhood: Assessments of Development*. New York: Int. Univ. Press.
GOLDBLATT, M. (1972). Psychoanalysis of the school child. In *Handbook of Child Psychoanalysis: Research, Theory, and Practice*, ed. B. B. Wolman, pp. 253–96. New York: Van Nostrand Reinhold.
HOFFMAN, L. (1989). The psychoanalytic process and the development of insight in child analysis: A case study. *Psychoanal. Q.*, 57:63–80.
KLEIN, M. (1975). *Envy and Gratitude and Other Works, 1946–1963*. New York: Delacorte.
PINE, F. (1990). *Drive, Ego, Object and Self: A Synthesis for Clinical Work*. New York: Basic.
SEGAL, H. (1972). Melanie Klein's Technique of Child Analysis. In *Handbook of Child Psychoanalysis: Research, Theory, and Practice*, ed. B. B. Wolman, pp. 401– 14. New York: Van Nostrand Reinhold.
SHORRIS, E. (1992). *Latinos*. New York: W. W. Norton.
TALAN, K. H. (1989). Gifts in psychoanalysis: Theoretical and technical issues. *Psychoanal. Study Child*, 44:149–63.
WEISS, S. (1985). How culture influences the interpretation of the Oedipus Myth. In *The Oedipus Papers*, ed. G. H. Pollock and J. M. Ross, pp. 373–85. Madison, Conn.: Int. Univ. Press, 1988.

APPLIED PSYCHOANALYSIS

Traumatic Memory and the Intergenerational Transmission of Holocaust Narratives

ANNE ADELMAN, Ph.D.

This paper investigates the roles of affect regulation, narrative cohesion, and symbolic representation in the intergenerational transmission of the Holocaust experience. A study of the reminiscences of mothers who are Holocaust survivors and their daughters' reflections about the Holocaust illustrates the process of the transmission of trauma by tracing the transgenerational evolution of narrative forms, dynamic themes, and affective organization. The quality of the survivor parent's organization and integration of affect has significant bearing on how her child assimilates her knowledge of the Holocaust and develops the capacity to tolerate and express painful emotions. Through the preservation, transformation, and transmutation of traumatic memory, children of survivors strive to assimilate, redeem, and transform their tragic historical legacy.

And still it is not yet enough to have memories. One
must be able to forget them when they are many and

Instructor, Yale Child Study Center and Department of Psychiatry, Yale University School of Medicine. This paper is rooted in research undertaken for my doctoral dissertation, entitled "Representation and Remembrance: On Retelling Inherited Narratives of the Holocaust," City University of New York, June 1993. I thank Dr. Michael Moskowitz for advising me in the early stages of my dissertation, for chairing my dissertation committee, and, ultimately, for giving me the courage to pursue this topic, which is of both personal and professional interest to me. I thank Dr. Deborah Dwork for following the development of my ideas, for her dedication to the subject, and for her devotion to my work. I am also most grateful to Mr. Steven Nagler, who helped me explore the contemporary clinical applications of these ideas.

one must have the great patience to wait until they
come again. For it is not yet the memories themselves.
Not till they have turned to blood within us, to glance
and gesture, nameless and no longer to be distinguished from ourselves—not till then can it happen
that in a most rare hour the first word of a verse arises
in their midst and goes forth from them.

—RILKE, "Blood Remembering"

In the quiet of her kitchen, Helena told me simply and
directly about her experience. "It will never be forgotten," she explained. "It's something—you cannot get
rid of it, never. Till you die, it's still fresh . . . You feel
close to people who went through the same. I have
friends, Americans here, my neighbors. I meet them, I
play cards with them, I take part in something. But,
you know, this is not real . . . Sure, I remember. I remember everything." Her daughter Tanya told me, "It
was like my mother was always feeding me stories . . .
And I think I probably became a writer in order to be
able to tell her story . . . My feeling is that it was always
really difficult for my parents. . . . I felt I was stuck in a
ghetto, a ghetto of my parents' making. I think I just
wanted to escape that . . . I started writing this poetry,
and the first poem I ever wrote was called 'Child of the
Holocaust.' I have to look it up, I can't remember it,
that's funny . . . 'I was born a child of the universe,
always a child of the Holocaust.'"

THIS IS A STORY OF HOW MEMORIES ARE SALVAGED FROM THE WRECKAGE OF
traumatic history through oral testimony. It is also a story of the replacement and regeneration of memory through narrative form. In
the following discussion, I draw upon findings from my research on
Holocaust-survivor mothers and their daughters. I interviewed twenty
pairs of mothers and daughters about their early experiences and the
mothers' memories of the Holocaust. Both early memories and memories of traumatic life experiences, obtained from a semistructured clinical interview, were used to assess individuals' psychic structure and
representational world. I proposed that memories of traumatic events,
like early memories, can be viewed as expressions of dominant psychological themes, as relationship paradigms, and as representations of
self and other, of internal conflict, and of defensive and adaptive operations. Through their form, content, and structure, memories of traumatic events reflect an individual's ways of synthesizing and organizing

painful experiences. They also reveal deficits and lacunae in that individual's efforts to process and integrate distressing memory fragments.

A central finding of this study is that traumatic events are encoded in memory in different ways than are nontraumatic episodes in terms of affective organization, representation, and cognition. Experiences of trauma lead to changes in the self, which provide the vehicle for intergenerational transmission of trauma. The Holocaust created a rupture in history that gave rise to a duality of experience with profound consequences for the post-Shoah generations.

Survivor parents' affective and representational organization influence their children's capacity to integrate traumatic memories. Mothers' levels and styles of communication influence their daughters' affectivity and representational worlds. There is an exchange between mother and daughter through verbal and nonverbal forms of expression, which permits psychological integration, acknowledgment, and acceptance. On the mother's capacity to tolerate her daughter's emotions depends the daughter's ability to put experience into words, to contextualize experience, and to approach a resolution of traumatic memory.

DIFFERENCES IN THE ENCODING OF TRAUMATIC AND NON-TRAUMATIC MEMORY

Lived experiences are encoded in memory not only as autobiographical facts but also as psychological structures that are woven together to form the fabric of our self-perceptions and our perceptions of others and the world. These internal representations of self and other are enduring structures of personality organization. Throughout the course of maturation, enduring traits and internally consistent modes of organizing experience persist as core dimensions of personality that ensure self-sameness and continuity of self-identity across developmental transitions and shifts. How we construe early experience forms the backdrop against which later experiences and relationships are interpreted and organized.

A common thread running through the clinical literature on massive psychic trauma is that of the pathogenic effects of traumatic experiences on personality organization. In the group of twenty pairs of mothers and daughters I interviewed, the narration of traumatic memories led to regressive shifts in affective and representational organization characterized by basic concerns with self-regulation and homeostasis. However, the stability of personality organization persisted despite these dramatic fluctuations in affectivity and object representation. These survivors and their daughters invoked a new set of organizing principles to integrate and make sense out of their memories of trauma. They passed from one mode of organizing experience to another, as if the Holocaust represented a pocket of the universe with unique laws of self-regulation and definitions of self and other. The narrative construction of particular episodes in which pretraumatic memory and traumatic experience clashed dramatically illustrates this point. These episodes—moments in which two fundamentally different types of experience unfolded in parallel but not related universes—were characterized by duality.

At one point in her narrative, for example, Irena recalled her arrival at Auschwitz and her separation from her father:

> I had a little bag where I had, you know, they call it in Europe "necessaries"—where I had a piece of soap and a washcloth and some cologne and a toothbrush, you know. And I was standing with my mother, my grandmother, myself, and all of a sudden I feel somebody tapping on my shoulder. It was my father, handing me that bag, you know? Red bag with a zipper, which he brought me from Budapest once. And I looked back, but I didn't see my father, 'cause I saw a Hungarian soldier hitting an old Jew, and I saw the blood trickling down his beard. And after that I was just very scared and I was never hungry and I didn't care or anything.

In this moment, Irena captures her experience of being caught midstream, on the threshold between the ordinary, benevolent, familiar, and comforting world of her childhood and the brutal, bizarre, inhuman, and "extra-ordinary" (Debórah Dwork, personal communication, 1993) universe of Auschwitz.

Esther recalls another moment of separation:

> We came to Auschwitz and—I always feel somehow, feel like I have a guilty conscience. It is not—then they separated the men from the women. And my mother took me by the arm, because if my father goes with the boys, at least we should stay together, I shouldn't get lost. It was such a turmoil, such a thing! And she only, only schlepped me by the arm, we should stay together. And this was the problem. 'Cause my mother was a young woman still—she was forty-five years old, she could have passed through, she was a strong woman—just because we were together, so Dr. Mengele separated us. So—I don't remember any more. He told me to go to the right, my mother on the left, and we didn't see her any more.

Esther's secure relationship with her mother and her unshakable faith that her mother's strong arm wrapped around her provided a safe haven, belonged to the set of basic assumptions that organized her prewar existence. The all too human malice of Mengele—an illogical structure which then forms the basis for its own set of assumptions ("just because we were together, so Dr. Mengele separated us")—exists in another, hellish universe in which fundamental human ties are ruptured. Yet Esther's memory reveals that neither truth eradicates the other. Her emotional tie to her mother, her feelings of guilt arising in the context of the prewar universe in which she acquired a moral conscience, is as present and as internally alive to her as the memory of trauma and its shattering psychological consequences.

Memories such as these reveal how Holocaust survivors and their children reconstruct two discrete but simultaneous ways of knowing and being in the world—in a sense, two worlds. It is in retrospective inquiry that these two worlds become interlocked. The narratives quoted above, which capture the collision of two universes, also capture—in the very moment of their telling—the process wherein the narrative itself creates a bridge that restores the severed connections in the self. Changes in the self occur at the moment of recognition, when the survivor turns to her face in the mirror and finds reflected back both the "me" of prewar existence and the "not-me" of the Holocaust. "Sometimes, sometimes," says Bella, "I don't believe it myself. I don't believe myself what I went through." Transformations in the self emerge as the face of the "me" turns its gaze upon the face of the "not-me" and slowly acknowledges its own reflection.

The following clinical vignette will serve to highlight the transgenerational evolution of traumatic memories and their narrative forms.

RUTH AND LILLY

Ruth, a sixty-seven-year-old Holocaust survivor, is an artist currently living and working in a large city. We met in her studio, a small room crammed with canvases, papers, and books. An old typewriter sat on a writing table covered with notes, letters, and evidence of work in progress. The paintings on the walls were striking in their intensity of color, movement, and graphic forms.

About Ruth herself there was an equal intensity. She was poised, articulate, and graceful as she told me her story. Once or twice she asked me to turn off the tape recorder, and then we sat in silence for a moment before she resumed her narrative. As Ruth spoke, I heard the tension between her wish to remain dry, imperturbable, matter-of-fact and the sharp undercurrents of intense emotions that she did not articulate. Although she seems to need not to feel them herself, these emotions are powerfully evoked in the listener. As we shall see, it is clear that her daughter Lilly feels them too.

Ruth's narrative was especially noteworthy for the minute, detailed descriptions that sometimes absorbed her quite fully. Often she seemed to forget that I was there while she searched inwardly for a reconnection to her to the thoughts and feelings she had had during her experiences in Warsaw. Sometimes she would come up against the blankness and loss of feeling she had experienced during the war: "I had no feelings or no thoughts." At other times, what she discovered in looking back were truncated connections to her past experiences. She was unable to rediscover and reexperience what she had felt then:

> At that time—I was alone—I wrote poetry. It just came and I wrote everything down, what came to me. It was a sort of salvation for me. I had, when the war ended, I had a rather large book filled with that, and somehow—I met a friend and she said "Let me have it, I'll publish it." So I gave it to her and that was the last I saw of it. She lost it somewhere along the way . . . This was—not possible to reconstruct. I had no more of those feelings I had then and I just didn't remember, it's impossible. No, I lost my language. When I came here I couldn't write, I had no . . . At that time it was just flowing, I guess, suffering . . . I don't know, I'm not going to go into it . . . You could not duplicate this.

Ruth's halting, disjointed narrative echoes these severed links to her past.

Ruth was fifteen years old when the war broke out. She spent the war years in hiding, smuggled out of the Warsaw ghetto by a Catholic woman who later led her to an underground bunker, where she remained for several months.

Early childhood had been a time of warm and sometimes pleasurable experiences for Ruth. She was reared primarily by her nursemaid, although she recalls a very close relationship with her mother, whom she idolized. Her descriptions of moments spent with her mother are evocative and sensory: "She was playing piano. That was just fine because she had tremendous technique. I remember myself sitting by the piano, with my ear towards, just listening. For hours I was sitting on the floor with the ear to the piano as she played. . . . I cannot describe this—that was heaven, I guess."

Of her father, Ruth's memories are more mixed. He was a journalist, educated and refined, who was well integrated into Polish culture and the Warsaw community. He was charitable and kind-hearted, but his temper terrified her. Her most vivid memories of him have to do with being badly frightened by his volatility and by a sense of humor that was morbid and scary to a child.

Ruth's memory of the beginning of the war is of an exciting, almost exhilarating sense of escapade. Yet as she describes her "adventures," what comes through as subtext are the terrifying and harsh conditions that confronted her as a fifteen-year-old school girl:

> It was an adventure. I was going places. I was afraid I'll miss something at that time . . . Jewish schools were closed, and the air raids were on Warsaw. We left. I was very happy going. After the first day of walking I was less happy. I was tired. My feet hurt. I was thirsty. I saw dead horses laying on the road. And I ran away into a ditch hiding from the planes that were shooting at us. But I never thought I was in any danger. There was adventure. And we slept outdoors. It was terrific. I never slept outdoors before, under the trees . . . This was a real adventure.

Although she denies being afraid, her narrative reveals the terror and uncertainty that lay just beneath the surface. It is striking that even in retrospect, she is unable to acknowledge the horrifying reality that confronted her. Indeed, it may well have been that the terror did not become real until afterwards (Debórah Dwork, personal communication). There is a broad gap between what she conveys nonverbally and what she is willing to put into words:

> When the war was being announced on the radio, I started to cry hysterically. *I have no idea why.* But I was crying so hysterically that they couldn't quiet me down. I had—maybe it was premonition, I don't know. But I don't even know why I was crying so. What did I know about the war? I had a good life, an exceptionally good life. What did I know about the war? Why was I crying? But I was hysterical. [*emphasis mine*]

Following that initial departure from Warsaw, Ruth lived on her own in an apartment in a small town near Bialystock, where her sister and brother-in-law lived. There, she tasted the freedom and independence of an adolescent emerging into adulthood. She attended school and went to dances and social events. However, this freedom was short-lived, for the school was closed, and Ruth had neither food nor money. Missing her mother and her family, Ruth took leave of her sister and returned to Warsaw. That was the last time she saw her sister. What became of her sister is the first of many questions regarding her narrative that remain unanswered, both in Ruth's mind and in the mind of the listener: "They [sister and brother-in-law] remained in the place that the Germans took over, and that was not too far from Babi Yar. And I think this is where they ended up, in Babi Yar. Because I know they did not go—we received a letter to that effect from . . . yes . . . Stop for awhile." The disruption in her narrative parallels the inner disjunction she experiences at the collapse of the knowable and the unuttered grief that rushes in to close the gap in her knowledge.

In the early stages of the war, Ruth was an adolescent on the threshold of achieving psychological separation and independence from her parents. Her thinking has a kind of magical quality typical of adolescents, who do not yet believe in their own mortality. Ruth recalls having an only superficial understanding of the deteriorating situation in Warsaw. To protect herself from increasing fear and despair, she immersed herself in books, social gatherings, and artistic pursuits.

At the same time, on a deeper level, Ruth was preparing for a new phase of her development. Her strong pull toward a dependent, childlike stance was giving way to a developmental thrust toward maturity and autonomy. This developmental transition, however, was suspended on the day her mother was taken to Treblinka: She recalls her attempts to tend to the oozing sore on her neck that her mother had nursed daily:

> I was sick because this [wound] started to act up. . . . So then it started to ooze and everybody was very concerned with that wound I had here. It had to be changed constantly because it started—a terrible odor was given out. I had so many bandages, that day that my mother didn't come back. I worked myself—almost twenty-five bandages, you know, gauze bandages. They were re-used constantly. I washed it myself that day. I was so proud that that day, for the first time in my life, I peeled potatoes and I cooked potatoes, for the first time in my life. And I was waiting to get that pat on the head, that I am such a hero, that I boiled potatoes. I never did. She never came home. And so many bandages that she usually washed, that day I did it myself.

Shortly afterwards, Ruth's father was arrested in the market place and taken to Treblinka. For Ruth, the process of separation and the development of autonomy was interrupted by the final and all too real separation from her parents, which came without warning. Her narrative conveys the impression of a moment frozen in time, defined in terms of its lack of resolution and closure. She never obtained the much-needed and wished-for affirmation of her step toward increased autonomy. Instead, she was left wondering whether her actions had any meaning or impact in the world.

Ruth now had to wrestle alone with a reality that she did not understand. Although she lacked definitive information about her mother's whereabouts, she realized that her failure to return home could have only one meaning. Nonetheless, the event retained an aura of mystery, confusion, and disbelief—an aura that permitted Ruth to hope against hope while simultaneously preventing her from mourning the loss. This engendered a profound duality in her experience: Ruth knew instinctively what she would not allow herself to acknowledge—that she would not see her mother again. Yet her powerful resistance against knowing permitted her to maintain the belief that her mother was alive and waiting for her. This belief sustained her long after her belief in her own ability to survive had dissipated. "I was sure I would not survive the war," she tells me, "although I tried very hard because I knew that my mother was going to look for me after the war. So that was my aim, not to disappoint her somehow and try to survive." This duality between knowing and not knowing is a dominant theme in Ruth's memory organization.

As she proceeded with her narrative, her sense of time as well as the tempo of her story ebb and flow, lingering over minute details one moment, then skipping forward to the telling of the next event as a way of firmly closing the door on the previous one. Her emotions, too, are frozen. Her narrative voice becomes grim and impassive:

> I was working at the time . . . making fabric from threads. First the threads were put on the row, and then this was put on the bar, and this was feeding the machine, and machine was making the fabric and the fabric was coming out. Was very interesting. First, I was working when it was going out from spools, and I was watching spools. And there was a man there, making big roll from the threads. And then one day there was a, they were taking people away, so they took that man. And he said to me, "You know how to work it, so now you go work this part." He was standing in the door, and he waved to me, said "Bye! I'll meet you on the shelf with the soap!" There were rumors that they were making soap out of Jews. But that was rumors. Who believes that? So he made the joke. "I'll meet you on the shelf with soap." I don't know whether he survived or didn't. I have no idea. One thing is for sure, I was not on the shelf with soap.

In the months following her parents' arrest, Ruth spent her time in various hiding places, being helped by some people, while others threatened or betrayed her. She recounts that she was taken in by a Catholic family and hidden in a crate on their balcony. She recalls a time when her life had lost all value and purpose. Once, someone confronted the Polish woman who was hiding her: "One day somebody came and said, 'What do you have, rabbits out there on the balcony?' So she said 'No, just garbage.' So that is what I was doing there." She goes on to say,

> It was not easy, and into the bargain I was sick. Forget about this neck that was oozing. I developed new things. I was hungry. I was swollen from hunger. And I also had crabs, I don't know whether you know what it is. A little spider, sort of, that sits in your skin. Doesn't go anyplace, but sits there and multiplies. My best pleasure was when I was scratching till I bled. Till whatever I was scratching started to bleed, then it didn't itch as much. That was my only pleasure at the time.

Ruth could gain access to her feelings only through reviving bodily sensations that provided, through pain, a pathway back to knowing that she was alive.

It was when Ruth ultimately joined a group of people hiding in an underground bunker that she began to feel again the stirrings of her active will to live. Being part of a group—having actions made meaningful by membership in a collectivity and orientation toward its causes—roused her determination to survive, so deeply tied to her fantasy that her mother would be waiting for her after the war was over. Ruth's liberation marked the return of emotion:

> At night, somebody walked out and heard from far away singing, Russian singing. And so he went further—was not too far—and heard singing in Yiddish. They couldn't understand this, and 'Maybe we are liberated?' And that is how it was. We were liberated. We went out from the bunker at night. We started to cry something awful. I knew already I was liberated. I couldn't control myself. I don't know why I was crying but I was. Terrible crying . . . . It's very hard to say why I was crying. I don't know why I was crying. I just felt alone, very much alone.

Her tears are reminiscent of the tears she cried at the onset of the war— tears without words. It is impossible for Ruth to put into words the emotions that flooded her. Liberation brought with it not only the revival of feeling but also the recognition of being utterly alone. She did not, however, completely relinquish her hope that another family member had survived. Immediately following liberation, she set off on a search for her mother, although, as she states, "At that time, you see, I already understood more than before that there was nobody alive anymore. I saw what was happening. But of course someplace down there I still believe that maybe somewhere . . . till the last moment you . . . But I know that time when my mother went, everybody went to Treblinka, nobody came out from there—I was still looking." Her narrative—its breaks, its shifts from past to present and back, its unfinished thoughts—recapitulates in its form the evanescent ties between the living and the dead. The absolute knowledge that her mother is dead collides with her yearning and the fantasy of reunion that endures, bolstered by the enormity of her need and the absence of some concrete marker of death.

For Ruth, becoming a mother was inextricably linked to her traumatic loss of her own mother and her truncated childhood. The birth of her first child brought with it a flood of grief, mourning, and terror. Feelings of guilt because she was alive while her own mother had perished pervaded the experience. Ruth deeply identified with what she recognized as her baby's utter aloneness and absolute dependence:

When she was born, I had one thought: "That little thing has nobody in the entire—in the world." I am the only one that she had. I didn't like her even. I am just looking at her. "Look what I did. That is my entire responsibility. She hasn't got anybody in the world." You see, later on comes to motherhood, I guess, but in the beginning, it was just "Look at this strange thing." I said, "She is ugly. She has hair all over the place." Of course, later on the hair evaporated and the eyes became less red, and she was a glorious baby according to the standard. And she liked to eat, she was always hungry and she had enough food and so she thrived, O.K.? . . . I really didn't know what to do with the baby. I was just holding her, I was telling her stories, I was singing to her, and she was everything I had at the time.

For Ruth, the very act of mothering brought with it vivid and devastating reminders of the brutal bodily assault she suffered during the war. She explains that, shortly after the birth, she developed a breast infection that required invasive surgery. She recalls not the pain but the terror that her baby would die without her, while she was in the hospital: "I was all covered with bandages, operated, and it still didn't hurt yet. I said 'I have to go home.' They said, 'How could you go home now?' I said, 'I have to go home, I have a baby home. I have to feed the baby. She is going to starve to death.'" However, when Ruth arrived at home, she became aware of the extent of the surgery: "Then I saw what was happening in my breast. It was open in three places and . . . at each opening there was a rubber thing [a tube], for drainage, not to let it heal. But I still fed her from one breast." Ruth estranged from and mystified by her daughter and fed her dispassionately and without pleasure. Her experience of mothering is characterized by polarization of positive and negative affect states. Though she feels as though the very life and vitality are drained out of her and emptied into the hungry mouth of her helpless and needy baby, she is determined to nourish her infant and sustain her life. Her baby experienced a mother who was feeding her through the sheer force of willpower but who could not hold her close to her heart, for fear of opening bottomless wounds.

The vivid intensity of these early moments of their relationship set the stage for the psychic drama enacted between this mother and her daughters over time.

Ruth's second daughter Lilly is a professional woman in her thirties who lives alone in a studio apartment in the same city as her mother. Her physical appearance presents a striking contrast to her mother's stateliness. Lilly is small and heavy, and palpably sad.

Lilly's early memories are characterized by vagueness and contradictions. When I asked her to recall her childhood, her first impulse was to describe her sense of being intimately connected, through her memo-

ries, to her earliest years. However, the promise of such a connection
did not bear fruit. As she spoke, Lilly seemed to lose the threads that
connected her to her childhood, and she began to question the authenticity of her experience.

Lilly's early memories portray a world that is bizarre and unpredictable. Her feelings and her reactions to events are bland, vague, and
emotionless. The memories are not clearly anchored in a definite time
or place. In addition, there is a striking lack of a reliable caregiving
presence. Instead, she conveys the sense that she accepted without
question the transitory and erratic nature of things. For example, she
describes how she was weaned from the bottle:

> I remember when my mother took my bottle away, by telling me that we
> lost it. And I wasn't, particularly, you know—I didn't care one way or the
> other, you know. (Laughs) It's funny 'cause I have this visual sense of her,
> like, being bigger than me, you know what I mean? You know, up there
> somewhere. And I think I remember thinking that it was strange that
> they lost it, but I don't remember being upset, I remember just accepting
> it, you know. Big deal. I guess I didn't have any particular attraction or
> attachment to a bottle. Very strange.

In retrospect, Lilly cannot explain this event to herself. Her memory
captures her confusion between her own feelings and her mother's
fantasies and seems to echo her mother's own traumatic experiences.
In particular, we are reminded of the death of Ruth's mother—a disap-
pearance that was similarly abrupt and unforeseen. Lilly seems to have
learned early on that it is not worthwhile to invest emotionally in anything, because it may simply disappear.

Lilly's early sense of her mother is of "her, like, being bigger than
me . . . up there somewhere." She experiences her as out of reach,
unattainable, and unable to help her with her own loss. Ruth's absorption in her own grieving process excludes her daughter. When Lilly
searches for her mother, she cannot find her. The only connection
available to her is through her mother's loss, grief, and pain—which
she makes her own.

Lilly views her knowledge of the Holocaust as intrinsic to her being, a
part of her very identity: "Well, you have to remember, it's like if I ask
you what was your reaction to learning the alphabet, you know what I
mean? It is something that you just did. You know, you learned *a,b,c,d,*
or you learned how to read." Although Lilly recalled asking her mother
many questions about her Holocaust experiences in her childhood, she
also experienced a sense—which she cannot fully articulate—that
something was being kept from her. It is as if her mother erected
imperceptible barriers that kept Lilly on the outside of the "magic

circle" of knowing. "I think that probably," she tells me, "if anything, I would probably want to know more than what she was telling me, thinking 'Well, there must be more than that.' You know, you can't really force somebody to tell you something." Lilly wasn't told about the Holocaust. Always knowing and yet never knowing her mother's history, she was compelled to discover it in her own history.

This tension between knowing and not being allowed to know was echoed in Ruth's narrative: "She never asked me. She knew everything. I mean, there was nothing. If she had a question, then she asked." She went on to say, "I didn't want to force it on her. I—when she was interested, she would know, but I did not want to stop her, say 'Hey, listen, so and so.' I never did . . . It was probably good that she is interested to a certain extent. Because there are some things that I felt she should know. But I didn't know what she wanted to know, so I couldn't initiate the telling." Ruth's ambivalence about telling arises out of her need for her daughter to understand and withstand her pain and her simultaneous recognition that would be an impossible feat. Mother and daughter jointly defend against intense despair and grief, fearing that, if the floodgates were to open, they both would be swept away in the torrent.

Lilly's narratives of the Holocaust are sparsely detailed, spun together out of the threads of her fantasies rather than out of stories her mother has told her. She herself finds it difficult to distinguish between the "truth" and what she has put together out of television images and dramatizations: "I don't know if this is true, it is just my sense of it"; "I don't know what life was like then"; "I just don't know." In telling her mother's story, she was dismayed by the great gaps in her recollections. Lilly cannot seem to hold onto a consistent and coherent narrative of her mother's history. Her knowledge of her mother's experience is characterized by a jumble of paradoxical images. For example, although she is certain that her mother had sufficient food while she lived underground ("at night they would go out and get whatever they want"), she also imagines starvation and degradation ("I don't know if there were rats or anything. I used to think my mother ate rats"). She describes her mother's home as ramshackle ruins, yet pictures lacy curtains in the windows. Thus, Lilly reveals the difficulty she has in reconciling the reality she has come to understand as an adult with the fantasies she had as a child. At those moments when there is a gap in her knowledge, her narrative wavers and her fantasies about her mother's experiences take the foreground. In this way she attempts to repair, through remaking, the broken link in the transgenerational chain.

In order to understand fully the transmission of knowledge of the Holocaust from Ruth to Lilly, we need to look beyond the direct communications that mother and daughter describe to the indirect, unconscious modes of transmission and transposition (see Kestenberg, 1982). Compare, for example, Ruth's first memory of *her* mother to Lilly's earliest childhood memory. Of her own mother, Ruth recalls:

> I don't know how old I was, but she was bending over me and putting compresses on my eyes. I remember it was like cotton, and was wet, and I remember opening my eyes under the cotton. She said, "Open the eyes, let the water go in." Something must have been wrong with my eyes. And she bent over the bed, or whatever it was, a crib, I have no idea, but I remember her face there. I was very little, because later on I found out, that must have been about a year and a half.

Lilly's earliest memory is this:

> I have very early childhood memories. I mean I remember being in a crib. You see, I think I've remembered it now—I sort of remember it by remembering it. You know? I think I can't remember it specifically now, but I have remembered it all the years. I mean, I remember lying in my crib and something getting in my eye and I remember thinking it fell down from the ceiling, you know? And I remember my sister's bed across from mine. I was in the crib and she had a bed. I remember thinking I wanted to be able to turn over, because I thought things were falling from the ceiling. Strange concept. I can't remember any more. It must have gone away. I must have gone to sleep.

In her memory, Lilly repeats the theme of Ruth's memory while she simultaneously represents in her inner landscape the gaping hole that was left by the Holocaust and that irrevocably altered her mother's psyche. Ruth's image is of her vision being carefully and tenderly healed by an idealized mothering figure. Lilly's image, reflected from the deep pool of traumatic memory, captures the utter absence of the mothering figure, as well as the desecration of the visual senses created by the Holocaust and the bleak, bizarre, and inexplicable collapse of the universe that ensued (that is, the caving in of the ceiling). Finally, the memories reveal that Ruth's absorption in her own grieving has kept her from constructing for her own daughter the protective maternal shield that her mother provided for her.

Out of this deeply buried sense of loss transmitted unconsciously from mother to daughter, the theme of missing parts has taken shape in Lilly's internal world. Lilly desperately misses something in her fragmentary knowledge of the Holocaust, in her relationship to her mother, and in her ties to her family of origin. At the end of our meeting, she spoke of her enduring wish to locate missing relatives. In particular, she yearns for the grandmother she has never known. Poignantly, Lilly relates that when she and her mother were in Poland recently, they had checked the listings in the telephone book and, startlingly, found Ruth's mother's name. Joining together in a fantasy, they telephoned the woman, their trepidation mingled with hope, only to learn that she was no relation to the family. "So I guess, for a fleeting minute, you know . . . But I think the reality was that my mother knew her mother didn't survive. It was . . . hope against hope."

This vignette exemplifies the exquisitely personal and singular ways in which memories of the Holocaust are borne across the span of generations. It also underscores the impact of trauma on mothering. While survivor parents often harbor the fantasy that they will impart to their children that which they themselves lost, trauma may impede such restitutive parenting. Daughters of survivors often live out their mother's pain through unconscious identifications and introjections. However, we shall also see that daughters may reach beyond their mothers' experiences, achieving greater psychological integration and, perhaps, through their own regeneration and mothering, some healing and some resolution of the past.

MOTHERING AND MOTHERLINESS

All of the mothers in this study had been traumatically separated from their own mothers under horrifying and brutal conditions. These losses profoundly transformed their representations of their mothers and of the mothering relationship. A baby brought into the world in the aftermath of the Holocaust came to represent both hope for the future and remembrance of the past, embedded in a deeply buried longing for resurrection of and reconnection with lost family members. Pregnancy and birth were made more difficult by the psychological and emotional isolation these women experienced. They experienced a profound sense of yearning for their own mothers. The birth of a child—in particular, a daughter—represented a fervent wish to restore the meaning and purpose of their lives and invest hope and belief in the future, while simultaneously searching for a link to the past.

The ambivalent attitudes toward pregnancy and motherhood that women frequently experience was intensified for those whose emergence from adolescence into womanhood transpired during imprisonment in a concentration camp. Starvation, deprivation, malnutrition, and illness in the camps assaulted the body and often led to dramatic physiological changes, such as amenorrhea. Resumption of the menstrual cycle following liberation served as a confirmation of the body's vitality, viability, and fecundity. Thus, the cessation of menstruation during pregnancy could have multiple and often intensely conflictual meanings for them.

Many women described medical complications involving the reproductive organs immediately following liberation. This occurrence frequently heightened both a wish to conceive and a deep ambivalence toward the actual pregnancy. For example, Esther's memories of becoming pregnant are interlocked with her recollections of ovarian surgery:

> They had to remove one ovary and I had, from the ovary I got, a cyst. [Cries.] The doctor said he doesn't know how I could have survived because, anyway, my appendix was completely rotten, infected, and how I didn't get poisoned from it. They couldn't even make the surgery because if they would somehow, just a little—they had to take the cyst out with the water, the cyst shouldn't burst. If it would burst I would get poisoned, my whole insides . . . I could hardly walk on my legs, I was terribly swollen. Then the doctor said to my husband, "You married, and you want to have children—" And you know, I just have one ovary— that we would have to try right away. It was very difficult, very difficult. because I had surgery and was—inside—I had from the surgery, you know, like wounds. My pregnancy, the doctor explained to me, "Your womb is stretching, this is why it's so painful—" because all over I was inside sewn—"but just if you conceive . . . And you are a very lucky woman if you want to have children." I knew I want very badly to have, and I knew my husband, he loves children.

For Esther the experience of fertility and the potential to bring forth new life were inextricably bound up with internal scars, loss of body integrity, and a sense of internal toxicity.

The acutely conflictual feelings surrounding the birth of a child often were heightened by intense identifications with the baby and fantasies of merger. The infant was invested with tremendous narcissistic value. Through identification with a "perfect" baby, a survivor mother could reestablish the link to her prewar, infantile self—and thus to her preverbal memory of herself being a mothered infant— and could simultaneously experience a sense of rebirth and renewed meaning in her own life.

The birth of the newborn also roused profound fears of abandonment and loss. Many women had learned not to hold anyone too close to their heart, for fear that he or she would be brutally snatched away.

To invest emotionally in a fragile new life evoked terror of loss and grave apprehensions about the infant's safety and well-being. These mothers found it difficult, at times, to let go of their children, and reacted to separations with heightened protectiveness and resistance to psychological differentiation.

In some of these women, their memories and depressive affect were accompanied by extremely conflictual responses to the helplessness of their infants. The infantile condition seemed to revive the traumatic memories of their own defenselessness and vulnerability. Often mothers moved back and forth between two poles: at one end, they experienced strong feelings of identification with their baby's helplessness and need for a life-sustaining, nurturing presence; at the other, they strongly repudiated that identification and these needs, split-off, disavowed aspects of themselves that were rooted in their experiences of trauma. Trying to summon up feelings of maternal warmth and protectiveness, they discovered within themselves only fear and despair.

These warring emotions could find expression in conflicts around feeding and nourishing their infants—for instance, fear that there wouldn't be enough food or breast milk, combined with a potent wish to nurse. The ability to provide vital nourishment might restore the link to a mother's own sense of vitality, and she would become immersed in the rituals of mothering. Alternatively, a mother's drive to nourish her infant might be complicated by profound feelings of rage stemming from their own abandonment and deprivation. Caroline was six years old when her father was arrested and her mother deported to a concentration camp. She spent several months fending for herself in the ghetto, roaming bombed-out basements until she was taken into hiding. She recalls with grief her early experiences of mothering her first-born child:

> It was very difficult. I was very unhappy with my own life, with myself. And if you're unhappy with yourself, you obviously can't give to your child. My daughter is, or was, a cranky baby. Or maybe what she needed was a calm mother. She didn't want to eat. I should have left her alone. But I force-fed her, you understand? If she threw up, I hit her, you know what I'm saying? . . . And uh, maybe deep down she didn't understand it, but maybe she realized that it's, you know, the anger in me reflected in her.

Caroline sought to fill up her baby but could not tolerate her baby's refusal to swallow her mother's rage. She achieved some resolution with her third child, born several years later.

My third daughter was born when I was thirty, and I really felt that that was the time when I came into maturity and into myself. And although I didn't want this third child, I must say that I was healed enough to finally know the joys of motherhood by having her. And she was everything a baby should be . . . She had two older siblings who adored her. She was a wonderful baby that proved to me that I can be a normal mother, so it was a wonderful experience. She was beautiful. *She was never demanding of anything, she just thrived and grew on her own.* I was, you know, a normal functioning human being. You know, I still had nightmares, but they did diminish by then. *And when she cried I was no longer angry, but she never cried.* [Italics mine]

In mothering an unwanted baby, Caroline essentially redeemed her own sense of herself and her capacity to sustain life. Her identification with this baby was especially powerful because she viewed her as dispossessed and, at the same time, inherently resilient and tenacious. This perception mirrors her own experience of herself in her traumatic childhood, and her sense that her infant's vitality can promote a process of healing within her. She relinquishes her rage and depression and draws strength from her baby's miraculous health. Although she remains conflicted about her own nurturing role, she can embrace her baby's spirit and participate in her thriving.

Childbirth often set in motion a process of reclamation of feminine identity, bodily integrity, and the capacity to nourish and sustain life. Simultaneously, bearing children reevoked painful feelings of depression, about abandonment, rage, helplessness, alienation, and despair. The mothers could see their children as narcissistic extensions, gratifying essential needs for fulfillment and replacement of lost parts of the self. These early, largely unconscious dynamics laid the foundation for patterns of verbal and nonverbal communication between mother and daughter and set the stage for the intergenerational transmission of trauma.

MODES OF COMMUNICATION AND TRANSMISSION OF MEMORY

Like many survivor parents, the mothers in this study were deeply ambivalent about what and how much to tell their children directly about their traumatic experiences. For example, one mother told me:

We don't talk about the past. I don't know how much she knows. No, we don't talk about it. I didn't talk about it. Why should I put horrible things—? . . . She knows everything, she knows enough . . . And there you have it.

Another said,

> I was deeply ashamed of the fact that I had lived such a—that I had
> experienced such a humiliating experience. Such an unbelievable, inhu-
> man kind of existence. It—it—I was very much ashamed of having lived
> that way . . . I wanted to bring up well-adjusted, strong, happy children
> and therefore it's probably much better that they should never know. I
> forgot that if I bring up these children without telling them the whole
> truth, then in fact they are poorer for it, not richer . . . I think the
> mystery of it may have been a greater burden than finally my unraveling
> the thing for them. But my unraveling didn't really come till very late.

And a third,

> When they were little and they asked "What is this?" [gestures to number
> on her arm]—"It is my telephone number." Not very original, but . . . I
> couldn't—what do you say to a child? I felt like somebody took my
> insides and squeezed it. [Crying] When they asked me, "How come I
> don't have a grandmother or grandfather?" the answer was, "Because
> Hitler killed them." My daughter says she had a picture of this man—
> she knew who Hitler was, one of us must have explained it to her, or she
> saw it, I don't know—and he went around asking with a gun, "Are you
> the grandparents of Karen L.?" and when he found them—boom. I
> didn't explain because I could not.

The decision about what, if anything, to convey to their daughters
about the Holocaust was fraught with anguish. For some, their experiences during the Holocaust, their memories of degradation and humiliation, felt like poison running through their veins, and they feared
that telling would contaminate their children. They bore their past in
silence, like a shameful secret. Sometimes, however, they would ad-
monish their children: "Don't forget. Always remember"—a confusing
and paradoxical injunction to remember the unknown. Others had a
strong wish for their children to know, to understand their past, or to
share their experiences of loss and suffering, often with a simultaneous
wish to protect the children from unimaginable horror. Thus, the
narratives they constructed served both to reveal and to conceal their
traumatic memories. Their descriptions contained denial of events,
distortions, or misrepresentations. This gave rise to narratives that
were confusing, splintered, and conflicting. These narrative disjunc-
tions and distortions can be understood in light of the fluctuations and
regressive flow in the mothers' affective regulation and representational capacities. Many mothers described their worst moments to me
as overwhelming bodily assaults—such as hunger, cold, and pain. In

contrast, their daughters rarely alluded to such experiences in their narratives of the Holocaust. It is likely that they never heard directly from their mothers about these times of bodily anguish.

The daughters also displayed great diversity in the quality of their object representations concerning Holocaust memories. Confronting their mothers' experiences had led to a qualitative shift in representational style, characterized by an inhibition in their capacity to understand others and engage with them in flexible, mutual, and meaningful ways. They tended to identify experiences of separation as the worst moments for their mothers. Their most dramatic regressive shifts and most poorly developed representations were associated with their fantasied representations of their mothers' forced, brutal, and irrevocable separations. Many daughters felt able to identify deeply with these moments of separation, relating them to their own worst experiences or fantasies. However, daughters often sensed that discussing separations was too difficult and upsetting for their mothers, and they learned to not ask questions about these occurrences. Because their mothers often could not help their daughters to regulate or organize the powerful emotions associated with separations, these events became highly meaningful in their inner lives.

Silence carries its own consequences for mothers and children. The mothers in this group who had never told their daughters about their experiences displayed the poorest affect tolerance and expression in both the domains of traumatic and nontraumatic memory. They typically revealed bleak, malevolent, and narrowly defined representational worlds. Their daughters tended to display significant regressive shifts in affectivity in the domain of traumatic memory, contending with their absence of knowledge about the Holocaust through rationalization, avoidance, or denial.

The silence of their mothers gives rise to intense conflict between wanting to know and not wanting to know. Without the freedom to inquire about their mothers' histories, the daughters are left with a sense of nameless dread (S. Nagler, personal communication). The knowledge missing from the fabric of their self-history takes on toxic or deathly meanings, as if the very act of knowing would be destructive, even annihilating. They are simultaneously possessed and dispossessed of their historical legacy. Their fear, that they might become absorbed by their mothers' pain illuminates the fragile nature of the boundaries they maintain between self and other. Silence about the Holocaust gives the illusion of safeguarding the boundaries between their own reality and their mothers' history.

Often, these daughters feel rage at their mothers for not being able to help them to understand and make sense out of their history. Because their mothers have been unable to acknowledge their traumatic experiences, the daughters have lost faith in their mothers' capacity to recognize their need for knowledge. Their mothers' silence leads to profound feelings of abandonment, loss, and anger. If the silence remains unresolved, daughters often turn away, relinquishing their right to their own history and their trust in their mothers' ability to acknowledge the authenticity of their own experience.

DIFFERENCES IN AFFECT EXPRESSION FOR TRAUMATIC AND NONTRAUMATIC MEMORIES

Trauma affects the capacity to verbalize emotion. Traumatic and nontraumatic events are differently encoded in memory, particularly along the dimension of affect expression. The act of narrating the Holocaust brought regressive shifts to the women's ability to articulate emotions and diminished access to a wide array of emotions whether as internal signals or in interpersonal communications. Difficulties in verbalizing narratives of the Holocaust arise in the context of disruptions in the organization of the verbal self (Stern, 1985).

Ellie spoke about her struggle to understand her mother's silence:

> It sort of seems to me that these aren't really things that you can tell so much, that they are more experiences and occurrences and things that happened. And that knowing a vagueness about the situation is really all you can, even if you are told things, because they are not going to bring you there. They are not going to bring you into the situation, you know? It is just—it just wouldn't be real enough to ask for, to ask to be told what it's about. Or to, you know—since you can't really touch it, you can't really be there, however someone would tell you about it. Unless it was to relieve the burden from themselves, somehow. I mean, I don't know . . . I don't think it is sufficient. The magnitude is so vast that it is not even fair to bring an eyedropper out of it. (Pause) The intensity of it. It's sort of an intimacy too, I guess.

Ellie goes on to say that searching within herself for a comparable realm of silence, she finds one related to her past experience of psychosis and psychiatric hospitalization. She is concerned in part with privacy and the limits of compassion, but at the heart of her dilemma lies recognition of the constraints of verbal relatedness: "The intimacy that I had, with being as sick as I was when I was sick, I just—I can't give it to you with words." In her description, she touches upon those aspects of human experience—intimacy and intensity—which lie at the heart of such silence.

The capacity to tolerate affect develops early in life from the child's repeated experiences of displaying affect and having it tolerated, acknowledged, and modulated by the primary caregivers. Through the gradual internalization of the caregiver's empathic responsiveness, attunement, and carefully titrated recalibrations, the infant becomes able to tolerate intense emotion. As these regulatory functions become a part of the ego, the need for a regulatory other is relinquished and intensity of affect is managed and regulated internally. Affect tolerance is not a stable, unidimensional construct, but rather a set of characteristic ways (Wilson, 1987) in which an individual calibrates the ebb and flow of emotional life. It is singular and private. Some affects are more or less disruptive than others and are tolerated in more primitive or less mature forms. Often strong emotions take us unawares, and the self is startled, jostled. Then we may hasten to regain equilibrium through more archaic modes of self-regulation. At other times, when our footholds are secure, it is possible to attend to subtle nuances in our emotional lives with maturity and wisdom.

The verbal self, however, is necessarily—though not solely—a social self. Attaining the capacity to verbalize one's inner life and to use affects effectively as signals and communications is a developmental achievement that succeeds the consolidation of the capacity for affect tolerance. It is made possible by the convergence of language acquisition, the development of a theory of mind, and the development of symbolic thought. Verbal emotional expressivity is a link to one's fellow human beings, so it is fundamentally a dyadic enterprise.

During the Holocaust, dyadic exchange became impossible. The expectation of an empathic response was obliterated. Annihilation of the potential "other" led to an abandonment of the hope for the construction and evolution of shared meanings through verbal relatedness. Dialogue with the other ceased, and silence ensued. And accompanying this silence, there was by necessity a turning inward, toward an interior dialogue. The process of meaning-making took place in the realm of the interior, speechlessly.

The "intimacy" which Ellie referred to is an intimacy with oneself, with the self's absorption in the psychological and physical intricacies of the effort to survive in a hostile universe. Where the other has been extinguished, where there is no predictability or basic trust in empathic human responsiveness, the realm of the inner life becomes profoundly intimate. Recognition and acknowledgement of this interiority is a crucial aspect of the process of narrating the Holocaust. The regressive shift we have observed in the realm of affect expression reflects the collapse of verbal relatedness and dyadic exchange; the process of remembering and organizing memory takes place unceasingly on an internal level. But between the interior dialogue and dyadic verbal expression there is a sweep of empty space which can be spanned. And it is spanned. As this study has shown, it is not accurate to refer to the trauma of the Holocaust as "unspeakable." The mothers and daughters whom I interviewed spoke courageously and cogently about their memories of this event and the meanings it has come to have in their lives. Direct parental communication, however, is only one of many ways in which children of survivors accrue knowledge of the Holocaust, develop an understanding of their mother's experience, and begin to contextualize their own history. But psychological integration depends on something beyond learning the facts. The daughter will be able to integrate her mother's traumatic memories to the degree in which the mother can provide reassurance and acceptance of her daughter's affective states. The mother must allow her daughter to express what she herself cannot put into words. Thus the process of integration is a reciprocal phenomenon that arises out of an exchange between mother and daughter. Together they can weave a shared narrative that becomes restorative. Within this dyadic interplay—the resumption of a ruptured dyadic exchange—the mother provides something essential for her daughter—the ability to tolerate her own shifting affective states. She must be able to accept something in return: her daughter's ability to put words to experience, to withstand her mother's anguish, and to participate with her in the process of restitution and regeneration. The stories of the Holocaust that children of survivors internalize emerge from the intricate interplay between the narratives told by their parents and the later meanings that children impart to them. Children's narratives are shaped, too, by the many tasks of remembrance. Through their memories, children of survivors seek to repair the broken chain of familial, cultural, and spiritual history. Narrating the legacy of the Holocaust becomes a quest for mastery and redemption and simultaneously a way to assimilate and transform tragic memory.

BIBLIOGRAPHY

Auerhahn, N., & Laub, D. (1984). Annihilation and restoration: Post-traumatic memory as pathway and obstacle to recovery. *Int. Rev. Psychoanal.*, 11:327–44.
Auerhahn, N., & Prelinger, E. (1983). Repetition in the concentration camp survivor and her child. *Int. Rev. Psychoanal.*, 10:31–46.

BASCH, M. (1976). The concept of affect: A re-examination. *J. Amer. Psychoanal. Assn.*, 21:759–77.

BEEBE, B., & LACHMANN, F. (1988). The contribution of mother-infant mutual influence to the origins of self- and object representations. *Psychoanal. Psychol.*, 5(4):305–77.

BEEBE, B., & STERN, D. (1977). Engagement-disengagement and early object experiences. In *Communicative Structures and Psychic Structures*, ed. Freedman and Grand. New York: Plenum.

CANTOR, M., & GLUCKSMAN, M., eds. (1983). *Affect: Psychoanalytic Theory and Practice.* New York: Wiley.

DEMERS-DEROSIER, L. (1982). Influence of alexythymia on symbolic function. *Psychotherapy and Psychosomatics*, 38:103–20.

DWORK, D. (1989). *Children with a Star.* New Haven: Yale Univ. Press.

EMDE, R. (1983). The prerepresentational self and its affective core. *Psychoanal. Study Child*, 38:165–92.

FRESCO, N. (1984). Remembering the unknown. *Int. Rev. Psychoanal.*, 11:417–27.

FREUD, S. (1901). Childhood memories and screen memories. *S.E.*, 6.

——— (1917). Mourning and melancholia.

GAENSBAUER, T. (1982). The differentiation of discrete affects. *Psychoanal. Study Child*, 37:29–66.

GRUBICH-SIMITIS, I. (1984). From concretism to metaphor: Thoughts on some theoretical and technical aspects of the psychoanalytic work with children of Holocaust survivors. *Psychoanal. Study Child*, 39:301–19.

JUCOVY, M. (1985). Telling the Holocaust story: A link between the generations. *Psychoanal. Inq.*, 5(1):31–50.

KATAN, A. (1961). Some thoughts about the role of verbalization in early childhood. *Psychoanal. Study Child.*, 16:184–88.

KESTENBERG, J. (1982). A metapsychological assessment based on an analysis of a survivor's child. In *Generations of the Holocaust*, ed. Bergman and Jucovy. New York: Basic.

KRYSTAL, H. (1978). Trauma and affects. *Psychoanal. Study Child*, 33:81–116.

LANGER, L. (1991). *Holocaust Testimonies: The Ruins of Memory.* New Haven: Yale Univ. Press.

LAUB, D., & AUERHAHN, N. (1989). Failed empathy: A central theme in the survivor's Holocaust experience. *Psychoanal. Psychol.*, 6:377–400.

——— (1988). Knowing and not knowing massive psychic trauma: Forms of traumatic memory. Paper presented at the Annual Meeting of the Division of Psychoanalysis of the American Psychological Association, San Francisco.

MICHEELS, L. (1985). Bearer of the secret. *Psychoanal. Inq.*, 5(1):21–30.

OGDEN, T. (1990). *The Matrix of the Mind.* Northvale, N.J.: Aronson.

SANDLER, J., & ROSENBLATT, B. The concept of the representational world. *Psychoanal. Study Child*, 17:128–45.

SCHAFER, R. How was this story told? *J. Projective Technique*, 22:181–210.

STERN, D. *The Interpersonal World of the Infant.* New York: Basic.

WINNICOTT, D. (1964). *The Child, the Family and the Outside World*. Harmondsworth: Penguin.

—— (1965). *The Maturational Processes and the Facilitating Environment*. New York: Int. Univ. Press.

—— (1975). *Through Paediatrics to Psycho-analysis*. New York: Basic.

YOUNG, J. (1990). *Writing and Rewriting the Holocaust*. Indianapolis: Indiana Univ. Press.

Models of Reflexive Recognition

Wallon's *Origines du caractère* and Lacan's "Mirror Stage"

SHULI BARZILAI, Ph.D.

Jacques Lacan drew on the empirical research of the psychologist Henri Wallon both in his 1938 theory of the mirror stage ("the intrusion complex") and in subsequent formulations. Yet, like Lacan's famous "return" to Freud, his recourse to Wallon is revisionary and, at times, antithetical. This essay examines the disparities between Wallon's and Lacan's work on the mirror experience, focusing especially on the status of the mirror and the identity of the reflected image. An analysis of these differences helps to clarify the meaning of the child's specular activity— "an ontological structure of the human world"—in Lacan's later view and the implications of reflexive recognition for his conception of parental agency.

CONTEXTS AND INFLUENCES

IN "THE MIRROR STAGE AS FORMATIVE OF THE FUNCTION OF THE *I* AS Revealed in Psychoanalytic Experience" (1949), Jacques Lacan describes the "startling spectacle" of a child between the ages of six and eighteen months before a mirror: "Unable as yet to walk, or even stand up, and held tightly as he is by some support . . . he nevertheless over-

Senior lecturer in English at the Hebrew University of Jerusalem; teaches courses in psychoanalytic criticism and contemporary literary theory.

Research for this article was supported in part by a grant from the Israel Science Foundation, administered by the Israel Academy of Sciences and Humanities.

The Psychoanalytic Study of the Child 50, ed. Albert J. Solnit, Peter B. Neubauer, Samuel Abrams, and A. Scott Dowling (Yale University Press, copyright © 1995 by Albert J. Solnit, Peter B. Neubauer, Samuel Abrams, and A. Scott Dowling).

comes, in a flutter of jubilant activity, the obstructions of his support and, fixing his attitude in a slightly leaning-forward position, in order to hold it in his gaze, brings back an instantaneous aspect of the image" (pp. 1–2). The act of seeing the mirror-image may have occurred previously. But now the child's jubilation indicates a recognition of the reflexive relations between the "me" who sees and the "me" who is seen. This insight is a complex achievement.

In addition to "The Mirror Stage" essay, Lacan provided highly condensed summaries of his theory in three papers delivered during the same period: "Propos sur la causalité psychique" (Remarks on psychic causality) (1946), "Aggressivity in Psychoanalysis" (1948), and "Some Reflections on the Ego" (1953). Lacan's initial conceptualization of the mirror stage, however, appeared several years earlier in "De l'Impulsion au complexe" (From impulsion to complex) (1939) and in a section called "The Intrusion Complex" in his contribution (1938a) to volume eight of the *Encyclopédie française*. This long article, entitled "Les complexes familiaux dans la formation de l'individu" (The family complexes in the formation of the individual) but widely known as "La famille" was commissioned from Lacan by the editor of the encyclopedia volume, Henri Wallon.

Lacan had become acquainted with Wallon, a fellow member of the Société de psychiatrie, in the early 1930s. During this period, he read Wallon's book-length monograph on the mirror experiences of children and animals (Roudinesco, 1990, pp. 142–43). Wallon first published his work, which cites and develops the studies of Charlotte Bühler, Charles Darwin, Paul Guillaume, Elsa Köhler, and W. T. Preyer, in *Journal de Psychologie* (November–December 1931). It was soon after reprinted in *Les origines du caractère chez l'enfant* (The origins of the infant's character) (1933). From the 1938 encyclopedia account of the mirror stage and throughout its subsequent permutations, Lacan relies on the extensive data and observations collected in Wallon's text.

In his essay on aggressivity (1948, p. 18), Lacan briefly acknowledges his debt to "Wallon's remarkable work," a debt that remains otherwise unmentioned in his writings. Disclosing "a certain forgetfulness or a curious lapsus," Lacan consistently "skips over" Wallon, as Bertrand Ogilvie puts it (1987, p. 113). Wallon is most notably absent from the 1949 essay on the mirror stage. Lacan also neglects to mention Wallon's influential research in "Some Reflections on the Ego" (1953), where he recapitulates *his* theory of the mirror stage for the British Psycho-Analytical Society: "I introduced the concept. . . . I returned to the subject two years ago. . . . The theory I there advanced, which I submitted long ago to French psychologists" (p. 14). Further, when Lacan presents his "antecedents" in *Écrits* (1966), Wallon's name is not among those singled out for recognition. He speaks of his "invention" of the ideas of the *moi* and specular encounter (p. 67). Whether the mirror stage is universally formative of the *I*-function or not, it would certainly seem to be so in the case of Lacan.

However, a different perspective can be brought to bear on the scandal surrounding this silence. Lacan's recourse to Wallon is complexly revisionary and, at times, antithetical. In this respect, it resembles his famous "return" to Freud. As I will presently show, Lacan assimilates and yet also transforms Wallon's observations to such an extent that, like the White Knight in Lewis Carroll's (1871) looking-glass world, he can proclaim, "It is my own invention" without egregious prevarication. In what follows I intend to examine the differences as well as the similarities between Wallon's and Lacan's ideas about the mirror-image. An exploration of this ideational dialogue will help to clarify the meaning of the child's specular activity—"an ontological structure of the human world"—in Lacan's view and, especially, to bring out his conception of parental agency (1949, p. 2).

SOME ZOOLOGICAL OBSERVATIONS

In the chapter of *Les origines du caractère chez l'enfant* entitled "The Body Proper and Its Exteroceptive Image," Wallon introduced a zoo of creatures to demonstrate, first, the disparity between animal and human modes of cognition and, second, the series of complex stages in which consciousness of reflexive reciprocity develops in the child. A dog or a monkey or a bird can perceive the mirror-image, but only the human infant, though still motorically uncoordinated, can grasp the reciprocal relation between the self and its reflection. Wallon cites the striking instance of a widowed drake of Turkey (*un canard de Turquie*). The drake acquired the habit, his partner being dead, of peering into a reflecting windowpane. "Without doubt its own reflection," Wallon writes, "could more or less fill in the void left by the absence of its companion" (1933, pp. 218–19).[1] The duck found consolation only because it was unable to identify the mirror-image; that is, it saw not itself but its mate in the glass. The animal, as opposed to the human infant, cannot grasp the relation between the virtual image seen in the mirror and the reality outside.

Wallon's text on mirror behavior vividly exemplifies the differences in the mental capacities among animal species, as well as among chil-

---

1. The translated excerpts from Wallon's text are given in my translation.

dren at various developmental stages. Similarly, in 1949 Lacan contrasted the behavior of the child and the chimp: "The child, at an age when he is for a time, however short, outdone by the chimpanzee in instrumental intelligence, can nevertheless already recognize as such his own image in a mirror" (p. 1; also Lacan, 1946, p. 185; and 1948, p. 18). The motoric advantage of the animal is offset by the spark of early human intelligence. Like Wallon, Lacan also mentions the experiments of Elsa Köhler and other psychologists who published their observations in the 1930s. In further keeping with these empirical arguments, Lacan refers to Leonard Harrison Matthews's study of ovulation in pigeons and Remy Chauvin's research on migratory locusts. Their studies demonstrate that visual stimulation links between mental and physical processes in these animals, even seeing the reflected image of members of the same species, can produce a physiological change. Matthews's experiments especially support the preeminence accorded the visual in Lacanian theory by proving that, for ovulation to occur in a female pigeon, either the sight of other (male or female) pigeons, or a mirror-image of herself alone is sufficient (see Lacan, 1949, p. 3; 1946, pp. 189–91; 1953, p. 14).[2]

It is very odd, as David Macey (1988) points out, that Lacan with his "reputation for militant anti-biologism" should thus repeatedly invoke experimental psychology, ethology, and biology (p. 99). But he had already done so earlier. Despite the polemical emphasis on culturally determined complexes—the social or the symbolic—as opposed to instinctual factors throughout *The Family Complexes,* Lacan had unhesitatingly recalled the "material base" of the complex in order to reinforce his conception of the enduring influence of the infant's separation from the maternal breast (*sevrage*). "The organic connection," he contends in his encyclopedia essay, "accounts for the fact that the maternal imago possesses the very depths of the psyche" (1938a, p. 32, and 1938b, p. 15). Because the mirror stage now replaces the nursing dyad and weaning as the governing structure of the psyche, it is not surprising to find Lacan's "anti-biologism" once again suspended.

Among other ideas specified in Wallon's work that resonate in Lacan's is the linkage between the child's acquisition of a unified body image and a preliminary understanding of symbolic representation. According to Wallon (1993), the human infant whose direct vision is limited to a partial body image ("only certain fragments and never assembled") accedes to a coherent image of the "total body" through

---

2. For a fuller discussion of the significance of Matthews's and Chauvin's research projects for Lacanian theory, see Wilfried Ver Eecke, 1983.

the mediation of the mirror (p. 227). Simple though this unification of the self in space may appear to adults, it implies a cognitive subordination of "the givens of immediate experience to pure representation." The mirror experience is thus also the "prelude to symbolic activity," enabling a transition from partial, sensorial perceptions to what Wallon calls the "symbolic function" (pp. 230–31).

Wallon's detailed experiments clearly established a conceptual paradigm for Lacan's understanding of the mirror stage. Yet Lacan decisively parts company with Wallon—and this departure is arguably the core of his theoretical innovation—on two points: the status of the mirror and the identity of the specular image.

THE STATUS OF THE MIRROR: REAL OR METAPHOR?

What is the phenomenological status of the mirror? Is it a real or metaphorical reflector? In Wallon's numerous descriptions of attitudes before the looking glass—be it those of dogs, cats, infants in their cradles, or a little girl admiring the straw hat on her head—a real mirror is involved. Wallon poses a literal reflector before his subjects, as do the several researchers whose data are cited in the pages of *Les Origines*. Lacan has a more complicated reflector in mind. It may (but need not) be a real one. Lacan does not rule out the perceiving subject's literal reduplication, yet, the mirror is also a metaphor and, as Lacan remarks in another connection, "it is not a metaphor to say so" (1957, p. 175).

In Lacan's theory, the mirror stage or phase functions as a figurative designation for two temporal modalities: first, a sudden moment or flash of recognition—the "jubilant assumption of his specular image by the child"—in which assimilation to the image of the counterpart (sibling, playmate, or actual reflection) takes place, and, second, a state of identification/alienation involving the other—"the mirror disposition"—that constitutes a permanent structure of the psyche (1949, pp. 2, 3). These modalities are closely implicated in each other but can nevertheless be elaborated separately. Whereas the first phase coincides with early childhood, the second characterizes a psychical tug-of-war, a dialectical tension ranging over the lifespan of the individual. The first specifies a moment of genesis in which the ego begins its formation. In this respect, Lacan adheres to Freud's suggestion in "On Narcissism: An Introduction" that "a unity comparable to the ego cannot exist in the individual from the start; the ego has to be developed" (1914, p. 77). The second entails an ongoing narcissistic, imaginary relationship based on aggression (as well as erotic attraction) between the ego and the other.

This second phase in particular bears the mark of another major influence on Lacan's thinking. As Jacques-Alain Miller recapitulates in a 1989 interview (eight years after the death of Lacan, his father-in-law): "Lacan reorganized the Freudian discovery from a point of view that was foreign to [Freud], the mirror-stage . . . which comes from Henri Wallon for its empirical basis and from Hegel revised by Kojève for its theory" (quoted in Borch-Jacobsen, 1991, p. 249n.11). In *The Family Complexes* and later writings, Lacan's mirror-stage theory not only draws on the psychologist Wallon's experimental research but is also mediated by his familiarity with Hegelian philosophy and, especially, with Alexandre Kojève's influential commentary on *The Phenomenology of the Mind*. Kojève began what was to become a legendary six-year series of lectures on Hegel at the École des Hautes Études in 1933. Lacan was among the Parisian avant-gardists (including also George Bataille, André Breton, Maurice Merleau-Ponty, Raymond Queneau and many others) who attended these lectures and discovered the key terms of Hegel's phenomenology via Kojève's teaching (Borch-Jacobsen, 1991, pp. 4–5; Macey, 1988, pp. 57–58, 95–98; Roudinesco, 1990, pp. 134–35, 140).

"Hegel speculated," Lacan writes in *The Family Complexes*, "that the individual who does not fight to be recognized outside the family group will never attain autonomy before death" (1938a, p. 35, and 1938b, p. 16). The dark, agonistic aspect of the mirror stage (which cancels or mitigates the jubilation it brings) derives from a Kojèvian version of the encounter between the subject and the other as a fight for "pure prestige," a life-and-death struggle for recognition on which independent self-consciousness is predicated. More needs to be said about this influence; but, for the purposes of the present comparison, it is noteworthy that Lacan transforms the real mirror that Wallon posed before his experimental subjects into a metaphor for a metapsychological concept of human genesis.[3]

To trace further this skein of similarities and dissimilarities, D. W. Winnicott, in his "Mirror-role of Mother and Family in Child Development" (1967), discloses an interest in the constitution of selfhood anal-

---

3. Roudinesco (1990) also observes that "a transition was . . . effected from the description of a concrete experiment to the elaboration of a doctrine" (p. 143). However, her analysis of this transition does not take into account the differences between Wallon's literal and Lacan's primarily metaphoric concepts of the mirror.

ogous to that of Lacan. At the very outset of the essay, Winnicott acknowledges Lacan's influential ideas on "the mirror in each individual's ego development" (p. 130), and, in his concluding statements, he also makes quite clear the metaphoric status of the mirror, a status that is implicitly (but not consistently) upheld in Lacan's writings. Thus, although it is possible to "include in all this [reflecting activity] the actual mirrors that exist in the house," Winnicott still insists, "It should be understood . . . that the actual mirror has significance mainly in its figurative sense" (p. 138). For Winnicott, too, a real mirror is not prerequisite for the maturational process of mirroring to ensue. In opting for a figural approach, Winnicott is closer to Lacan's views than Lacan is to Wallon's.

Yet whose face appears *as* the mirror? What body forms or attitudes can function in reflexive relation to the perceiver? Winnicott designates a range of individual forms and even entire familial attitudes: "when a family is intact . . . each child derives benefit from being able to see himself or herself in the attitude of the individual members or in the attitudes of the family as a whole." But, as his essay title suggests, he gives precedence to the mother's role. Under normal circumstances, her responsiveness to the child ("giving back to the baby the baby's own self") confers a positive experience of formation (p. 138). Winnicott thus draws on Lacan's mirror-stage theory but also indicates where his own stance differs. As he notes in his mirror-role essay, "Lacan does not think of the mirror in terms of the mother's face in the way that I wish to do" (p. 130). The mirror remains a metaphorical concept. However, in the terminological alteration from "stage [*stade*]" to "role," an abstract setting becomes an actual habitation: a familial setting in which the mother's face serves as primary reflector for the young child.[4]

This distinction carries over into the rhetoric that Lacan and Winnicott use to conceptualize what occurs during the analytic situation. Winnicott, in his 1967 essay and throughout his work, develops an analogy between the infant-mother and the analyzand-analyst relationships.[5] That is, in exploring what analysts actually do, the "holding" environment they provide for those under their care, Winnicott alludes to aspects of maternal care. Psychotherapy, according to Win-

---

4. In another connection, Gerald Fogel (1992) makes the analogous point that Winnicott's work "creates not a theory, but an antitheory." "Theories ordinarily explain, but Winnicott is more interested in grasping or describing the nature of personal experience, not its causes or its components. Almost everything he deals with refers to a relational or existential *process*" (p. 207).

5. On Winnicott's subtle deployment of this analogy in four additional papers published between 1941 and 1971, see Elsa First, 1994.

nicott, "is a complex derivative of the face that reflects what is there to be seen": "I like to think of my work this way, and to think that if I do this well enough the patient will find his or her own self" (pp. 137–38). Doing it "well enough" casts the analyst in the mirror-role of the mother. Lacan too, in his "Direction of the Treatment and the Principles of Its Power" (1958) and other writings, draws analogies between the "metaphor of the mirror" and the analyst's task; however, he typically evokes a "*smooth surface* that the analyst presents to the patient" (1958, p. 229; emphasis added). Lacan stresses the element of "abnegation," or self-imposed absence—"an impassive face and sealed lips" instead of the resilient, affective reciprocity suggested in Winnicott's recourse to the mirror analogy. While Lacan describes the analyst as bringing to the session "what in bridge is called the dummy (*le mort*)" (p. 229), Winnicott, contrarily, envisages the mommy (*la mère*) in the analysis.

The conceptual connections sketched here (Wallon-Lacan-Winnicott) constitute a line of disrupted continuities in more ways than one. Given Lacan's sustained reticence about Wallon and the general obscurity of the psychologist's work outside of France (*Les Origines* is to this date not translated into English), it is unlikely that Winnicott was directly acquainted with Wallon's research. And yet despite the distance between Wallon's literal and Winnicott's figural notions about the mirror, their views converge in two respects that differ from Lacan's formulations.

The first can be compared to the divergent inflections of rising and falling tones. Wallon evokes the child's triumph at the resolution of the mirror "ordeal [*épreuve*]" and Winnicott, the potential for growth and self-enrichment as a result of maternal mirroring. By contrast, Lacan describes a short-lived moment of jubilation. A sense of radical, unalterable alienation pervades his account. He envisions the ego whose formation is precipitated by the visual image of the counterpart in terms of a negativity derived from Kojève's reading of Hegel: "The dialectic which supports our experience . . . obliges us to understand the ego as being constituted from top to bottom within the movement of progressive alienation in which self-consciousness is constituted in Hegel's phenomenology" (Lacan 1966, p. 374, quoted and translated in Macey, 1988, pp. 97–98). Both Michael Eigen, in a comparison of Winnicott and Lacan, and Elisabeth Roudinesco, in a more recent comparison of Wallon and Lacan, comment on the negativistic aspect of the Lacanian vision (Eigen, 1981, pp. 421–22; Roudinesco, 1990, p. 143). Significant though this aspect may well be, I would propose that the second point of divergence discussed below is the more fundamental to

Lacan's conception of subject formation. It enables or seems to enable an exorcism of the powerful maternal presence.

THE IDENTITY OF THE IMAGE: WHO'S IN THE MIRROR?

Where the question "who's in the mirror?" is concerned, Lacan provides a Hegelian-based determination. Unlike Wallon, for whom the identity of the triggering image is indifferent, and most unlike Winnicott, for whom the image is usually—and preferably—an average devoted ("good-enough") mother, Lacan posits the conjunction between the ego and its antagonist-double as a necessary precondition for the moment of recognition. The self sees the *self-same* image in the dialectical encounter. A sharp contrast in content as well as in tone thus sets apart Lacan's theoretical formulations.

In particular, Wallon's text about the origins of the child's character provides an origin that is also a point of new beginning (or departure) for Lacan's definition of the specular image. According to Wallon, the reflected body of the perceiving subject need not be the one to trigger the mental integration of model and image. Other bodies may serve the same function. Wallon gives the example of a little boy who smiles at his own and his father's image in the mirror; however the child, still in an intermediate stage of development, turns in surprise upon hearing his father's voice behind him. He has not as yet grasped the connection between the reflection and the real presence of the father (1933, p. 223). In Wallon's analysis, the difficulty seems to lie in a spatial realism that prevents the child from linking the actual figure with the virtual one. The pre-mirror-stage child does not yet understand that the two bodies located at two points in space—the tactile body here and the visual body there—constitute, in fact, only one body. The child attributes an independent reality to each object or person occupying a different space (p. 225).

Yet, after the child has grasped the distinction between reality and its symbols or representations, a ludic element can enter into these interrelations. If asked "Where is Mommy?" a post-mirror-stage child may point to her image in the mirror and then turn toward her, laughing. The child now plays with the duality. "Slyly, he pretends to grant preponderance to the image," Wallon writes, "precisely because he has just clearly recognized its unreality and purely symbolic character" (p. 232).

For Wallon, then, the essential factor is the recognition of spatial values or, more precisely, the coordination of what was perceived as two bodies in two distinct places. The child's behavior suddenly demonstrates a comprehension of the reciprocity between model and image.

The realization of their subordinate rather than independent relation is the turning point. Wallon does devote separate sections in his work to children's specular relations with others ("L'enfant devant l'image speculaire d'autrui") and with their own bodies ("L'enfant devant sa propre image speculaire"), and he also discusses the different mental operations involved in withdrawing reality from the images of other bodies and from the self-image. Less crucial, however, than the identity of the person seen in the mirror is the elimination of the schism between the felt "me" and the visual "me."

In "The Child's Relations with Others," Merleau-Ponty (1960) comments on the Lacanian extension of the ideas found in *Les Origines:*

> In reading Wallon one often has the feeling that in acquiring the specular image it is a question of a labor of understanding, of a synthesis of certain visual perceptions with certain introceptive perceptions. For psychoanalysts the visual is not simply one type of sensibility among others. . . . With the visual experience of the self, there is . . . the advent of a new mode of relatedness to self. . . . The sensory functions themselves are thus redefined in proportion to the contribution they can make to the existence of the subject and the structures they can offer for the development of that existence. (pp. 137–38)

For Lacan, Merleau-Ponty suggests, the perceptual synthesis achieved during the mirror stage is a first steppingstone in a far more complicated process of formation. This process involves unconscious as well as conscious mental activities. Moreover, as I already indicated, the identity of the specular image is not an indifferent one. The reflected body belongs neither to the mother nor to any adult caretaker. On the contrary, Lacan's formulations repeatedly underscore the ego's captivation by its own image: "the mirror-image would seem to be the threshold of the visible world, if we go by the mirror disposition that the *imago of one's own body* presents in hallucinations or dreams" (1949, p. 3). This emphasis recurs in his "Propos sur la causalité psychique" (Remarks on psychical causality) and "Some Reflections on the Ego." He speaks of "the autonomy of the *image of the body proper* in the psyche" and of the infant's jubilant interest in "his own image in a mirror" (1946, p. 185; 1953, p. 14). The figure in the glass is none other than the counterpart of the self.

Adopting the stance of an objective or external focus, Lacan describes an observer's reaction to this drama of reflexive identification: "one is all the more impressed when one realizes"—and I take the impersonal "one" as a sign of special investment on his part—"that this behaviour occurs either in a babe in arms or in a child who is holding himself upright by one of those contrivances to help one to learn to walk without serious falls" (1953, p. 15). At this juncture, then, the question of the subject (or, to borrow Carroll's looking-glass conundrum, "Which Dreamed It?") might arise: how can one see what the child sees without putting one's self in the frame? Lacan's description conjures the child before the mirror in such a way that the presence of other persons is minimalized ("arms") or eliminated ("holding himself"). Likewise in his mirror-stage essay, he renders the mother or caretaker a virtually invisible factor: "Unable as yet to walk, or even stand up, and held tightly as he is by some support, human or artificial (what, in France, we call a 'trotte-bébé'), he nevertheless overcomes, in a flutter of jubilant activity, the obstructions of his support" (1949, p. 1).

Thus the hand the proverbially rocks the cradle (and, more ominously, rules the world) is whisked away. What remains is a contraption—a baby walker or a pair of disembodied arms—holding the infant. Lacan makes it abundantly clear that the image in the mirror is *not* the mother's. He reiterates this cardinal point: It is the "*imago* of one's own body" (1948, p. 25; also 1949, p. 3). Even when an adult holds the infant before the mirror, Lacan asserts that the crucial identification occurs only between the self and its semblable. If such repetition may be considered the site of a symptom (or symbol), then Lacan's evocations of an infant overcoming the actual obstruction of various supporting agents, however literally intended, acquire an added resonance. His insistence brings me, at the risk of a certain implausibility, to offer the following interpretation: in the small world of the infantile ego striving to surmount its supports, the venerable injunction "Thou shalt have no other image before me" has a revisionary, projective meaning. The ego (*moi*) receives a message from the *grand Autre* or big Other that originally emanated from itself.

Some commentators, however, refuse to allow the radical absence of the mother in the mirror-stage theory. Hence there is a tendency to reintroduce her. Mario Rendon, for example, cites Lacan's 1949 essay as a source for the observation that "the image of the self is originally constructed around the perceived image of the mother" (1981, p. 350). Elizabeth Grosz writes of "the (m)other/mirror-image," making the mother integral to this acanian concept of reflexive identification (1990, p. 32). These readings fail to grasp the literal meaning of the mirror stage and its doctrinal significance. As described in *The Family Complexes*, "the intrusion complex" already entails a scene of ego formation through the mirroring of the child's own body. That is, from the very beginning of his fifty-year career, Lacan posits a psychical mechanism—"narcissistic intrusion" as he calls it—that requires "the subject's recognition of his image in a mirror" (1938a, pp. 45, 42, and 1938b, pp. 18, 17).

SOME CONCLUSIONS

Critical differences notwithstanding, Wallon and Lacan both maintain that the unity of the specular image, the total bodily form or *Gestalt*, is an indispensable part of the maturation process. Lacan writes in 1938, "What the subject welcomes in [the image] is its inherent mental *unity;* . . . what he applauds in it is the triumph of its *integrative power*" (p. 44 [1938b, p. 18; emphasis added]). On this point, *The Family Complexes* anticipates Lacan's later formulation of the mirror stage as a drama involving self-reflection and self-integration: a perception of one's-*own*-body and of one's-*whole*-body.

Lacan singles out both of these factors in 1948: "What I have called the *mirror stage* is interesting in that it manifests the affective dynamism by which the subject originally identifies himself with the visual *Gestalt* of his own body: in relation to the still very profound lack of coordination of his own motility, it represents an ideal unity, a salutary *imago*" (1948, pp. 18–19). Appropriately enough, "ideal [that is, unreal or imaginary] unity" is endowed by a reflected totality. The celebratory sense of the *I* is a function of the formal constellation of parts in the mirror. The term *affective dynamism* in this passage should be glossed by the "triumphant jubilation" frequently associated with the child's identification of the image: "what demonstrates the phenomenon of recognition . . . are the signs of triumphant jubilation and playful discovery that characterize, from the sixth month, the child's encounter with his image in the mirror" (p. 18). For Lacan (as for Wallon), the behavioral evidence for the child's momentous insight is a joyous kind of playfulness.

The question arises: why joy? Why indeed does recognition of the specular other initially bring with it such jubilation? It is after all accompanied, in Lacan's agonistic view, by an inevitable estrangement, or "assumption of an armour of an alienating identity" (1949, p. 4). Lacan accounts for the child's joyful antics before the mirror as follows: the good *Gestalt* equips the child with a unitary mental image. This image ("the total form of the body") allows some compensation for the malaise accompanying the prematurity and discordance ("the fragmented body-image") of birth. Hence he calls the totality glimpsed in the glass "orthopaedic" (p. 4). After the neonate's experiences of separation and fragmentation, the specular counterpart puts Humpty Dumpty together again, however temporarily and phantasmatically.

One source of the widespread appeal of the mirror-stage theory, I therefore suggest, derives from this account of human genesis that, painful and fraught with psychical dangers (fantasies of fragmentation, acute narcissism, alienation) though it might be, takes place without mediation: sans mother and sans father. To a largely secular and skeptical readership, Lacan's mirror stage presents a new myth of genesis. It is a powerful creation myth whose passion and investment is overlaid by the dignity that an abstract and "scientific" terminology confers upon conjecture.[6] Unlike the myth of the goddess Athena (Freud's favorite artifact in his large collection) who sprang forth from Zeus's forehead, in Lacanian theory, the function of the *I* does not emerge as a result of any parental intervention. The birth of the ego takes place in and through the looking glass. In Lacan's view, the mirror is the mother of the ego. But the mother is not in the mirror.

In effect, the mirror stage also marks a complex moment of separation for Lacan. First and foremost, he undermines the primacy of Freud's theory of the Oedipus complex: identification with the fraternal counterpart prepares the way for identification with the paternal rival. The mirror stage replaces the Oedipal conflict as the linchpin or turning point of human development. Next, in orienting the psychoanalytic focus toward the fraternal (and, secondarily, the paternal) function in the formation of the ego, Lacan challenges the influence of Melanie Klein and the growing inclination since the 1930s to place the mother at the center of the child's world. As Lisa Appignanesi and John Forrester (1992) observe, "the Lacanian scheme guaranteed that psychoanalysis was removed from the ambiguously *ewige mutterliche*, or eternally maternal, tendencies that British Kleinian and other object-relations theories were encouraging" (p. 462). With these two revisionary moments, Lacan could be said to put himself in place of the (Freudian) father and the (Kleinian) mother. So with a single innovation, Lacan constitutes himself. The mirror stage represents his emergence as an embattled but full-fledged contender for theoretical preeminence in the Freudian field.

Briefly to pursue these speculations, critics and historians such as Borch-Jacobsen (1991), Ver Eecke (1983), Ogilvie (1987), and Roudinesco (1990) have traced the idea of the mirror stage back to numerous sources. The theory presents a stunning synthesis of several strands of thought in psychoanalysis, philosophy, and experimental psychology. Although Lacan would cast aside most precursors or supports, these

---

6. Lacan refers to psychoanalysis as a "conjectural science" on several occasions; see, e.g., his *Écrits*, 1966, pp. 472, 863.

same neglected ones merely wait to be recalled. They seem to impose or, at least, contribute to the alienation that curtails Lacan's jubilant assumption of his own invention. He thus tells the truth when he says that the sense of fragmentation is never fully overcome, even in those pleasurable moments in which an image of totality is glimpsed. His famous theory is itself a kind of body-in-pieces, a dream composed of diverse concepts. The vision of the self-constituted individual, or what could now be called "the good-enough *Gestalt*" indeed turns out to be a mirage. Humpty Dumpty, the seemingly complacent but ever-fragile ego ("*hommelette*," in Lacan's own punning phrase), is what the idea of the mirror stage defends against.

BIBLIOGRAPHY

APPIGNANESI, L., AND FORRESTER, J. (1992). *Freud's Women*. New York: Basic.

BORCH-JACOBSEN, M. (1991). *Lacan, the Absolute Master*, trans. D. Brick. Stanford, Calif.: Stanford Univ. Press.

CARROLL, L. (1871). *The Annotated Alice: Alice's Adventures in Wonderland and Through the Looking Glass*. New York: New American Library, 1963.

EIGEN, M. (1981). The area of faith in Winnicott, Lacan and Bion. *Int. J. Psychoanal.*, 62:413–33.

FIRST, E. (1994). Mothering, hate, and Winnicott. In *Representations of Motherhood*, ed. D. Bassin, M. Honey, and M. Mahrer Kaplan, pp. 147–61. New Haven: Yale Univ. Press.

FOGEL, G. I. (1992). Winnicott's authority and Winnicott's art: His significance for adult analysis. *Psychoanal. Study Child*, 47:205–22.

FREUD, S. (1914). On narcissism: An introduction. *S.E.*, 14:73–102.

GROSZ, E. (1990). *Jacques Lacan: A Feminist Introduction*. London: Routledge.

KOJÈVE, A. (1947). *Introduction to the Reading of Hegel*, trans. J. H. Nichols. New York: Basic, 1969.

LACAN, J. (1938a). *Les complexes familiaux dans la formation de l'individu*. Paris: Navarin, 1984.

——— (1938b). The family complexes. Trans. C. Asp. *Critical Texts*, 1988, 5:12–29.

——— (1939). De l'impulsion au complexe. *RFP*, 11:137–41. Reprinted in *Ornicar?* (1984), 31:14–19.

——— (1946). Propos sur la causalité psychique. In Lacan, 1966, pp. 151–92.

——— (1948). Aggressivity in psychoanalysis. In Lacan, 1977, pp. 8–29.

——— (1949). The mirror stage as formative of the function of the *I* as revealed in psychoanalytic experience. In Lacan, (1977), pp. 1–7.

——— (1953). Some reflections on the ego. Trans. N. E. Beaufils. *Int. J. Psychoanal.*, 34:11–17. Read at the British Psycho-Analytical Society in May 1951.

——— (1957). The agency of the letter in the unconscious or reason since Freud. In Lacan, 1977, pp. 146–78.

———— (1958). Direction of the treatment and the principles of its power. In Lacan, 1977, pp. 226–80.

———— (1966). *Écrits*, Paris: Seuil.

———— (1977). *Écrits: A Selection*. Trans. A. Sheridan. New York: W. W. Norton.

MACEY, D. (1988). *Lacan in Contexts*. London: Verso.

MERLEAU-PONTY, M. (1960). The child's relations with others [*Les relations avec autrui chez l'enfant*], trans. W. Cobb. In *The Primacy of Perception and Other Essays on Phenomenological Psychology, the Philosophy of Art, History and Politics*, ed. J. M. Edie, pp. 96–155. Evanston, Ill.: Northwestern Univ. Press, 1964.

OGILVIE, B. (1987). *Lacan: La Formation du concept de Sujet (1932–1949)*. Paris: Presses Universitaires de France.

RENDON, M. (1981). Narcissus revisited: A venture outside the intrapsychic. *Am. J. Psychoanal.*, 41:347–54.

ROUDINESCO, E. (1990). *Jacques Lacan & Co.: A History of Psychoanalysis in France, 1925–1985*, trans. Jeffrey Mehlman. Chicago: Univ. of Chicago Press, 1990. First published as *La bataille de cent ans: Histoire de la psychoanalyse en France*, 2. Paris: Éditions du Seuil, 1986.

VER EECKE, W. (1983). Hegal as Lacan's source for necessity in psychoanalytic theory. In *Interpreting Lacan*, ed. J. H. Smith and W. Kerrigan, pp. 113–38. New Haven: Yale Univ. Press.

WALLON, H. (1933). *Les origines du caractère chez l'enfant*. Paris: Presses Universitaires de France, 1949.

WINNICOTT, D. W. (1967). Mirror-role of mother and family in child development. In *Playing and Reality*, pp. 130–38. Harmondsworth, Middlesex: Penguin Books, 1971.

The Child Is Father of the Man

Wordsworth's *Ode: Intimations of Immortality* and His Secret Sharers

JULES GLENN, M.D.

William Wordsworth's "Ode: Intimations of Immortality" is manifestly about both the poet's loss of inspirational perceptive powers and emotional intensity with age, and the compensations of maturity. It also refers to the poet's fear that he might lose his "secret sharers," real or fantasied, consciously or unconsciously conceived parent substitutes for whom and with whom one creates. Wordsworth anticipated that with his upcoming marriage he would lose his sister Dorothy and his close friend and collaborator Samuel Taylor Coleridge, who played important roles in his creativity. Optimism and relief replaced sadness when he realized that he was not deprived of his sharers. The concepts of "secret sharers" and "collective alternates" for whom one creates are intimately related.

WILLIAM WORDSWORTH'S "ODE: INTIMATIONS OF IMMORTALITY FROM REC-
ollections of Early Childhood" is one of his most admired and beloved poems. Although it has been repeatedly interpreted, it can bear further psychoanalytic examination. I will attempt to show how the death of Wordsworth's mother when he was seven and his impending marriage when he started to write the poem in 1802 influenced its content. His fear that his marriage would result in the loss of his "secret sharers" (Meyer, 1967, 1972, 1987), his sister Dorothy and his close friend Sam-

Clinical professor of psychiatry and training and supervising analyst emeritus, Psychoanalytic Institute, New York University Medical Center.

This article was presented in modified form as the Marianne Kris Lecture at the Association for Child Psychoanalysis on April 12, 1992.

The Psychoanalytic Study of the Child 50, ed. Albert J. Solnit, Peter B. Neubauer, Samuel Abrams, and A. Scott Dowling (Yale University Press, copyright © 1995 by Albert J. Solnit, Peter B. Neubauer, Samuel Abrams, and A. Scott Dowling).

uel Taylor Coleridge, was instrumental in his writing of the poem. A
secret sharer is a real or imagined, consciously or unconsciously conceived parent substitute for whom and with whom one creates.

SOME PSYCHOANALYTIC PERSPECTIVES

Noyes and Hayden (1991), who are not particularly psychoanalytically
oriented, nevertheless see in the *Ode* an expression of loss and the
compensatory effects of maturing. In the first section, written in 1802,
shortly before his marriage, Wordsworth said that he no longer saw
things "appareled in celestial light," as he had done as a boy. In the last
section, composed several years later, he contended that despite the
loss of the powers and perceptions of youth, "we will grieve not, [but]
rather find strength in what remains behind."

As Turner (1988) puts it, the poem expresses the paradox that with
maturity one loses powers one possessed as an immature infant. Trosman (1990) has observed that Trilling (1940), approaching the *Ode*
from a psychoanalytic perspective, saw it as a poem about "growing
up," rather than about loss, a statement that the author is no longer a
youth and now sees things differently. Trilling, Trosman writes, understands the *Ode* in terms of Ferenczi's (1950 [1913]) "Stages in the Development of a Sense of Reality." Trilling asserts that the earlier strophes
"lament . . . the passage of childhood" and reflect "grief for the loss of
maternal love" and that the latter section "deals with the development
of a sense of reality which compensates for the loss of the dream" (see
Trosman, 1990, p. 11).

As Trosman further notes, Helen Vendler (1988) disagreeing with
Trilling, says:

> If it is truer to say, as I believe it is, that the Ode represents the
> acquisition of the power of metaphor; that to rest in either the splendor
> of sense or in blank misgivings is not to be a poet; that to join the external
> world of sense-experience with the interior world of moral conscious-
> ness is to become an adult; that to express that juncture in metaphor is to
> become a poet—then all of Wordsworth's great poetry is the result of the
> process of the humanizing of sense and the symbolizing of inner experi-
> ence described in the Ode. Affectional feelings (and not, as Trilling says,
> "the knowledge of man's mortality" alone) "replace[s] the 'glory' as the
> agency which makes things significant and precious." It is "thanks to the
> human *heart* . . . , its *tenderness*, its *joys* and *fears*" that a common flower
> can bear new weight of meaning. . . . It is this capacity of the Muse—
> absolutely unattainable by the six-years' darling, however blessed his
> Soul's immensity—that is celebrated in the Ode. (pp. 112–13)

Trosman interprets this to signify that the last part of the poem "is not an expression of a diminished personality regretting what is no longer present. It is an expression of the imaginative life, the capacity to join the external world of sense experience with the internal world of unconscious fantasy, the synthesis of sense and symbolization of inner experience. . . . We can understand the Ode in terms of the relation of external perception, symbolic language and the capacity of the ego to find meaning and relevance through the transformations of primitive experiences" (p. 12).

There is a shift from preoccupation with early perceptions of the external world to the influence of the imaginative ego which integrates such perceptions, Trosman continues. He suggests that to differentiate self from object was problematic in Wordsworth's development and that he later became able to use his integrative ego to surmount the disorganizing fragmentation of his early life. I would add that the developing ego partly neutralizes instinctual energy (Hartmann, 1965) as well as integrating and synthesizing it to produce a mature, controlled, and still emotional poetry.

I would also add that the disorganization Trosman speaks of resulted from the loss of Wordsworth's mother in latency and of his father when the poet was thirteen. Although the literature I have cited dwells on the loss of capacities with maturation, it is necessary to emphasize the importance of *object* loss in the poet's development and its influence on his creativity.

THE CONCEPT OF SECRET SHARERS

Meyer (1967, 1972 1987) has noted that many creative people produce their artistic work under the grip of a number of interrelated compelling fantasies, about which he coined the term *secret sharers*. The creator writes for his sharer, with his sharer in mind. He also fantasies a union with a double—the equivalent of a mother or, in the case of a male, an unconscious homosexual attachment to a father—as part of the creative act, from which the baby/creative product emerges.

The term itself comes from the title of a story by Joseph Conrad in which the hero sees a man who looks like himself in the sea next to the boat he commandeers. At great risk to himself and his crew, the captain saves his double by taking him aboard and then helping him to escape from the men who are pursuing him. Meyer suggests that Conrad had a secret-sharing relationship with Ford Maddox Ford, with whom he had mutually stimulating interactions. When their relationship ended, Conrad's creative capacity lapsed. The working with and for the sharer is often quite overt, but the fantasies behind the working alliance are unconscious and in that sense secret.

The secret-sharer fantasy may well be a universal requirement for creativity. We can infer it in Freud's relationship with Fliess, which resulted in "the parenthood of psychoanalysis" (Blum, 1990); in Peter and Anthony Shaffer's twinship and mutuality (they even wrote as co-authors under the name of Peter Anthony [Glenn, 1983]); and in Thornton Wilder's fantasy of speaking to and writing for his twin brother, who died shortly after his birth (Glenn, 1986). Meyer's concept of the secret sharer is broader than the concept of a self object (Kohut, 1977). It may involve a more mature relationship in which oedipal heterosexual and homosexual fantasies may dominate rather than an immature reaction of doubles with preoedipal fantasies.

Coltrera (1981) confirmed the secret-sharing aspects of creativity by citing the interaction of T. S. Eliot and Ezra Pound as well as the editorial work Maxwell Perkins performed on the novels of Thomas Wolfe, F. Scott Fitzgerald. In these cases the sharer provided material cooperation as well as a fantasied and psychologically personal attachment. Coltrera warns that analytic interference with an artist's attachment to secret sharers can block creative activity. It is also possible, however, that in some cases the loss of the sharer in reality may spur creativity by fortifying the fantasied attachment; losing an object can result in a fantasied incorporation of that object (Freud, 1917).

EVENTS IN WORDSWORTH'S LIFE

William Wordsworth was born in 1770 in Cumberland, England.[1] He was the second son of John Wordsworth, a lawyer, and Ann Cookson Wordsworth. William had four siblings, including one sister, Dorothy, born a year after William, and brothers Richard, Christopher, and John. Ann died of pneumonia when William was almost eight. It was "a vicious blow" (Gill, 1989, p. 18). "She left us destitute," wrote Wordsworth (1979) in the *Prelude,* a long autobiographical poem published posthumously. The family broke up; William did not see Dorothy for nine years. The four boys were sent to live with Ann Tyson, who took in boarders. She and her husband supplied the love William needed, but repeated separations seem to have interfered with his conviction of constancy. After his father died, when the boy was thirteen, his uncles became his guardians. In his poems Wordsworth recalled feelings of

---

1. This brief account of Wordsworth's life is based on Daiches (1971), *Encyclopaedia Brittanica* (1957), Gill (1989), and Harper (1960).

guilt and longing. He referred to his father's demise as "that dreary time" and a "chastisement." During school sessions he continued to live with the Tysons until he went to college. He lost these caretakers repeatedly when school was out and he had to move elsewhere for a period of time. His anger appeared in a screen memory of an unstated age in which he struck a lash through a family portrait of an elderly lady; in another recollection he angrily desired suicide. These two memories appear in writing directly after a reference to his mother's death (Wordsworth, 1988).

William attended Cambridge from 1787 to 1791, when he was graduated. He spent time in France during the Revolution in 1790 and then again in 1792, when he sired a child with Annette Vallon (still another Ann!), whom he did not marry, but about whom he felt guilty. He was in England when his daughter, Caroline (baptized Anne-Caroline), was born, and he could not join mother and child because of war between France and England. They did keep contact through letters.

Following a period of wandering and "breakdown," Wordsworth settled in Dorset in 1795 and later in the Lake District of England with his sister, Dorothy, who was to become a fine author in her own right and an inspiration to William. He felt that she had saved his life. She was family, compensating for his lost parents. She was, he wrote, "the woman of my soul," "nature's inmate." So intimate was their relationship that some have suggested it was incestuous; certainly they had incestuous fantasies.

William started writing poems at the request of a teacher when he was fourteen, in the second half of 1784, possibly as a reaction to his father's death on December 30, 1783. His father had had William read and memorize "portions of the works of great British poets" (Gill, 1989, p. 17). Wordsworth recalled the influence of his teacher, William Taylor, while gazing at Taylor's grave in August 1794 and entered the recollection in the *Prelude*.

Wordsworth became a full-time poet, and in 1798, he and Samuel Taylor Coleridge, who at times lived near William and Dorothy, published a joint work, *Lyrical Ballads*.[2] The poems in this volume, a result of close association between the two men, included Coleridge's *Rime of the Ancient Mariner* and Wordsworth's *Tintern Abbey*. They were not-so-secret sharers with complementary and overlapping conceptual con-

---

2. One wonders whether it was a coincidence that his collaborator had for a middle name his teacher's last name, Taylor—that is, whether Wordsworth may have developed a friendship with Coleridge partly because of the name connection with a favorite teacher.

cerns. Wordsworth's ideal was to capture the quality of the relationship between man and nature through calm remembrance of tumultuous past experiences. Coleridge tended to start his poetry with a philosophical premise in mind.

On October 4, 1802, Wordsworth married Mary Hutchinson, who then shared the house with William and Dorothy. A baby boy was born on July 1, 1803, the first of their five children. Just prior to the marriage William and Dorothy visited Calais, where they spent a month with Annette and Caroline and made "financial arrangements" of some sort.

The marriage evoked ambivalent reactions from both Coleridge and Dorothy. Wordsworth wrote the first four stanzas of *Ode: Intimations of Immortality* seven months before his wedding and completed the poem two years later, in 1804. In 1807 he published it in a two-volume collection which is said to be the peak of Wordsworth's poetic creativity. "By the end of the first decade of the nineteenth century his thinking, in religion and politics, loses that speculative rebel quality from which it drew so much of his early strength, and his imagination . . . tends to hoard barren incidents and trivial perceptions" (*Encyclopedia Britannica*, 1957). Wordsworth lived until he was eighty. In his later years he was honored with a sinecure and then a pension; he was appointed Poet Laureate in 1843.

Years after Wordsworth's marriage, Dorothy's physical and mental health declined (although she survived William by five years); she suffered from arteriosclerosis. He had prolonged but intermittent fallings-out with Coleridge; the final breakup occurred years later. The sudden death at sea of William's brother John in 1805 "affected deeply a temperament to which melancholy was nature, inducing in Wordsworth a regress upon religious orthodoxy, and upon orthodoxies less banal" (*Encyclopedia Britannica*, 1957).

WORDSWORTH'S SECRET SHARERS

Wordsworth, his sister Dorothy, and Coleridge shared intimacy and poetic creation. Wordsworth felt that Dorothy had helped him reorganize his life and that she and Coleridge gave him stability. They believed themselves a quasi-religious Trinity. Coleridge once said, "Tho' we were three persons it was but one God" (Gill, 1989, p. 205). The three of them took long walking tours together. In 1797, as the trio started on one of their treks, they planned to write a poem together to help pay for the trip. Coleridge decided to base the ballad, which became *The Rime of the Ancient Mariner*, on a story he had heard about a beleaguered ship. Wordsworth contributed the myth of the albatross and the scene of the dead sailors navigating the ship. He even composed several lines that remained part of the poem. But the joint enterprise was not sustained, and Coleridge completed the work himself. Gill (1989) states: "Fired though he was by Coleridge's conversation and by his *creative fertility*, Wordsworth proved incapable of writing to order or to another man's plan" (p. 132) [italics mine].

While the three made a sharing trinity, Dorothy and William were a sharing pair and Coleridge and William another dyad. Dorothy was a mother-substitute who stabilized William's life and helped him overcome the "breakdown" he is said to have suffered before they remet and started to live together. His poetic statement in *The Sparrow's Nest* (Wordsworth, 1990), "She gave me eyes, she gave me ears," suggests his dependence on her, his feeling that she created him and his potential to be a poet who observed nature and its glory. The oedipal implication is clear. The poem also suggests that Dorothy's astute observations, which appear in her diaries, stirred Wordsworth as he heard and read her descriptions (Professor Arthur Zeiger, personal communication). The Lucy poems, which I will describe below, point to incestuous sexual fantasies about his sister. Her writings inspired William as his did her work. She read, transcribed, and criticized much of his work. He thus wrote for her, with her in mind, and fantasied union with her.

Wordsworth and Coleridge's intimacy has also been acknowledged. Their close association began in 1797. Trilling (1940), McFarland (1981), and Ruoff (1989) describe it as "symbiotic." Magnuson (1988), in *Coleridge and Wordsworth: A Lyrical Dialogue,* says that their writing has to be considered "one work" consisting of individual contributions, an "'amalgamation' [that] must have been a poetic and intellectual one" (p. 4). He adds that Wordsworth struggled against such a union as he tried to write original work and not to be influenced by Coleridge. In a later edition of *Lyrical Ballads,* for instance, Wordsworth's antagonism showed itself in his deprecation of Coleridge's contribution. "Nursing his conviction that . . . *The Ancient Mariner* had damaged the 1798 volume [of *Lyrical Ballads*], Wordsworth encouraged Coleridge to revise its diction" (Gill, 1989, p. 186). He removed the poem from the first position in Volume I of the 1800 edition and wrote an extremely critical note about it. The pair attempted to write two other poems together, but Wordsworth withdrew from these collaborations, too. Nevertheless, many of the poems they wrote as individuals resulted from mutual stimulation. The two would read each other's poems and address poems to each other. Each would refer to the work of the other in his poetry. And they would of course discuss their work directly.

Throughout their years of friendship Wordsworth and Coleridge engaged in many arguments, heated and cordial, about creativity, philosophy, and psychology. Coleridge was an even more prolific reader than Wordsworth and provided him with information and philosophical background beyond what Wordsworth would ordinarily possess. The doctrine of preexistence which William maintained in the *Ode* was introduced to him by Coleridge. In that poem he even referred to Coleridge's six-year-old son as an example of the glowing perceptions of children that grow dim as the children mature, a concept basic to this doctrine. Indeed, a mood of Coleridge's stimulated the poem.

In mid-March 1802, about seven months before Wordsworth was to marry Mary Hutchinson, a depressed Coleridge visited him and complained of a loss of creative powers (Noyes and Hayden, 1991, p. 111). Coleridge's dark mood affected Wordsworth, who tried to counteract his own worry on the same score; within five days of Coleridge's departure Wordsworth (1990) composed two optimistic poems (*To a Cuckoo* and *My Heart Leaps Up*) and the opening stanzas of the *Ode: Intimations of Immortality*, which, while intermittently optimistic, ends with a heavy sense of loss. A recovery of optimism appeared two years later, when he finished the poem, but this recovery was not complete.

Coleridge reacted strongly when he read the first four stanzas. In the spring of 1802 he addressed Wordsworth directly in a verse letter to Sara Hutchinson, the sister of Wordsworth's bride-to-be. This poem, according to Ruoff (1989), who was influenced by Bloom, is an "antithetical completion" (p. 74) of Wordsworth's 1802 *Ode*. In the verse poem, Coleridge first anticipates Wordsworth's marriage happily by asserting that Mary and Sara will join the Wordsworths in "one happy Home/One House, the dear and abiding Home of All." Then gloomily he adds: "Ours is her wedding garment, ours her Shroud."

As the date of the marriage approached, both Coleridge and Dorothy responded poorly. By April 1802, Coleridge, who a few months earlier had referred to William, Dorothy, and himself as a trinity, was "aware" and resentful that the trinity had expanded. His *Dejection: An Ode*, a condensed derivative of his verse poem to Sara Hutchinson, appeared in print on October 4, the very day of Wordsworth's wedding and the anniversary of Coleridge's own unhappy marriage. Intended as a wedding gift, it does attempt to achieve optimism, but its title tells of the pessimism and gloom against which Coleridge struggled. It expresses some of his anger at and envy of Wordsworth. A week later he published an attack on Wordsworth, indicating that William was sanctimonious and hypocritical.

Dorothy, too, was disturbed by the breakup of the trinity. She was distraught on the wedding day and "succumbed completely to hysteria" (p. 211), Gill asserts. She did not attend the ceremony. Indeed, Sara Hutchinson had to press her to greet William and Mary afterwards. No wonder! Shortly before the wedding Dorothy had written in her journal: "Poor Mary! Wm fell asleep, lying upon my breast and I upon Mary. I lay motionless for a long time, but I was at last obliged to move" (D. Wordsworth, 1987, p. 170). Dorothy obviously kept herself between the prospective bride and groom. The night before the wedding Dorothy wore the wedding ring. The next day William placed it back on her finger. Dorothy wrote, "I gave him the wedding ring—with how deep a blessing! I took it from my forefinger where I had worn it the whole night before—he slipped it again onto my finger, and pleased me fervently" (p. 13). The two lovers, possibly unaware of the full nature of their tie, were losing each other. Dorothy, having no intimate sexual replacement, would suffer more.

Dorothy's physical and mental health deteriorated after a considerable period of time. Living in the same house as William and Mary may have been a consolation and, as she helped to rear the children, may have involved a pleasurable enactment of a wish to parent William's child. (William and Dorothy had previously reared another child, Basil Montagu, for three years from the ages of three to six after his mother died [Moorman, 1957].) It must also have accentuated her recognition of the loss of her brother to another woman. A baby boy named John, after Wordsworth's father, was born on June 1, 1803. He was conceived around the time of the marriage, and his presence too must have upset Dorothy and Coleridge.

Wordsworth had anticipated the loss of his secret sharers as his marriage had approached, and the first four stanzas of the *Ode* expressed his depressive mood associated. The poem is about loss, not just of the acute perceptions of childhood, but also of Dorothy and Coleridge. Diminution of intense joyous reactions to nature must have recurred as Wordsworth became saddened by the probable loss, just as it had done when his parents died. Identification with Coleridge must have accentuated his sadness. The final section, written two years later, was a successful attempt at a more optimistic response. By that time, Wordsworth was assured that he had not lost Dorothy; his closeness to Coleridge also was sufficiently intact at that time.

Other factors played a role in the poet's sadness. With the birth of John, a rival appeared. Seeing mother and child together must have revived unconscious wishes to be with his mother. Hence the desire to return to the days of vivid sensations, his own birth, according to the doctrine of preexistence, when he was closest to his mother. John—

named, as he was, for Wordsworth's father—must also have served as a replacement for his lost parents. In this context the *Ode*'s epigraph, "The child is father of the man," acquires a new significance. This line, from Wordsworth's poem "My Heart Leaps Up," was written shortly before he began the *Ode* and was not added to the *Ode* until the 1815 version.

A telling confirmation of the suggestion that Wordsworth associated the *Ode*, his marriage, and the birth of his child appears in the epigraph Wordsworth chose for the 1807 version of the text: *"Paulo majora canumus"* (Let us sing a nobler song).[3] This line comes from Virgil's Fourth Eclogue (see Manning, 1983; Levinson, 1986; Magnuson, 1988), a work about the desired consequences of a wedding between Antonius and Octavia, and the miraculous birth of a child whose coming will restore the golden age.

THE LUCY POEMS

A discussion of the Lucy poems will provide further evidence for Wordsworth's incestuous attachment to Dorothy (Bateson, 1954) and his antagonism to her (Matlak, 1978) as well as his unconscious equation of Lucy and Dorothy with his mother. In addition I will suggest that Wordsworth's affection for Coleridge could turn to antagonism when Coleridge spurned and separated from him. The Lucy poems thus add to our knowledge of Wordsworth's intimacy with Dorothy and Coleridge that is part of the secret sharer fantasies.

In 1798 William and Dorothy Wordsworth paid a prolonged visit to Germany with Coleridge and John Chester, an admirer of Coleridge whom Coleridge had invited for a stay. Within a short time Coleridge, on his own, rented room and board for Chester and himself in Ratzeburg, a lovely town near Hamburg that was too expensive for William and Dorothy's budget. Wordsworth found quarters that he could afford in Goslar, which was quite a distance from Ratzeburg. As a result, William and Dorothy shared tight and poorly heated quarters without the diluting effect of the presence of others. Since the local citizens believed that Dorothy and William were illicit lovers living together rather than sister and brother, they shunned their company. Under these conditions, affectionate feelings between brother and sister were accentuated, as Wordsworth's comparison at that time of his state and that of a lonely cold fly indicates (see Wordsworth, 1990):

> No brother, no mate has he near him—while I
> Can draw warmth from the cheek of my love

---

3. I am grateful to Marjorie Levinson for pointing this out to me.

The first three Lucy poems, composed within the first three months of the stay at Goslar, were formally written to Coleridge, but Dorothy read them first. They were thus written to her as well. The first poem, *Strange Fits of Passion* (Wordsworth, 1990), was addressed to "the Lover's ear alone":

> When she I loved looked every day
> Fresh as a rose in June,
> I to her cottage bent my way
> Beneath an evening moon.

As he approaches his love on horseback he thinks:

> What fond and wayward thoughts will slide
> Into a lover's head!
> "O Mercy" to myself I cried
> "If Lucy should be dead!"

In "She Dwelt among Untrodden Ways" (Wordsworth, 1990), his beloved Lucy dies.

> . . . few could know
> When Lucy ceased to be;
> But she is in her grave, and, oh,
> The difference to me!

According to Matlak (1978), Wordsworth wrote the fourth Lucy poem after a reunion with Coleridge (*Three Years She Grew*) and the fifth and final one after a threatened loss of Coleridge (*I Travelled among Unknown Men*). The Lucy poems suggest an interplay of love and anger toward Lucy (identified as Dorothy by Coleridge) in a setting in which he lost and regained Coleridge.[4] The hatred, Matlak says, arises because Dorothy/Lucy interferes with Wordsworth's closeness to Coleridge. The love, I suggest, is an oedipal love of Dorothy/Lucy, Wordsworth's mother substitute and creator, the woman who is so close to Wordsworth, especially while they are in Goslar.

It is not unusual for antagonism to serve as a defense against incestuous wishes, and that appears to be the case with Wordsworth's feeling for Dorothy. Reiman (1978) believes that "the origin of the dream or premonition of Dorothy's death . . . may be in William's subconscious struggle to avoid focusing his obviously strong sexual drive on the sister he lived with" (p. 250). I suggest that the association of Dorothy and their mother makes things more complicated; the mother died when

---

4. Reiman (1978) notes that in certain interrelated poems Coleridge calls the Lucy-figure Dorothy. Wordsworth identified the Lucy-figure in the Glow-Worm poem as Dorothy in an 1802 letter to Coleridge (Noyes and Hayden, 1991, p. 49).

William was seven, evoking images of a dead Lucy in the poems. The loved one's death is a repetition of a childhood experience, created partly in an attempt at mastery of the early loss, partly out of rage at one who died and left him. The loss of Coleridge gave rise anew to these same images.

Matlak suggests that the sleepy trancelike state of the rider as he approaches Lucy in *Strange Fits of Passion* represents a "decathexis" of libido due to a wish that Dorothy die, a forbidden wish counteracted by censorship. He does not suggest that the sleep avoids forbidden oedipal contact with Lucy/Dorothy/Mother or the death a forbidden orgasm (*la petite mort*). However, it seems likely that the sleep serves as both a defense and a wish fulfillment.

I was surprised that Matlak recognizes neither Wordsworth's fury toward Coleridge deriving from his loss of him, nor his intense affection for Coleridge and his jealousy of Chester. Although I am not suggesting that the loving or sexual aspects of this affection were conscious, it seems likely that they existed as a potent motivating force. Through displacement Lucy becomes a stand-in for Coleridge as well as for Dorothy. In fact Lucy is a multifaceted poetic symbol for Dorothy, Coleridge, and Wordsworth's mother. The poem expresses and defends against love and hatred for each of them.

Secret Sharers and Collective Alternates

The concept of secret sharers developed by Meyer overlaps with that of "collective alternates" (Greenacre, 1957, 1958). Greenacre did not discuss Wordsworth in any detail, but she provided insight into creativity that is particularly applicable to Wordsworth, who experienced his surroundings intensely in childhood and had vivid and detailed memories as a grownup. His adult perceptions were also of remarkable strength.

Greenacre (1958, p. 52) asserts that artists (including poets) possess unusually great "sensory responsiveness" to their environment, even as children. They also enjoy immense capacities "to organize sensory impressions into related engrams with special sensitivity to rhythm and form" (p. 528) as well as remarkable empathy with other humans and even with nature. Their faculties are so great that their relationships with the outer world of nature are unusually intense. The world and the people who inhabit it become powerful objects or, more accurately, object representations. The artist creates not only for his parents or their substitutes (secret sharers) but also for "collective alternates" that form in part through displacement from the representations of parents. The highly cathected objects in nature contribute mightily to the collective alternates' representations. Collective alternates, although less specific than secret sharers, are similar in structure and play a significant role in creativity.

It appears, then, that Wordsworth created the *Ode* and other works not only for Dorothy and Coleridge—specific sharers who were parent surrogates—but also for collective alternates that were amalgams of nature and of his mother. Displacement occurred *from* nature as well as *to* nature.

Onorato (1971), using psychoanalytic knowledge, is interested in the displacement from mother to nature. He seems to ignore the poet's primary perceptual acuity, sensitivity, and cathexis as he demonstrates that Wordsworth's enormous sensitivity to nature arose out of his relationship with the mother whom he had lost. McFarland (1981) agreed with Onorato that William's "projection" of this mutual relationship "fixated itself as a denial of the loss" (p. 48). More accurately, Wordsworth displaced cathexis from mother to nature, which came to symbolize mother. This displacement facilitated denial of the loss.

Wordsworth (1979), writing about his infancy in the *Prelude,* said:

> blest the Babe,
> Nursed in his Mother's arms, who sinks to sleep
> Rocked on his Mother's breast; who with his soul
> Drinks in the feelings of his Mother's eye!
> (Wordsworth, p. 79, 1850 version, lines 234–37)

With his mother's death, he wrote:

> I was left alone
> Seeking the visible world, nor knowing why.
> The props of my affections were removed,
> And yet the building stood, as if sustained
> By its own spirit!
> (Wordsworth, p. 80, 1805 version, lines 277–81)

Immediately after this passage about his mother's death, the poet continued:

> All that I beheld
> Was dear to me, and from this cause it came
> That now to Nature's finest influxes
> My mind lay open . . .
> (Wordsworth, 1805 version, lines 281–84)

In this poem Wordsworth reveals that he turned to nature as a substitute for his mother. He could create for nature as well as for his secret sharers. Or perhaps we should say that nature became one of his sharers. Nature became an admired presence for whom and with whom he created.

BIBLIOGRAPHY

BATESON, F. W. (1954). *Wordsworth: A Reinterpretation.* London: Longmans.

BLUM, H. P. (1990). Freud, Fliess, and the parenthood of psychoanalysis. *Psychoanal. Q.*, 59:21–40.

COLERIDGE, S. T. (1950). The rime of the ancient mariner. In *The Portable Coleridge*, ed. I. A. Richards. New York: Viking Penguin.

COLTRERA, J. T., ed. (1981). *Lives, Events and Other Players: Directions in Psychobiography.* Of the Downstate Psychoanalytic Institute Twenty-Fifth Anniversary Series, volume 4. New York: Aronson.

DAICHES, D., ed. (1971). *The Penguin Companion to English Literature*, S.V. "William Wordsworth." New York: McGraw-Hill.

ENCYCLOPAEDIA BRITANNICA, 1957 ed., S.V. "William Wordsworth."

FERENCZI, S. (1950 [1913]). Stages in the development of a sense of reality. Trans. E. Jones, 213–39. In *Sex in Psychoanalysis.* New York: Basic.

FREUD, S. (1917). Mourning and Melancholia. *S.E.*, 14:239–58.

GILL, S. (1989). *William Wordsworth: A Life.* Oxford: Clarendon.

GLENN, J. (1983). Twins in the theater: A study of plays by Peter and Anthony Shaffer. In *Blood Brothers*, ed. N. Kiell, 277–99. New York: Int. Univ. Press.

———— (1986). Twinship themes and fantasies in the work of Thornton Wilder. *Psychoanal. Study Child*, 41:627–51.

GREENACRE, P. (1971 [1957]). The childhood of the artist. In *Emotional Growth* 2:479–504. New York: Int. Univ. Press. Originally published in *Psychoanal. Study Child*, 12:47–72.

———— (1971 [1958]). The family romance of the artist. In *Emotional Growth* 2:505–32. New York: Int. Univ. Press. Originally published in *Psychoanal. Study Child*, 13:9–36.

HARPER, G. M. (1916). *William Wordsworth: His Life, Works, and Influence.* New York: Russell and Russell.

HARTMANN, H. (1965). *Essays on Ego Psychology.* New York: Int. Univ. Press.

KOHUT, H. (1977). *The Restoration of the Self.* New York: Int. Univ. Press.

LEVINSON, M. (1986). *Wordsworth's Great Period Poems: Four Essays.* Cambridge: Cambridge University Press.

MC FARLAND, T. (1981). *Romanticism and the Forms of Ruin.* Princeton, N.J.: Princeton University Press.

MAGNUSON, P. (1988). *Coleridge and Wordsworth: A Lyrical Dialogue.* Princeton, N.J.: Princeton University Press.

MANNING, P. (1983). Wordsworth's intimations ode and its epigraphs. *Journal of English and Germanic Philology*, 82:526–40.

MATLAK, R. E. (1978). Wordsworth's Lucy poems in psychobiographical context. *PMLA*, 93. Reprinted in *Critical Essays on William Wordsworth*. ed. G. H. Gilpin, pp. 267–99. Boston: G. K. Hall, 1990.

MEYER, B. C. (1967). *Joseph Conrad: A Psychoanalytic Biography*. Princeton, N.J.: Princeton University Press.

———(1972). Some reflections on the contributions of psychoanalysis to biography. *Psychoanal. and Contemp. Sci.*, 1:373–91.

———(1987). Notes on the uses of psychoanalysis for biography. *Psychoanal. Q.*, 56:287–316.

MOORMAN, M. (1957). *William Wordsworth: A Biography, Early Years: 1770–1803*. Oxford: Clarendon Press.

NOYES, R., & HAYDEN, J. O. (1991). *William Wordsworth*. Updated ed. Boston: Twayne.

ONORATO, R. J. (1971). *The Character of the Poet: Wordsworth in "The Prelude."* Princeton, N.J.: Princeton University Press.

REIMAN, D. H. (1978). Poetry of familiarity: Wordsworth, Dorothy, and Mary Hutchinson. In *The Evidence of the Imagination*, ed. D. H. Reiman, M. C. Jaye, and B. T. Bennett. New York: New York University Press. Reprinted in *Critical Essays on William Wordsworth*, ed. G. H . Gilpin, 237–67. Boston: G. K. Hall, 1990.

RUOFF, G. W. (1989). *Wordsworth and Coleridge: The Making of the Major Lyrics, 1802–1804*. New Brunswick, N.J.: Rutgers University Press.

TRILLING, L. (1940). *The Liberal Imagination*. New York: Viking.

TROSMAN, H. (1990). Psychoanalysis and the imaginative life. Paper presented at the Meeting Commemorating the Fortieth Anniversary of the Psychoanalytic Institute, New York University Medical Center.

TURNER, J. (1988). Wordsworth and Winnicott in the area of play. *Int. Rev. Psycho-Anal.*, 15:481-98.

VENDLER, H. (1988). *The Music of What Happens*. Cambridge, Mass.: Harvard University Press.

WORDSWORTH, D. (1987). *The Grasmere Journal*. New York: Henry Holt.

WORDSWORTH, W. (1990). *The Poems*. Volume 1. London: Penguin Group.

———(1979). *The Prelude 1799, 1805, 1850*, ed. J. Wordsworth, M. H. Abrams and S. Gill. New York: W. W. Norton.

———(1988). *Selected Prose*, ed. J. O. Hayden. Harmondsworth: Penguin.

"Lazarus Stand Forth"

H. D. Encounters Freud

WILLIAM D. JEFFREY, M.D.

H. D., the noted writer Hilda Doolittle, wrote three differing accounts of her first analytic session with Freud, held on March 1, 1933. The first account was written on the same day as her session in a letter to her friend Bryher; it indicates that Freud did not meet H. D.'s preformed transference expectation. Although H. D. focused on her fear of Freud's rejection, her deeper concern was her disappointment in Freud and her fear of loving a person who might die soon. In 1944, five years after Freud's death, H. D. wrote a second account of the session in "Tribute to Freud" in which she attempted to recall an idealized memory of Freud. To do this her description split the session into a part in which she projected her anger onto Freud and a part in which she reconciled with Freud in a mystical, wordless communication by means of her relation to his dog, Yofi. Her third account, "Advent," was written in 1948, following a period of psychosis. At that time H. D. was able to acknowledge that she had been frightened of loving a man who was vulnerable to death and to restore Freud's presence by identifying with his analytic ability.

Clinical assistant professor at the Psychoanalytic Institute at New York University School of Medicine; attending psychiatrist at Maimonides Medical Center, Brooklyn, New York.

A shorter version of this paper was presented at the spring meeting of the Division of Psychoanalysis of the American Psychological Association, April 12, 1991, and at the 37th International Psychoanalytical Congress, July 29, 1991.

The author thanks the Beinecke Rare Book and Manuscript Library of Yale University for permission to quote from their collection of Hilda Doolittle manuscripts. Excerpts from *Tribute to Freud* by H. D., Copyright © 1974 by Norman Holmes Pearson, and *Helen in Egypt* by H. D., Copyright © 1961 by Norman Holmes Pearson, are reprinted by permission of New Directions Publication Corporation.

The Psychoanalytic Study of the Child 50, ed. Albert J. Solnit, Peter B. Neubauer, Samuel Abrams, and A. Scott Dowling (Yale University Press, copyright © 1995 by Albert J. Solnit, Peter B. Neubauer, Samuel Abrams, and A. Scott Dowling).

OF THE FEW OF FREUD'S ANALYSANDS WHO WROTE EXTENSIVELY ABOUT their experiences with him, the best known is Hilda Doolittle, the prominent poet and author known as H. D. H. D. was in analysis with Freud from March 1, 1933, to June 12, 1933, and then again from October 31, 1934, to December 2, 1934. She wrote not one but three accounts of her treatment: a series of unpublished letters written at the time of her analysis (H. D. 1933–34); "Tribute to Freud," written in 1944 (H. D., 1944); and "Advent," written in 1948 (H. D., 1974).

Psychoanalysts have made few comments about these accounts. Holland (1969a, 1969b) wrote two articles in 1969 about "Tribute to Freud," but since then the only analyst to write about H. D. has been Richards, in 1992. There has been much recent interest in H. D.'s life and work in academia, however, particularly among feminist critics. Major works include two biographies (Robinson, 1982; Guest, 1984), four critical studies (Friedman, 1981, 1990;) Du Plessis, 1986; Chisholm, 1992) and a series of critical essays (King, 1986).

This paper will examine H. D.'s memoirs of her first session with Freud to gain understanding into her psyche and conflicts, not only at the time of her initial encounter with Freud but at the times of recalling her experience. The following biographical information on H. D.'s often turbulent life is drawn from Friedman's account (1986a) in the *Dictionary of Literary Biography* unless otherwise noted.

H. D. was born on September 10, 1886, in Bethlehem, Pennsylvania, to Charles Leander Doolittle, a noted astronomer, and Helen Wolle Doolittle. She attended Bryn Mawr College but withdrew under unclear circumstances, perhaps after suffering a "breakdown" (Friedman, 1981, p. 27). In 1911 she settled in England. She began publishing her poetry and soon became noted as the foremost poet of the Imagist school. She married the writer Richard Aldington in 1913.

During the years of World War I she suffered a series of traumas. In 1915, she had a stillborn child. The following year, Aldington entered the army, and their marriage began to disintegrate. In 1918, H. D.'s brother Gilbert was killed in France, and shortly thereafter, early in 1919, her father died. H. D. was pregnant, not by her husband, but by Cecil Gray, a music historian. She developed influenza that almost killed both her and her unborn child; however, her daughter, Perdita, was born on March 31, 1919. She and Aldington then separated. This sequence resulted in an emotional breakdown, for which she consulted with Havelock Ellis (Friedman, 1990, p. 11).

In July 1918 H. D. became closely involved with Annie Winifred Ellerman, who became her lover and a source of support for the rest of her life. Ellerman, the daughter of a wealthy English shipping magnate, was later recognized as a writer under her pseudonym, Bryher. In the early 1920s, Ellis showed Bryher an article about psychoanalysis, and Bryher soon became a dedicated supporter of psychoanalysis. She met Freud in 1927 and began analysis with Hanns Sachs in 1928.

In 1927, Bryher married the artist Kenneth Macpherson, a lover of H. D. The following year she and Macpherson adopted H. D.'s daughter. Also in 1928, H. D. became pregnant by Macpherson and on the advice of Sachs had an abortion in Berlin (Guest, 1984, pp. 193–94).

Influenced by Bryher's interest, H. D. began to read about psychoanalysis. She and Bryher attended psychoanalytic lectures in Berlin (Friedman, 1981, p. 18). H. D. first entered analysis (for twenty-four sessions) in April 1931 with an analyst friend, Mary Chadwick, and had at least three sessions with Hanns Sachs in the winter of 1931–32 (Friedman, 1981, p. 18). Sachs suggested that she enter analysis with Freud and wrote her a letter of introduction. She was accepted by Freud, but the start of the analysis was delayed by Freud's illness (Friedman, 1986b, p. 321). During this time, H. D. read widely about analysis (Friedman, 1981, pp. 18–19). Finally, on March 1, 1933 she began a relationship that was to have a profound effect on the rest of her life.

LETTER TO BRYHER

Until Freud discouraged it as a resistance, H. D. recorded each analytic session in her dairy. Unfortunately, she probably destroyed the notes in 1948 (Friedman, 1990, p. 283). During her analysis, however, she also wrote detailed letters to Bryher, which have been preserved. H. D.'s March 1 letter to Bryher describes her dramatic first encounter with Freud. ("Cat" refers to H. D.; "Chaddie" is Chadwick; "Turtle" is Sachs; and "Puss" is H. D.'s daughter, Perdita.)

Wed. after dinner. March 1.

I wrote Alice, and will see her, at her convenience, to-morrow or day after.

I staggered down Berg Gasse, having timed it to take about ten slow minutes, or eight fast, this morning. The entrance was lovely with wide steps and a statue in a court-yard before a trellis and gave me time to powder, only a gent with an attache case emerged and looked at me knowingly, and I thought, "ah—the Professor's last" and found the door still open from his exit, to let enter cat, who was moaned over by a tiny stagemaid who took off the gun-metal rubbers and said I should not wear my coat. I stuck to the coat, was ushered into waiting room, and before I could adjust before joyless-street mirror, a little white ghost emerged at my elbow and I nearly fainted, it said, "enter fair madame" and I did and a small but furry chow got up in the other room, and came and stood at my feet. God. I think if the chow hadn't liked me, I would have left, I was so scared by Oedipus. I shook all over, he said I must take off my coat, I said I was cold, he led me around the room and I admired bits of Pompeii in red, a bit of Egyptian cloth and some authentic coffin paintings, A spynx faces the bed. I did not want to go to bed, the white "napkin for the head" was the only professional touch, there were dim lights, like an opium dive. I started to talk about Sachs and Chaddy and my experience with ps-a. He said he would prefer me to recline. He has a real fur rug, and I started to tell him how turtle had none, he seemed vaguely shocked, then remarked, "I see you are going to be very difficult. Now although it is against the rules, I will tell you something: YOU *WERE* DISAPPOINTED, AND YOU *ARE* DISAPPOINTED IN ME." I then let out a howl, and screamed, "but do you not realize you are everything, you are priest, you are magician." He said, "no. It is you who are poet and magician." I then cried so I could hardly utter and he said that I had looked at the pictures, preferring the mere dead shreds of antiquity to his living presence. I then yelled, "but you see your dog liked me, when your dog came, I knew it was all right, as it would not have liked me if you had not." He said, "ah, an English proverb but reversed, like me and you like my dog." I corrected him, "love me, love my dog" and he growled and purred with delight. He then gave me a long speech on how sad it was for a poet to listen to his bad English. I then howled some more and said he was not a person but a voice, and that in looking at antiquity, I was looking at him. He said I had got to the same place as he, we met, he in the childhood of humanity—antiquity—I in my own childhood. I cried some more and the hour was already more than half gone. It was terrible. I go now at five regularly. I could not tackle him about money but will try to-morrow. He is not there at all, is simply a ghost and I simply shake all over and cry. He kept asking me if I wanted the lights changed. He sat, not at, but on the pillow and hammered with his fist to point his remarks and mine. I am terrified of Oedipus Rex. What am I to do? He finally made me stand beside him and said though I was taller, he was nearly as tall. I had said maybe I was disaappointed that he was not a giant, as being taller made me grown up; in my dreams now I was always a child. We compromised . . . but he seemed to have won. Then I got as far as the door and the porfessor [*sic*] said, "ah" and there, snug under the rug, were my bags (I had taken two small ones instead of a big one). So I did win after all, he saw then that I was not disappointed in him . . . but it was too awful, I shall never get over Oedipus and I go to-morrow and on and on. He is terrible, dope and dope and dope. We talked of race and the war, he said I was English from America and that was not difficult, "what am I?" I said, "well, a Jew—" he seemed to want me to make the statement. I then went on to say that that too was a religious bond as Jew was the only member of antiquity that still lived in the world. He said, "in fragments." O Lord . . . you said he would not talk and he talked half the time and he would not let me lie

and dream and made me talk; not with T. and Chaddie, I was never at a
loss for a word, but this old Oedipus Rex has got me . . . I told him so,
sobbing, and said I had not cried in the other hours. O Lord, write me!
 This is to you both . . . I can't think of you separate as you both saw me
off . . . O Gawd!
 Then I couldn't come back here as I was sobbing so.
 I found a most exquisite old, old, wooden place where they serve white
wine and apples, off a courtyard through snow. I asked some girls in a
bake-shop for a restaurant for "ladies". They showed me this which is a
real old old trouvaille, I doubt if even Alice knows it, O marvelous with
old mellowed brown paintings on the wall and such apples. Well . . .
come. I will show you that "Wien and der Wein" still exists, so funny.
How did it happen that I fell in on that? No film has ever done more . . .
it is old stuff that people say is non est. Come to Wien . . . in lilac time.
 This is silly, hysterical and mad. There was no returned wire, so I
judged you had it, so did not send your pre-paid. If the return "not
known" comes to-morrow, I will get them to call up the house.
 Must stop, the dog is called yo-si or fi-yo or something Chinese. It
came and sat in a chair at my feet . . . but I suppose it is trained to give
the analysands confidence. SAnyhow [*sic*] . . . long live Oedipus.
 Love to all and sundry. I don't dare write in a frivolous and lightsome
manner except to you two. Tell T. what it means to me, Dr. F. spoke of
him and he knew of Chaddie but didn't want me to talk of them.
 Love to old Puss, tell her about it and the chow. It is faun and buff. H.
D.   [H. D., 1933–34]

A few considerations should be kept in mind when examining this
letter and the others. The account of any analysand trying to recall a
session would be distorted. What is more, H. D. wrote her letters to
Bryher immediately after her sessions; therefore, there was no retrospective revision in response to later understandings and insights. The
letters were not written for publication, and in them H. D. is candid
about her sexuality and engages in much unflattering gossip about
friends and acquaintances.

 In the first letter, H. D. conveys her almost overwhelming anxiety in
regard to Freud during their initial meeting. Although she begins by
casually mentioning a mutual acquaintance, Alice Modern, a former
governess of H. D.'s daughter, and flippantly describes her arrival at 19
Berggasse, making a pun ("joyless-street mirror"; *Freud* means joy), her
view of Freud on this day certainly reflects her fears. In rapid succes-
sion, she reports that she almost fainted, was scared, shook all over,
howled, screamed, yelled, and sobbed.

 Early in her letter, H. D. introduces the theme of her anxiety about
her relationship to Freud and reassurance by Freud's dog, Yofi. In the

most dramatic part of the letter—the crux of the session—she writes of her overwhelming distress at Freud's comment that she will be "difficult": "You were disappointed, and you are disappointed in me." Although it is later in her letter that she mentions Freud's "hammering," it must have been at this point that it happened.

H. D. deals with Freud's interpretation as if it were a rejection, reacting with anxiety to the loss of Freud's love. In response to his comment she not only denies any disappointment on her part but claims that, to her, Freud is everything. She then uses her imagined relationship to Yofi in an attempt to convince Freud (really to convince herself) that Freud likes her, claiming, "[Yofi] would not have liked me if you had not." H. D.'s peculiar logic is based on her hope. She reports that Freud then commented that she had reversed the proverb "Like me and you like my dog." H. D. then "corrected" Freud by intensifying the affect, shifting from "like" to "love." However, she never actually addressed Freud's interpretation that she was disappointed in him. Although, midway through her letter H. D. writes that she was able tentatively to acknowledge Freud's comment, this seemed to reflect desire not to displease him, rather than insight, since she then uses her parapraxis, forgetting to take her bags, as further evidence that she was not disappointed.

Her concern that Freud does not love her pervades the letter, and she frequently recalls the session in such a manner as to reassure herself of Freud's love. At the beginning of the letter, she portrays Freud as solicitous, if not seductive. She mentions Freud's charming greeting, "Welcome, fair madame." She resisted beginning the analytic relationship and reports that Freud said she must take off her coat, that he led her about the room (which she associated to an opium dive), and that he said he preferred her to lie on the couch.

As H. D. writes of the session, she emphasizes other special ways in which Freud treated her. In fact, she prefaces Freud's devastating comment, "You were and are disappointed in me," by reporting that he said his statement was "against the rules." She enumerates various ways in which Freud broke "the rules" and therefore gave her special treatment: He complimented her, calling her "poet and magician." He showed "delight" at her correction of the proverb. He gave her "a long speech," mentioning "how sad it was for a poet to listen to his bad English." He asked if she wished the lights changed, had her stand next to him, discussed race and war, and "talked half the time."

In her session and when writing her letter, H. D. attempted to deal with her wish for Freud to love her and her anxiety that he would not, but this focus avoided her greater anxiety—"loving an idealized object who was vulnerable to death. Freud's comment that she was disappointed in him was a painful truth, and recognizing this was too frightening for her. What he perspicaciously noted was a key to H. D.'s conflict. Her first description of Freud, as "a little white ghost," is important for understanding H. D.'s conflictual relationship to him, since one significant attribute of a ghost is that he both succumbs to death and overcomes death.

H. D. appears to have brought into her first session an intense, preformed transference. (She later wrote, "I did feel that I had reached the high-water mark of achievement . . . to be accepted by him as an analysand or student, seemed to crown all my personal contacts and relationships [H. D., 1944, p. 64].) But the Freud H. D. saw was not her idealized powerful vision of Freud. In 1933 Freud was small and old and had suffered from cancer and from cancer operations since 1923. H. D. must have been very disappointed in the real figure of Freud, who did not measure up to her preformed transference expectation and need. Even if she did have his love, it would be of questionable value—the love of a defective, not an idealized, object.

H. D.'s awareness of Freud's vulnerability to death is evident throughout her letter. With the statement "in looking at antiquity, I was looking at him," she means to deny disappointment, but that meaning is belied by her description of the antiquities: "bits of Pompeii in red, a bit of Egyptian cloth [recovered from a burial?] and some authentic coffin paintings." H. D.'s later words, "dead shreds" and "living presence," again reveal fear of Freud's physical vulnerability. Finally, she mentioned that the Jew was "the only member of antiquity that still lived in the world," and her repetition of Freud's reply, "in fragments," poignantly reflected her apprehension.

H. D.'s conflation of Freud and Oedipus, similarly alludes to a conflict about developing a relationship with the aging analyst. Her complaint, "I shall never get over Oedipus and I go to-morrow and on and on," conceals her wish that the relationship with Freud will not end through his death, and the statements "this old Oedipus Rex has got me" and "long live Oedipus" again refer to this issue, which underlies much of H. D.'s anxiety. When she writes that "he is not there at all, is simply a ghost and I simply shake all over and cry" and that Freud is "not a person but a voice," she may be indicating a problem in maintaining the mental representation of the Freud she expected.

H. D. deals with her fears of Freud's rejection and his potential death by emphasizing their closeness. She reports that after she told Freud that he was a priest and magician, he called her a poet and magician; Freud himself indicated their similarity—both are magicians. As another mark of similarity, H. D. mentions Freud's intervention that they met in the same place, he in the childhood of humanity—antiquity—and she in her own childhood. Even when she notes that Freud alluded to a difference between them—he was a Jew and she English and American—H. D. tried to forge from it a closeness to Freud by claiming "that too was a religious bond as Jew was the only member of antiquity that still lived in the world." Freud's reply, "In fragments," alludes to H. D.'s initial contemplation of the fragments of antiquity in Freud's office, signifying Freud's mortality.

In her description of standing beside Freud, she claims that Freud said he was almost as tall as she. This appears to be another aspect of a wish for closeness since H. D. was five feet, eleven inches, in height, significantly taller than Freud, who measured five feet and seven or eight inches (Knight, 1937, p. 113). Finally, leaving her bags behind probably represented a wish to avoid separation as much as a denial of disappointment.

When H. D. reports that Freud hammered, she writes that he sat "on," not by, the pillow. This too seems to represent a wish for closeness to Freud, which at times has aspects of a wish for merger. She mentions, for example, that Freud hammered "to point his remarks and mine," a doubtful surmise since it would not make sense for Freud to hammer to point *her* remarks. Her inference seems to be a blurring of self and object boundaries. A stronger image of merger occurs as she describes Freud "growling and purring." Freud (the dog Yofi) and H. D. (whose nickname was Cat) become one. Another merging with Freud occurs when she paraphrases the conversation: H. D.'s own words and Freud's words are combined. For example, the report, "he said that I had looked at the picture, preferring the mere dead shreds of antiquity to his living presence," sounds more like the poetry of H. D. than the words of Freud.

H. D.'s feeling of a need for intimate closeness continued, past the session, to the time at which she wrote to Bryher. After again mentioning that she cried during the hour, H. D. begs Bryher to write and then says, "I can't think of you as separate as you both saw me off." (She probably is referring to Bryher and Perdita.) Then she asks Bryher to come to her in Vienna. As she struggles to end her letter, she mentions confusion about a wire she sent to Bryher, an association to her difficulty maintaining a relationship. Her letter goes on and on, as if she cannot bear to end it.

H. D.'s description of her comfort at the restaurant for ladies appears to be a derivative of a wish for maternal nurturing, and she again refers to Alice Modern in this passage, resuming a theme of reuniting with an absent maternal figure. Susan Stanford Friedman (1990, pp. 340–42), has written about *The Gift*, H. D.'s insightful memoir of childhood written in the early 1940s, in which she recalls her father returning home one evening with his head bloodied. The family feared that he might die. Friedman reconstructs H. D.'s fantasy of the death and rebirth of her father, who, resurrected but damaged (that is, castrated), would be a less frightening figure. Two weeks into her analysis, H. D. wrote to Kenneth Macpherson, "Freud is simply Jesus-Christ after the resurrection, he has that wistful ghost look of someone who has been right past the door of the tomb" (Friedman, 1981, p. 19). H. D.'s perception of an aging and ill Freud during her first session conforms to the fantasy of a once powerful, now damaged man and might have been an additional factor in her distress around Freud. She may have felt that her wish for a less intimidating, albeit wounded, paternal figure had somehow come true.

When H. D. first encountered Freud she was faced with a conflict: to love Freud was to love a person who soon might die, adding to the long series of losses and deaths that ran throughout her life. She writes, in fact, that she entered analysis to learn to deal with these losses. But Freud did not fit H. D.'s initial transference expectations of a parental figure who could protect her from the dangers of the world (and the dangers of her internal world). An even worse possibility existed: in her fantasy, her anger might destroy the weak, ill, and fragile Freud. Not only would she have no relationship, she would be burdened with guilt.

However, H. D.'s idealization of Freud quickly returned, and her analysis moved forward. Unfortunately, she left Vienna and analysis abruptly in June 1933, after a tram on which she was riding almost triggered a bomb on the tracks. Although Freud advised her to return in the fall, she did not (Friedman, 1986b, p. 321). The following summer, H. D. learned that a fellow analysand of Freud's had died in a plane crash. She had a "brief, but severe breakdown" (ibid.) and returned to Freud in the late fall of 1934 for one month.

Although her analysis proved of lasting benefit to her creative abilities, H. D. nonetheless continued to have emotional difficulties and was in therapy with Walter Schmideberg from 1935 through 1937.

TRIBUTE TO FREUD

H. D. first wrote for publication about her analysis ten years after it ended, from September 19 to November 2, 1944, in London (H. D., 1944). Her diaries of her analysis, which were in Switzerland, were unavailable because of the war. She revised the draft, probably in the winter of 1944–45, and the memoir was first published in May, June, August, and September 1945 and January 1946 as a series of articles in the English magazine *Life and Letters Today* under the title "Writing on the Wall." The memoir was republished with minor changes in 1956 as *Tribute to Freud.*

The book's eighty-five sections proceed not sequentially, but in a manner similar to free association. H. D.'s description of her first session with Freud appears near the end of the book in sections 74, 75, and 76. In the following excerpt the material deleted from the original draft is in brackets and the material added is in bold face.

> I HAVE SAID that these impressions must take me, rather than I [the impressions] **take them.** The first impression of all takes me back to the beginning, to my first session with the Professor. Paula has opened the door. . . . She has divested me of my coat and made some welcoming remark which has slightly embarrassed me, as I am thinking English thoughts and only English words come to prompt me. She has shown me into the waiting-room with the lace-curtains at the window. . . . I know that **Prof.** Dr. Sigmund Freud will open the door which faces me. Although I know this and have been preparing for some months for this ordeal, I am, none the less, taken aback, surprised, shocked even, when the door opens. It seems to me, after my time of waiting, that he appears too suddenly.
>
> Automatically, I walk through the door. It closes. Sigmund Freud does not speak. [He is waiting for me to say something. I cannot speak.] I look round the room. A lover of Greek art, I am automatically taking stock of the room's contents. Pricelessly lovely objects are displayed here on the shelves to right, to left of me. . . . I know that he had a very grave **recurrence of a former serious illness,** some five years or so ago, [a malignant cancer—and was miraculously saved.] **and was again operated on for that particularly pernicious form of cancer of the mouth or tongue, and that by a miracle (to the amazement of the Viennese specialist) he recovered. It seems to me, in some curious way, that we were both "miraculously saved" for some purpose. But all this is a feeling, an atmosphere—something that I realize or perceive, but do not actually put into words or thoughts.** . . .
>
> He is the infinitely old symbol, weighing the soul, Psyche, in the Balance. Does the Soul, passing the portals of life, entering the House of Eternity, greet the Keeper of the Door? It seems so. I should have thought the Door-Keeper, at home beyond the threshold, might have greeted the shivering soul. Not so the Professor. But waiting and finding that I would not or could not speak, he uttered. What he said—and I thought a little sadly—was, "You are the only person who has ever come into this room and looked at the things in the room before looking at me."

But worse was to come. A little lion-like creature came padding toward me—a lioness, as it happened. She had emerged from the inner sanctum or manifested from under or behind the couch; anyhow, she continued her course across the carpet. Embarrassed, shy, overwhelmed, I bend down to greet this creature. But the Professor says, "Do not touch her—she snaps—she is very difficult with strangers." *Strangers?* Is the Soul crossing the threshold, a stranger to the Door-Keeper? It appears so. But, though no accredited dog-lover, I like dogs and they oddly and sometimes unexpectedly "take" to me. If this is an exception, I am ready to take the risk. Unintimidated but distressed by the Professor's somewhat forbidding manner, I not only continue my gesture toward the little chow, but crouch on the floor so she can snap better if she wants to. [It turns out] Yofi—her name is Yofi—snuggles her [muzzle] **nose** into my hand and nuzzles her head, in delicate sympathy, against my shoulder. . . .

[So again I can say the Professor was not always right. That is, he was right in so far as the actual presumption the Yo-fi might snap was concerned. So far he was right. His mind was right in its assumption; even his unconscious mind was right. But "we have tunnelled very deep" he said one day. Deeper than conscious mind or even deeper than the layers of the unconscious mind so far explained and labeled, is another great stream of consciousness. Perhaps the old truism "love me love my dog" not consciously in my thought at that moment (but this sort of truism is a sign-post in the partly mapped out region of the unconscious mind) gave a clue to still deeper regions of cause and effect, prompted me in spite of the Professor's injunction that Yo-fi snaps at strangers, to hunch on the floor beside her. It was a sudden, unpredicted gesture and was in a sense a reply to his comment "you are the only person who has ever come into this room and looked at the things in the room, before looking at me." For "if I like Yo-fi and if Yo-fi likes me" was my unspoken answer" then] **"We'll show him," . . . and, without forming the thought, the words, "love me, love my dog" are there to prompt me. "He will see whether or not I am indifferent," my** *emotion* **snaps back, though not in words. . . . My intuition challenges the Professor, though not in words. That intuition cannot really be translated into words, but if it could be it would go, roughly, something like this: "Why should I look at you? You are contained in the things you love, and if you accuse me of looking at the things in the room before looking at you, well, I will go on looking at the things in the room. One of them is this little golden dog. She snaps, does she? You call me a stranger, do you? Well, I will show you two things: one, I am not a stranger; two, even if I were, two seconds ago, I am now no longer one. And moreover I never was a stranger to this little golden Yofi."**

The wordless challenge goes on, "You are a very great man. I am overwhelmed with embarrassment, I am shy and frightened and gauche as an over-grown school-girl. But listen. You are a man. Yofi is

a dog. I am a woman. If this dog and this woman 'take' to one another, it will prove that beyond your caustic implied criticism—if criticism it is—there is another region of cause and effect, another region of question and answer." Undoubtedly, the Professor took an important clue from the first reaction of a new analysand or patient.

(HD., 1944; HD., 1956, pp. 145–51)

In this description of her first session, H. D. does not mention that Freud hammered; she does, however, mention a hammering episode earlier in "Tribute" in sections 9, 10, 11 and 12.

I did not know what enraged him suddenly. I veered round off the couch, my feet on the floor. I do not know exactly what I had said. . . .

[I say, I veered round on the couch. This is my way of recalling my impressions. I may or I may not have noted the date, jotted down in some detail the dream and events of the day preceding the night of the dream, the dream day as the Professor termed it. I have these notebooks, though some of the letters and materials were left in Switzerland. It was there that I heard of the death of the Professor but it is here that the Professor died.]

I veer round, uncanonically seated stark upright with my feet on the floor. [But] The Professor himself is uncanonical enough; he is beating with his hand, with his fist, on the head-piece of the old-fashioned horsehair sofa that had heard more secrets than the confession box of any popular Roman Catholic Father-confessor in his hey-day. . . .

Consciously, I was not aware of having said anything that might account for the Professor's outburst. And even as I [swing round] veered around, facing him, my mind was detached enough to wonder if this was some idea of *his* for speeding up the analytic content or redirecting the flow of associated images. The Professor said, "The trouble is—I am an old man—*you do not think it worth your while to love me.*"

THE IMPACT of his words was too dreadful—I simply felt nothing at all. I said nothing. What did he expect me to say? Exactly it was as if the Supreme Being had hammered with his fist on the back of the couch where I had been lying. Why, anyway, did he do that? He must know everything or he didn't know anything. He must know what I felt. Maybe he did. . . . The Professor had said in the very beginning that I had come to Vienna hoping to find my mother. Mother? Mamma. But my mother was dead. I was dead; that is, the child in me that had called her mamma was dead. Anyhow, he was a terribly frightening old man, too old and too detached, too wise and too famous altogether, to beat that way with his fist, like a child hammering a porridge-spoon on the table. . . .

I smoothed the folds of the rug, I glanced surreptitiously at my wrist-watch. The other day the Professor had reproached me for jerking out my arm and looking at my watch.

One day he said to me, 'You discovered for yourself what I discovered for the race.' To **all** that I [will] hope to return to later. At the moment, I [have veered round and] **am lying on the couch. I have just** readjusted the rug that had slipped to the floor. **I have tucked my hands under the rug. I am wondering if the Professor caught me looking at my wristwatch.** I am really somewhat shattered. But there is no answering flareback.   (H. D., 1944; H. D., 1956, pp. 19–26)

Examining "Tribute to Freud" as a work of historical accuracy is fraught with serious problems. It was written a decade after H. D.'s analysis, from memory, without any notes. Its structure is not in a temporal sequence. It was written for publication and is self-censored (for example, there is no direct mention of H. D.'s homosexuality). Comparing this memory (or creative fantasy) of her first session written ten years after her analysis with her letter of the session written shortly after it actually occurred reveals several discrepant areas.

In "Tribute" H. D. describes much less actual interaction with Freud in this first session than she reported in her letter. In "Tribute" Paula takes her coat, Freud silently greets her, and H. D. looks around the room; in her letter, Freud greets her with "Enter, fair madame," asks her to remove her coat, and leads her around the room. In "Tribute" the proverb, "Love me, love my dog," remains a thought in H. D.'s mind; in her letter, it is part of the conversation between herself and Freud. In "Tribute" H. D. writes that she thought that by looking at the things in the room she was looking at Freud; in her letter, H. D. says to Freud that in looking at the antiquities she was looking at him. In "Tribute" it is she and Yofi who are reconciled; in her letter, she is reconciled with a "growling" Freud.

In her "Tribute" account, as in her letter, H. D. tells of being hurt by Freud. She reports that she did not speak, and Freud's first comment was, "You are the only person who has ever come into this room and looked at the things in the room before looking at me." This differs from the account of the letter. In the letter, Freud first was solicitous, but then hammered, saying that she was disappointed in him; following this tirade, he explained that H. D. preferred to look at the pictures rather than him.

In "Tribute" H. D. tells an elaborate story about Yofi that occupies about a quarter of the account. Although H. D. mentions Yofi in her letter, she does not tell the long story of Yofi and does not mention Freud's calling her a "stranger" to Yofi. In both "Tribute" and her letter, the imagery of Freud and death appears. In "Tribute" Freud becomes the "Keeper of the Door" of "the House of Eternity," a grander entity than the Freud of her letter, "a little white ghost."

A possible explanation for H. D.'s writing of much less interaction with Freud in "Tribute" is that in 1944 she was losing the recollection of her actual encounter with Freud, and writing "Tribute" was an attempt to bolster her fading memory of an idealized Freud, the "blameless physician," to whom she dedicated "Tribute." Freud may not have been entirely blameless, however. At the time she wrote "Tribute" H. D.'s worst fears of the first meeting had occurred: Freud had died. In her memoir, she attempts to resurrect him in her memory.

The most parsimonious evaluation of the separate hammering episode in "Tribute" is that when H. D. recalled her first session, she was unable to remember that Freud's hammering occurred then. She does mention in the draft of the hammering episode that she "may not have noted the date."

The reports of the hammering episode in "Tribute" and in the letter to Bryher differ quite significantly in emphasis. In "Tribute" Freud is "enraged"; in the letter, he is "vaguely shocked." In "Tribute" it appears that Freud's wounded feelings prompted his hammering; but in the letter, H. D. learns from Freud that it was her looking at the pictures and not at him. In both accounts, H. D. reports that Freud criticized her for being disappointed in him. In "Tribute" H. D. writes that Freud said it was because he is "an old man"; in the letter, it is because he is "not a giant." In "Tribute" it is Freud who says, "You do not think it worth your while to love me," but in the letter, H. D. fears Freud will not love her and it is she who writes of the word *love*. Her recollection in "Tribute" of Freud's saying, "You discovered for yourself what I discovered for the race" is a variation of her recollection in her letter of Freud's saying they had met: Freud in the childhood of humanity and H. D. in her own childhood. But recalling that this conversation happened "one day" removes it from the first session.

H. D. in "Tribute" describes Freud as a person who suffers from narcissistic vulnerability. She portrays him as a man who is disappointed and reacts with inappropriate rage because he feels that H. D. thinks he is too old to love. In her letter, it appears that it was H. D., not Freud, who was disappointed, and that Freud's age was a major factor in her disappointment and fear of loving him. In "Tribute" H. D. projects her unacceptable feelings; in her letter, she denies them.

It would seem that at the time of writing the first-session sections of "Tribute" H. D. was attempting to preserve or restore her memory of a relationship with a benevolent and protective Freud. To help accomplish this, she split the first session into two parts and projected her disappointment and anger onto the description of Freud that appears at the beginning of her memoirs. She leaves a more idealized description of Freud, with whom she has a reconciliation, for the conclusion. But even here she does not reconcile with Freud directly but rather through a surrogate, Yofi.

She continued to revise her manuscript for the published version. She added the anecdote of Freud reproaching her for looking at her wristwatch "the other day," which definitely splits the hammering scene from the initial encounter. Significantly, she wrote the infamous description of Freud as "a child hammering a porridge-spoon on the table"—a further projection of her own feelings of disappointment and anger—after she had finished writing of her reconciliation with Freud in the draft. That she still had these intense feelings indicate that her attempt to preserve the memory of an idealized Freud by writing "Tribute to Freud" was not successful.

In the later sections of "Tribute" H. D. added passages which heightened the atmosphere of miraculous cure. Also, the communicative meaning of the story of Yofi was greatly revised. H. D. dropped some spoken dialogue between Freud and herself. She added her unspoken address to him. In both versions she describes a mystical region of the mind. The published version is the more dramatic. In these changes, H. D. intensified her wish for a mystical, unspoken connection and communication with Freud.

H. D. had a lifelong interest in mysticism, to which her Moravian religious upbringing contributed. The Moravians believed in "the gift" of vision and wisdom of the holy spirit. In the early 1940s H. D. became involved with a Brahman mystic and, beginning in 1943, she embraced the beliefs of Lord Hugh Dowding, a hero of the Battle of Britain, who wrote a book claiming that during seances he could communicate with the souls of lost R.A.F. pilots. It was during this period of involvement in Dowding's ideas that H. D. wrote "Tribute to Freud." Her interest in the occult intensified, and she experienced visions during seances. In September 1945 she maintained that dead R.A.F. pilots were rapping messages to her on a seance table. However, Dowding repudiated H. D.'s claims in February 1946. She developed an overt psychosis, and in May was hospitalized at Kusnacht Klinik in Switzerland for six months. During the course of her treatment she received a form of convulsive therapy.

In 1946–47, H. D. wrote an unpublished autobiographical novel, *The Sword Went Out to Sea,* in which she described her psychic and psychotic experiences. She wrote of delusions that World War III had begun and a small atom bomb had been dropped on St. Paul's Cathedral; that London had been evacuated because of plague; and that secret tunnels ran under Europe (H. D., 1946–47, pp. 104–5). In the novel she wrote, "There were avenues of scaffolds—whole populations were condemned to death. . . . The dogs had been bred with lions and were of enormous size. They were used to track down offenders and rescue individuals and parties of 'displaced persons,' who were dangerously wandering at large" (H. D., 1946–47, p. 105).

These delusions appear to contain projections of her fear of the destructive force of her anger. Her delusions involving "whole populations . . . condemned to death" must refer to the Holocaust, and one wonders if the "dogs . . . bred with lions," which were used to rescue displaced persons, was a reference to Yofi-Freud.

"ADVENT"

While in Switzerland, in December 1948 H. D., using her now-available diary of her sessions with Freud, completed another account of her analysis, which had occurred thirteen years previously (Friedman, 1990, p. 283). It, like "Tribute," was written for publication and was self-censored. "Advent," in which H. D. recounts the first four weeks of her analysis, was first published in 1974 as part of a new edition of "Tribute to Freud."

H. D. dates the first section of "Advent" March 2, but in it she writes of her first session, on March 1. (The second section appears to be a continuation of the first but is actually her second session.) Lacking details, the first section appears to be a recollection of the initial encounter with Freud. H. D. seems not to have used diary notes here, unlike the other sections of "Advent." (Perhaps she did not write in the diary after her frightening first session and long letter to Bryher.) "Advent" begins:

> March 2, 1933
> I CRIED TOO HARD . . . went to the old wooden restaurant with the paintings, like the pictures that my mother did. . . . There are a few still-life studies, apples with a brown jug and the usual bunched full double-peonies with a stalk of blue delphinium. . . .
> My mother and I visited an Austrian village, like these pictures . . . I remember my mother talking on a wooden bridge to one of the village women. . . . My mother spoke perfect German. . . .
> I wandered alone across the bridge but did not get far. . . .
> I cried too hard . . . I do not know what I remembered: the hurt of the cold, nun-like nurses at the time of my first London confinement, spring 1915; the shock of the *Lusitania* going down just before the child was still-born; fear of drowning; young men on park benches in blue hospital uniform; my father's anti-war sentiments and his violent *volte-*

face in 1918; my broken marriage; a short period with friends in Corn-
wall in 1918; my father's telescope, my grandfather's microscope. If I let
go (I, this one drop, this one ego under the microscope-telescope of
Sigmund Freud) I fear to be dissolved utterly. . . .

When I told Professor Freud I was married in 1913, he said, "Ah,
twenty years ago."

Sigmund Freud is like a curator in a museum, surrounded by his
priceless collection of Greek, Egyptian, and Chinese treasures; he is
"Lazarus stand forth"; he is like D. H. Lawrence, grown old but matured
and with astute perception. His hands are sensitive and frail. He is
midwife to the soul. He is himself the soul. Thought of him bashes across
my forehead, like a death-head moth; he is not the sphinx but the
sphinx-moth, the death-head moth.

No wonder I am frightened. I let death in at the window. If I do not let
ice-thin window-glass intellect protect my soul or my emotion, I let
death in.

But perhaps I will be treated with a psychic drug, will take away a
nameless precious phial from his cavern. Perhaps I will learn the secret,
be priestess with power over life and death.

He beat on my pillow or the head-piece of the old couch I lie on. He
was annoyed with me. His small chow, Yofi, sits at his feet. We make an
ancient cycle or circle, wise-man, woman, lioness (as he calls his chow)!

He is a Jew; like the last Prophet, he would break down the old law of
Leviticus: death by stoning for the vagrant, and unimaginable punish-
ment for the lawless. The old Victorian law is hard; Havelock Ellis and
Sigmund Freud have tempered it for my generation.

Kenneth Macpherson called me "recording angel." I will endeavor to
record the grain in the painted apple, in the painted basket, hanging to
the left of the wooden dresser, directly in line with my eyes, as I glance
up from my notebook   (H. D., 1974, pp. 115–17).

This section of "Advent" contains only a few facts compared with the
letter to Bryher and with "Tribute to Freud." In all three accounts she
mentions that she was anxious and that she cried; however, in "Advent"
she says she cried about the series of traumas during World War I, not
because Freud mistreated her. She mentions a wooden restaurant in
both "Advent" and her letter; however, in "Advent" the apples are
painted and in the letter the apples are real. In each account she mentions Yofi, but in "Advent" she gives the dog even less importance than
in her letter. She places the hammering scene back in the context of the
first session, as it is in her letter but not in "Tribute." The intensity of
the hammering in "Advent" is attenuated in comparison with that
scene in the letter and in "Tribute." She describes Freud as "annoyed,"
not "vaguely shocked" as in the letter, or "enraged" as in "Tribute." In
"Advent," unlike in "Tribute," H. D. does not split Freud into a ham-

merer and reconcilee, nor does she need to prove his love for her and hers for him by using her relationship to Yofi. She comments in "Advent" that Freud is a Jew who is not harsh, and her fear of punishment or criticism from him is minimal.

The content of "Advent" has less to do with describing H. D.'s relationship with Freud during her first session than with her associations and self-reflections. A major set of associations is to her mother, and maternal issues seem to dominate. Even her association to father, grandfather, and Freud, "I fear to dissolve utterly," focuses on a danger associated with the maternal transference—the loss of self.

She does continue to idealize Freud. She yearns for him to be omnipotent: "He is Lazarus stand forth." He is not; he has been dead for nine years. But her memory of him as a good, protective object, as reflected in this recall of her first encounter, has returned. Perhaps this is a result of her recovery from psychosis, perhaps because of further therapy, or perhaps because she had retrieved her diary notes.

Most significant, H. D. now has an understanding that was missing from the letter to Bryher and from "Tribute." She realizes that a major theme in her first encounter with Freud was her fear of loving a dying man. She compares Freud with the death-head moth and realizes that she did "let death in." (In the March 8 section of "Advent," she writes, "I cannot be disappointed with Sigmund Freud, only I have this constant obsession that the analysis will be broken by death. I cannot discuss this with the Professor" [H. D., 1974].) Although she still writes of her wishes for a more tangible or magical cure, to "take away a nameless precious phial," to be "priestess with power over life and death," she seems aware of the impossibility of her desire.

Unlike the recollection in 1944 in "Tribute" of her first session, in 1946 H. D. used an analytic approach to understand a deeper meaning of the session. She recognized the importance of the painful issues of the past and her desire for her mother. She now had some knowledge of her fear of Freud's death. His "resurrection" could not happen by means of a wishful recall of her session with Freud; however, a "resurrection" of sorts could occur by identification with Freud through the process of self-analysis.

In July 1953, H. D. returned to Kusnacht Klinik for a surgical operation and developed a close relationship with another psychoanalyst, Erich Heydt. This relationship was to last the rest of her life. In 1956, after a fracture of her hip, she returned once more to Kusnacht Klinik and remained there, living a protected but productive life, until her death on September 27, 1961. Her need to write of an idealized Freud continued. She made slight revisions of her manuscripts for the 1956 republication of "Tribute to Freud." In one of her last major works, *Helen in Egypt*, written in 1952 through 1956 and published in 1961, Freud appears in the guise of Theseus, the hero who returns from the underworld and consoles Helen (H. D.):

> It is one thing, Helen, to slay Death,
> it is another thing to come back
> through the intricate windings of the Labyrinth
> . . . .
> belovèd Child, we are together,
> weary of War,
> only the Quest remains.
>
> (H. D., 1961, pp. 163–64)

BIBLIOGRAPHY

CHISHOLM, D. (1992). *H. D.'s Freudian Poetics*. Ithaca: Cornell Univ. Press.

DU PLESSIS, R. (1986). *H. D.: The Career of That Struggle*. Brighton, England: Harvester.

FRIEDMAN, S. S. (1981). *Psyche Reborn: The Emergence of H. D.* Bloomington: Indiana Univ. Press.

——— (1986a). *Dictionary of Literary Biography: American Poets, First Series, 1880–1945*, Vol. 45., S.V. "Hilda Doolittle (H. D.)." ed.

——— (1986b). A most luscious *vers libre* relationship: H. D. and Freud. *Annual of Psychoanalysis*, 14:319–43. New York: Int. Univ. Press.

——— (1990). *Penelope's Web: Gender, Modernity, H. D.'s Fiction*. Cambridge: Cambridge Univ. Press.

GUEST, B. (1984). *Herself Defined: The Poet H. D. and Her World*. Garden City, N.Y.: Doubleday.

H. D. (1933–34). Letters to Winifred Bryher. Typescript. Beinecke Library, Yale University, New Haven, Connecticut.

——— (1944). Tribute to Freud: "Writing on the wall," Notebook. Beinecke Library, Yale University, New Haven, Connecticut. Published as *Tribute to Freud*. New York: Pantheon, 1956.

——— (1946–47). The Sword Went Out to Sea. Typescript. Beinecke Library, Yale University, New Haven, Connecticut.

——— (1961). *Helen in Egypt*. New York: Grove.

——— (1974). "Advent" (written in 1948). In *Tribute to Freud, Writing on the Wall, Advent*. Boston: D. R. Godine.

HOLLAND, N. N. (1969a). Freud and H. D. *Int. J. Psycho-Anal.*, 50:309–15.

——— (1969b). H. D. and the "Blameless Physician." *Contemp. Lit.*, 10:474–506.

KING, M., ed. (1986). *H. D.: Woman and Poet*. Orono, Maine: University of Maine.

KNIGHT, R. P. (1937). A visit with Freud. In *Freud as We Knew Him*, ed. Hendrik M. Ruitenbeek, pp. 112–15. Detroit: Wayne State Univ. Press, 1973.

RICHARDS, A. (1992). Hilda Doolittle and creativity: Freud's gift. *Psychoanal. Study Child*, 47:391–406.

ROBINSON, J. S. (1982). *H. D.: The Life and Work of an American Poet*. Boston: Houghton Mifflin.

The Examination Dream Revisited

A Clinical Note

MORTIMER OSTOW, M.D.

In each of three dreams reported to me fortuitously within a few days of each other, the patient was anxious about a forthcoming medical examination. Two of the patients reported a sense of guilt for immoral behavior; the feared illness could be interpreted as punishment.

IN *THE INTERPRETATION OF DREAMS* (1900, P. 274) FREUD SUGGESTS THAT dreams about failing an examination or being unprepared for one occur "whenever, having done something wrong or failed to do something properly, we expect to be punished by the event—whenever, in short, we feel the burden of responsibility." The subject of the examination dream has scarcely been neglected in the psychoanalytic literature. Renik (1981) and Kafka (1979) reviewed the literature; Kafka, in his paper, emphasizes early disagreeable medical experiences as associations and precursors to the examination dream. (See also Myers, 1983, and Sterbe, 1928.) The purpose of this note is to record some clinical observations that I have made in recent months. I have found that every time a patient reports a typical examination dream to me, either spontaneously or in response to my question, he or she will tell me of some medical examination that is anticipated in the near future. The word examination itself links the manifest content and the latent content.

President, Psychoanalytic Research and Development Fund; attending psychiatrist, Montefiore Medical Center, New York City.

The Psychoanalytic Study of the Child 50, ed. Albert J. Solnit, Peter B. Neubauer, Samuel Abrams, and A. Scott Dowling (Yale University Press, copyright © 1995 by Albert J. Solnit, Peter B. Neubauer, Samuel Abrams, and A. Scott Dowling).

Let me illustrate with what seems to me a particularly transparent example. The patient was a middle-aged woman who had had a lump removed from her breast about a year before the dream. Because pathologic examination disclosed malignancy—though fairly well circumscribed—she was subsequently treated with a full course of chemotherapy and then a full course of radiotherapy, the latter having been concluded only a few months before the incident here reported. One morning, just before awakening, the patient dreamed:

> I was in a cafeteria, a large room like a gymnasium. I was getting ready for an examination. I hadn't studied. I didn't even read the book or go to class. I turned the pages and anxiously read a little before the examination. I thought that I wouldn't be able to write an essay. All the others were taking seats at large tables. I got a chair and brought it to a table. One guy who had gone to school with me and another fat guy, whom I didn't know, sat at my table. The examination was about munitions, how to assemble a gun. It was very technical. I had two pencils in front of me.

Without stopping, she continued:

> Speaking of two, I'm worried about my breasts. I have an examination coming up, or rather a few examinations—mammography, bone scan, chest x-ray and blood tests. I've been reassured that everything is okay, but I can't help worrying.

My own clinical observations concur, for the most part, with Freud's comment that "it is but rarely that the material with which the dreamer provides us in associations is sufficient to interpret the dream" (1900, p. 275). What follows is an exception to that generalization, for my patient led me directly into the reality concerned. Her dream differs from the typical examination dream in another way—namely, that the examination with which she is having difficulty, is an examination that she never took in reality. Therefore it does not carry the reassurance that Freud mentioned, that just as one had passed the given examination previously, so one would successfully negotiate the upcoming ordeal.

The fact that the examination is to take place in a cafeteria reminds me of one of the patient's childhood fantasies, the fear of being consumed by the witch of the Hansel and Gretel story. In dealing with her illness and treatment, she felt that it was the breast that was being devoured. A remark she made in the following session can be taken as an association to the book she was paging through in this dream. The session had been preceded by further anxious ruminations about the upcoming medical examinations, and during these ruminations she had fantasied that she was a book composed of many pages that had been created by sectioning her body into very thin slices, an allusion to the principle of tomography. When she was a young adolescent, her mother had teased her about her small breasts. Analysis had focused on her preoedipal fears of being destroyed by her mother—who incidently had sustained a full mastectomy several decades earlier for malignant disease and had survived. In the complex to which the dream calls our attention, the breast, which had been attacked first by the biting and consuming cancer and then by the surgeon, was now being attacked—in fact sliced into thin sections—by the posttreatment examinations. The phallic images are less easily interpreted, though the dream suggests that she viewed a possible mastectomy as a castration.

I do not know that every examination dream alludes to a feared medical examination but I suppose it would be fair to say that what is anticipated with anxiety in an examination dream is an approaching ordeal. That ordeal is often a worrisome medical examination.

The day after I had written the above, one of my patients began her session as follows:

> I have just come from the eye doctor. He says that I'm all right. One day last week while I was working, suddenly my vision got blurred. It lasted a few minutes. I wasn't scared but I saw the eye doctor that day. He wanted me to come back to complete the examination. Last night I had a dream about some tests that I had to take that I wasn't prepared for.

My patient then told me that a girlfriend of hers had just divorced her husband because he had been promiscuous, not only before the marriage but also during marriage. As a result she had to "take an AIDS test." My patient is a young divorcee, religiously observant, who is willing to engage in intercourse only with the immediate prospect of marriage but will permit herself some lesser liberties with a man she is fond of. Recently, however, she had been somewhat more indulgent than she wished and was remorseful. She did not find it necessary to take an AIDS test, but she did feel guilty.

The examination dream in this case may allude not only to the medical examination but also to the moral examination that warranted punishment by disease. In Jewish liturgy, with which my patient is quite familiar, Jer. 11.20 reads: "For the Lord of hosts is a just judge, He examines reins and heart." This dream represented anxiety about examination for somatic disease and also about examination for moral integrity.

A few days later, a third patient reported an examination dream:

> I was with my mother and daughter and my friend. We were trying to get a place to live. I was going from place to place. There was a tree called

a sea grape tree and I was eating from it. I was also taking a test. My daughter was little. Someone called out to me from a high window. My friend was hanging out with me. I told her about school. I had to take a test.

She then added, "I feel I'm not in good health. I'm too fat, I've had no exercise, I feel tired, that is, depressed." She was concerned that she had lost interest in graduate school and felt "disconnected from it." She believed she had done poorly on a test she had taken in preparation for her doctorate a few weeks earlier. She wondered whether she had damaged her mind through overindulgence in drugs when she was an adolescent. She thought she should have surgery because her neck was too fat. She was ashamed of her "bad mothering skills."

This woman's continuing attempts to retrieve the gratification of early contact with her mother take the form of food craving, which she has constantly to resist because she is already too heavy. She had used street drugs years ago when she was very young and currently is taking antidepression medication. This dream, like the one reported immediately above, combines somatic anxiety with moral concerns.

It may be merely coincidence that the three vignettes I have just described were reported by women; examination dreams are also reported by men. Galenson (1978) suggested, however, that women experience special test anxieties.

Reviewing these three examples, I observed that each of these patients was struggling with depressive tendencies. The first exhibited an almost continuous low-level depressive tendency, exacerbated from time to time by a strong response to traumatic events. The second patient is actually a manic depressive in remission for whom recent life events have been rather disappointing and who is trying to resist recurrence of depression. The third woman is a burned-out borderline patient who had recently started medication for a recurrence of mild depression. Somatic anxiety occurs commonly in depression, and so does guilt. The examination anxiety then represents fear of the judgment of the superego, which is activated by the depressive state. Judgment is the prelude to punishment. The depressed patient believes that his depression is a punishment and that he will be punished further by somatic illness, disability, and death.

DEVELOPMENTAL ASPECTS

The first patient had come to see me years before for treatment of hysterical blindness. This symptom receded quickly as a result of transference influence and the analysis of early voyeuristic experiences. If I am to believe her, these occurred only during the first two years of her life, when, as an infant in her crib, she was aware of exciting sounds in the dark through which she attempted to peer. But we learn also that as a small child she always found any physical illness distressing because her mother would become angry with her for being ill. Her mother was a schoolteacher and the child's illness posed the problem of whether she could leave the child alone in the house or, instead, had to stay home from her job. The mother was an unhappy, troubled woman and often treated the child harshly for no reason the child knew. She also was a poor cook, who prepared unappetizing meals and offered only small amounts. Judging from the mother's current behavior, these memories are probably fairly accurate. The patient's mother increased the child's fixation on her body by frequent critical references to her thick lips, curly hair, and small breasts. At that time the child did not associate illness with misbehavior. She was impressed by fairy tales about witches, especially, as I have noted, by the story of Hansel and Gretel, in which the children were in danger of being devoured by the witch and in self-defense pushed her into an oven. To this day, when things go badly, she reports feeling as though she had been cursed by a witch.

Her oedipal phase was stunted by her mother's refusal to allow any relation between the child and her father. She married a man who has filled the role of a good mother to her. However, the sexual relation bears the mark of the incompleteness of oedipal development. That is, she participates happily in intercourse but will not permit her breasts to be touched. As a child, she was told by her mother that touching her breasts would cause cancer, and this fear intensified when the mother subsequently sustained her own mastectomy. When the patient developed her breast malignancy, she thought of her mother's warning, although she still thought even more of being cursed, rather than being punished for sexual or other misbehavior.

The third patient grew up in a fairly chaotic home and early on found her chief gratification in eating. She was exposed to intense sexual stimulation even before puberty. Thereafter she sought out sexual experience frequently and inappropriately and ultimately supported herself by prostitution. During adolescence especially, oral orientation led her to the use of street drugs. The development of a true oedipal structure was impeded by her father's frequent absences and the divorce of her parents when she was seven or eight. Although she had some early religious exposure, first in the Catholic Church and subsequently to various Protestant denominations, she became aware of the issue of morality only in adult life, when she became seriously interested in the subject. When circumstances made it possible for her to pursue intellectual interests, she studied the history and mythology of religions.

Clinically she presented as a borderline personality, now in her forties, burned out or stabilized. What was left was a cyclothymia. Her attitude toward the psychiatric drug therapy, to which she responded well, was ambivalent because of her early experience with street drugs. In the incident I reported, she attributed her complaints to having been poisoned by the street drugs, but at the same time she was inclined to find fault with her medication, although she knew and acknowledged how helpful it had been. The patient interpreted her present state of physical and mental distress as punishment for her early indulgence, although she did not believe literally in religious doctrines of reward and punishment.

In these two instances, (case 1 and case 3) the somatic fixations were traceable to oral and rapprochement phases of development manifest by early memories, preferred mode of gratification, and perceived sources of distress. The specific view of illness as punishment for sin was absent in the first case and present but not prominent in the third case. It was, however, of moment in the second case, presumably because the girl had grown up in a religious environment and continued religious practice and a fairly fundamentalist belief in adult life. Since she was seen in only superficial, though very helpful, psychotherapy, I do not have childhood information, but despite her evident panic in response to the medical problem that precipitated her examination dream, there was no evidence of undue somatic involvement. Relevant to these concerns is the clinical fact that melancholic patients often display profound hypochondria. One hears delusions or fantasies that there is a living creature in the abdomen devouring the viscera.

In these patients, at least, the somatic fixations and anxieties that led to examination dreams related to medical examinations derived from the experiences of the oral phase. The interpretation of the feared disease as punishment for immoral gratification points to elaboration of the complex into the oedipal process.

BIBLIOGRAPHY

FREUD, S. (1900). *The Interpretation of Dreams, S.E.*, 4.
GALENSON, E. (1978). Examination anxiety in women. Paper presented to the meeting of the New York Psychoanalytic Society, May 16, 1978. Abstracted in R. Shaw, *Psychoanal. Q.* (1980), 49:183–84.

KAFKA, E. (1979). On examination dreams. *Psychoanal. Q.*, 48:426–27.
MYERS, W. A. (1983). Athletic example of typical examination dream. *Psychoanal. Q.*, 52:594.
RENIK, O. (1981). Typical examination dreams, "superego dreams," and traumatic dreams. *Psychoanal. Q.*, 50:159–89.
STERBE, R. (1928). Communication: An examination dream. *Int. J. Psycho-Anal.*, 9:353.

Index